ENCOUNTERING
THE
WORD

—ENCOUNTERING—

THE
WORD

365 DEVOTIONS

PUBLISHING GROUP

NASHVILLE, TENNESSEE

Introduction

Books come in all shapes and sizes. Even when you narrow it down to wanting a devotional, how do you choose?

Do you look for one by your favorite author? One that is focused on a certain topic. Maybe God has put a specific book of the Bible on your heart to study. The possibilities are endless! The most important thing when looking for a devotional is to find one that will pull your heart closer to God and give you a deeper understanding of who He is, and it's our greatest desire that this is exactly what you will find in these pages.

Through these devotions you will find a wide variety of voices. Some days you'll laugh, some days you'll cry, and some days you will learn something new. This devotional was designed so that as you are diving into God's Word and spending time with your Father, you can also get a taste of some of the most popular female authors of today. Our hope is that even when you finish this book, it will continue to be a resource to find books and devotionals from authors who you never knew, but now have a connection with.

While the voice may be different, what you are guaranteed to get each day is a verse to meditate on and a story or lesson to pull your heart into an encounter with God. Allow these excerpts to bring you encouragement as you transform your life into a love letter for your Creator.

The God Who Speaks

*In the beginning God created the heavens and the earth.
Now the earth was formless and empty, darkness covered
the surface of the watery depths, and the Spirit of God was
hovering over the surface of the waters. Then God said, "Let
there be light," and there was light. (Genesis 1:1–3 HCSB)*

Words change things. When a pastor stands next to a gushing groom and a beaming bride and says, "I now pronounce you husband and wife," their status changes. They become united before God and God's people. They are ushered into the union of holy matrimony. The spoken word changed them forever because it was spoken with authority. But words have no authority in themselves. Words are only powerful when spoken by someone with power.

Notice the power of God at creation. He spoke two words and suddenly, light existed. He spoke again and planets started spinning, oceans started crashing, birds started flapping their wings. God created by *speaking*. He spoke the whole world into existence. And the result of His speaking demonstrates how powerful He is.

Responding to the powerful nature of God's speech, the psalmist praised God for His creative authority: "Praise Him, sun and moon; praise Him, all you shining stars. Praise Him, highest heavens, and you waters above the heavens. Let them praise the name of Yahweh, for He commanded, and they were created" (Ps. 148:3–5 HCSB).

Words matter. Words carry weight. And the weightiest words are those uttered by the most glorious Being in the universe. His words matter because of who He is. He speaks with the ultimate authority.

The truth that God speaks is what separates Him from all idols. In the Old Testament, we see frequent showdowns between the true God of Israel and the false gods of pagan peoples. Whether it be the plagues God sent on Egypt, showing up the Egyptian gods (Exod. 7–11) or Elijah calling down fire on Mount Carmel after the prophets of Baal cried out in vain (1 Kings 18), the writers of the Bible delight in showing the power of God over idolatry.

In Psalm 115:3–5, we read: "Our God is in heaven and does whatever He pleases. Their idols are silver and gold, made by human hands. They have mouths but cannot speak, eyes, but cannot see" (HCSB). The contrast is clear. God is Spirit. He has no physical mouth, and yet He speaks. The idols, on the other hand, are physical. They have mouths but are silent. God alone has authority. God is the God who speaks.

God's words aren't reserved for creation or to put in check ancient idol worshippers. God still speaks to us today. His words still have the power to bring light and life and to kick our idols off their throne. Where does God speak? How can we hear Him? By running to the Word of God!

"For our gospel did not come to you in word only, but also in power, in the Holy Spirit, and with much assurance" (1 Thess. 1:5 HCSB).

Excerpt taken from *90 Days with the God Who Speaks* (© 2017).

For God So Loved the World

Then God said, "Let us make man in our image, according to our likeness . . . So God created man in his own image; he created him in the image of God; he created them male and female. God blessed them, and God said to them, "Be fruitful, multiply, fill the earth, and subdue it. Rule the fish of the sea, the birds of the sky, and every creature that crawls on the earth." God also said, "Look, I have given you every seed-bearing plant on the surface of the entire earth and every tree whose fruit contains seed. This will be food for you, for all the wildlife of the earth, for every bird of the sky, and for every creature that crawls on the earth—everything having the breath of life in it—I have given every green plant for food." And it was so. God saw all that he had made, and it was very good indeed. (Genesis 1:26–31 CSB)

Can you imagine the fellowship of the Trinity on the seventh day? As they rested and looked upon the very good work they had accomplished, one planet had been tended like no other to our knowledge. Perfectly placed in the universe with adequate distance from sun, moon, and stars to sustain human life, it was chosen for divine infiltration.

"For God loved the world." Scripture doesn't tell us He loved the sun, the most impressive of the heavenly bodies we can see. Nor are we told that He loved the stars, even though He knows every one of them by name. John goes out of his way, however, to tell us that God loved the world.

In a universe so vast, so incomprehensible, why does God single out one little planet to love? Beloved, absorb this into the marrow of your bones: because we are on it. As despicable as humanity can be, God loves us. Inconceivably, we are His treasures, His prized creation. He can't help it. He just loves us. So much, in fact, that He did something I, with my comparatively pitiful love for my children, would not do for anyone. He "gave His One and Only Son, so that everyone who believes in Him will not perish but have eternal life" (John 3:16 HCSB).

Let it fall afresh. Elohim is so huge; we are so small. Yet the vastness of His love—so high, so wide, so deep, so long—envelops us like the endless universe envelops a crude little planet God first called Earth.

Of his God, the psalmist wrote, "Your right hand sustains me; you stoop down to make me great" (Ps. 18:35 NIV). The Amplified Version says it this way: "Your gentleness and condescension have made me great." And when the God of all the universe stoops down and a single child recognizes the tender condescension and bends her knee to stoop as well, the heart of God surges with unbridled emotion. And there they are. Just the two of them.

Excerpt taken from *Portraits of Devotion* by Beth Moore (© 2014).

A Space of Delight

*The LORD God planted a garden in Eden, in the east,
and there He placed the man He had formed. The LORD
God caused to grow out of the ground every tree pleasing
in appearance and good for food, including the tree of
life in the middle of the garden, as well as the tree of the
knowledge of good and evil. (Genesis 2:8–9 HCSB)*

The garden of Eden has become a euphemism for perfection of dwelling and lifestyle. Unfortunately, for most women, the picture of a perfect home is a dream dwelling with a prestigious location, picturesque structure, exquisite furnishings, helpful neighbors, and a loving family. We want an "Eden" of our own, with everything decorated and cleaned to perfection. Our goal is simply to have a beautiful house, but did God design our homes to be something more?

The Creator's plan begins with a clear statement that He—"the LORD God"—plants you where He wants you to be geographically, which often is not where you want to be. This divinely appointed "garden" ("a place hedged around" or "protected") is a wonderful metaphor for what the Creator designed as home. Gardens set apart a particular space; they suggest beauty—whether flowers or fruit trees or just a touch of green and some natural stones; some produce food and sustenance; they often create a sense of peace and quiet rest and provide a perfect setting for conversation and building relationships (Gen. 2:9–10, 21–23).

How fitting that God decided to name this garden "Eden" (a Persian loan word meaning "delight"). Here then is the challenge:

Can you create a home of "delight" for those whom you love the most and for the strangers who pass your way? Can you do more than simply keep the closets organized and the front door decked out in seasonal décor by intentionally creating a space that makes others feel "hedged" or "protected" from the many cares and pressures of this world? I truly have happy memories from all the dwellings in which I have lived—some more than others, several that demanded far less creativity and energy to pull together, none that I was privileged to design or even decorate exactly as I wanted. But I am grateful that this challenge to create "delight" in my home found me early in my journey! Understanding the Creators plan and opening my heart to dream of more than just a beautiful house but rather, "House Beautiful." My goal isn't to create a space worthy of a magazine cover, but rather a place of delight for me and my family, I have found the Lord faithful to provide creativity and energy in the journey.

How can you make your house delightful to others? Regardless of the neighborhood in which you are living, whatever the age or size of your home, despite the quality of your furnishings—you can create a garden of delight using your own creative energies and developing an attitude of faithful service to those whom you love the most.

Excerpt taken from *The Devotional for Women* by Rhonda Harrington Kelley and Dorothy Kelley Patterson (© 2015).

One Is the Loneliest Number

*"It is not good for the man to be alone. I will make
a helper suitable for him." (Genesis 2:18 NIV)*

Adam was living in paradise and had a relationship with God, yet God determined he needed a companion. God intended marriage to minister to our aloneness. However, it's possible to be married for many years and feel desperately alone. The key to reducing our loneliness in marriage is to nurture a deep and intimate friendship with our husbands—apart from our children. The only way to accomplish this is to make time for the friendship. Share common interests together. Flirt with each other. Laugh together. Share your dreams. Hold hands. Hug often. Be goofy. Send each other texts throughout the day. Plan getaways. Take up a hobby together. Don't put it off any longer. We make time for the things we deem to be important.

Many Christian families have bought into the lie that the needs, wants, and desires of the children should come before the needs, wants, and desires of the parents. Kid-centric homes have become the norm in our culture, and as a result, the marriage relationship has been put on a back burner in many homes. In fact, one woman who answered my question about creative date night ideas said, "If we go on a date night, it is rare. Maybe twice a year. But we do have family night a few times a week, which is like a family date."

This is a dangerous line of thinking that many Christian couples have adopted. Family date nights do not prioritize the marriage— they prioritize the children. Of course, there is nothing wrong with having family date nights as long as you have carved out time for your marriage first. Take it from this empty nester: those kids are going to leave you someday. I know it's hard to imagine that day will come when you are right smack in the daily grind of parenting. The truth is, you will spend the majority of your years with your husband, not your children. You need time alone with your husband away from your kids. Children who grow up seeing their parents prioritize the marriage are more secure and confident in the long run.

In his book *The Meaning of Marriage,* Tim Keller writes that God "didn't put a parent and a child in the Garden," but "a husband and a wife. When you marry your spouse, that must supersede all other relationships, even the parental relationship. Your spouse and your marriage must be the number one priority in your life. Keller goes on to say that the purpose of marriage is for "helping each other to become our future glory-selves, the new creations that God will eventually make us." Putting a Christian friendship at the heart of a marriage can only strengthen it, giving it the foundation it needs to withstand both trials and time. But it can also "lift it to a level that no other vision of marriage approaches."

Excerpt taken from *Everafter* by Vicki Courtney (© 2013).

Leave and Cleave

So the LORD God caused a deep sleep to fall upon the man, and while he slept took one of his ribs and closed up its place with flesh. And the rib that the LORD God had taken from the man he made into a woman and brought her to the man. (Genesis 2:21–22 ESV)

God provided Eve for Adam. Maybe God forced Adam to sleep through the creation process so that there would be no illusion that Adam drummed up the woman for himself. God created the need for connection then *He* provided the solution.

With this truth in mind, one verse jumps out at me from the Genesis account: "Therefore a man shall leave his father and his mother and hold fast to his wife, and they shall become one flesh" (Gen. 2:24 ESV).

God gives permission here to "cleave" or to hold on tightly to human relationships, but He must be talking about more than Adam and Eve in this verse. You see, Adam and Eve had no father or mother to leave. They were not born of a man and a woman; God created them. So all of that leaving father and mother to hold fast to another business must have been prescriptive, not descriptive. God was talking about us.

When it comes to our relationships, God intends for us to cling. We have a tendency to distort things. We conjure up images of being a clingy girl who is whiny and needy and we say "no thanks." But what if we are throwing the baby out with the bathwater? What if by refusing to be needy we deny God the opportunity to meet a deep, genuine need?

In Matthew Henry's commentary on Genesis 2, he writes, "Perfect solitude would turn a paradise into a desert, and a palace into a dungeon."[1]

And yet solitude is what we often choose. We isolate ourselves. We neglect our relationships with God and with others and then we wonder why we feel so sad.

God met Adam's need for relationship, and everything was rainbows and butterflies and romantic walks on the beach for a while. Ah ha! So the answer to our loneliness problem must be a great marriage, right?

Not exactly.

We girls can be a fickle bunch. Either we withdraw and isolate ourselves, keeping our relationships at the surface level to keep things neat and tidy, or we put all of our eggs in one basket, looking to others—especially the men in our lives—to fill every single relational void.

Neither path will take us somewhere pleasant.

Adam didn't trade in his relationship with God for his relationship with his wife. He had both. He needed both.

Only God can supply all of our needs (Phil. 4:19). When we neglect our relationship with Him, we will find ourselves very lonely, but one way God provides is through human connection. When we refuse to accept that gift or look to our human relationships to be everything we need, we will find ourselves badly off-kilter.

Excerpt taken from *Connected* by Erin Davis (© 2016).

---

1. Matthew Henry, *Genesis*, Matthew Henry Commentary on the Whole Bible, accessed September 12, 2013, http://www.biblestudytools.com/commentaries/ matthew-henry-complete/genesis/2.html.

The Enemy's Battle Plan

*Then the woman saw that the tree was good for food
and delightful to look at, and that it was desirable
for obtaining wisdom. So she took some of its fruit
and ate it; she also gave some to her husband, who
was with her, and he ate it. (Genesis 3:6 HCSB)*

God has given us the battle plan of Satan in His Word. No temptation to be drawn into disobedience and sin falls outside of what is detailed in Genesis 3. Here Satan chose to disguise himself as a cunning serpent (v. 1). He was crafty and shrewd, suggesting a well-planned and sensible attack on the prey.

As we study the Enemy's tactics, it's worth pausing to consider: Why did Satan approach Eve? Adam was created first. Perhaps Satan approached Eve since she, unlike Adam, had not received directly from God the prohibition concerning the fruit of the tree. Likewise, when we are untethered from the Word of God, we become sitting ducks open to attack.

Satan makes his approach in the same general way—whatever the test may be. You can stop at any point and refuse to be drawn into disobedience—until you reach the final step. Here is the adversary's battle plan:

- **Has God indeed said . . . ?** (v. 1 NKJV). Did God really say that? Questioning God is the beginning of every slippery slope in your life.
- **You shall not eat it, nor shall you touch it, lest you die** (v. 3 NKJV). Eve adds her own interpretation to Gods' words. Whether she was trying to make God's words more

restrictive and thus unjust or simply carelessly exaggerating the words of God, she erred in putting her personal words in the mouth of the Creator God.

- **You will *not surely* die** (v. 4 NKJV). The devil contradicted God, twisting words coming directly from God.
- **You will be like God, knowing good and evil** (v. 5 NKJV). At the root of every temptation is the desire to go your own way instead of God's way. Satan moves to surpass God— offering you more! He uses a half-truth; Eve's knowledge would be increased through experience. She would now "know" evil by doing it.
- **She took of its fruit and ate** (v. 6). Eve chose to disobey God. She saw the fruit as appealing to appetite, beauty, and ambition. We stumble when we follow the cravings of our eyes as well (1 John 2:16); she took and drew into her own heart; she ate. But she did not stop there—she also gave to her husband, extending the sphere of her disobedience.

Paul warned his protégé Timothy, "flee from youthful passions" (2 Tim. 2:22 HCSB). Instead of fleeing, Eve engaged in a conversation with her adversary, lingered in his presence, then allowed herself to be drawn into his net of deceit. Refuse to allow Satan to pull you into disobedience lest you, too, are guilty of disobedience and a conduit for the ravages of your sinful choices to extend to any with whom you have influence.

Excerpt taken from *The Devotional for Women* by Rhonda Harrington Kelley and Dorothy Kelley Patterson (© 2015).

The Unimaginable

"Do not be afraid, Abram. I am your shield; your reward will be very great." (Genesis 15:1 HCSB)

Life changes in an instant. But even when that change is unwelcome, we can give thanks because God is good.

A lot of men and women in the Bible were fighting for permanent just like us.

Take Abraham, for example.

Abram's permanent was his family's land and his wife, Sarai. (Later they would be known as Abraham and Sarah. Not even names are permanent!)

Sarai's permanent was that she was barren. This was life as they'd known it for all of their married life. At ages seventy-five and sixty-five, barrenness was their reality. Together they lived in the land of Ur and had a family lineage that included worshipping false gods (Josh. 24:2–3).

Well. With God you're never too old for your circumstances to change. God came to Abram and said, "Go from your country, your people and your father's household to the land I will show you" (Gen. 12:1 NIV). Just like that, their permanent passed away forever. Life would never be the same.

The land in which they lived and the God they worshiped weren't the only circumstances that changed. It turns out even barrenness in your nineties isn't a permanent situation when God ordains something else. God promised Abram and Sarai a son. Not just a son, but descendants so numerous, they would outnumber the stars in the heavens and the sand in the sea.

If you're keeping track, that's us, you guys. We're the sand and the stars.

God's promise to Abram (known to theologians as the Abrahamic Covenant) meant He was going to make him the father of a great nation. God would bless Abraham, make his name great, curse anyone who curses him, and "all the peoples on earth will be blessed through [him]" (Gen. 12:2–3 HCSB). This one-time, never-broken promise began the history of the people of Israel.

From Abraham and Sarah's small-picture view, leaving their home country and trusting the call of a God they barely knew must've been tough. In fact, the Bible tells us they were zoomed in tight on the details of how they would possibly conceive in their old age and how they would know where they were going and who to take with them.

But from God's whole-picture view, these complicated roadblocks were simply minor details. This was the beginning of a nation and a promise of faithfulness that would be kept and honored forever. It was a great blessing. In His goodness, God helped Abraham and Sarah take their eyes away from the lens of the telescope of their present circumstances to see the entire sky of stars, saying, "Look toward heaven, and number the stars, if you are able to number them. . . . So shall your offspring be" (Gen. 15:5 ESV). Not just one son, but an entire sky's worth of sons and daughters—more than he could ever ask or imagine.

Excerpt taken from *She Reads Truth* by Raechel Myers and Amanda Bible Williams (© 2016).

Abused But Not Abandoned

*So she called the LORD who spoke to her: The God
Who Sees, for she said, "In this place, have I actually
seen the One who sees me?" (Genesis 16:13 HCSB)*

Hagar's life was truly heartbreaking. As the innocent maidservant of Sarah, she had no personal rights or physical protection. When Sarah was unable to conceive a child, she conceived a plan for Hagar to bear Abraham's child. Sarah's plot violated God's perfect plan for marriage and for her life and put Hagar in an extraordinarily difficult position.

You may already know where the story goes from there. Soon Ishmael was born to Hagar, and her problems intensified. Hagar despised her mistress and Sarah dealt harshly with her maid. Things went from bad to worse. Because of abuse and mistreatment, bitterness and conflict, Hagar fled. She needed an escape. Alone and afraid in the desert, this innocent victim realized she was not abandoned.

The angel of the Lord spoke to Hagar at her time of despair. She responded in faith to the God Who Sees. She dared to ask, "Have I also here seen Him who sees me?" (Gen. 16:13 NKJV). She had! Despite her difficult circumstances and human injustices, Hagar experienced the protection and provision of a just, loving God.

Innocent victims are all around us. So are women who are abused, cast out, mistreated, and shunned. Perhaps you are among them. God has not abandoned such women. He loves them and wants to care for them. Are there hurting women in your family or your church? Have they suffered mentally and emotionally due to mistreatment? Are there abused women in your community who have been exploited or battered? Have their rights been violated and their freedom been withheld? Are there impoverished women in the world? Have they been mistreated or massacred unjustly. Yes. There are hundreds of thousands of wounded women in our world. In the face of this war on women, we look to God's Word for hope and for marching orders.

I'm reminded of a New Orleans shelter that provides protection for homeless women and their children. It is a biblically-based ministry providing physical, emotional, and spiritual support to women in their times of greatest need. Whether exploited by others or battered by husbands, they receive help and hope from a loving staff. Many also receive job training and assistance with transitional living arrangements. It's a wonderful ministry to wounded women and a model we can apply in our own lives.

There are similar ministries in this country and around the world for women who are hurting. The God Who Sees them loves them and offers them protection. So can we.

Because God notices their needs and provides for them, we can do the same.

Because God sees their loneliness and comforts them, we can seek to bring lonely women into the fold.

Because God recognizes their bondage and offers them freedom in Christ, we are compelled to share the gospel with wounded women.

Excerpt taken from *The Devotional for Women* by Rhonda Harrington Kelley and Dorothy Kelley Patterson (© 2015).

The Promise Kept

God himself will provide the lamb for the
burnt offering. (Genesis 22:8 NIV)

Abraham was intimately acquainted with God.

He'd been given the promise of generations as numerous as the stars and He took God at His Word. Those words must have held Abraham through many seasons of doubt and loss, but none greater than the test he would be given when his son Isaac was nearly a grown man himself.

And then God spoke words Abraham never could've anticipated.

"Take your son, your only son Isaac, whom you love, and go to the land of Moriah, and offer him there as a burnt offering on one of the mountains of which I shall tell you" (Gen. 22:2 ESV).

I don't know what Abraham felt in that moment, but if his actions are an indication, he was prepared for obedience. He rose early the next morning, saddled his donkey, and gathered two of his men and Isaac, cutting the wood for the burnt offering himself. God hadn't told him where exactly they were going, so he just began walking.

Three days pass.

Sound familiar?

On the third day, Abraham "lifted up his eyes and saw" (v. 4 ESV) the mountain where he was to sacrifice his son. He told the two men he and his son were going to go there, and that *they* would be back. Not *I* will be back; *we* will be back. Hebrews 11 tells us

Abraham knew God was able to raise Isaac from the dead. As a result of that faith, he and his son go and worship before continuing.

Worship.

They expressed praise in spite of circumstance.

I don't know when Isaac realized (or was informed) he was going to be sacrificed, but it's clear he accepted it on the same faith as his father. After all, Abraham was an elderly man and could hardly have kept his son on the altar if Isaac had fought him. Yet we see, even as Abraham bound him, he wasn't struggling to get loose or even questioning the situation.

As Abraham lifted his knife in the air, an angel of the Lord cried mercy.

"Abraham, Abraham!"

"Here I am" (v. 11 ESV).

Here I am, Lord. With my arm raised and ready to take the life of the son I love if You should say the word. Not because I understand it, but because You told me to and I trust what You know more than what I can see.

As Abraham and Isaac climbed the mountain, Abraham assured his son with the words,

"God will provide for himself the lamb for a burnt offering" (v. 8 ESV).

That was the promise.

Not a thicket.

Not a ram.

A Lamb.

The Lamb.

He is a God who cannot break His Word and around two thousand years later, God would provide exactly that: our perfect, spotless Lamb, who came to swallow our sin and provide our eternal security. He was the promise, and the promise was kept.

Excerpt taken from *Chasing God* by Angie Smith (© 2014).

A Satisfied Life

*This is the length of Abraham's life: 175 years. He took his
last breath and died at a good old age, old and contented,
and he was gathered to his people. (Genesis 25:7–8 CSB)*

So how do we find the best in life? Abraham found it, dying as
"an old man and satisfied with life" (Gen. 25:8 NASB). This capstone statement reveals a life rewarded with a deep sense of personal
fulfillment and gratification. It also suggests a life with few regrets.
In short, life worked for Abraham. It came together with a "Wow!"
rather than a whimper, and paid rich dividends. Is there a woman or
man alive today who wouldn't want a life like this? So what's the
secret to living such a satisfied life?

We look to many different things for satisfaction. It's easy, for
example, to consider life as good and satisfying if we have a happy
marriage, rewarding kids, or a fulfilling job. Some people look to
unhealthier things. It's a particular temptation in America today to
look to money to somehow "buy" happiness. The truth is, of course,
that it often buys the opposite, especially when it becomes the goal
of life.

Really, *anything* we rely on for happiness or contentment other
than God is going to be toxic for happiness in the end. So if love of
money, for example, is toxic for happiness, what's the tonic?

The big-picture answer is a relationship with God that is so
vibrant we don't rely or lean on anything *but* Him. But the specific
way that God—through relationship—leads His people to a satisfying life is this: *purpose.*

God has a purpose for every person, and deep down, we all long to find it. So how do we know which way is the right way? How do we find our purpose? For us, we know studying and searching the Bible are huge assets in this undertaking because it contains a treasure trove of proven guidelines.

Yet many of us are already trying to live a godly life and follow the Bible's specific precepts, and we *still* aren't sure exactly which choices to make among all our opportunities and demands on our time. We're still stressed and torn. Many of us might doubt whether, in fact, the Bible can even provide that sort of ultra-practical, day-to-day direction for us as modern women, since the choices that are open to us today couldn't have even been imagined thousands of years ago when the Bible was written.

While our world has changed around us, certain things have remained. Our design as human beings hasn't changed from two thousand years ago. Nor has our design as women. God's design has given us both universal and individual gifts and callings for His purposes—that hasn't changed either.

No matter what your life looks like, God has a calling and a place that He has specially designed for you. And He *wants* each of us to find it.

Excerpt taken from *The Life Ready Woman* by Shaunti Feldhahn and Robert Lewis (© 2011).

God Alone

And she conceived again, gave birth to a son, and said, "This time I will praise the LORD." Therefore she named him Judah. Then Leah stopped having children. (Genesis 29:35 HCSB)

I can sometimes grow distant from God when I get so close to someone else that I feel like maybe that person can take a little of His responsibility or accomplish some of the things in my life that I should truly get solely from Him.

I remember walking through a season where this was particularly evident to me. I was a newlywed and I believed that my new husband had hung the moon, relying on him to help me process every emotion, being every person I needed, and depending on him in a way that I allowed to hinder my relationship with the Lord. I didn't feel the need for God the way I should have.

Well, the Lord loves an opportunity to draw us close to Him, doesn't He? Several months into our marriage we found out I was pregnant with twins and my husband was on the road quite a bit at that time. I threw up all day (and night) long, crying myself to sleep because I felt so alone. I would wait for him to call me after work and when he did I would unload my mental artillery and wait for him to come up with a solution. My mental health pretty much depended on him picking the right thing to say. I was a wreck. No matter how hard he tried, or how much he wanted to be enough, he couldn't be.

He wasn't meant to be.

Think of the story of Rachel and Leah. Two sisters married to one man, Jacob. The Bible cuts right to the chase in telling us that

Jacob was over the moon in love with Rachel but that Leah was unloved. I imagine Leah weeping night after night as she wrestled with the fact that her love was sharing a bed with her sister while she cared for his children. As much as I sympathize with Leah, I admire the way she chose her God over her husband and set out on a new path to bring Him glory.

Those of you who are familiar with this particular story probably know that from the line of Judah comes our Christ. The Lord chose the woman who had been rejected to be part of the lineage that brought the Redeemer Himself. What a beautiful, profound image for all of us who are tempted to believe that our pain can't be transformed into glory.

What we see as someone failing us is the chance to see God refuse to do so. Sometimes I think He allows us to go down our little bunny-trails of expectation with others because we have to learn the hard way in order for it to be real to us. He is the only One Who can love us in a way that truly satisfies our souls.

Excerpt taken from *What Women Fear* by Angie Smith (© 2011).

Who Are You Now?

*"You have struggled with God and with men
and have prevailed." (Genesis 32:28 HSCB)*

In the book of Genesis we meet a pregnant woman who is carrying twins. As she delivers them, one holds onto the heel of the other. He is born second, but it seems that from the time he enters the world he is trying to get ahead. His name is Jacob, which means "heel-grabber, usurper, deceiver."

True to his name, Jacob lives a life of deception. At one point he tricks his father into believing he is his twin brother Esau in order to steal his blessing. He succeeds, and when his brother discovers what has happened he despises Jacob and fantasizes about killing him, so Jacob flees.

Some time later Jacob is on the run again. This time he is traveling with his wives and children and is told that his brother Esau is coming to meet with him. Jacob is fearful of an attack. The night before he is to see Esau, he settles his family in a safe area and then goes off on his own.

At this point Jacob becomes engaged in a wrestling match with the Lord, and in the process of the hours-long battle he is asked a question that will change everything, both for him and for us.

The sun starts to come up after a night of struggle and Jacob refuses to let go. It is as if he realizes this could be the night that will make God the victor over much of the ugliness in his life. Jacob insists upon a blessing. At this request, the Lord simply asks him, "What is your name?"

Let's take a moment and consider the question in its truest form.

"Who are you, now?"

I've been there with the Lord.

I've wrestled until the break of dawn, begging the Lord to save me from my circumstances and bless me in spite of my transgressions. I have stared at myself in the mirror, wondering who I was underneath the makeup, underneath the mistakes, underneath the moments I wish I could do differently. I have felt shame as He asked me to say it, knowing that it was only by His grace that it would be different.

I believe in every one of those moments we have a Savior who is asking the same of us . . . *What is your name? Who have I truly intended you to be?*

And so we wrestle.

I love the fact that Jacob's wrestling happened through the night, where things are hard to see and equally hard to comprehend. You can't quite wrap your brain around what is happening, other than knowing you are in the fight of your life. And even though you do not know where you are getting the strength, just like Jacob, you do not let go. Suddenly, it is daybreak. The shadows disappear and the light casts awareness on the situation. We see that it is not foe we are up against, but rather the One Who came to be our ever-present help.

Excerpt taken from *What Women Fear* by Angie Smith (© 2011).

What's in a Name?

*God said to Moses, "I AM WHO I AM." And he said, "Say
this to the people of Israel: 'I AM has sent me to you.'" God
also said to Moses, "Say this to the people of Israel: 'The
LORD, the God of your fathers, the God of Abraham, the
God of Isaac, and the God of Jacob, has sent me to you.'
This is my name forever, and thus I am to be remembered
throughout all generations." (Exodus 3:14–15 ESV)*

When I'm pregnant, I want to find out the gender of my baby
ASAP. When I can start calling the bundle of joy stirring
inside me by name, a connection is made that I lacked before. Their
names distinguish them. In naming our children, we took care to
select names that meant something desirable, not that just sounded
lovely, in case they lived up to their names.

Names help define.

There are different names for God that He revealed to His people to distinguish and define Himself from among other gods. "The
LORD" in Hebrew is *Yahweh*, the secret name for God. A name so
holy and sacred the Israelites would not utter it.

Abraham was a man called by God to leave his family, his people, and his country to go to a land the Lord promised to give him.
Through false starts and faith-testing delays, God fulfilled His
promise of a son to Abraham. His wife, Sarah, gave birth in her old
age to Isaac who eventually became the father of Jacob, also known
as Israel, from which we get the term "Israelites."

One of Jacob's sons, Joseph, was sold by his brothers into slavery
in Egypt. Although it seemed a bleak prospect, God used the
betrayal of Joseph's brothers to bring about salvation for their

family. By God's favor and grace, Joseph rose from slave to overseer of Pharaoh's house. When the land in which Jacob and his sons lived was depleted by famine, they were able to seek refuge in Egypt because of Joseph's gracious forgiveness and covering. All the sons of Jacob and their families "were fruitful and increased greatly; they multiplied and grew exceedingly strong, so that the land was filled with them" (Exod. 1:7 ESV).

A new king rose to power in Egypt who did not know Joseph. He looked at the Israelites not as a blessing but as a threat. So he oppressed them. They became slaves. Along with their chains, a great darkness laid on God's people. No light at the end of the tunnel, only an endlessly black corridor.

But God remembered His promise to them. He heard their cries and lit up the interminable night with a burning bush. In Exodus 3:14–15, God finally introduces Himself to Moses as the LORD: Yahweh, "I AM WHO I AM" (ESV).

Names help define.

God has no beginning and no end. He has always been and will always be. Nothing and no one made Him. He just is. And what He is He will always be.

Excerpt taken from *Steadfast Love* by Lauren Chandler (© 2016).

Protection in the Wilderness

*But God led the people around by the way of the
wilderness toward the Red Sea. (Exodus 13:18 ESV)*

If it troubles you to think of God allowing you to travel through a
rough patch just so you can know Him better—if that sounds
incredibly heavy-handed, borderline heartless—consider that the
wilderness is often safer than the alternative.

All we know for sure is what we see in our own situation. From
that grass-is-greener vantage point, it's easy to dress up our imaginary fantasy lands in colors to match the rainbow. But we can't
know, as God does, the harsh realities we'd have faced in places we've
never been. So in order to shelter us from danger, He sometimes
hedges us inside areas that, although perhaps extremely uncomfortable and unwanted, are much safer than we realize, much less painful than what we *could* be experiencing.

Yes, He's protecting us from dangerous outsiders and situations,
but He's also protecting us from ourselves. Take a look, for example,
at the Hebrews marching out of Egypt, assembling themselves "in
martial array" (Exod. 13:18 NASB), as though they really knew what
they were doing. It's almost funny, the image of them flexing their
reedy muscles and strapping on their homemade gear, a bunch of
skinny bricklayers pretending to be skilled in the art of battle—who
were they trying to kid? What kind of enemy did they think they
could overpower?

God knew they weren't going to strike fear in the hearts of savage armies by shaking their fists and slinging rocks. Besides, the
battle they would ultimately be called upon to wage was to be a

spiritual battle. They may have *thought* they were ready to take on all comers, but God knew their meeting with the Philistines would no doubt end in utter defeat and dissuade them from His purposes. And besides, there was a lot of preparation still to be done in their hearts and souls.

We simply cannot know who we'd be if it weren't for the wilderness. Even the great apostle Paul was dispatched to Arabia and other lonely places for three years after his dramatic conversion to Christ (see Gal. 1:15–18), where he got to know God in pivotal ways that would prepare him for his historic ministry to the first-century world—and to us. Peter certainly found himself stumbling and off balance in the wilderness after his denial of Christ, but this was valuable time if he was to become the firebrand preacher of Pentecost. John, late in life, was exiled on the island prison of Patmos—a wilderness if ever there was one, but apparently the ideal spot for God to reveal Himself in all His galloping glory.

From the dry, dusty middle of our wilderness, we may not be able to see any good reason for it or any good intentions on God's part for bringing us here. But again, figuring out the wilderness is not our job. If we'll just yield to God's purposes for us in the wilderness, He'll protect us from ourselves and prepare us for our destiny.

Excerpt taken from *One in a Million* by Priscilla Shirer (© 2010).

Dead Ahead

*They set out from Succoth and camped in Etham on
the edge of the wilderness. (Exodus 13:20 NASB)*

There it was. The wilderness. Settled at Etham, they could see
it—coughing and swirling in the hot desert wind. The last place
their tired feet wanted to take them. The wild, time-wasting
wilderness.

We know from Exodus 13:21–22 (NASB) that God had already
been "going before them in a pillar of cloud by day . . . and in a pillar of fire by night," a manifestation of His presence He did not take
away from them for one minute. For the last little while, His hovering cloud had held stationary over Etham, the place where God
wanted them to camp out and catch their breath. From this settled
location they could look north and see the easiest, most convenient
route to Canaan. But they could also sit and look to the south,
where they saw nothing but wilderness—dry, dusty wilderness—
and God's pillar of cloud, beckoning them to follow Him into the
bleakness.

What do you do in a situation like that? How will you respond
when you're at Etham with a clear view of a more comfortable route
but also a sure certainty that God's presence is leading you another
way? The Israelites had that kind of decision to make: should they
turn back and take what seemed to be the most simple path to where
they were headed, or should they continue pursuing God, knowing
full well that the direction He was going would lead them on a more
difficult route?

Maybe you're at a place like that, camped out at your own personal Etham. Do you stay in this tough marriage? Do you keep trying to parent these difficult children? Do you accept singleness as a way of life, at least for now? Do you suffer in some way or another without letting it turn into bitterness, without letting it veer you off the path God knows you need to take to experience fullness of life with Him?

Let me make something clear at this point: *the wilderness is not a necessity to reaching spiritual abundance.* Yes, we live in a fallen world, and the wilderness will likely be a part of everyone's experience at one time or another (John 16:33). But "God is love" first and foremost (1 John 4:16 NASB), and "the LORD is righteous in all His ways and *kind* in all His deeds" (Ps. 145:17 NASB, author emphasis). He will use the wilderness when He knows we need it, when it's part of His purpose for how He desires to grow us and use us.

You needn't be terrified of God, always wondering when or how He's going to allow a season of trouble. Nor should you be terrified of tragedy, as though you could never endure it. Yet each of us does need to consider how we'll respond if we indeed discover that a wilderness experience—for us, for now—has become His will.

Excerpt taken from *One in a Million* by Priscilla Shirer (© 2010).

Glory, Glory

"I will receive glory by means of Pharaoh and all his army, and the Egyptians will know that I am the LORD." (Exodus 14:4 CSB)

R eadiness for Canaan. Nearness to God.

These are healthy motivators for us to keep our focus upward and our goals eternal. But there's still one thing that matters more while we're in the waiting: Glory. *God's* glory. The Lord tipped His people off to this grand purpose for the wilderness when He proclaimed victory, even as Pharaoh had set out with his troops to corral them at the Red Sea.

This is what God was after: to be fully believed and trusted, and given the immense weight and credibility He deserves. He wanted this not only at the Red Sea but also in the days and years that followed—even in the in-between times. He wants your life to give daily evidence of His presence as seen in the way you handle everything from prosperity to heartbreaking loss, everything from buzzed-up excitement to complete boredom. He wants His influence to weigh more heavily over your actions and decisions than all those me-first and people-pleasing attitudes that often come quickest to mind. He may even want you to be squeezed into a situation where no other explanation can suffice for your deliverance than that God has done something special for you.

Give Him glory.

I can look back at some of our past difficulties and dry patches and see the ways God eventually intervened to change things for the better. I remember the miracles He performed. I recall the unexpected convergence of events He caused to occur, citing how He performed a mighty rescue of our health, finances, and prospects for the future. I see (at least I *hope* I can see) how we gave Him glory for that—not perfectly but at least purposefully—and how anyone who either witnessed or heard of it should've been able to recognize it as the obvious work of God.

That's great. That's what's supposed to happen.

But here's how we test whether or not we're learning what God is teaching in His wilderness lectures. Here's how we know if we've been paying attention when He's made the circuit through our lives: when we have spiritual vision and anticipation to *expect* God to wring glory out of this in-between situation—a tight, uncomfortable spot that's a whole lot easier to gripe about than to pray over. (Now this—*this*—is what I've got to work on.) If we've grasped the fact that nearness to God and a developing readiness for Canaan are more valuable than anything else. If we can keep ourselves fixated on reflecting His glory rather than repeating our self-consumed complaints.

What's He going to do to fix our situation? I don't know.

But what's going to happen if we yield to Him while we're in it? God's gettin' glory.

And I can live with that. How about you?

Excerpt taken from *One in a Million* by Priscilla Shirer (© 2010).

The Reeds

The LORD will fight for you; you need
only to be still. (Exodus 14:14 NIV)

A baby was drawn out of the water to be used by our Lord. God had great things planned for him. The providence of the Lord allowed his mother to keep him hidden at his birth, ordained that Pharaoh's daughter would be bathing at the exact time his basket would be in the reeds to draw her attention, and made sure Moses' sister was near enough to connect them all back to Moses' mother (see Exod. 2:1–10). It is beautiful to see them in my mind's eye, as the Lord orchestrated the life of Moses.

From the life of Moses we can see the sovereignty of God, who uses the details of life to bring about His plans. For Moses this meant being rescued as a baby and used mightily for the Lord. And oftentimes for us His providence leads to experiences on this earth that bring great joy and deliverance as literal as what the Egyptians experienced when God fought for them and parted the sea. But is that it? Promise of happiness for all?

Well, not so quick. Moses led God's people through the wilderness, but he never got to experience the Promised Land himself. Just as for Moses, our lives are also a mixture of circumstances that lead us to rest and revel in the providence of God, and circumstances that drive us to our knees and question how such things could happen.

The Lord walks beside me as He walked beside Moses. He knows me by name. He loves me and I love Him. I've learned to trust Him in the reeds, and yet, here I am, worshipping the God who allows it. I still believe that He will fight for me and that I can be still. I believe in the providence of God, even when it feels contrary to what my heart desires.

But I'm certain you have faced circumstances that felt overwhelming. You have lived with things you wish you could have changed. And you have probably questioned why God would allow you to experience such things.

None of us knows how long we have or how many trials we will face. We do not know whether we will see victory on this earth or in eternity. You can know the God who knows all of this, though. The God whose hand was on Moses in the basket has His hand on you. Be still and let Him fight for you (Exod. 14:14). Trust not in your circumstances, but in His power to overcome.

He has not abandoned you, and He has not abandoned me. He is the God powerful over the universe. He is the God powerful over broken dreams and hopeless situations. He created you.

Be still and let Him fight for you.

Excerpt taken from *Mended* by Angie Smith (© 2012).

Emotional Healing

*And he cried to the LORD, and the LORD showed
him a log, and he threw it into the water, and the
water became sweet. (Exodus 15:25 ESV)*

God can work a miracle in your emotions, you know.

His goal for our journey isn't just that we see His power at work in our *experiences*. He also wants us to see His miraculous power at work in our *emotions*. That's why when Moses cried out to God, in one swift move of vulnerability and obedience, he found God ready to act, relieving both the Israelites' thirst and their tired emotions. That which was bitter had been made sweet.

Are you bitter because of the hand you've been dealt? Sometimes He'll allow us to come face-to-face with an experience that could potentially breed bitterness, just so we can see His ability to work miracles in the way we feel. He wants us to know that our natural slide into bitterness and anger can be caught by the rescuing hand of His grace, then transformed into a state of mind, mood, and motivation that could only come from the Lord Himself. One word from God, and the bitter can become sweet, my friend.

Only God can bring a smile to the face of one who's going through a bitter divorce.

Only God can call up a sigh of relief from the dry mouth of one who's fighting disease.

Only God can usher peace into the heart of one who's brokenhearted.

Only God can quiet the screeching fears of one whose worries keep her up at night.

Only God can stir feelings of contentment in one whose financial condition is in peril.

So when Moses, who was just as thirsty as everyone else, either tasted the bitter water himself or heard the raucous complaining of the crowd, he didn't shake his fist at such bad misfortune. He knew how to handle bitterness. His first response was to cry out to the Lord, the only place he knew his help could come from.

"And the LORD showed him a tree" (Exod. 15:25 NASB).

Now if Moses had gone to throwing things, if he'd joined the crowd in wanting to go back for some decent drinking water in Egypt, if he'd been fed up with the challenges of living in the wilderness, he might've missed the miracle God was waiting to perform. We can sometimes get so focused on one thing, the one way we want God to act on our behalf, that we close ourselves off from His greater purposes.

This all comes from trying to *fix* the wilderness rather than *yield* to the wilderness. But if you lean into what God's doing in the midst of your struggle, He'll show you, just as He did Moses, how to take that huge heartache of yours and turn it into a sweet spot that daily reminds you how big and powerful your God really is.

Excerpt taken from *One in a Million* by Priscilla Shirer (© 2010).

Enough to Match Your Need

*They came to Elim where there were twelve springs
of water and seventy date palms, and they camped
there beside the waters. (Exodus 15:27 NASB)*

Elim was the most extensive watercourse in the area, estimated to be about a mile wide, an oasis adorned with a great variety of trees. Imagine the thirsty, discouraged Hebrews squinting through the blurry haze of sand, seeing in the distance what appeared to be a palm tree. Imagine how the buzz of surprise must have spread through the ranks when, not just one, but *dozens* of trees were spotted. Palm trees meant nearby water, and nearby water meant these thirsty travelers had refreshment waiting on them just beyond the next rise. It must have seemed like a love letter sent to them straight from God.

An oasis.

In the wilderness.

And this is what makes a wilderness different from a desert. A desert is nothing more than a barren expanse of sand dunes that can't support wildlife or vegetation. A wilderness may certainly have long, arid regions like that, but the withering dryness is sprinkled at various places with springs and oases. Here and there grassy upland plains form a restful contrast to the rugged, inhospitable wasteland below. Although there were stretches of travel in the Israelites' journey where refreshment seemed scarce, their particular wilderness contained lush oases like that of Kadesh in the north, as well as the Wadi Feran near Sinai in the south, plus various brooks to break up the dryness. God's people might have died if He had marooned them in the desert, but no, He had led them into the wilderness, where just-in-time refreshment was at least occasionally on tap. God doesn't lead His people to a place where survival is not possible but rather to a stretch of land where they can be sustained. Thank God for choosing to allow wilderness travel for you and me, forgoing the road through the desert.

Look, in fact, at how precise God's provision was. "Twelve springs of water" to match the twelve tribes of Israel. What a great illustration of God's overwhelming care and specific concern for His people. He knows *exactly* what it takes to refresh you. When He chooses to encourage your heart with a dose of divine comfort, it won't look like what He gives to somebody else. You can be sure it's what He *knows* will be just the right amount and quality to refuel your tanks and recharge you for the journey. Whether it's a hug given at just the right moment, a word spoken in due season, an unexpected card or email, or a conference that refreshes you with fellowship and messages that seem to have your name on them, it'll be a $500 story uniquely designed for you—to keep you going when you don't think you can.

Please don't miss Him when He comes by to offer an "Elim" to you as you trudge along.

And don't lose track of the times He already has.

Excerpt taken from *One in a Million* by Priscilla Shirer (© 2010).

Jesus Honored the Sabbath

Tomorrow is a day of solemn rest, a holy
Sabbath to the LORD. (Exodus 16:23 ESV)

When Jesus retreated from His usual pace, He was modeling the practice of the Sabbath—a subject with more than a hundred and fifty mentions in Scripture, beginning in Exodus and wrapping up in Hebrews. The concept literally bookends much of God's Word.

We first see the word *Sabbath* in Exodus 16:23, after the Exodus, as the Israelites were learning to live in the wilderness. God promises to feed them manna from heaven, and then commands them to a holy day of rest, the Sabbath. We pick up two key parts of God's plan for the Sabbath here. The Sabbath is designed to be a day of solemn rest and it's to be holy.

This theme is woven through the rest of God's Word. In Exodus 20:8, Sabbath makes it into the Ten Commandments: "Remember the Sabbath day, to keep it holy." Notice what God isn't asking of us. He does not say, "Remember the Sabbath day, to keep it busy."

We associate Sabbath with the day we go to church. Certainly, a church service could be a valuable part of our Sabbath, but we tend to leave out the rhythm of space and rest that God modeled and then called us to emulate. I know that's been true in our house. We've been involved in every church activity that we possibly could, resulting in a Sunday schedule that looks like the rest of a busy work week.

No wonder we're lonely. We're empty and tired and have nothing to give. The people around us are in the same state. At this pace, we cannot nurture the intimacy with God and others that we are wired for.

God must've known we'd be slow learners in this area because He repeats His command to Sabbath over and over and over. In Exodus 31:13, He commands the Israelites to keep His Sabbath day "above all" (ESV). Clearly, when it comes to Sabbath rest, God means business.

In Leviticus 26:34, God reminds us to enjoy His Sabbath—that it was made for us (Mark 2:27). It is a gift to us. God asks us to honor the Sabbath because it's for our good. He hardwired us for connection, and then gave us a slot in which to connect.

For Jesus, Sabbath wasn't about rules or rigid scheduling. In Matthew 12, Jesus puts the Pharisees in their place when they tried to condemn He and His disciples for eating grain together on the Sabbath. That same passage describes Jesus healing a man with a withered hand on the Sabbath. He shows us the Sabbath is a space for connecting. If you have a chance to eat a meal with your friends, do it. If you can meet the needs of someone else, do that. Busyness chokes out these opportunities. Jesus shows us that part of Sabbath is making yourself available to be with and respond to others.

Excerpt taken from *Connected* by Erin Davis (© 2016).

Hold Me Up

When Moses' hands grew heavy, they took a stone and put it under him, and he sat down on it. Then Aaron and Hur supported his hands, one on one side and one on the other so that his hands remained steady until the sun went down. So Joshua defeated Amalek and his army with the sword. (Exodus 17:12–13 HCSB)

The body of Christ, His Church, is one of the most tangible evidences here on this temporary earth of the permanence of the gospel.

She gathers her people for worship and prayer, for confession and edification. She invites them to the table to remember the sacrificial death of Jesus, to give thanks for the indwelling of the Holy Spirit. Throughout space and time, from the first disciples to now, the Church has stood like a neon arrow pointing to the gospel by which it exists.

We don't just see the arrow on Sundays when we stand and sing the call to worship or sit and listen to the sermon. We see it in the Church's people, in day-to-day life, reminding us of what's true. The Church holds the gospel up high for us to see.

When the Israelites were wandering in the desert, they were attacked by the Amalekites. This was after the Lord delivered them from slavery and parted the Red Sea. After He rained down bread from heaven and caused water to pour from a rock, satisfying their thirst. Just as He'd rescued and sustained them so many times before, God would do the same during this battle. And He would choose to do so through a familiar image: Moses' arms raised in the air.

We see this image as Moses stood by the Red Sea, staff in hand, when God divided the water into two walls (Exod. 14:21), and when Moses raised his arms to strike the rock with his staff, producing water for the people at Horeb (Exod. 17:5–6). And as Joshua led the people into battle against Amalek, Moses' upraised arms determined the outcome of the fight. As long as Moses held up his arms, the Israelites prevailed; when he lowered them, the Amalekites prevailed. So Moses held up his arms.

Then something wonderfully ordinary happened. Moses' arms got tired. Moses, the man God had chosen to deliver His people from bondage and lead them to the Promised Land, needed help. Israel needed Moses to hold up his hands so they could win the battle. And Moses needed Aaron and Hur to help him hold up his hands.

We all need holding up. We all need our arms or our faith propped up by the arms or faith of another. When others live in the gospel and live it out, it helps us do the same. Like Moses and Aaron and Hur, we are all part of the great "cloud of witnesses" and it is our responsibility to point our brothers' and sisters' eyes to Jesus, "the source and perfecter of our faith" (Heb. 12:1–2 HCSB).

Excerpt taken from *She Reads Truth* by Raechel Myers and Amanda Bible Williams (© 2016).

A God of His Word

"I am the LORD your God, who brought you out of the land of Egypt, out of the place of slavery." (Exodus 20:2 HCSB)

When we speak about someone's character, we sometimes use the phrase "He's a man of his word" to describe trustworthiness. Sometimes politicians are accused of making "hollow promises," a term that means their words can't be trusted. One of the reasons words are so is important because they convey the character of the person speaking them.

God is the Master Communicator. His law reflects His perfect moral character. God never speaks hollow words. Just as you can know what kind of mother a woman is to her children by the words she speaks to them, God's words reflect who He is. The rules He gives us reflect His character as a loving Father.

Consider the first words Moses recorded when God spoke the Ten Commandments: "I am the LORD your God" (Exod. 20:2 HCSB). This is covenant language that carries with it not only a statement of fact but of promise. With two simple words He reveals that He is the eternal and unchanging God.

Watch what comes next. See how God's name becomes synonymous with what He has done for Israel: "I am the LORD your God, who brought you out of the land of Egypt, out of the place of slavery." Though He is the God of all nations, He established a unique relationship with Israel. He became her Redeemer and Rescuer so that she would be His own possession, a kingdom of priests and a holy people. This is the relationship that forms the foundation for all of the Ten Commandments. It is precisely because He has rescued her and restored relationship with her that He demands moral fidelity from her. Israel's new identity is now tied to God's identity!

Imagine getting married and then, after the ceremony, continuing to live as though you were not married. No bride would go for that! Wedding ceremonies are always an outward expression of a commitment intended to shape and protect an ongoing, intimate relationship. Once married, it is right to have expectations of complete fidelity from your spouse.

In the same way, God did not just deliver Israel from the bondage of Egypt, He delivered them into His own presence! They were saved from slavery for God. God's love is signified not only in His delivering us from the bondage of sin but also in His expectations of fidelity from us. Failure to have those expectations would convey apathy and lack of affection, that we don't really belong to Him.

God's law was a gift to Israel that told them how to live as God's chosen people. Ultimately Israel's obedience would make them a "light to the nations" (Isa. 42:6; 49:6 HCSB) and "a city situated on a hill" (Matt. 5:14 HCSB) so that God's global plan of redemption would advance to all peoples. As undeserved recipients of grace from "I AM," we are living proof that He is a God of His Word.

Excerpt taken from *90 Days with the God Who Speaks* (© 2017).

Remember the Sabbath

"Remember the Sabbath day, to keep it holy." (Exodus 20:8 HCSB)

Are we so addicted to constant movement (even to our stress!) that we just don't know how to relax anymore? Are we so driven to performance and perfection that we can't see any value in a slowly paced day?

The woman resolved to live with grace rebels against our culture's resistance to rest. She understands that peace can only be experienced in her home if she purposefully creates margins to help herself and her family at least *occasionally* part ways from the hectic, demanding cycle of their usual activities. So she takes responsibility for planning deliberate opportunities for the age-old disciplines of rest and quiet. She is convinced that to "be still, and know that I am God" (Ps. 46:10 KJV) remains the most likely way for her and those she loves to sense His presence in her home.

I believe this principle is precisely what was on God's mind when He gave detailed instructions for Moses to relay to His beloved children of Israel. After nearly four hundred years of constant, grueling, daily servitude to Pharaoh in Egypt, this chosen generation had finally tasted freedom. And in the shower of God's deliverance, they were given (among others) instructions to "remember the Sabbath day, to keep it holy."

"Sabbath" is from the Hebrew word *Shabbat,* meaning "stopping" or "cessation." God was requiring His people to do something exactly opposite from what they'd grown used to doing. Instead of endlessly working, one day after another, engaging in every demanded activity, they were to *stop*—to purposefully carve out time to be still and enjoy Him—to celebrate a time of rest, rejuvenation, and spiritual focus that would perpetuate their experience of freedom, not just in theory but in the most practical terms. In other words, the Sabbath principle was the total reverse of the slavery they had already experienced in Egypt and a protection against sliding into bondage of another form.

And while we are no longer subject to the Old Testament law, this principle of Sabbath still carries fresh impact for us.

Our inclination toward incessant activity shows up in all of our crowded spaces—packed calendars, stuffed closets, jumbled minds that can't be turned off and quieted. We become slaves to busyness, slaves to the schedule, slaves to the disorder in our homes and our lives. We can't keep a single thought in our heads for more than thirty seconds. The roar never stops. We rarely just leave room for . . . *nothing*. Like Israel, we've grown so accustomed to constant activity that even when the opportunity arises to be still, we can't help but feel unsettled.

So in order to protect ourselves from being controlled and enslaved by our chaos, we must become women who intentionally create "Sabbath spaces"—margins in our lives that are left purposefully clean and clear so we can enjoy the liberty we've been granted by God Himself. Failure to do so will continue to result in more and more bondage.

Excerpt taken from *The Resolution for Women* by Priscilla Shirer (© 2011).

Seeing Vertically and Horizontally

Moses responded to the people, "Don't be afraid,
for God has come to test you, so that you will fear
Him and will not sin." (Exodus 20:20 HCSB)

To fully understand God's purpose in giving the Ten Commandments, it's helpful to examine how they are structured. The first four commands focus vertically on our relationship to God. The last six commands focus horizontally on our relationship to others.

As in all things of God, there in intentional order, in place for our good. It's of primary importance that we understand the character of God first, causing us to prioritize our relationship with Him. It is only ever as an outflow of that primary relationship, and God's work in us, that we can have right relationships with our fellow image bearers all around us.

Jesus may have alluded to this structure when He answered the question in Matthew 22:36–40 regarding which command is most important. Quoting Deuteronomy 6:5 Jesus said, "Love the LORD your God with all your heart, with all your soul, and with all your strength" (HCSB).

This summarizes the vertical nature of commandments 1–4.

Do not have other gods besides Me.

Do not make an idol for yourself.

Do not misuse the name of the LORD your God.

Remember the Sabbath day, to keep it holy (Exod. 20:3–8 HCSB).

Then Jesus went on to emphasize Leviticus 19:18: "Love your neighbor as yourself" (HCSB).

This summarizes the horizontal nature of commandments 5–10.

Honor your father and mother.

Do not murder.

Do not commit adultery.

Do not steal.

Do not give false testimony.

Do not covet (Exod. 20:12–17 HCSB).

It seems Jesus was saying that the two orientations, God-ward and man-ward, are tied together.

Just as the commandments have both a vertical and horizontal orientation, violation of the Ten Commandments has both vertical and horizontal consequences. God has given His commands to us as a gift, both to help us flourish in our walk with Him and to help us flourish in our relationships with each other.

Let's take King David, for example. One evening while his army was off to war without him, he went out on his rooftop and saw a beautiful woman bathing. He wanted her for himself, violating God's command not to covet. He took her and had sex with her as if she was his own even though she was married to another man, violating God's commands not to steal or to commit adultery. He lied about it, violating God's command not to give false testimony. He had the woman's husband killed to cover it up, violating God's command not to murder. But in his prayer of confession, he told God, "Against You—You alone—I have sinned and done this evil in Your sight" (Ps. 51:4 HCSB). David's transgression of commandments 6–10 was rooted in his pride and violation of the spirit of the first four. Break one commandment and it's like a house of cards: they all come tumbling down!

Excerpt taken from *90 Days with the God Who Speaks* (© 2017).

In His Presence

Now show me your glory. (Exodus 33:18 NIV)

The most beautiful, sacrificial, God-glorifying moments don't necessarily come when we feel fully convinced. I believe the times when I stand, face to the wind, telling Him I am choosing to trust Him even though I can't emotionally sense His presence are the instances He rejoices over my faith the most.

More often than not, we aren't going to have that radical revelation, and yet it is our will that continues to bow before Him with the words that rattle hell with their faith.

I don't see You, but I am believing that You see me.

As Christians, we don't always have a strong sense of His voice or presence as far as tangible, earth-shattering evidence, but we do have the gift of the Holy Spirit within us. We might not "hear" God, but we learn to trust the promptings we are given by His Spirit, and we act in accordance with that urging. God isn't making it a game where some people wander around wondering what they're supposed to be doing, while others have a navigation-like voice directing their every step.

The mistake we make is in assuming our feelings indicate the quality of our faith.

As a result, some people "are waiting to have an inward feeling that His words are true, before they will believe them. They look upon them as beautiful things for Him to say, and they wish they could believe them, but they do not think they can be true in their own special case, unless they have an inward feeling that they are; and if they should speak out honestly, they would confess that, since they have no such inward feeling, they do not believe His words apply to them; and as a consequence they do not in the least expect Him to actually care for their affairs at all. 'Oh, if I could only feel it was all true,' we say; and God says, 'Oh, if you would only believe it is all true!'"[1]

When we spend more of our time searching for assurance than we do acting out of belief, we are chasing God.

This came as a startling realization to me, because I am an emotional, experiential, and very intuitive person. So when I couldn't have that with the Lord, I saw myself as a failure, or worse yet, someone who hadn't tried hard enough to achieve it.

Maybe you want to shout along with Moses, "Show me Your glory!" But allow yourself to ask which two words are more important, and your answer will reveal your true devotion.

I chased God, shouting, *"Show me."* Truly abiding in Christ means whispering in every instance, *"Your glory. Only Your glory, Lord."*

We will have moments where we experience a sense of Him that is overwhelming and poetic, where the curtain is pulled back a bit on His essence. We may see His glory and we may not, but we do well to remember that His glory remains regardless.

Excerpt taken from *Chasing God* by Angie Smith (© 2014).

---

1. Hannah Whitall Smith, *The God of All Comfort* (Chicago, IL: Moody Publishers, 1953), 44.

Dropping Anchor

Then the LORD passed in front of him and proclaimed:
"Yahweh—Yahweh is a compassionate and gracious
God, slow to anger and rich in faithful love and truth,
maintaining faithful love to a thousand generations,
forgiving wrongdoing, rebellion, and sin. But He will not
leave the guilty unpunished, bringing the consequences of the
fathers' wrongdoing on the children and grandchildren to
the third and fourth generation." (Exodus 34:6–7 HCSB)

Of all the descriptors God could have used to describe Himself (holy, just, or righteous), He chose merciful, gracious, slow to anger, faithful, and abounding in steadfast love. He gave the Law and not ten seconds after He picked up His heavenly stylus from sacred stone did the people break it. And just like their father and mother, Adam and Eve, they dealt blame to whoever fit the bill. Sin upon sin. The LORD had every right to say, "I'm done. That's it." But He didn't. Instead, He demonstrated His *hesed*—His loyal, covenant-keeping love. He invited Moses to come near and intercede on behalf of the people. He granted Moses' request to let His presence remain with them. And He started over again. New tablets. Another chance. Mercy and forgiveness on thousands.

This is where *hesed* between humans and *hesed* from God toward His people differs. The mutuality of *hesed* humanly speaking is not the same with God. Even though Ruth freely showed kindness to Naomi, she mutually benefited from the wisdom and encouragement Naomi had to offer. And although Boaz freely showed kindness to Ruth and Naomi, he benefited by acquiring property, producing an heir, and continuing his own bloodline. God, however, needs nothing from us (Acts 17:25). Although the LORD requires faith and obedience from His people, He knows we are but dust and prone to wander, every one of us.

So, He made a way. The Way's shadow is cast long over the account in Exodus. There was a people created in the image of God for the display of His glory. But in their impatience and brokenness, they fashioned a replacement with their own hands. The law was broken. Instead of stone tablets breaking at the foot of a mountain, a body was broken on a cross atop a holy hill. Like Moses, the LORD interceded for the rebellious people. For "we have this as a sure and steadfast anchor of the soul, a hope that enters into the inner place behind the curtain, where Jesus has gone as a forerunner on our behalf" (Heb. 6:19–20 ESV). He gives, and becomes, another chance for us. Jesus embodies *hesed*. We know *hesed* because of Jesus.

By faith, we are invited to respond. We are beckoned to drop this anchor of hesed in our souls. To say, *I am guilty of trading the real God for a fake one; but You, oh God, have made a way according to Your steadfast love, Your* hesed, *through Jesus' perfect life on earth, death on the cross, and resurrection from the dead.*

Christ is the only anchor that truly holds.

Excerpt taken from *Steadfast Love* by Lauren Chandler (© 2016).

God's Plan for Rest

The LORD spoke to Moses on Mount Sinai: "Speak to the Israelites and tell them: When you enter the land I am giving you, the land will observe a Sabbath to the LORD." (Leviticus 25:1–2 HCSB)

God established the principle of Sabbath rest from the beginning: "He rested on the seventh day from all His work that He had done" (Gen. 2:2 HCSB). He also "blessed the seventh day and declared it holy, for on it He rested from His work of creation" (v. 3 HCSB). The fourth of the Ten Commandments—"Remember the Sabbath day, to keep it holy" (Exod. 20:8 HCSB)—is so fundamental that not only does explanation immediately follow the command, but also the rationale for the law is reiterated right away: "For the LORD made the heavens and the earth, the sea, and everything in them in six days; then He rested on the seventh day. Therefore the LORD blessed the Sabbath day and declared it holy" (v. 11 HCSB).

In Leviticus 25:2, God commands His people to apply the same principle of Sabbath rest to the land. This instruction would go into effect with the Israelites entered the Promised Land, where they were supposed to exemplify living abundantly under God's rule. If they were obedient, the Israelites—people who belonged to the Lord— would keep the seventh day holy by resting and honoring the Lord. Likewise, they would enforce a Sabbath year "of complete rest for the land in the seventh year, a Sabbath to the LORD" (v. 4 HCSB).

To observe the Sabbath day or year or planting season—whether as individuals, families, or farming communities—required the Israelites to exercise faith in the Lord and to keep His promises. At face value, these Sabbath commands make no sense to sinful minds. "What shall we eat in the seventh year if we don't sow or gather our produce?" (v. 20 HCSB). The Israelites wondered, as though God would command them to stop cultivating and harvesting for an entire year only to let His people starve. He promised them bumper crops for the sixth year and crops continuing to grow on their own during the seventh. They would have plenty to eat even during the eighth year of planning crops anew (vv. 21–22).

Observing the Sabbath as a day of rest doesn't make any more sense to us than it did to the Israelites, does it? We all know, "A woman's work is never done." Whatever the work is—housework or office work, home-based work or homework, volunteer work or busy work—how often we wear ourselves out trying to do it all our own way, using all seven days of the week, instead of living God's Sabbath way. Is it time to exercise your faith in the Lord to keep His promises so you can set apart "the seventh day" for worship and real rest?

Ask the Lord to make you aware of at least one change you can make today to enable you to establish God's principle of Sabbath rest in your life.

Excerpt taken from *The Devotional for Women* by Rhonda Harrington Kelley and Dorothy Kelley Patterson (© 2015).

A Sacred Vow

The LORD instructed Moses: "Speak to the Israelites and tell them: When a man or woman makes a special vow, a Nazirite vow, to consecrate himself to the LORD, he is to abstain from wine and beer. He must not drink vinegar made from wine or from beer. He must not drink any grape juice or eat fresh grapes or raisins. He is not to eat anything produced by the grapevine, from seeds to skin, during his vow. . . . He is holy to the LORD during the time of consecration." (Numbers 6:1–4, 8 HCSB)

God has always been interested in drawing men and women closer to His heart and His purpose for their lives. Just prior to the beginning of their journey from Mt. Sinai toward the land of Canaan, God gave a specific word to Moses to give to His people concerning a very special personal vow. The taking of this "Nazirite" vow was voluntary, not required. However, anyone who entered into the vow automatically bound themselves to fulfill it. Taking a vow is a very serious commitment in the eyes of God.

The Nazirite vow did not mean you came from Nazareth. Rather than describing a geographical location, this Hebrew word *nezer* means "separation." The person taking the Nazirite vow was making a personal decision to "separate" himself in distinctive ways for a period of time in order to walk more closely with God in an observable lifestyle of holiness.

Three "no touch" requirements were to be observed by the Nazirite:

- No razors.
- No dead bodies.
- No grapes.

Nazirites wore long hair untouched by a razor. Their physical appearance was unique. They were willing to appear differently in public. Nazirites refrained from the immediate defilement incurred with touching a dead body. They desired to remain eligible, fully qualified worshippers. Contact with dead bodies excluded individuals from worship for a time and required a special ceremony of cleansing. Nazirites refused to enjoy the fruit of the grapevine in any form. They chose to find their joy completely in the Lord, not in physical pleasure. Outward deeds gave testimony to their inward commitment.

According to Numbers 6:2, the opportunity to enter into the Nazirite vow was offered to both men and women. Biblical examples include Samson the judge (Judges 13), Samuel the prophet (1 Samuel 1), John the Baptist (Luke 1) and Paul the apostle (Acts 18:18).

Perhaps you desire a closer walk with God. On this side of the Cross of Calvary, please know that the key to understanding this passage of Scripture is not found in the keeping of requirements. Jesus died to set us free to live as willing, faithful, daily bondservants of His Father. The true definition of a modern-day Nazirite is discovered in a phrase that is repeated more than ten times in Numbers 6—"to the LORD" (NKJV). Turning our backs on things that bring sorrow to God will immediately focus the eyes of our hearts toward Him. Lives that lean toward God will begin to look more like Jesus.

Excerpt taken from *The Devotional for Women* by Rhonda Harrington Kelley and Dorothy Kelley Patterson (© 2015).

Covenant Promises

Know that the LORD your God is God, the faithful
God who keeps his gracious covenant loyalty for a
thousand generations with those who love him and
keep his commands. (Deuteronomy 7:9 CSB)

Facts are facts, and they are ever-changing in our lives.

Truth is different. Truth remains.

Promises are flimsy on a good day. They're just the stuff of life—mostly mundane. But that doesn't stop me from arranging my life around them and hoping for the best. And I expect life to go a certain way in return. The promises of the world aren't certain by any means, but that doesn't stop me from treating them like guarantees.

The Bible, too, is a collection of facts and promises. In day-to-day life, it's easy to expect the same thing from God's promises as I do the world's, treating them both like they're unshakable. Even worse, I'm prone to see the world-promises as sure footing while suspecting the Scripture-promises may shift.

God's promises to us, thankfully, are different. Because God is who He is—good, holy, faithful, just—His promises are, by nature, unbreakable. His promises are part of a covenant, an everlasting, over-arching capital-P Promise to His people. The promises are true because the Promise is true.

When I need proof of the Promise—which is every single day—I turn to Scripture.

I read about the God who created mankind from dust and in love, sealing that love with a promise, and not withdrawing when they rebel against Him (Gen. 3:15). This vow is our first glimpse of the covenant the Creator established with His creation: "I will not leave you to your sin. I will rescue you."

I see the covenant continue with Noah as a holy God wiped the earth clean of rampant evil, but not before stretching out His hand to cover one imperfect family (Gen. 6:17–18).

I read as God so poetically conveyed His covenant to Abraham, taking him outside to gaze at the stars and saying to him, "Your offspring will be that numerous" (Gen. 15:5 HCSB).

And then to David, the shepherd boy God plucked from the pasture to rule over Israel, God confirmed His covenant once more (2 Sam. 7:11–13).

In the pages of Scripture, we see God's covenant passed down from generation to generation, perfectly kept along the way and made new in the life, death, and resurrection of Jesus.

At the Last Supper with His disciples, Jesus gave thanks and broke the bread, saying, "This is My body, which is given for you." Then after supper He took the cup and held it up, saying, "This cup is the new covenant established by My blood" (Luke 22:19–20 HCSB). The new covenant in Christ still holds, from that supper table in Jerusalem to us here today.

"There's no such thing as a guarantee," the world generally agrees, and we know from experience that it's true. But we know God's promises are good. We know they are meant to be kept.

You and I were made for an unbreakable promise. We can have a guarantee. The one true covenant comes from the one true God, and we'll find it in His Word.

Excerpt taken from *She Reads Truth* by Raechel Myers and Amanda Bible Williams (© 2016).

The Promise or the Promise Giver?

*Remember that the LORD your God led you on the entire journey
these 40 years in the wilderness, so that He might humble you
and test you to know what was in your heart, whether or not
you would keep His commands. (Deuteronomy 8:2 HCSB)*

What had become clear from the Hebrews forty years of wandering in the wilderness was that God had used it to "humble" them. Not to *humiliate* them as Egypt's Pharaoh had done but rather to strip away the pride that would keep them from being submissive, teachable people who could handle abundant living with gratitude and perspective. By humbling them, the true intentions of their hearts and their level of commitment to obedience would be revealed.

The wilderness is often God's reminder that we're not as big, strong, and independently capable as we think we are. Wilderness travel causes us never to wake up to a day when we're not totally in need of His love, provision, and care. It reminds us of the reality that even when we're the most healthy, the most self-disciplined, the most on top of our daily schedule, we're still living off His blessings. We're here because of Him. Sometimes the wilderness is what it takes to help us remember that.

And the Lord knows that being humbled will inevitably reveal to us who we really are and what's in the depths of our hearts. The wilderness is designed "to test you to know what is in your heart," which is a good thing to know now because it'll come in handy later.

Like any good teacher, God wants us to know if the facts we're learning are just a bunch of names and dates in our minds or if they're finally starting to come together in something that resembles understanding. He wants us to know, if we're ready to make the leap from having His Word on the page to having His Word in our hearts, to see if all this pew-sitting is translating into pavement-walking.

So do we want the Promise Giver, or do we just want the Promised Land? The wilderness has a way of revealing our true intent, then leading us to love the former so we can genuinely experience the latter. God employed the wilderness to see "whether or not you would keep His commands." And without the wilderness, we don't possess the muscle tone and endurance to try that hard. Without His fatherly willingness to stretch us and test us and prove us and strengthen us, we can't call up the courage to obey God in the face of a challenge.

It's in the wilderness that you get to know God more intimately than you've ever known Him before. Here you develop the hard-won treasures of humility, authenticity, and obedience, becoming more prepared than ever to embrace fully the Promised Land life He has in store for you.

Excerpt taken from *One in a Million* by Priscilla Shirer (© 2010).

Leaving a Legacy

*See, I have set before you today life and prosperity, and
death and adversity; in that I command you today to love
the LORD your God, to walk in His ways and to keep His
commandments and His statutes and His judgments, that
you may live and multiply, and that the LORD your God
may bless you in the land where you are entering to possess
it. . . . So choose life in order that you may live, you and
your descendants. (Deuteronomy 30:15–16, 19 NASB)*

Are you making today's decisions with their impact on tomorrow
in mind? When you're arranging your priorities and forming
your habits, do you think about your children, your grandchildren,
about the kind of character they'll remember about you and inherit
from you? Do you ever stop to consider that you're perhaps playing
a role in the attitudes and observations of a young woman you
hardly know, maybe even a total stranger who one day hears someone telling what you were like?

These are the kinds of questions to keep in mind when thinking
about what you will do today. How you will respond in this moment.
What type of resolutions you will make and live by. These decisions
matter right now, and . . .

They *keep on* mattering. They are your legacy.

We know that a legacy, generally speaking, is an inheritance, a
gift bequeathed to others after a person's death. Usually the terms of
this transfer are carefully spelled out in an organized, legal document, detailing exactly how gifts of land, money, property, and possessions are to be distributed to a person's loved ones. As valid and
honorable as it is to make these kinds of arrangements, cementing

the tangible connection between generations, people tend to spend more time planning their physical inheritance than their spiritual one.

Our legacy of faith, compassion, gratitude, perseverance, forgiveness, patience, and love should be carefully crafted and then purposefully passed on.

Just you. Choosing to live today as if someone's tomorrow depended on it.

This seemed to be paramount in Moses' mind as he stood on the outskirts of the land of promise, having sojourned with God's people forty years in the wilderness. Here he was, 120 years old, nearing the end of his life, sharing the crucial messages on his heart in these final hours with his beloved friends and fellow citizens (Deut. 28–30).

He spoke of legacy.

He spoke of spiritual inheritance.

He encouraged God's people to make today's decisions with tomorrow in mind.

By choosing to love the Lord, to cling to Him, and commit themselves to Him in faithful obedience—*today*—the people of God could expect a long, prosperous existence as a nation *tomorrow*, filled with a lifetime supply of His joy and peace. In return for their faithful choices, they would be assured of "life"—a promising legacy of divine protection and provision to be handed down to their children and grandchildren as a heritage and birthright.

Pause and consider the way today's choices build a legacy for others to cash in tomorrow.

Excerpt taken from *The Resolution for Women* by Priscilla Shirer (© 2011).

A Choice to Make Today

See, today I have set before you life and prosperity,
death and adversity. (Deuteronomy 30:15 HCSB)

In Deuteronomy 28–30, Moses stands on the edge of the Promised Land with the people he's led for forty years and gives an inspiring speech about legacy.

I wonder if the men and women hearing Moses' words, thinking about what God was offering—I wonder if they looked down at their children, milling and playing around their feet, picturing them all grown up and experiencing the full, rich benefits of their parents' obedience—a mom and dad who chose to live in a way pleasing to the Lord.

I wonder, too, if they were equally lost in thought and in visions of the future when Moses presented the second alternative: *death*. Making this selection would result in consequences that were equally explicit—things like misery, loss of divine favor, the insecurity of living outside God's protection. Terrible stuff. Horrible, long-lasting side effects. Worse than the kind they rattle off on those prescription drug commercials that come on while you're cooking dinner.

Two choices. Life. Death.

Was there really a choice to make?

It all starts today.

With the decisions you'll make right now.

This was Eileen's reason for living well. She was a mother with eight children. Her husband worked like a madman to provide for the family. It was no easier on Eileen, who lost two of her children to death at birth, struggled with her own health, life was hard. Every day harder than the one before. But she had decided as a young woman that she would cultivate a legacy worth leaving to those she loved. So despite the many difficulties and challenges, she made each day of her life a decision to pay her legacy forward. To stay committed to her family and faithful to the Lord. To sit all eight of her children around her knees to read Scripture and pray over them. To invest herself fully in the work God had for her. It was difficult, but it was worth it.

Today, at ninety-two, with thirteen grands and twenty-one greats to go with her already enormous brood, you can see the sparkle in her eye when surrounded by the fruits of her labor. As she watches her posterity soaking in the favor of God's protection and provision, she takes that breath of a woman satisfied. You can see the framework of God's blessing in the lives of those who trace their history to her door. You can see that her wise decisions paid off.

This can be your legacy. It's not too late.

Today—truly, within the next twenty-four hours—an eye-opening choice is set before you. It's disguised as your next opportunity, your next option, your next decision, your next offer. Now's your chance to see these through the lens of Moses' biblical description. See them as small yet significant choices between death and life.

Is there really a choice to make? Choose life.

Choose wisely.

The legacy you are leaving depends on it.

Excerpt taken from *The Resolution for Women* by Priscilla Shirer (© 2011).

He Blesses What He Commands

*For I am commanding you today to love the LORD your
God, to walk in His ways, and to keep His commands,
statutes, and ordinances, so that you may live and multiply,
and the LORD your God may bless you in the land you
are entering to possess. (Deuteronomy 30:16 HCSB)*

We don't have to prove anything to God. He is the *kardiognostes*, the Knower of Hearts. He knows exactly what we're made of and exactly what He invested in us. He knows the immensity of the treasures He tucked way down inside of us in a place that can only be tapped by turmoil. God knows precisely how He gifted us and to what unfathomable degree He empowered us through His own Holy Spirit. He knows to the minutest detail how thoroughly He has equipped us. God cannot be conned. He requires no proof to quell His own curiosity. Confusion is human, not divine. God knows exactly how real or pretentious our faith is.

But we don't. That's the thing. Neither do the people in our homes, our workplaces, our churches, our social environments, or our spheres of influence. Neither do angels or demonic principalities. God tests us to bring out the real us. He tests us to prove our faithfulness to Him in front of a devil who bets we're fakes. God tests us to prove us genuine to *a large cloud of witnesses surrounding us* (Heb. 12:1). For crying out loud, He tests us to prove us genuine to ourselves, the last ones to usually know. God knows what is inside of you. That's the person He's trying to surface. If He's knocking the cover off of you, He's trying to get to the light.

And He does this out of deep love for us. A love that not only fuels endurance, but also feeds obedience. Look at John 14:15: "If you love Me, you will keep My commands" (HCSB).

Everything commanded by God commands blessing. It may come sooner. It may come later. But it will come. His way is the way of wholeness, goodness, rightness, and of glad and gleeful reaping.

We who live on this side of Christ's cross and resurrection dwell under the New Covenant where divine promises find parallels primarily in spiritual terms, which, incidentally, far surpass anything temporal. Jesus promised that our lives rather than our lands would bear much fruit. He promised that we would have, not just life but life more abundantly. He promised to multiply disciples all over the earth, invading every nation and people group with the gospel before He returns. And He's chosen to do that primarily through His own followers. What He commands, He blesses.

And listen, you can't live an obedient life and miss an adventure. When you give your heart over to the outrageous occupation of the glorious love of God, He will flabbergast your mind with a living, breathing reminder of 1 Corinthians 2:9:

> *What eye did not see and ear did not hear,*
> *and what never entered the human mind—*
> *God prepared this for those who love Him.* (HCSB)

Excerpt taken from *Audacious* by Beth Moore (© 2015).

The God Who Sees

*It is the LORD who goes before you. He will be with
you; he will not leave you or forsake you. Do not
fear or be dismayed. (Deuteronomy 31:8 ESV)*

Hagar was the Egyptian servant of Abram's wife Sarai. You can
read her story in Genesis 16. I'll give you the Wikipedia
version.

Sarai was old and infertile. Her craving for a baby was so intense
that she lost her mind for the briefest of moments and asked her
husband to sleep with another woman in order to give her a child.
Anyone who has seen an episode of *The Jerry Springer Show* could
have predicted that this was going to go wrong, but Abe said okay
and soon enough Hagar was pregnant with his baby.

As soon as the stick turned pink, the mean girl stuff started.
Hagar and Sarai couldn't stand each other and Abram excused himself from the situation. Eventually Hagar ran away into the
wilderness.

The story of Hagar's life teaches a profound lesson about loneliness. Her loneliness was deep and urgent. Her circumstances were
forced upon her. When things went bad, no one stuck with her. She
was abandoned and alone. A pregnant woman sitting by a spring in
the desert is a pretty vivid image of loneliness.

But she was never really alone. (Remember, neither are we.)

An angel of the Lord appeared to Hagar and before she could
even tell her side of the story, the angel made it clear that God knew
what was going on. He had seen this situation develop. He knew
her.

"So she called the name of the LORD who spoke to her, 'You are a God of seeing,' for she said, 'Truly here I have seen him who looks after me'" (Gen. 16:13 ESV).

The name for God we see in this passage is *El Roi*—"the God who sees me." Seeing us is part of who He is. He sees me. He sees you. He is thinking about you. He knows even the parts of your life that happen behind closed doors. He is always, always, always looking after you. If He needs to, He can chase you down in lonely deserts or alongside parade routes to remind you that He is with you.

This is just the tip of the iceberg when it comes to the promises of God. "It is the LORD who goes before you. He will be with you; he will not leave you or forsake you. Do not fear or be dismayed" (Deut. 31:8 ESV).

Do you feel lonely because no one is thinking about you? The truth is, since before you were even born, God hasn't stopped thinking about you.

Do you feel like no one notices just how hard life can be? God keeps a record of every heartbreak.

Do you feel friendless? Betrayed? Walked out on? The God who created everything out of nothing, who always was and always will be, whose name is Faithful and True, calls you His friend. His offer always stands.

Excerpt taken from *Connected* by Erin Davis (© 2016).

No Fair!

*The Rock—His work is perfect; all His ways are
entirely just. A faithful God, without prejudice, He is
righteous and true. (Deuteronomy 32:4 HCSB)*

A few months ago I bought a gift for one of my sons. My husband and I made the decision based on that particular son's needs. When my youngest son found out, he protested with cries of "No fair!" He felt as though we had done him a great injustice.

But his perception of justice is different from ours. We are the parents. He is the child. We make decisions taking into account factors he has no awareness of. As parents, we continually make decisions that our children could perceive as unfair. We paid for braces for one son's teeth. But not all of our sons got braces. We bought a new bicycle for one son; the other got a secondhand one.

We love our children equally, but we interact with them differently based on their age, their personality, their gifts, the character traits they need to develop in their lives, and a myriad of other factors, some of which have nothing to do with them at all. Our love and their equality of worth do not demand that we treat them exactly the same. According to my children, this sometimes appears unfair. But we know better. We are more mature and have a better sense of justice than they.

Justice means acting in accordance with what is right. It signifies "straightness" or acting correctly. God is just. He acts correctly. His ways are entirely just.

Psalm 45:6 says, "Your throne, God, is forever and ever; the scepter of Your kingdom is a scepter of justice" (HCSB). Those passages tell me that justice is no passing whim for our God. Justice is so built into the fabric of His nature that from eternity past to eternity future He will never for one moment act in any way that is not just.

Many times people treat us in ways that are unjust. When such injustice arises, you can do at least two things. You can draw the mistaken conclusion that God is also unfair, or you can learn to see earthly injustice as a contrast to God's character. Just as the black night is necessary to appreciate the brilliance of a sunrise, earthly injustice is but the absence of God's justice, and Scripture tells us that such injustice is but a precursor of the glory that is to follow.

Just as my sense of justice is more perfect than my children's, so the Father's sense of justice is more perfect than mine.

David said that the Father's righteousness is like the mighty mountains and His justice like the great deep (Ps. 36:6). This is a fitting analogy, for the ways of the Father are too high and too deep for us to comprehend fully. We cannot always know why, but when life seems unfair we can trust that the Father's ways are entirely just.

Excerpt taken from *In My Father's House* by Mary Kassian (© 2005).

Crossing Over

*Those which were flowing down toward the sea of the Arabah, the
Salt Sea, were completely cut off. So the people crossed opposite
Jericho. And the priests who carried the ark of the covenant of
the LORD stood firm on dry ground in the middle of the Jordan
while all Israel crossed on dry ground, until all the nation
had finished crossing the Jordan. (Joshua 3:16–17 NASB)*

Joshua gave the word, the one he had heard from the Lord, the
one that made this forty-year odyssey seem as though it were
finally going to end in triumph. It was finally going to take them
where they'd been headed all this time. After decades of roundabout
wandering, the children of Israel were about to walk a miraculous
straight line into the Promised Land.

The people woke up on that expectant morning, brought their
entire families out of their tents, and approached the swirling rapids
of the Jordan. The priests who carried the ark of God stepped off
the bank into the shallow east edge of the water.

At first it would have appeared as if nothing was happening
since the water didn't immediately divide right in front of them. But
what the children of Israel didn't know as they craned their necks to
the north was that far upstream God was already working His miracle for them. Though the roar of the current continued to drown
out conversations, clearly mitigating against a mass river crossing,
"the waters which were flowing down from above stood and rose up
in one heap, a great distance away at Adam, the city that is beside
Zarethan" (Josh. 3:16 NASB). Adam was thirty miles away. At this
place, far out of sight, the Jordan was even then starting to become

a dry riverbed. It was going to take a little while for the runoff to spill through at the Israelites' downstream location, but the miracle was already in progress.[1]

From your current vantage point you may not be able to see how God is going to work out His purposes in your life, the ones that seem far away and impossible to detect. You've gotten your feet wet, but life just seems to roll on like it always has, oblivious to your prayers and the faith you've placed in God's clear word to you. But be convinced that even though God may be working "a great distance" away, He is working. He has not forgotten His promises. He has not run into a snag that may prevent Him from following through. As you faithfully incorporate the new paradigm of Joshua's leadership into your life, be assured that God will carry out the miraculous plans He has for you. And you will see them with your own eyes, just as the Hebrews did when the remaining waves, stripped of their energy source, emptied out before them like water down a storm drain.

"All the nation."

Across.

They made it.

And so can we.

Excerpt taken from *One in a Million* by Priscilla Shirer (© 2010).

---

1. *A Commentary and Critical and Explanatory on the Old and New Testament*, Joshua 3:16, Logos Bible Software.

Keeping a Record

Then Joshua set up in Gilgal the 12 stones they had taken from the Jordan, and he said to the Israelites, "In the future, when your children ask their fathers, 'What is the meaning of these stones?' you should tell your children 'Israel crossed the Jordan on dry ground.'" (Joshua 4:20–22 HCSB)

Your legacy. It needs a script for others to follow. Both you and they need a way to remember.

Now let me preface what I'm about to share with you by confessing that I'm not all that fantastic when it comes to journaling. I wrote a little something in my journal last week, and it was my first entry since, oh, nine months ago? How's that for consistency?

Even though I've not been terribly dependable in this department, I'm grateful that the Lord has kept journaling an important part of my life. I'm the type of woman who journals when . . .

- something is pressing on my heart and mind.
- a specific milestone has been reached.
- the Lord has been doing an important, transformative work in me.
- I'm in the middle of a particular life occurrence that seems to hold implications I just know will matter in the future.

Fairly average days and events, in most respects. And yet the only thing that really makes them forgettable is when I fail to record them.

The day will certainly come when those to whom you desire to leave a vibrant spiritual heritage will be interested in seeing how you handled even an ordinary moment from an ordinary morning, how God's faithfulness and care and protection and guidance intersected your path one day and turned it into much more than just a routine traffic stop. They'll be curious to see how He moved and worked, through both your successes and your failures, your high spots and your biggest mistakes, wrapping them all in His sovereign grace and (with your cooperation) sealing them in ink on these simple pages.

It's good reading. Legacy making.

My point is—I'm not really asking you to resolve to journal—to do it in this one way and this one way only. I know the pen-and-paper method just doesn't match up for everybody. I get that. But I *am* asking you to find your own way to store up your legacy. To gather stones.

Obviously the life you live is much more important than the one you write down. The way you respond in practical, consistent ways to Christ's lordship is of much greater real-world importance than how some book of yours remembers it. But as a woman of resolutions, you bear a responsibility to others. This is not just about whether you like to do something. It's about priority. Purpose. Promises.

Just find your own unique way to do it, but don't leave your children and grandchildren without something to see and touch and feel and hear—something that shows what God has done to bring you and them to this moment in time. It's a masterpiece in the making.

Excerpt taken from *The Resolution for Women* by Priscilla Shirer (© 2011).

Exhausted Pursuit

Gideon and the 300 men came to the Jordan and crossed it.
They were exhausted but still in pursuit. (Judges 8:4 HCSB)

What are the areas in your life that you feel this fear most intensely? Do you fear you will be a failure as a spouse? As a parent? As an employee? As a friend?

Maybe you fear that you will fail at being a good Christian.

I wonder if that last one touched a nerve in you like it does in me. We struggle to get through the day feeling like we did faith "right" and we focus intently on our own missteps. We are all naturally sinners and the battle of the flesh is terrifically difficult to win. It's no wonder that we can get to a place where we feel like we aren't ever going to get it right.

Have you ever worried that maybe you were running out of chances?

I'm not going to give you some trite quote about this because anything I say will pale in comparison to the truth, which is that God loves and forgives us because once we have trusted in Christ for salvation, ultimately He does not see our sin when He looks at us. He sees Jesus' perfection.

Is that hard for you to comprehend? Well then. You're in good company.

What I want to encourage you to do is to try to change the way you think of "failing" God. First of all, if you are a believer in Christ, there is nothing you can do to separate yourself from Him (Rom. 8:38–39). You will continue to sin but you don't have to believe you are one big epic flop. Instead of spending your time lamenting your errors, pray about why those patterns of sin are present. Seek the counsel of those who have been there and ask them for advice. Tell the Lord every day that you need His help to serve Him wholeheartedly, and be disciplined in spending time in the Word.

After you have repented and committed your sin to the Lord, don't allow the enemy to tell you that you need to keep going back to it in your mind, because the more you dwell on it, the more likely you will repeat it. You will start to define yourself by your poor decisions instead of your great Redeemer, and it is far too easy to fall into old habits as the helplessness sets in. Instead, as you begin to set a pattern of repentance and submission to Him, you will see Him glorify Himself and redeem your sin.

In each day the Lord gives us, let us become consumed with the obedient pursuit instead of the perceived victory. Let us become exhausted as we seek the face of a God who delights in giving us power through our weaknesses. Let us reevaluate failure in light of the gracious God who calls us in the same breath He called Gideon.

Excerpt taken from *What Women Fear* by Angie Smith (© 2011).

A Vow Fulfilled

I prayed for this boy, and since the LORD gave me what I asked Him for, I now give the boy to the LORD. For as long as he lives, he is given to the LORD. (1 Samuel 1:27–28 HCSB)

Hannah named him Samuel. So precious. So prayed for. So deeply loved. And so very important to the Hebrew nation. "She named him Samuel, saying, 'Because I asked the LORD for him'" (1 Sam. 1:20 NIV). Hannah vowed to give the son she'd prayed for to the Lord; the child would be a Nazirite.

Imagine how much easier it would've been to make that promise about a hypothetical baby—before holding him in your arms. Imagine the emotion that must've flooded Hannah's mama heart. When Elkanah went up to make the annual sacrifice, Hannah stayed behind, but she told him, "After the boy is weaned, I will take him and present him before the LORD, and he will live there always" (v. 22 NIV).

And that's just what she did (v. 24 NIV).

God had a marvelous plan. He allowed Hannah to be childless so she'd petition God for a child instead of assuming it would be the normal result of marital relations. He also allowed Hannah to be deeply desirous of a child so she would dedicate him entirely to the Lord. He sovereignly planned for His word to come through Eli at the temple so that she would return him to the exact place where she made the vow. Why? Because God had a plan for Samuel that was far more significant than even the most loving set of parents could devise.

Surely while nursing him, Hannah looked into the face of her precious son, and with love overflowing, rehearsed the faithfulness of God in his tiny ears. No doubt he was weaned to know he was appointed to grow up in the house of the Lord. What did the child do when she took him there? "He worshiped the LORD" (v. 28 NIV).

How in the world could a child that age have such respect for the God of the universe? We get a clue from Hannah's prayer of praise, found in 1 Samuel 2:1–10 . . .

> There is no one holy like the LORD; there is no one besides you; there is no Rock like our God. (v. 2 NIV)

Samuel learned faith from his mother—a woman whose faithfulness evidenced her faith, a woman with compulsory praise on her lips. She met painful sacrifice with a song.

God does not ask of us that we take our children to the temple and leave them there to be reared by priests, but we must give them to God in other, equally important ways.

Remember the faith of Hannah. She sought God in her deep need. She made a vow that, by its very nature, was either a deep commitment or a hollow mockery. Then she fulfilled her vow with a mother's sacrifice.

Excerpt taken from *Portraits of Devotion* by Beth Moore (© 2014).

A Wise and Faithful Son

Saul's son Jonathan said to the attendant who
carried his weapons, "Come on, let's cross over to the
Philistine garrison on the other side." However, he
did not tell his father. (1 Samuel 14:1 HCSB)

Saul, a man with such potential, squandered the kingdom through his disobedience. His son Jonathan, however, was vastly different from his father—he was as noble as Saul was disappointing.

Once again Saul, Jonathan, and the Israelite army faced a far superior force of Philistines. The Israelites were hiding in fear, but Jonathan knew the army of the mighty God need not hide. Jonathan said to his armor-bearer:

> Come, let's go over to the outpost of those uncircumcised fellows. Perhaps the LORD will act in our behalf. Nothing can hinder the LORD from saving, whether by many or by few. (1 Sam. 14:6 NIV)

They challenged the Philistines, and God led them in the attack. Before the day ended, the Israelites had won a great victory.

Jonathan and his armor-bearer were worthy men. His keen perception of the Lord far exceeded that of his father Saul's. Jonathan knew the Lord. He knew the Lord could save, no matter who or how many were fighting the battle. In fact, he knew that if God chose to save, nothing could hinder Him! (1 Sam. 14:6). His faith in God's strength was solid.

Jonathan began the battle that quickly turned into a rout. God sent panic on the Philistines until they killed one another. The Israelites merely chased the Philistines in a mopping-up operation.

Then King Saul entered the picture. He saw the Philistine army in disarray and ordered the Israelites into battle. His actions were impulsive and unwise, forcing the army into an ill-advised and non-God-directed fast (1 Sam. 14:24).

We can learn a lot from Saul's rash behavior. No one should make decisions on impulse and certainly not without consulting God. Hasty, self-centered vows come at a cost. As the army chased the Philistines, they became exhausted. Since Jonathan wasn't in the camp, he didn't hear his father's command. When they came to a place where a beehive had been broken open, Jonathan ate some of the honey.

In this story we encounter an amazing and humbling truth: God expected the people to obey the king—even when his edicts made no sense. So the next day when they inquired of God, He remained silent. Through a process of elimination, they discovered that Jonathan had disobeyed the command of Saul. The king would've put his own son to death, but the men wouldn't allow it.

God tried to teach Saul a very serious lesson that day: His pride could've caused him to keep a foolish vow. Better to repent than to add foolishness to foolishness.

In the account of the battle and its aftermath, we see evidence that God is for us, not against us. He wants us fortified before our enemy with faith like Jonathan's, obedience like the armor-bearer's, and with the proper fuel like Saul's army should have received.

Excerpt taken from *Portraits of Devotion* by Beth Moore (© 2014).

A Better Gift

Then Samuel said: "Does the LORD take pleasure in burnt
offerings and sacrifices as much as in obeying the LORD?
Look: to obey is better than sacrifice, to pay attention is
better than the fat of rams." (1 Samuel 15:22 HCSB)

Sometimes when we're caught red-handed in our rebellious running, we react to the pain by making promises to change. We
decide to go back to our Monday night Bible study. We pray more.
We don't begin eating a meal, even in public, without saying a blessing. We do the things that make us feel spiritual, renewed, connected with God again.

Good.

But God is still seeking *relationship* with us and *obedience* from
us, not just a religious reaction. He would prefer that we get *right*
with Him rather than just behave for Him. And if we don't realize
that, then the same evasions and avoidances we'd been displaying
before—the ones God has been working to reveal to us by interrupt-
ing us, by intervening in our lives—may still persist even after we've
said we're sorry and tried to patch things up with Him.

"To obey is better than sacrifice," the prophet Samuel had said
to a misguided King Saul, who thought his disobedience to a clear
command from God could be overlooked by engaging in a religious
exercise that showed what a big, spiritual guy he was. But although
Yahweh had *allowed* sacrifices as a means of atoning for sin, they
were not his ultimate desire. He longed for people who had a heart
to obey Him and remain in fellowship with Him, not people who
chose their own path and then ran to the altar to gain forgiveness for

their actions. Offering a sacrifice was an easier option for Saul than his willing obedience.

We, too, have been known to disguise a measure of disobedience behind our "sacrifices"—well-meaning and heartfelt though they may be—thinking they cover and excuse us from having to deal any more deeply or personally with God. If we're faithful in church and singing in the choir and going on short-term mission trips, would He still expect us to deal with His latest command, to yield to His last set of instructions? Maybe, just maybe, we think we can do enough religious stuff to satisfy Him so He'll leave us alone. Hopefully, then, we won't have to say "yes" to any prompting of God that's always gotten a solid "no" from us before. Won't have to worry about responding to interruptions any differently than we ever do, not stopping to consider that they might be divine interventions—an invitation to participate with God in something eternally significant and supernatural.

Excerpt taken from *Life Interrupted* by Priscilla Shirer (© 2011).

Enough Already

*But the LORD said to Samuel, "Do not look at his appearance
or his stature, because I have rejected him. Man does
not see what the LORD sees, for man sees what is visible,
but the LORD sees the heart." (1 Samuel 16:7 HCSB)*

God is only concerned with the temporal as it relates to the eternal. He cares about my body as it pertains to my health, my self-discipline, my self-respect, my modesty, and my self-worth. The rest is neutral. He cares about the way your living room is decorated only to the degree that it reflects your spiritual condition: if you overspent, that matters. If you use it to entertain, love, grow children well, that matters. If you tend to it in such a way that allows you to be grateful and peaceful and happy, that matters. Beyond that, it's neutral, so don't fret so much about it. God is only ever concerned with what matters; He never needs a perspective shift. He IS the big picture. He IS wisdom. He IS the truth. And the thing that God cares about, the thing He looks at, is hearts.

God cares not one iota about the bags under my eyes. He is concerned with whether I pursued Him or my coffee more zealously this morning.

There is this incredible story in the New Testament where some guys brought Jesus a man that was paralyzed and lying on a mat. Jesus rewarded their faith by telling the man, "Your sins are forgiven"—because He knew that the man's biggest problem wasn't his legs; it was his heart. Of course, everyone around thinks Jesus is (1) blasphemous, (2) crazy, and (3) a little bit of a jerk for not healing the guy, if He can in fact heal people. And get this:

Knowing their thoughts, Jesus said, "Why do you entertain evil thoughts in your hearts? Which is easier: to say, 'Your sins are forgiven,' or to say, 'Get up and walk'? But so that you may know that the Son of Man has authority on earth to forgive sins." (Matt. 9:4–6 NIV)

Which is more difficult to deal with—paralysis or sin? Which matters more—legs or souls? The obvious answer is implicit: souls, hearts. This is what matters to God. Nobody had to die for God to heal paralytics, but someone had to pay in blood for the sins of the world; perfect justice requires it. No wrong can be overlooked; no one is off the hook. The redemption of our souls is why Jesus came; all the healing was just to get our attention.

And so, if God, in His omniscience and holy zeal, sees all my ugliness of heart and still declares me enough, why should I ever despair?

It is our hearts that matter, and our hearts are loved. It is our souls that endure, and our souls are redeemed. The externals are neutral—temporary and fading fast (see Prov. 31:30). The inside is where our value lies, and our insides are enough.

Excerpt taken from *Enough* by Kate Conner (© 2014).

The Shepherd's Heart

*So Samuel took the horn of oil, anointed him in the presence
of his brothers, and the Spirit of the LORD took control of
David from that day forward. (1 Samuel 16:13 HCSB)*

David's occupation made him a candidate for kingship.

Do you find God's activity as fascinating as I do? We might be tempted to go overboard and believe only His grace matters—that we are the hole in the proverbial doughnut. Of David we might think, "God called him in spite of the fact that he was a common shepherd." The facts prove otherwise. God was working in David's life from the beginning.

David received invaluable experience in the process of keeping sheep. Psalm 78:70–72 states, "He chose David his servant and took him from the sheep pens; from tending the sheep he brought him to be the shepherd of his people Jacob, of Israel his inheritance. And David shepherded them with integrity of heart; with skillful hands he led them" (NIV).

God takes the building blocks of our lives and uses them to His glory. Never assume that to follow Him means to throw away who He has made you to be. Few things seem less spiritual than keeping a bunch of smelly sheep, yet God used David's skills for eternal purposes.

When David arrived at home, Samuel saw that he was "ruddy, with a fine appearance and handsome features" (1 Sam. 16:12 NIV). Still, Samuel did not move. He'd already made a mistake based on appearances. Then God said, "Rise and anoint him; he is the one," commanding Samuel to anoint David in the presence of his brothers (1 Sam. 16:12–13).

The Holy Spirit just can't seem to arrive without power, can He? As we study the life of a shepherd boy, we will no doubt see testimony of that power again and again. Samuel stood before a young lad and with awe and reverence poured the oil on his head. Although the oil surely blurred the vision of the one whose eyes it bathed, God's vision was crystal clear. He had said, "I will send thee to Jesse the Bethlehemite: for I have provided me a king among his sons" (1 Sam. 16:1 KJV).

The Hebrew word for "provided" is *ra'ah*. It means "to see, to look at, view, inspect, regard, to perceive; . . . to feel; to experience."[1] Second Chronicles 16:9 says, "For the eyes of the Lord run to and fro throughout the whole earth, to show Himself strong on behalf of those whose heart is loyal to Him" (NKJV).

That day so many years ago, the eyes of the Lord looked throughout the whole earth and fell upon an obscure little village called Bethlehem. There He found a heart—one like unto His own. He found a heart tender to little lost sheep, and He showed Himself strong on behalf of that heart, just as He promised.

Excerpt taken from *Portraits of Devotion* by Beth Moore (© 2014).

---

1. Warren Baker, general editor, *The Complete Word Study Old Testament* (Chattanooga, TN: AMG Publishers, 1994), 2363.

Souls Knit Together

*As soon as he had finished speaking to Saul, the soul of
Jonathan was knit to the soul of David, and Jonathan
loved him as his own soul. (1 Samuel 18:1 ESV)*

David was certainly loved. Throngs of women cheered his name in the street (1 Sam. 18:7). But what did that love gain him? Let's take a quick look at David, and the people who loved him.

King Saul: In 1 Samuel 17, David impresses Saul by offering to whip up on the oppressive enemy soldier Goliath. You know the story. David hits the giant with a rock, cuts off his head, and brings it to the king. Apparently, dismembered body parts were Saul's love language, because he's immediately enamored with David. But Saul's love was short-lived. He becomes insanely jealous of David and plots to kill him.

Michal: "Now Saul's daughter Michal loved David. And they told Saul, and the thing pleased him" (1 Sam. 18:20 ESV).

Michal loved David so much that she wanted to marry him, and so she did. But if we fast-forward in David's story a bit we read, "As the ark of the LORD came into the city of David, Michal the daughter of Saul looked out of the window and saw King David leaping and dancing before the LORD, and she despised him in her heart" (2 Sam. 6:16 ESV).

Saul and Michal loved David, but the love didn't last, eventually giving way to jealousy and resentment.

Jonathan: Jonathan was Saul's son and David's best friend. The Bible tells us that Jonathan gave David his robe, armor, sword, bow, and belt—friendship offerings given from one warrior to another.

When Saul intended to kill David, Jonathan worked as a mediator, and when that didn't work, he helped David escape.

David and Jonathan's friendship provides the definition we need to understand being known. 1 Samuel 18:1 tells us, "As soon as he had finished speaking to Saul, *the soul of Jonathan was knit to the soul of David,* and Jonathan loved him as his own soul" (ESV, author emphasis).

Knit-together souls. This is the image of knowing.

Knowing says, "I see who you are and choose to weave my life into yours." Better than a simple, "I love you," right?

I understand the analogy. This was a relationship that took intentionality. It required concentrated effort. That's why knit-together souls are such a beautiful description of knowing. It's the process of mining someone else's heart to discover all the jewels within. It's seeing someone for who they really are and willfully tying your own self to them.

Sometimes, we're lonely because we're so wrapped up in loving and being loved that we miss the opportunity to know and be known.

Love is based on what you can do for each other and what you look like when your best foot is pointing forward. Knowing and being known only happens when we allow the roots of our relationships to grow deep.

Excerpt taken from *Connected* by Erin Davis (© 2016).

One Bad Decision

*The LORD considered what David had done
to be evil. (2 Samuel 11:27 HCSB)*

I f anyone knows how a few bad decisions can leave behind a huge mess to clean up, it's King David.

You surely know the story. First, he opted out of a responsibility so he could hang back home at the palace. Then, while (perhaps innocently enough) taking a late-night stroll around his rooftop during a bout of wakefulness, he spied a beautiful woman taking a bath in some nearby location down below. Talk about an explosive combination—a moonlit night, an undressed woman, a lonely man of power, influence, and persuasion. All the elements were in place for a fall from grace.

At this point David had an option. He could have marched himself back to bed, tried to clear his head of the temptation. Instead he chose to linger on that rooftop. Chose to breathe the oxygen that allowed his lusts to spark into flame. Unable to stop himself from desiring what he'd set in motion, he sent a messenger to invite the woman up to his room (after discovering that her warrior husband was away in battle) and slept with her.

From there, those first, fateful decisions led to a desperate cover-up, a senseless murder, the ordeal of watching his illegitimate son's death, a lifelong loss of trust and relationship with his children, and—always most importantly—the displeasure of God.

Wonder how stunned David was as he considered the downward spiral of events in his life. Wonder how many times he thought back to that starry night on the rooftop, the same starry sky he could have been scanning from outside his tent on the battlefield, doing his duty.

One bad decision can take a person down.

First decisions. Acceptable compromises. Lazy judgment calls that don't feel like any big deal at the time. Rejections of Christ's lordship in areas that seem like only minor disobediences.

They're some of the first things Satan latches onto when he believes he's got a hot prospect for taking down. Those initial urges of ours to run from God's Word, to resist His divine plans and opportunities for us, are how lusts and desires of every kind give "birth to sin, and when sin is fully grown, it gives birth to death" (James 1:15 HCSB).

A year from now, a decade from now, a generation from now, you'll know whether or not you've walked with God in a faithful, trusting manner or whether you've left yourself wide open to doubt and bitterness and all the biting regrets of picking and choosing your obedience options.

Every David who sneaks up onto the rooftop for another look will end up trapped in a web of deception. Every prodigal son who thinks he knows more about life than his "Father" will find himself in a pigsty. And every Jonah who runs in the opposite direction of God's calling will see the storm clouds gathering behind him. It's only a matter of time.

Excerpt taken from *Life Interrupted* by Priscilla Shirer (© 2011).

Heart of Stone

*So he gave the pillar his name. It is still called Absalom's
Monument today. (2 Samuel 18:18 HCSB)*

The story of David and Absalom is a tragedy, two opponents—
father and son—torn apart by love and hate. We can't change
the story. We can only agree to be changed through it.

At one time Absalom was a handsome and compassionate man.
He loved his sister deeply, grieving the shame Amnon had heaped
on her. He made a place for his desolate sister in his own home. He
named his daughter Tamar in her honor. He tried to do the right
things for Tamar, but he ended up doing all the wrong things for
himself.

Absalom didn't feel better after Amnon was in the grave. He
didn't feel better when David let him return to Jerusalem without
punishment. He didn't feel better after he was summoned to the
king's quarters and reunited with his father. And after stealing the
hearts of his father's people, he still didn't feel any better. Absalom
ultimately possessed as little self-control as the brother he despised.
His lack of self-control finally killed him.

Can you imagine the thoughts going through the head of that
beautiful but troubled young man as he struggled to set himself free
from the tree branches? The picture of his death was the picture of
his life: the noose of bitterness choking the captive's cry. In the end,
those close enough to hear him choking no longer cared.

There's great irony in the fact that the record of Absalom's
grave—the "huge mound of stones" piled over him by Joab's men—
and the account of the monument he erected to himself appear

together in Scripture (2 Sam. 18:18). The verses demonstrate that Absalom's death as a traitor remains far more memorable than his self-absorbed life. Through bitterness, Absalom's heart became as hard and cold as the pillar he raised. Even though David committed many sins and was unfair to others, his heart did not grow cold.

After Absalom's death, word reached the waiting David. He cried out, "O Absalom, my son, my son!" (v. 33 NIV). The words send chills up a parent's spine, don't they? Suddenly, a heart of tragically suppressed love exploded. Tears he should've cried long ago poured from his eyes. Words he should've said the moment he first saw his prodigal finally burst from his lips: "My son, O, my son!" He didn't speak about him. He spoke right to him, as if his voice would carry to the depths of the pit where the body lay.

"If only I had died instead of you!" (v. 33 NIV).

Death would've been far easier than life without him. What grieving parent hasn't cried those same words? Felt those same emotions? And where was God when David lost his son? Where was He when a king's own countrymen pierced his son? Where was He when the blood poured forth? The same place He was when He lost His own Son.

Excerpt taken from *Portraits of Devotion* by Beth Moore (© 2014).

Old Song, New Heart

*I called to the LORD in my distress; I called to my God.
From His temple He heard my voice, and my cry for
help reached His ears. (2 Samuel 22:7 HCSB)*

Nothing is more appropriate than celebrating a victory God has sovereignly and majestically won for us! After all the ups and downs of David's journey, in 2 Samuel 22 we get to experience the sheer pleasure of attending a celebration. Anyone who has ever experienced victory in Jesus is invited to attend—otherwise, they just wouldn't understand.

> David sang to the LORD the words of this song when the LORD delivered him from the hand of all his enemies and from the hand of Saul. (2 Sam. 22:1 NIV)

Think about what motivated David to sing. Sometimes God puts a new song in our mouths—a hymn of praise to our God! Other times He brings us back to an old song, one that fell from our lips many years ago and has gathered a film of dust only a fresh breath could blow away. No doubt about it, sometimes God wants to hear an old song from a new heart. This was the case for David.

David remembered the words he had sung many years before, after God delivered him from the hand of Saul. Perhaps his recent victory over the Philistines rekindled the remembrance of his victory over Saul because of several similarities. Both conflicts seemed they would never end. Both conflicts sapped his strength. Both conflicts caused him to rely on another's strength.

Decades wedged their way between the solos of this one song. How different the sound of the same singer's voice—so young and daring when first he sang. Now the voice was old, but suddenly, unexpectedly filled with the passion of a young warrior. I believe the words comprise the testimony of an old man with a fresh passion. Praise God, we need never get too old to experience a young passion!

Second Samuel 22 is a lengthy song of praise, as David catalogued the ways God had worked in his life: "He reached down from on high and took hold of me; he drew me out of deep waters. He rescued me from my powerful enemy, from my foes, who were too strong for me" (vv. 17–18 NIV).

David is serving us a slice of his personal history with God. He's testifying to his close relationship with His Maker. In Psalm 18, David simply declares, "I love you, O LORD, my strength" (v. 1 NIV).

"I love you, Lord."

No demands. No despair. The psalmist considered his delivered state and his Father's stubborn love, and he burst forth with the words: "I love you, Lord."

The One who delivered David from his enemies was no distant deity. David deeply loved God. David was a man after God's own heart because his desire was also the sheer pleasure of the Father. The Father's deepest desire is to be loved—genuinely loved—by His child.

Excerpt taken from *Portraits of Devotion* by Beth Moore (© 2014).

High Places

Solomon loved the LORD by walking in the statutes of his father David, but he also sacrificed and burned incense on the high places. (1 Kings 3:3 HCSB)

The *high places.*

Throughout the Old Testament, beginning almost immediately after Israel's Exodus from Egypt and continuing throughout the remainder of its historical and prophetic books, we continue to encounter the tempting allure of these "high places."

Historians describe them as elevated sites, usually found on top of a hill or mountain, sometimes situated over cave openings, which symbolically represented the underworld. These high places were most commonly shrines or altars employed in worship to pagan deities, where the indigenous populations of Canaan held their various religious rites. And to hear God's repeated injunction to His people about what He wanted done to these structures as Israel moved to occupy the land, there was only one acceptable use for a high place—to be demolished, smashed, chopped up, and torn down.

But these high places, which maintained a provocative interest for the Hebrews, proved remarkably resistant to demolition. And as long as they were still there, able to be accessed and explored, they continued to be magnets for the people's fascination with religious experimentation, if not outright rejection of the one true God. These venues contributed to a "playing the odds" pattern of worship that sort of covered all possible bases of prayer, but always resulted in a deteriorating dive into deeper rebellion.

High places bring people down.

The original words for "pride" and an "arrogant spirit" in Proverbs 16:18 each carry the idea of *height*. They are high places for us to live. But unlike the *high places* of Canaan, which the people could choose to leave intact if they so desired, the high places of pride and arrogance leave us no other option. They will eventually come tumbling down. "Pride comes before destruction, and an arrogant spirit before a fall." Even Solomon, whose reign began with such promise, ended up leaving a divided kingdom as his legacy. The kind of pride that results in several hundred wives from all over the known world turned his "heart away from the LORD" (1 Kings 11:3 HCSB), making him ripe for a fall.

"When pride comes, disgrace follows, but with humility comes wisdom" (Prov. 11:2 HCSB). "The proud speech of a fool brings a rod of discipline, but the lips of the wise protect them" (14:3 HCSB). "Everyone with a proud heart is detestable to the LORD; be assured, he will not go unpunished" (16:5 HCSB).

The language of Proverbs 16:18 is so well-known, we can almost skim over it without its full weight landing on us. But its warning is so sacred and so severe, we can't afford to let it escape our complete attention.

Put it "high" on your list of reminders that help guide the kind of character you seek to maintain.

Excerpt taken from *100 Days in Proverbs* (© 2016).

Chasing God

Behold, heaven and the highest heaven cannot contain you;
how much less this house that I have built! (1 Kings 8:27 ESV)

O ne can hardly deny the appeal of a good chase.

It's beautiful in concept: we seek after that which eludes us, longing for something just out of reach. Anticipation builds as our hearts beat faster, wondering if we're about to turn the final corner and catch the object of our affection.

Our minds are wild with possibility, intoxicated by the sense of adventure. Before we know it, we've forgotten the objective because we're caught up in the thrill of wondering. Either that, or we simply give up, forgoing the chase altogether because we're exhausted and discouraged. Either we *catch up* or we *give up*.

We try to fill in the gray instead of living in the black and white. We shape theology to suit our taste, our times, our situations, and our desires. It's the mess we've made by desiring to understand Him more than we want to know Him, and we're growing more exhausted than inspired every day. What was meant to be a gift has become an obligation, a source of guilt, or a way to fight fear.

Don't misunderstand me; we're not called to be passive in our journey with Christ. In fact, being a disciple of Christ necessitates that we press forward until we can hardly believe we can do it anymore. The problem comes when we use our energy in ways He never asked us to because we're more concerned with our own feeble sketches of God than we are with *God Himself.*

We rely on our own standards, rules, opinions, agendas, and measurements of holiness instead of His. And as the books pile one on top of another, so do the questions. *It's the difference between following and chasing.* We're called to one and not the other.

We stare at the rest of the pew, wondering why we aren't as far along as they are, secretly resenting those who unswervingly claim their faith while we enter another Bible study group, hoping something will stick.

If I just do this, I'll catch Him.

My misguided understanding of responsibility, control, and ability led me to despair of all the wrong failures and to celebrate successes that God Himself doesn't recognize as such.

It's what happens when you try to use religion to fill in the gaps of your faith.

Religion is what we build with our own hands when we can't stand to feel like observers. When it crumbles, we blame God. We have determined the man-made ceiling to be our own instead of the heavens themselves, and we have allowed our insatiable hunger for understanding to strangle the mystery we're supposed to embrace.

He is the Architect, and our lives were given only to thank Him for His creation. When we spend our time gazing at the church ceiling instead of His sky, we fail to see Him, to thank Him. We miss the Creator for His creation.

Excerpt taken from *Chasing God* by Angie Smith (© 2014).

Shortcuts Won't Cut It

*Elisha sent a messenger to him, saying, "Go and wash
in the Jordan seven times, and your flesh will be restored
to you and you will be clean." (2 Kings 5:10 NASB)*

If you remember your Old Testament, you've likely heard of
Naaman, the grizzled army captain who contracted leprosy and
in his desperation sought help from an Israelite prophet, Elisha. But
he sure didn't like Elisha's prescription for healing: "Go and wash in
the Jordan seven times, and your flesh will be restored to you and
you will be clean" (2 Kings 5:10 NASB).

Naaman wasn't happy with *what* he was being told to do, *how*
he was being told to do it, or *where* he was being told to go. He'd
been hoping for more of a bingo, bango, instant relief kind of healing. And even if the whole dipping in the river thing was a necessary
part of the plan, he thought a much cleaner, much more convenient
alternative would be to use the water sources in his own hometown
that were a lot nicer to swim in, plus a lot easier to get to.

Shortcuts. Bargains. Counterproposals.

Nice try, Naaman.

For what he obviously didn't understand when he "turned and
went away in a rage" (v. 12 NASB) was that his cure wasn't in the
water; it was in his obedience to the word of God. The work that
God is trying to accomplish in and through us can only be found in
our doing *what* He says, *how* He says to do it, and *where* He says to
go. Full participation is the price of full reward.

As my friend Shundria often says to her three children, after giving them a task or chore to complete, "You can do it now, or you

can do it later, but guess what: you're *gonna* do it." I can't help but think of Jonah's story. You might remember that he disobeyed God's call the first time resulting in a three-day sentence in the belly of the whale. God gave Jonah a second chance, but His calling on Jonah's life didn't change.

Yes, it's encouraging to see that "Jonah arose and went to Nineveh according to the word of the LORD" (Jonah 3:3 NASB). After all of that running and messing around, he'd been brought back to square one by the fatherly, sovereign, supervising hand of God—not to shame him but just to show him that shortcuts won't cut it. Not where following the Lord is concerned.

If you're sitting on a second chance, let it take you back to where you came from, where you last ran from an interruption, when you couldn't bring yourself to follow along with what God was sending you into. What you'll find on your return trip is a new, repentant heart, a greater sense of God's presence, and a fresh opportunity to obey—and then just see what happens next.

For Jonah, it was "rinse and repeat." Out of the fish and back into God's service.

What'll it be for you?

Excerpt taken from *Life Interrupted* by Priscilla Shirer (© 2011).

Day 51

From Entitlement to Gratitude

*Now I know that there is no God in all the world except in Israel.
So please accept a gift from your servant. (2 Kings 5:15 NLT)*

Naaman was a great man. He was courageous, important, highly regarded, a valiant soldier; and he had leprosy. Naaman's wife's servant came to him, told him there was a prophet named Elisha who could heal him, and Naaman went to his master. The master saddled him up with lots of material credibility and sent him not to the prophet but to the king. When the king had no idea what to do, Elisha came to him and said he'd take care of it. So Naaman pulled his chariots and intimidating entourage up to a prophet's humble house. When Elisha's servant came to tell him how to be healed, Naaman was furious. Naaman, with all of his expectations and entitlement, was angry that Elisha delivered his news by lowly messenger and the news involved immersing himself in a dirty river. He surely deserved more than that.

Once again the servants shared the truth. They caught up to Naaman after he "stomped off, mad as a hornet" according to *The Message*. (Sound familiar?) They appealed to his arrogance by saying that surely Naaman would have done whatever the prophet asked if it was something courageous. Surprisingly, the great man dipped himself seven times in the dirty river. As a result, not only his skin but also his spirit came out clean. Naaman's response was, "Now I know." He walked away with a sense of gratitude. He walked away from that river wanting to give back to the one who had healed him of both a skin disease and a sense of entitlement.

Maybe our role is that of the servants. We are the agents of humility in this culture of entitlement. We remind our children that there is and can be healing. We take them back, again and again, to that river of humility. The first servant reminded Naaman that he needed cleansing. The second servant creatively showed him the way.

Our children are not just great boys and girls. They are made in the image of a wise, wonderful God. But they don't "deserve" to ride up in their chariots and order us or anyone else around. They can't expect that every want they have will be met and met right now. Their demands will cause them more insecurity. Our children are great. They are courageous and valiant and they need healing. They need healing from their struggles, from their entitlement, . . . from their sin. They are dignity and depravity. And, as they come to know both—as they learn what it means to bow their entitled knees to a God who can and does heal them—they will know the power of grace. They will walk away with a sense of gratitude saying, with Naaman, "Now I know."

Excerpt taken from *Modern Parents, Vintage Values* by Melissa Trevathan and Sissy Goff (© 2010).

Open Your Eyes

"Don't be afraid!" Elisha told him. "For there are more on our
side than on theirs!" Then Elisha prayed, "O LORD, open his eyes
and let him see!" The LORD opened the young man's eyes, and
when he looked up, he saw that the hillside around Elisha was
filled with horses and chariots of fire. (2 Kings 6:16–17 NLT)

The story of an experience between the Old Testament prophet
Elisha and one of his servants can help us understand what we
fail to see when we're not looking at our lives through the lens of
God's truth.

Immediately on the heels of the floating ax head miracle in
2 Kings 6, the Bible tells of war breaking out between a neighboring
nation (the Arameans) and the people of Israel. While the king of
Aram was working out his attack strategy, the Lord kept tipping off
Elisha to the king's intentions and movements. Then Elisha would
deliver these divinely accurate spy reports to the king of Israel, who
would redeploy his soldiers into perfectly placed, perfectly timed
position to defend themselves.

This drove the king of Aram crazy enough to go hunting among
his men, only to find that Elisha had really been serving Israel all
along. He surrounded the city where Elisha was located, ready to
take him out by force.

The prophet's attendant woke up early that morning, went outside, and—*whoa!*—the whole place was teeming with horses, chariots, and sharpened artillery ready to strike. The servant ran back
inside, stammering to his boss about their imminent danger.

Elisha, cool as ever, told him not to worry because "those who are with us are more than those who are with them." Then he prayed to the Father: "O LORD I pray open his eyes that he may see" (2 Kings 6:16–17 NASB).

Then the terrified servant turned around to see, not the *physical* reality of fire-breathing army troops itching to attack, but rather the *spiritual* reality of a mountainside filled to the brim with angelic chariots of fire, surrounding, protecting, holding the enemy back.

Prayer made him *aware* of all the resources and strength and protection that God had already placed on their side. Without this renewed perspective he was already defeated before the battle had even begun.

That's what the enemy wants. He wants you living in a state of defeat. Your defenses down. Your resolve weak and flimsy. Surrendering to an army of insecurities and misdiagnosis instead of courageously thriving in the sophisticated security of your identity in Christ.

Makes you wonder, then, why we tend to only see our flaws, inadequacies, failures, and weaknesses. The enemy wants us distracted, so we don't see the real battlefield—the place primed for God's glory. No matter what's against you, it's no match for the power, authority, and overriding ocean of His grace He's given you access to. And prayer will *open your eyes* so you can see it.

Excerpt taken from *Fervent* by Priscilla Shirer (© 2015).

The Adventure You Crave

Who knows, perhaps you have come to your royal
position for such a time as this. (Esther 4:14 HCSB)

My best friend, Brooke, is of the quiet variety. She quietly started her own business, and it quietly became a smashing success. She quietly carries big hurts and forgives big wrongs. She quietly lavishes generosity, and she quietly inspires thousands.

She can change the world in the same way as Mother Teresa or Emily Dickinson.

A part of even the most staunch homebodies (of whom I am The Queen) fantasizes about adventure like Sacagawea's—leading men through the wilderness, strong, capable, and brave—the heroine of her own story. Our souls need passion and purpose. When we can't find it authentically, we manufacture it in the form of drama and daydreams to feed our hungry hearts. The problem is that a woman subsisting off of drama and daydreams is like a lion subsisting off of grass, berries, and bugs. We might survive, but we will never be healthy, and we will never be satisfied.

Women crave adventure because we were created this way. God is on mission and, as His followers, so are we. He has a plan for you. The more I read through Scripture, the more likely it seems that it is not a safe plan.

Sarah left her life behind to follow her aging husband into some unknown "promised land" that she was just supposed to take on faith. She also ended up having a baby when she was nearly one hundred years old.

Rahab looked square into the eyes of the armed guards at her door and lied to them while harboring enemy spies.

Deborah led a battle. You guys, she led a battle.

Ruth knowingly settled in a hostile land and endured racial discrimination to preserve a relationship with her mother-in-law.

Esther went before the king on behalf of her people, knowing her beheading was likely. BEHEADING. Her cousin encouraged her, "Who knows, perhaps you have come to your royal position for such a time as this?" and Esther responded, "I will go to the king even if it is against the law. If I perish, I persish."

That is a sense of purpose.

Life is a series of "for such a time as this" moments that are either seized, or not. Our souls know that the world, time, *life* is about something bigger than ourselves. When we feel disconnected from that, we try to amplify our lives to get just a taste of purpose. We are so hungry for it. We spin, stir, and fret; we busy ourselves and we talk, talk, talk to get a whiff, a drip, just a morsel of connectedness to the bigness of God that our hearts are after.

Do it loud, or do it quietly. It doesn't matter if it is flashy, simply obey the call Christ has placed on your life and step into the adventure God has for you for such a time as this.

Excerpt taken from *Enough* by Kate Connor (© 2014).

Where Were You?

"Where were you when I established the earth? Tell
Me, if you have understanding." (Job 38:4 HCSB)

So often we base our self-worth on the chatter going on around us instead of the Lord Himself. That in itself can be crippling, but imagine what it would be like to put your full weight into Him and then feel like maybe you had really been duped. What if you walked with Him day in and day out, only to become fearful that you had been abandoned and deceived?

Those of us who have fears of rejection, abandonment, or betrayal with people around us will no doubt have those same concerns about God. The truth is, we have gotten used to being disappointed in ourselves for being so vulnerable. We assume, even if unconsciously, that God is another rung on the ladder of misplaced trust.

He is not.

Scripture is very clear in saying that He will not abandon us, and we must know Him well enough to believe Him. The world is not going to teach us how to love God; only God can do that. Don't believe the lie that Satan longs to use against you; God has not, and will not, forsake you.

Ever.

Period.

Remember the story of Job. Interestingly, when Job goes to the Lord with his anger and confusion, God asks him a simple question that will rock our world to the core even to this day. At first glance it may seem callous that in the midst of Job's suffering, the best God can do to comfort him is to ask, "Where were you when I laid the earth's foundation?" (Job 38:4 NIV).

Well that's one way to end a conversation.

And He doesn't stop there. In fact, He goes on to ask Job over thirty more questions in this chapter alone.

I'm thinking Job didn't feel real solid about his case when God finished His little pep talk.

This conversation would be comical if it didn't hit such a nerve in me. I get hurt and I immediately hurl my side of things to the Lord, ignoring any response He might be trying to fit in as I rage on about the unfairness of it all. In my haste I can forget a very simple truth that would serve me well when I'm convinced the world needs to revolve around my disappointment.

I have a question to answer, and maybe you do too. I pray I will remember that He is the Beginning and the End, and He doesn't take it lightly when I blame Him for my misconceptions. He longs for us to love Him, and the more I rely on Him, the stronger I find Him. In times where I have faced the sting of rejection and the agony of feeling forgotten, I have found the Love of my life faithful. That is the steady foundation for all other relationships, and the more I find my balance in Him, the less I will fret about what the world says.

Excerpt taken from *What Women Fear* by Angie Smith (© 2011).

Seeing Is Believing

*I have heard of You by the hearing of the ear;
But now my eye sees You. (Job 42:5 NASB)*

O ften our first reaction to a difficult turn of events is to look and see what we've done to cause it. And granted, God is faithful enough to know that the short-term pain of correction is worth the long-term prize of character. But generally speaking, the Bible seems to say that the wilderness isn't a one-to-one reaction to some specific thing we've done—it's not typically the spiritual equivalent to discipline. The wilderness is often just God's chosen plan for us.

Can you believe that? *Will* you believe that?

I can't explain it, but I can tell you from experience and from the Word of God that the road He chooses to lead us on as we travel into a life of abundance is often more challenging, tedious, lonely, indirect, and costly than we ever expected. Not always, but often.

The historical account of Job certainly bears this out in dramatic detail. The first verse of the first chapter clearly points out that this was a man who was "blameless, upright, fearing God and turning away from evil." Everybody who knew Job would tell you he was righteous. He had a wife who loved him, a big houseful of kids, and all kind of property and possessions. He sat comfortably within the "hedge" God had provided to protect everything he owned from decay, ruin, and destruction (Job 1:10 NASB). Job had it going on! And seemed to be the one-in-a-million kind of guy who could have all of that and not let it go to his head.

Then, as we know, God allowed the enemy to run rampant through Job's life—not because Satan had outsmarted or strong-armed the Lord. No, God had pointed Job out: "Have you considered My servant Job? For there is no one like him on the earth, a blameless and upright man, fearing God and turning away from evil" (1:8 NASB). Well, you know what happened next. In rapid succession his servants were put to death, his livestock either stolen by bandits or struck dead in a storm, even all ten of his children killed in a common tragedy. Soon his physical health had taken such a beating, the friends who came around to survey the damage didn't even recognize who he was.

This was a man who loved God, a man whose initial reaction to this horrific turn of events went something like this: he "arose and tore his robe and shaved his head, and he fell to the ground and"— he *what?*—he "worshiped" (1:20 NASB). Why would God lead a person like this to the wilderness?

Maybe the answer we're seeking comes at the end of Job's ordeal. After a long, torturous run through some of the driest, dustiest conditions ever known to man, Job was able to articulate something he could never have put into these kinds of words before: Now I know You by *experience*.

Excerpt taken from *One in a Million* by Priscilla Shirer (© 2010).

Day and Night

*How happy is the man does not follow the advice of the
wicked or take the path of sinners or join a group of mockers!
Instead, his delight is in the LORD's instruction, and he
meditates on it day and night. (Psalm 1:1–2 HCSB)*

There are morning people, and there are stay-up-late people.
Early risers and night owls. Yes, perhaps somewhere in the world
today are individuals who are so steady, so regulated, so right-down-
the-middle that they wake up religiously at 7:00 and go to bed precisely at 10:30. Neither exceptionally early nor exceptionally late.

But for the rest of us, whose body clocks lean one way or the
other, Psalm 1 introduces a life plan that can *double* our number of
access points to spiritual joy and blessing. To spiritual victory and
power.

This *happiness* that Psalm 1 talks about is not just nice, smiley
happiness. It's blessedness. It's the feeling of actually experiencing
God's redeeming favor—something you've already been given as a
believer in Jesus Christ.

But something called *sin*—this whole problem of ours that
necessitated God's redemption of us in the first place—remains
wickedly capable of shutting down our full enjoyment of God's love
and acceptance. Our sin is the source of ongoing disconnect between
what God has done for us and the freeing experience of actually living in it.

That's because we still have a weakness for liking the sound of
sin's "advice." We still head down that "path" like someone who

hasn't learned the first ten million times that, yes, bad things are always waiting for us down there at the bottom.

And so the writer of Psalm 1 invites us back into the Word. Into the "delight" of the "Lord's instruction." We're invited to the always-available place where God's truth counteracts the habitual part of our human natures that still wants to rebel against His counsel, preferring our own stupid way instead.

But the Word of God is not just for coffee and back porches and the soft colors of the sunrise. Nor is it just for the quiet, lamp-lit, final moments of the evening, when you're out of your dress clothes and into something more comfortable.

It's for both.

So if you're reading this in the morning right now—your morning quiet time—these same words of Scripture can also be there to sing you off to sleep tonight, as you choose to *meditate* on Him throughout the day and make His Word your last thoughts before an early bedtime. Or if you're reading this at night, fighting to stay awake at the end of a long day, you can keep the circle of blessing going by choosing to let this Word be your first thought of the new morning—while you're groggily coming up from under a deep oversleep. Let a moment in His Word, first thing tomorrow, be your true jolt of reality for the hours ahead.

Don't settle for being a morning person or a night person. Experience the all-day delight of being a *happy* person.

Excerpt taken from *100 Days in the Psalms* (© 2016).

Leaves and Fruit

He is like a tree planted beside streams of water that
bears its fruit in season and whose leaf does not wither.
Whatever he does prospers. (Psalm 1:3 HCSB)

We are meant to be relational people, not just religious people. The freedom given to us in Christ means no amount of do-gooding is required in order to please or impress God, any more than He's pleased with us already. Jesus' righteousness has washed completely over our unrighteousness. Our only job now is simply to live in pure grace and gratitude for the utterly undeserved righteousness we've been given.

So the thing we're shooting for, when we spend time reading our Bibles, is not a set number of minutes or hours committed to it every day. That's *religious* thinking. The experience we're seeking is to let the Word simmer and percolate within us, feeding on it, drinking of it—not so we can try proving our piety, but so we can experience our full privileges as people rescued from certain death, recipients now of abundant life.

Here's what happens when we do.

Two things, among many things.

First, we produce *fruit*. We become like a "tree planted beside streams of water that bears its fruit in season." The way we bear fruit as believers is by planting ourselves in the Word. Jesus said, "The one who remains in Me and I in him produces much fruit, because you can do nothing without Me" (John 15:5 HCSB). This fruit of the Spirit is said to include things like "love, joy, peace, patience, kindness, goodness, faith, gentleness, self-control. Against such things there is no law" (Gal. 5:22–23 HCSB). Like apples on an apple tree, like lemons on a lemon tree, they're simply the natural result of being true believers planted in Christ. "My Father is glorified by this," Jesus said, "that you produce much fruit and prove to be"—give evidence of being—"My disciples" (John 15:8 HCSB).

But second, along with fruit, trees also produce *leaves*. And the leaf of a tree whose roots go down deep into God's Word is the type that Psalm 1 says "does not wither." Doesn't turn brown and crinkly. Stays lush and green, able to be easily identified as coming from the life of someone marked by relationship with Jesus.

Think of leaves as more like your reputation, your known identity as a Christian. They're not the actual fruit you produce, but they should constantly match up with the kind of tree you claim to be. Where hypocrisy, fakeness, and double standards can cause people to wonder what kind of Christian you really are—and even cause you yourself to feel the unsettled difference between what you preach and what you actually practice—the authenticity of being a Word-based believer keeps your outer package in line with your profession. Everything works together the way it should . . . the way that truly makes a person "happy."

Leaves and fruit. The Word is how you keep both of them growing and looking good.

Excerpt taken from *100 Days in the Psalms* (© 2016).

That's Not Funny

Why do the nations rebel and the peoples plot in
vain? . . . The One enthroned in heaven laughs;
the Lord ridicules them. (Psalm 2:1, 4 HCSB)

They used to say if you ever saw the late Mike Wallace striding up to your office door, lead investigative reporter for the long-running CBS news program *60 Minutes*, you knew you were in big trouble. Probing questions were about to be asked. And any attempt to duck or dodge allegations would be met with a suspicious, truth-knowing smirk and snicker. This probably wasn't going to end well.

Just imagine, then, what's coming next if *God* ever starts laughing at you. Not *with* you. At you. And according to Psalm 2, people who persist in their rebellion are inviting it. They're mocking the power and sovereignty of God, selfishly rebelling against His claims of ultimate authority over their lives. They're like blades of grass trying to slow down a lawn mower, only to soon realize what a *real* blade can do.

Now undervaluing the infinite superiority of God is not something that only the unsaved are capable of doing. We, too, can minimize God in our minds. When faced with some of the hard questions and challenges of life, we can sometimes wonder if He's really there and (if so) wonder if He really knows what He's doing.

But there's a proper response when tempted to question the size and smarts of God. And we get the whole knee-buckling experience of it through the eyes of the Old Testament character Job.

Job's reputation is one of remarkable patience. *The patience of Job.* And in some places throughout his narrative, yes, he embodies the squared shoulders and backbone of a man with deep humility and perseverance. But not always. His stiff upper lip quivers at several points, melting into rants of accusation against God as well as moans of self-pity and hands-in-the-air, who-cares surrender.

In the end, though, after God had delivered a stunning case for His absolute rule and dominion over all things (Job 38—41)—truly some of the most dazzling, colorful prose in all the Bible, perhaps in all of ancient literature—Job did what the defiant kings and rulers of Psalm 2 refuse to do.

He shut up. He knew he'd been licked.

"I know," he said to the Lord, "that You can do anything and no plan of Yours can be thwarted. . . . Surely I spoke about things I did not understand, things too wonderful for me to know. . . . I had heard rumors about You, but now my eyes have seen You. Therefore I take back my words and repent in dust and ashes" (Job 42:1–3, 5–6 HCSB).

In every battle of wills between man and God, God wins every time. Hundred times out of a hundred. So in order to win at life, we must be on His side to begin with. Because our odds of winning otherwise . . . they're not even funny.

It's All Good!

Many are saying, "Who can show us anything good?"
Look on us with favor, LORD. You have put more
joy in my heart than they have when their grain
and new wine abound. (Psalm 4:6–7 HCSB)

Many scholars believe that Psalm 4 is a second response to the same historical event that inspired Psalm 3—an attempted coup by David's son Absalom, which led to the great king fleeing his palace in Jerusalem, accompanied by those who were loyal to him. You can read all about it sometime in 2 Samuel 15–18. (Don't be surprised if someone ends up with his head caught in a low-hanging limb, dangling in midair, while his animal rides right out from under him.)

So this was a tense period of fear, change, and upheaval in Israel's history. It didn't look at first as though David was going to survive this assault on the throne from within his own family. So "who can show us anything good?" many were asking, begging God for relief and protection from this savage downturn in their circumstances.

But David, even in the face of his son's rebellion and betrayal, even when badgered by others' accusations and pessimism, even while wrestling with his own inner churning of failure and regret, found something that calmed him down and kept him steady.

First, he knew the Lord was like a "shield" around him (Ps. 3:3 HCSB), offering protection greater than the most elite army or security team could provide.

Second, he knew God was hearing and answering his prayer, that God hadn't abandoned him to struggle alone. "I cry aloud to the LORD, and He answers me from His holy mountain" (v. 4 HCSB). "Answer me when I call," he asked. "Be gracious to me and hear my prayer" (Ps. 4:1 HCSB).

Third, he was confident that the Lord's will would ultimately prevail. "Know that the LORD has set apart the faithful for Himself;" so that we can "offer sacrifices in righteousness" and simply "trust in the LORD" (vv. 3, 5 HCSB).

Although other people seemed to be holding the upper hand at the moment, and though it looked from all outward appearances that David was about to lose everything, he still considered himself blessed. He embraced an illogical joy that defied the grim colors of his surroundings.

That's why he was able to do something *all* of us as believers can do and experience. After fighting all day (like you do), giving it every last ounce of bravery and backbone (like you do), David curled up in thankful prayer at night and did something maybe you *don't* do. "I lie down and sleep; I wake again because the LORD sustains me" (Ps. 3:5 HCSB). "I will both lie down and sleep in peace, for You alone, LORD, make me live in safety" (Ps. 4:8 HCSB).

Has it been a tough day? I know.

But end it by saying these sweet, strong words of faith.

Good night. And *see you tomorrow.*

Excerpt taken from *100 Days in the Psalms* (© 2016).

Making A Case

*At daybreak, LORD, You hear my voice; at daybreak I plead
my case to You and watch expectantly. (Psalm 5:3 HCSB)*

Anyone who thinks prayer is all soft and sweet, murmured in
hushed tones, confined to the codebook of spiritually acceptable terms and phrases—they've obviously not spent much time in
the psalms.

Take this fifth psalm, for example. We don't know exactly what
was stuck in David's craw on this particular morning, at this "daybreak" moment when he awakened to "plead my case" at the justice
bench of God. But whatever had lately been happening to him, and
whoever was giving him the hardest time in the middle of it, David
was not in the peppiest of moods today. By the time he really got
wound up—and was getting really personal—he was saying things
about these enemies of his, like, "There is nothing reliable in what
they say; destruction is within them; their throat is an open grave;
they flatter with their tongues" (Ps. 5:9 HCSB). Furthermore, if God
was interested in taking one man's advice on what to do with these
guys, David's idea of payback would be to "punish them, God; let
them fall by their own schemes. Drive them out because of their
many crimes, for they rebel against You" (v. 10 HCSB).

Apparently, since God chose to place this chapter in the Bible
for our ongoing instruction, He must be telling us that a bad mood
can apparently still be a prayerful mood. Because *every* mood is
meant to be a prayerful mood.

Now if David had already been up and dressed, if he was railing
against these people's reputations with his friends or staff over

morning coffee, there wouldn't be much to admire or emulate about what he was saying. The raw heat of his heart and passion—even the legitimate justice of his arguments—did not give him spiritual permission to blast away at his opponents in public and try getting everyone to agree with him on the wrongness of their actions. But in the privacy of his prayer closet, alone with God in startlingly honest conversation, he could feel the clearance to just baldly share his heart.

Because, yes, we enter God's presence with a deep awareness of our smallness compared to His greatness. David himself said, in this very psalm, "I enter Your house by the abundance of Your faithful love; I bow down toward Your holy temple in reverential awe of You" (v. 7 HCSB). We enter also with humility, recognizing our own sin and our personal need for repentance and direction. "LORD, lead me in Your righteousness," he prayed. "Make Your way straight before me" (v. 8 HCSB). But God's shoulders are big and broad enough to handle even our angry, hurtful streams of thought—the weariness of our soul and our frustration with what we're being forced to deal with.

So feel free to plead your case to Him. And then leave it in His hands to take care of it from there.

Excerpt taken from *100 Days in the Psalms* (© 2016).

Both Small and Great

When I observe Your heavens, the work of Your fingers,
the moon and the stars, which You set in place, what
is man that You remember him, the son of man
that You look after him? (Psalm 8:3–4 HCSB)

O Lord, our Lord, *"how magnificent is Your name in all the earth!"*
(Ps. 8:1 HCSB).

Psalm 8, like several others, is what's known as a creation hymn. Its focus is on the earth, the heavens, the wonder of God's created world. For while life is filled with questions, with challenges, with reasons for doubting both God's power and compassion, we are often able to be brought back to our senses by recognizing the unexplainable mystery and majesty of creation. By staring up into the night sky. By observing the natural habits of quirky animals and wildlife. By watching an angry scrape on our elbow scab over and soften and heal without a trace.

It is wonderful. It is amazing.

It is evidence of an indescribable God.

Beyond our thoughts. Beyond all thoughtfulness.

Sometimes, of course, we vainly imagine ourselves the center of our universe. If we're hurting, we think everyone should notice and care and sympathize. If we're happy, any incoming threat to our peace and rest is viewed as unjust, unfair, a ripe reason for complaining. If we've made plans and scheduled the day's appointments, no one who alters or disrupts them should expect not to feel our displeasure.

We are strong. We matter. We are of utmost importance.

But then there are *other* times . . . when we are made keenly aware that we are one of seven some-odd billion souls on the earth. Invisible and unknown to all but a relative handful of people. Showing signs of age in the skin on the back of our hands. Horribly outweighed by a medical diagnosis that could mean we seriously might not see this calendar date roll around more than once, twice, maybe three more times.

We are weak. We are small. We pale in comparison.

Why, then, would God ever stop long enough to darken His thoughts with someone like us? These cares and concerns which are so top-of-mind to us, which have occupied the bulk of our praying all week long—why would God filter through the millions of other prayers emanating from every pocket on the planet right now and pay even a half-second's worth of attention to ours?

Why?

Because we are His prized creations. Man and woman—you and I—have been crowned by our Creator with "glory and honor" (v. 5 HCSB). And O Lord, our Lord, that makes us sort of want to say, "How magnificent is Your name throughout the earth." For among the most touching evidence of His matchless magnificence is His grand decision to engage and esteem us (little old us) with a matchless love.

> We are small, yes. But in Him we are great.
> In Him we matter and are made important.
> How utterly magnificent.

Excerpt taken from *100 Days in the Psalms* (© 2016).

What Is This World Coming To?

*When the foundations are destroyed, what can
the righteous do? (Psalm 11:3 HCSB)*

Enough of the hand-wringing already.

Every decade has its doomsday scares and current events. Its scandalous revelations. Its horrifically cruel wars. Its gasps of moral ruin and decadence. But if you remember God's assessment of mankind before the flood, He said that "every scheme his mind thought of was nothing but evil all the time" (Gen. 6:5 HCSB). So we ought to be used to it by now without flipping our lid. Bad things happen, but we're still here, and God is still in control.

And yet, like the nervous squirrels surrounding King David during another sky-is-falling moment in human history, the chatter continues: "Escape to the mountain like a bird! For look, the wicked string the bow; they put the arrow on the bowstring to shoot from the shadows at the upright in heart. When the foundations are destroyed, what can the righteous do?" (Ps. 11:1–3 HCSB).

Well . . .

They can trust. David said he'd taken "refuge" in the Lord (v. 1 HCSB). The stronghold of God's name, His power, His faithfulness, and His track record were enough to help David weed out the panic he might've felt otherwise.

They can remember. "The LORD is in His holy temple; the LORD's throne is in heaven" (v. 4 HCSB). Despite what actually did feel like the ground shifting under his feet, David knew what his faith had always told him. He realized no earthly calamity could occur without being overseen from the throne room of heaven, and that whenever this current crisis had done its worst, God would still be anchored in His immovable place.

They can relax. There's simply a confidence that comes from putting God first in your mind and heart, believing His Word and living it out, day by day, over time. Paul the apostle later talked about how standing in God's grace means we can rejoice even in our afflictions, "because we know that affliction produces endurance, endurance produces proven character, and proven character produces hope" (Rom. 5:3–4 HCSB).

Hope is the exclusive territory of the believer. The righteousness we've been given by Christ makes us eternally accepted by God. Because of that, we can be truly hopeful. But look here: When we allow this faith-based gift to transform us into people who actually live the righteousness we've been given, hope becomes an even more natural by-product. We are comforted, rather than mortified, by knowing "His eyes watch; He examines everyone" (Ps. 11:4 HCSB), because we know we're devoted to Him, following Him both in public and in private. We're experiencing the wraparound gift of "proven character" that isn't just the right thing to do, but is tangible evidence that God is here, He is active, and He is clearly redeeming things. Because if He can change us—as stubborn and resistant and rebellious as we know we can be—He can change anything.

"What can the *righteous* do?"

We can live in confident hope.

Excerpt taken from *100 Days in the Psalms* (© 2016).

The Bad News of the Gospel

The LORD looks down from heaven on the human race to see if there is one who is wise, one who seeks God. All have turned away; all alike have become corrupt. There is no one who does good, not even one. (Psalm 14:2–3 HCSB)

I've got some good news, and I've got some bad news. Which one do you want first? The bad news?

Okay then, let's get this over with.

Because this is the worst news of all.

We're horrible sinners. We came into this world already broken, lost, and dying. Guilty by association with the original sin of Adam. There was no hope for us. We couldn't be good enough. We couldn't reach high enough. We can never improve enough.

We, by nature, are "enemies" of God (Rom. 5:10 HCSB), our hearts choose sin as an ally, making us at war with Him. We don't want Him. We don't want to follow Him. We don't think we need Him. We think we're better off without Him. We are fools . . . corrupt . . . vile . . . worthy of nothing but His hatred and our death.

It's not just *you* we're talking about; it's all of us. And there's not a single one of us who can do a single thing about it.

That, my friend, is the bad news of the gospel.

And not everyone is willing to believe it.

But until we do, there is no good news for us. Sure, a few good things may happen here and there. God, in what's known as His *common grace*, has given us glimpses of His beauty in the mountain peaks, the ocean's surf, and the radiant colors of the sunset. Glimpses of joy in the faces of our family, the love of others, and the deep sighs of hard-fought goal attainment.

Yet nothing but horror awaits us because of this fundamental flaw in our character—the spiritual depravity that prevents us from ever escaping the death sentence that may as well be placed in the little cribs they wheel into the hospital nursery with our little babies inside them.

I'm sorry that stings. It's just the truth.

Our problem is really that bad.

But there's *good news*, remember? And hopefully by now, it sounds even better than it did before. Christ's salvation—His perfect life, His sacrificial death, His conquering of the grave, His eternal seat of resurrection at the right hand of the Father—means that all this bad news can be remedied and overcome. Not wiped away, as if God's decided just to overlook it, and the crucifixion wasn't really necessary. But for those who have believed on His name and put their faith in Christ's righteous blood, all the guilt for all our sins has been placed on Him and paid in full, now and forever. We are His. We are loved. Redeemed, reborn, and rescued. From beyond all hope to hope beyond our wildest dreams.

There's good news for you. For us.

But only in the name of Jesus.

Excerpt taken from *100 Days in the Psalms* (© 2016).

When You Don't Know What to Do

You reveal the path of life to me; in Your presence is abundant joy; in Your right hand are eternal pleasures. (Psalm 16:11 HCSB)

Sometimes I get frozen.

When twelve things need to happen at once and each one is dependent on the others—when there is no right order, no efficient course of action, I feel like I can't move my extremities. My brain locks up and I feel simultaneously over-stimulated and paralyzed—hearing everything and affecting nothing.

It happens most often when it's 6:00 p.m., I have no dinner plan, the house is a disaster, all three kids are screaming, the baby needs to be nursed, another kid has homework, and everyone needs to be in bed in ninety minutes. This happens at least twice a week.

My mantra when I get frozen and overwhelmed is this: "When you don't know what to do, do what you know to do."

It is my mantra when I feel aimless, like whatever mystical thing that holds my thoughts together, like skin, is gone, and I'm dissipating, drifting away from myself. When simple choices look like advanced calculus, I recite, "Just do what you know to do."

Deep breath, one foot in front of the other.

In my frozen 6:00 p.m.'s, what I know to do is to pick a child, any child, and hug it. I can't fix all the hurts, but I can fix one. Next, I clear one little corner of a room to function as a sanctuary. I throw armfuls of toys and laundry out of the way, wrap the babies in blankets, and sit them in the sanctuary with juice boxes. In clearing a space I clear my brain. My living room and my brain are connected in a mystical, spiritual way. When one is clean, so is the other—and vice versa. When I don't know what to do, I just do something—anything—that I know is right.

This principle—doing what you know to do—works on a grand scale as well as it does on a daily 6:00 p.m. scale.

The Bible, the Word of God, tells us what is right in every situation. It speaks to our actions, words, thoughts, and attitudes—it addresses our whole selves and how those selves interact with the world around us.

It demystifies life, snapping us out of our haze. We are not left without a guide. We have God's Word in front of us and the Holy Spirit inside of us. That is more than enough to help us take the next right step toward love, joy, and peace.

When we are frozen or floating, we can pick something, anything, that God tells us is right and do it.

When you don't know what to do, it is better to follow Scripture than it is to follow your passions, your dreams, your skills, your brain, your intuition, or anything else. Scripture is the only safe choice. It's a simple but liberating action plan. When you don't know what to do, open God's Word.

Excerpt taken from *Enough* by Kate Connor (© 2016).

The Ripple Effect

*I called to the LORD in my distress, and I cried to my
God for help. From His temple He heard my voice, and
my cry to Him reached His ears. (Psalm 18:6 HCSB)*

The sailors on board the vessel with Jonah were most likely
Phoenicians, pagans who came from a polytheistic culture.
They worshipped a plethora of gods, each of which governed a different aspect of nature and was easily offended. So when trouble
arose, like the savage storm they faced on the Mediterranean, these
men never knew *who* had done *what* to anger a particular deity.
That's why "every man cried to his god" (Jonah 1:5 NASB) as the
waves grew uncontrollable in an effort to make amends and tidy up
any spiritual messes they may have unknowingly made.

Yet after Jonah had been exposed as the source of this monsoon
and declared himself related to the one God "who made the sea"
(v. 9 NASB) on which they were being tossed, these same grizzled
sailors were not praying to their personal gods anymore but to the
God of Jonah. From verses 14 to 16, they were addressing Him by
the name Yahweh, the specific covenant name given to Israel.

As the first chapter of the book of Jonah nears its end, the
Scripture confirms that these men "feared the LORD greatly, and
they offered a sacrifice to the LORD and made vows" (v. 16 NASB).
Turns out Jonah's storm didn't just do *him* some good. The thunderous rainstorm caused enough fear among the unbelieving to prepare
them for a God encounter of their own.

Are you discouraged because of the storm your decisions may
have caused others around you to endure? God is truly a

multitasking whiz. He'll use the same storm that shivers our spiritual timbers to create changes in other people as well. Whether from watching our response or facing similar repercussions right along with us, they may discover their own opportunity to do business with God.

Yes, our Lord can get a lot done with a divine intervention. He will not allow fair weather to keep us from knowing Him, not just in a ceremonial way but in a serious, sensitive way—not just in a technically transacted way but in a real, responsive way. How often we throw our hands up in the air, beg for mercy, resent the interruption. But God wisely knows when only a storm will do, when no lighter form of inconvenience can alert us to who we really are and who He desires to be in us.

So wake up. Set your feet on the floor. Stand under the revealing shower of reality. Smell the clear-headed coffee of His Word and His truth.

Sometimes it just takes a storm to get us back to our senses, back to where we realize that no desire, distraction, or diversion can ever satisfy the deepest hungers of our souls. And your Father loves you too much not to send one.

Excerpt taken from *Life Interrupted* by Priscilla Shirer (© 2011).

The Heavens Declare

The heavens declare the glory of God, and the sky proclaims the work of His hands. Day after day they pour out speech; night after night they communicate knowledge. There is no speech; there are no words; their voice is not heard. Their message has gone out to all the earth, and their words to the ends of the world. (Psalm 19:1–4 HCSB)

Just like the presence of a watch indicates a watchmaker, our finely tuned bodies living in this finely tuned world hanging in this finely tuned cosmos point to the logical existence of a Creator. Nobody looks at a Mercedes Benz, for example, and assumes there was an explosion at a junkyard. According to the direct revelation of Psalm 19:1–4 (HCSB), the heavens and the sky are every day "pouring out speech" and every night "communicating knowledge" that God exists.

The sense we receive in verses 1–2 is of continual revelation. Creation never presses "pause" on its proclaiming that it is an effect, not a cause, and that it has an Originator. Verse 3 can be difficult to sort out, but the context of the passage gives us two most likely interpretations.

The first is that despite the nonstop speech and communication, some people simply ignore it as if it doesn't exist; the voice is not heard. Nevertheless, they cannot say they were not told, only that they did not listen. It is for a similar reason that Jesus said, "For this people's heart has grown callous; their ears are hard of hearing, and they have shut their eyes; otherwise they might see with their eyes and hear with their ears, understand with their hearts and turn back—and I would cure them" (Matt. 13:15 HCSB).

The second possible interpretation of Psalm 19:3 is simply that David is noting the nature of general revelation. It is not a speech that comes in an audible voice or literal words. The communication and knowledge is proclaimed, but not in the direct way that special revelation is. A watch tells us it has a watchmaker, but not in the same way as shaking the watchmaker's hand and hearing his voice say, "I made that."

Both of these senses are true of Psalm 19:3. It is true that creation is proclaiming its Creator, but many either don't hear it or they hear it but reject it. It is also true that the way creation proclaims its Creator is not as direct as the way the Creator proclaims Himself.

In any event, verse 4 tells us that the "message has gone out to all the earth, and their words to the ends of the world." In other words, no place is absent general revelation, every corner of the globe is teaching about God.

Nature's "music" points us to look for the Conductor. Nature's beauty points us to look for the Artist. The vastness of the Sahara Desert and the Arctic tundra and the mighty oceans, in making us feel small and vulnerable, point us to God, the strong Tower.

Excerpt taken from *90 Days with the God Who Speaks* (© 2017).

The Threshing Floor

He renews my life;
he leads me along the right paths
for his name's sake.
Even when I go through the darkest valley,
I fear no danger,
for you are with me;
your rod and your staff—they comfort me. (Psalm 23:3–4 CSB)

The idea of God doing some kind of sorting inside of us has struck me many times when I'm in the midst of "pruning seasons." Years ago, I was reading about the threshing floor and became fascinated by it. Basically, it was a place high on a hill (so the wind could assist the workers), where the chaff and the wheat were separated. The chaff, which was useless, blew away in the wind because of how light it was. The grain was heavier, so it fell to the ground and was gathered to be harvested.

God has brought this image to me many times in the midst of feeling "threshed." He's reminded me that His hands are doing the sorting. I began reading through all the "threshing floor" references in the Bible, becoming more engaged with the way it showed up in beautiful stories I've loved for years.

The first is in Genesis 50:10–11, where Joseph and his brothers were mourning the death of their father, Israel (formerly Jacob). Later, Ruth—commanded by her mother-in-law—went to the threshing floor and lay at the feet of Boaz, begging to be "redeemed" by him (Ruth 3:6–9 ESV).

In 1 Chronicles 21:18–28, David was purchasing a threshing floor from Ornan. Although Ornan told David that he would give it to him free of charge, David insisted on paying full price. He stood on the ground of "sifting" and explained that he would not take the easy way. He'd do what was right in the eyes of the Lord, regardless of the price. I'll stand before the Lord one day, and I want to tell Him that I did the same. I want to say that I was sifted and that I did what David did at that threshing floor.

"So David paid Ornan 600 shekels of gold by weight for the site. *And David built there an altar to the LORD*" (1 Chron. 21:25–26 ESV, author emphasis).

He built an altar to worship the God who threshes.

And here is the best part.

"Then Solomon began *to build the house of the LORD* in Jerusalem on Mount Moriah, where the LORD had appeared to David his father, at the place that David had appointed, on the threshing floor of Ornan the Jebusite" (2 Chron. 3:1 ESV, author emphasis).

Only God Himself knows why we each stand on the ground we're on, but there is something that you and I can do from here. I choose to build an altar to the Lord. The God of Jacob, of Ruth, of David, of Solomon, and of you and me wants to help us build where the hurt has been. Even in the wake of devastation, may we worship Him with eager expectation of the harvest.

Excerpt taken from *Mended* by Angie Smith (© 2012).

Let It Happen

*"One thing I have asked from the LORD, that I shall
seek: That I may dwell in the house of the LORD all the
days of my life, To behold the beauty of the LORD and
to meditate in His temple." (Psalm 27:4 NASB)*

Are you in a wilderness season right now, reeling from some tragic circumstance that seems to make no sense to you? Or perhaps you're just in a particular season or phase of life that, for whatever reason, you're really not that happy about. Would you consider for a moment that this is not a punishment, an accident, or a bit of negligence on the part of God, who apparently doesn't really care whether you live or die or whatever happens to you?

Would you ask yourself what you're really wanting in life? Is it just to be happy, at peace, at ease? Is it to be left alone to do what you want without having to live with challenges, difficulties, and shortages? Or is it to be in intimate relationship with a Father whose purpose in drawing you is to give you the opportunity to know— really *know*—this One who made you, wants you, loves you?

The psalmist Asaph admitted to getting pretty fed up with being in the wilderness. Not just being in the wilderness, but at the same time having to watch people who didn't even think, care, or have any interest in God seem to scoot along just fine without having to deal with the wilderness. *What's up with that?* "Surely in vain I have kept my heart pure and washed my hands in innocence; for I have been stricken all day long and chastened every morning" (Ps. 73:13–14 NASB).

That's honestly the way he felt until he "came into the sanctuary of God" (v. 17 NASB) . . . until he drew close to the One who'd been using the pressure of problems not to bury him but to beckon him. And in that place of nearness and fellowship, he discovered that being actively pursued by God was far more precious than merely having his problems alleviated by God (vv. 25–28).

It's awfully easy to get disillusioned with God out here in the wilderness, to think He's forgotten you, doesn't care about you, doesn't love you. It's easy to start asking why your best isn't good enough to earn you at least a little bit of relief from this constant upset and turmoil.

You don't have to figure out the wilderness. You don't have to fix it. You don't have to be able to explain to your church friends why you're going through the wilderness. Your job as a much loved, highly treasured child of God is simply to *yield* to the wilderness because it's often only in the wilderness where our runaway desires yield to His.

The wilderness is God's way of making us want the only thing that's really worth having. The wilderness, my friend, is worth it.

Excerpt taken from *One in a Million* by Priscilla Shirer (© 2010).

Nowhere to Turn

*I would have despaired unless I had believed
that I would see the goodness of the LORD in the
land of the living. (Psalm 27:13 NASB)*

God can work a miracle in your experiences, you know.

We tend to forget the miraculous ways God has dealt with us in the past—even the recent past—when a new experience presents itself that requires supernatural intervention. We fail to remember how His often unknown, unseen hand of protection and deliverance kept us going when we didn't think we could handle any more. We look back to a time before our problems reached such a danger point, before they turned into real emergencies, and we envy the seeming sense of ease we used to enjoy (forgetting that we complained just as hard then as we do now).

All we can feel are the walls closing in. All we can be sure of is that there's no way out. All we can see are the Egyptian hordes on one side and the vast Red Sea on the other—the rock, the hard place. But, my friend, this is God's place—the place where He wants to show His miracle-working power in your experience.

The Israelites' position at the lapping mouth of the Red Sea was no mistake. God knew they needed to see a mighty display of His power—one that would make a lasting impression on them, one that would be a visual reminder later on in their journey of exactly what He can do when all hope is gone. He wanted them in a place where the only available option was a miraculous move of God on their behalf, an incident that would serve as a bedrock of remembrance for the entire nation throughout the centuries to come.

David had heard stories like these recounted to him. He had witnessed God's deliverance himself with his own eyes, in his own life. This is what our Red Sea circumstances are for—not to frustrate and discourage us, not to leave us writhing in despair, but rather to foster in us an enthusiasm and anticipation for what God is preparing to do.

Are you in a Red Sea circumstance today? Are you caught between a rock and a hard place? Are you pinned against a decision that has to be made in the next forty-eight hours? Are you lost inside an impossibly complex problem without enough money to buy your way out of it and no good answers even if you did?

Then you're in a spot to be envied—like the Hebrews who were actually there when the waters of that sea piled up in a sloshing heap on either side of them. Feeling the surge of adrenaline that coursed through their veins as they hightailed it across on dry land, looking down and seeing no mud collecting on their sandals. Nothing like watching four hundred years of Egyptian oppression being yanked to the seafloor by the undertow of God's almighty power.

That power is at work in your life and mine, even today.

Excerpt taken from *One in a Million* by Priscilla Shirer (© 2010).

He Wrote It for You

For the word of the LORD is right and true; he is
faithful in all he does. (Psalm 33:4 NIV)

I am not going to master the Bible. *Not ever.*

I'm not going to dissect every Hebrew verb tense or be able to close my eyes and trace the path of the Israelites through the desert as they wandered for forty years. Many people can do that and they may very well be the most godly folks you've ever met. But I can tell you with certainty and from experience that there is only one motive that matters to God when we read His Word.

He wants us to know Him so we can glorify His name.

He wrote it for us. He wrote it for you.

You don't have to have a degree, a literary bent, or even above-average intellect in order to experience God through His Word. God does not love Bible scholars more than non-scholars. (Scholars, we'll chat after class. Find something shiny and Greek for a few minutes.) He doesn't count the minutes people spend with their Bibles open in order to determine their heavenly rewards or their earthly influence. There isn't a magazine rack in heaven featuring covers of people who memorized the most verses.

This Bible of mine? It is the breath of God spoken into my weary bones. It is the armor I need to walk the roads He has chosen for me, and it's the confirmation of promises that withstand the test of hours and adversity.

It's a love letter, and it has my name on it.

It has your name on it.

Hard to fathom, isn't it?

I believe that one of the most powerful ways the enemy has distracted us is by convincing us we aren't smart enough to understand the complexities of Scripture, and therefore, we won't get too much out of reading it. He wants us to feel like it's beyond our reach because he knows it's the best way to keep us weak and doubtful.

It's not supposed to be contained by the human intellect in its fullest profundity. It isn't a project to be aced. And if I go into it with an agenda or a feeling of obligation, I'm bound to end up frustrated. Additionally, "not being smart enough" isn't a valid excuse. He did that on purpose. You might not feel like you're smart enough to get as much as you want to out of it, but God promises you will get what you need from it as long as you are diligent.

We come away most impacted when we go to Scripture wanting to gaze at Him, not to search around for signs of Him. He is there. And if you haven't heard Him or been impacted by the Word, go back. Slow down. Listen.

And please, please don't think you're not going to be able to make sense of it.

To some, they are words. Just *words*. But to us, *they are everything*.

You might not realize it at first, but He will give you treasures in darkness. He loved you enough to share His words with you, and He promises you it's worth it.

Excerpt taken from *Chasing God* by Angie Smith (© 2014).

Surprisingly Delicious

Taste and see that the LORD is good.
How happy is the person who takes refuge
in him! (Psalm 34:8 CSB)

The Hebrews didn't get it, and many times, neither do we.

What was apparently lost on the Hebrews is the same thing we, too, can misplace when comparing God's steady, clockwork provision with Satan's full-range food court of empty-calorie options: *the manna was awesome!* The Bible describes it in Numbers 11:7 as being "like coriander seed" (an aromatic herb native to the region) and tasting "like wafers with honey" (Exod. 16:31 NASB). It may have looked something like porridge, some scholars believe, but it actually tasted more like Krispy Kreme doughnuts. It was indeed the "bread of heaven" (Ps. 78:24 NKJV), the original angel food cake!

So *this* was the food they turned up their noses at?

Just because the sharp, strong bite of their beloved Egyptian foods had become preferred tastes of choice in their mouths did not mean that nothing else had the power to satisfy them. In fact, God likely created the moist, sweet manna to serve as a marked contrast to their monster-breath favorites, those fire-breathing flavors that had so long grown delectable to palates poisoned by Egypt's influence. The purity of God's nightly manna against the harsh, high-heat quality of onions and garlic was not merely an ongoing gift of nourishment but also the beginning of a long process to wean the Hebrews from their former loves.

It was a clear change of taste.

God seemed eager, didn't He, to get the taste and desire for sin out of their lives—just as He desires to get it out of ours—so that we can become "wise in what is good and innocent in what is evil" (Rom. 16:19 NASB). While the enemy works overtime to keep us addicted to past likes, God relentlessly shapes us through wise amounts of blessing and correction to make us want what's really good for us. He refuses to offer us anything that would excite our prior obsessions, knowing that if we are ever to start living like free men and women, we need to start eating like it.

The manna He's asked you to chew on right now may be tough to swallow, but it's the process through which your taste buds will be renovated and refined. I know it's different. It's supposed to be. Anything less, and years from now you'll still be longing for a seat at Pharaoh's table.

Like always, simple purity and a determined desire for God's holiness carried the day. The tastes and textures prescribed by the Lord for the people He loves were the ones that were really best for them. God never fails to bring about abundant living in those who receive His gifts with confident gratitude. Rather than grumbling and complaining, at which the Hebrews became quite proficient (not that we haven't given their poor record a run for its money), we must accept His ways, knowing that they are designed as much for our good as they are for His glory.

Excerpt taken from *One in a Million* by Priscilla Shirer (© 2010).

Moving the Spotlight

They are filled from the abundance of Your house; You let them drink from your refreshing stream, for with You is life's fountain. In Your light we will see light. (Psalm 36:8–9 HCSB)

The religious person's approach to sin is to try to stop it. *Stop it! Don't do that!* It's a simple equation, right? If we'll just *stop it.* That ought to take care of it.

But there's something within this form of sin management that, first, doesn't work, and second, doesn't really feel like we're winning even when it *does* work. That's because when the goal is mainly to avoid sin, we unwittingly keep sin at center stage. Even in trying to beat it, overcome it, and work our way around it, we still let it occupy a place of undue prominence in our mind.

That's because sin is primarily not something to *defeat* but to *displace.* Sin has already been defeated—trampled underfoot by the resurrected Christ. The job's already been done. No need for us to try doing it again (and again) (and again) (and again). The best way to neutralize sin now is to minimize its footprint on the stage. And we do that, not by rallying to an anti-sin cause, but by elevating Christ above everything else.

Psalm 36 is a point-counterpoint portrayal of the stark difference between wickedness and righteousness, between sin and obedience. The first half covers the usual ground, how the person caught up in bad behavior has "no dread of God before his eyes" (v. 1 HCSB), how he "flatters himself too much to discover and hate his sin" (v. 2 HCSB). He has "stopped acting wisely and doing good," (v. 3 HCSB), enough that "even on his bed he makes malicious plans. He sets himself on a path that is not good and does not reject evil" (v. 4 HCSB).

Okay, we get it and it sounds terrible. Though all of us have been there, none of us want to stay there.

So as David prepares to flip the script beginning with verse 5, we're ready for him to tell us how to get this no-fear, self-flattering failure out of our lives for good. But we won't do it by simply telling ourselves to *stop it*! We'll do it by loving what is so true and revitalizing about our God, even more than by hating what is sometimes so false and shameful within ourselves.

We're talking about the "faithfulness" of God's love (v. 5 HCSB), the towering "mountains" of His righteousness (v. 6 HCSB), the "abundance" of His house, as well as the "refreshing" experience of drinking deeply from His pure streams of blessing (v. 8 HCSB).

"For with You is life's fountain," we say, standing in awe of His presence at center stage. "In Your light we will see light" (v. 9 HCSB). *In You I find everything I need.* And therefore find a lot less of what we *don't* need . . . without even trying not to do it.

Excerpt taken from *100 Days in the Psalms* (© 2016).

For Desert Wanderers

*As a deer longs for streams of water, so I long
for You, God. (Psalm 42:1 HCSB)*

I've had my share of howling and panting in the desert, and I'm only three and a half decades in. One desert season I can recall with clarity. It was early in our marriage. I was finishing up my last semester of college and my husband was in the thick of ministry.

His calling was clear: preach the gospel and lead people. Everywhere I turned I saw confirmation. Whatever he found to do, it flourished. The Bible study grew from a few hundred to over a thousand. The college ministry thrived and multiplied. On staff, he was being groomed to eventually be a pastor himself. Congregants regularly shared stories of the Lord using him to bring their friends and family to Christ or a breakthrough in their own relationship with the Lord.

From all appearances, he might as well have been chugging from the canteen while I watched with a sandy stare. Don't get me wrong, I was thrilled my husband was enjoying fruitfulness and drinking deeply from the well God provided. Being his wife, I got to appreciate the benefits. But only so far.

What about me, God? I'm here too!

Contentment eluded me. I was doing everything I was supposed to be doing. I dove into the life of our church. I served in the youth ministry. I discipled younger women. I went to class and made good grades. I sang on the worship team at the college Bible study.

Oh, that last one.

That's where I wanted to be fulfilled most. And that's where I felt the driest, the loneliest, the least fulfilled. The tension was strange. I struggled when I sang because I didn't like what I heard. I didn't feel as though I was offering my best. I didn't feel good enough. But I also struggled when I didn't sing. My pride was hurt when I wasn't invited to sing with the worship band. I felt an unceasing pull toward using my voice.

At one point I was so exasperated that I said to God, "If it's going to be this way, I'd rather You just take this desire from me completely!"

A little oasis in the desert came when He responded. Through someone I didn't know nor who knew little to nothing about me, God assured me that He had a purpose in this struggle and in using my voice to bring Him glory.

I pressed myself as hard as I could into the Lord. I found Him there. In my desiccation, He became a spring of water, a canteen, if you will.

Maybe you've felt this before—numb, aimless, discontent— maybe you're right smack dab in the middle of it now. Fellow sojourner, there's hope. Although the desert is daunting and you feel helplessly unable to find your way out, He is up to something. Take heart and hold on.

Excerpt taken from *Steadfast Love* by Lauren Chandler (© 2016).

The Big Event

In her chamber, the royal daughter is all glorious,
her clothing embroidered with gold. In colorful
garments she is lead to the king; . . . led in with
gladness and rejoicing. (Psalm 45:13–15 HCSB)

The psalms just don't miss a beat. They cover everything from exasperating frustration to exhilarating joy, from heaving regret to heavenly worship. Then look here at Psalm 45—a wedding song. Right here in the middle of the Bible stuff.

But we really shouldn't find it so out of place. Marriage was the first institution that God established on the earth, uniting Adam and Eve as husband and wife in the garden of Eden at the dawn of Creation. Every wedding continues to be a celebration of God's blessing and favor.

And yet it goes even deeper and more eternal than that. We know from the writings of the New Testament that the marriage relationship is representative of Christ's love, care, and protection for the church. "As the church submits to Christ, so wives are to submit to their husbands" (Eph. 5:24 HCSB). "Husbands, love your wives just as Christ loved the church and gave Himself for her" (v. 25 HCSB) . . . "for no one ever hates his own flesh but provides and cares for it, just as Christ does for the church" (v. 29 HCSB). When Paul talked about marriage, he said he was also talking "about Christ and the church" (v. 32 HCSB).

So when Jesus referred to His Second Coming as being like a "groom" arriving for the "wedding banquet" (Matt. 25:10 HCSB), He was indicating the type of relationship He's chosen to embody with His people. When John described the New Jerusalem "coming down out of heaven from God, prepared like a bride adorned for her husband" (Rev. 21:2 HCSB), he was saying that we've been sought and pursued by the Lover of our souls and made worthy through His blood of being in relationship with Him forever. "The marriage of the Lamb has come," is how John described these end-time events, and Christ's "wife," having prepared herself, will be "given fine linen to wear, bright and pure" (Rev. 19:7–8 HCSB).

That's the theologically rich, biblical heritage of marriage.

Psalm 45, now, seems to specifically be the ancient equivalent of a society page write-up, complete with listings of the attendants and the fashions worn by the wedding party. Yet it's also much more than that. It is an early picture of Christ, situated within these sacred writings, centuries before His physical appearance on Earth. He is the "king" and "mighty warrior" whose throne is "forever and ever," and whose arrival from "ivory palaces" is able to bring such joy. And we are His bride, who has left behind our attachments to old allegiances in order to bow down before Him in honor, gratitude, and devotion, made beautiful and "glorious" for Him through the relationship He's established with us.

So welcome to the big event. You're not just invited; He's made you a central part of what He's been planning for His people.

Centrifuge

God is within her; she will not be toppled. (Psalm 46:5 HCSB)

In a moment of bravery or stupidity, depending on your perspective, I once rode one of those carnival rides that demonstrates the principle of a centrifuge. The one my kids thrill to ride every year is called the Gravitron. You stand in a circular "room," which begins to spin faster and faster. Eventually the ride is going so fast that you are pressed against the wall by the force of the spinning. That's when the floor drops from underneath you, and you are suspended against the wall by nothing but a principle of physics. The kids scream with delight as they abandon themselves to the experience.

I scream right along with them, but my screams are not of delight but terror. For me, this experience does not inspire feelings of great joy but rather feelings of great nausea. I vowed to participate in no further explorations of centrifuges, or any other nausea-inducing principles of physics, in the future.

Sometimes I feel as though I live my life, especially as it relates to other people, inside that carnival ride, thrown against the wall by forces beyond my control, hoping that the principles holding me there will keep me from plummeting to the ground. It isn't so much that my relationships are completely out of control, but that they are out of *my* control. Though I want to throw my head back and laugh at the thrill of it all, I am more often hunched over the toilet, head forward, sick with fear. Fear of getting hurt, fear of disappointing, fear of rejection. Fear that if I get off the ride altogether, I will miss out on something really great. So I stay on and just hope I don't throw up all over my fellow riders.

As I struggle to hang out in this life-sized version of the Gravitron, I often curse the forces that hold me in place and highlight my helpless state. I want to be in harmony with those around me rather than always performing this dance of give and take in which someone always has to lose. The spiritual nausea that rises in my soul is a clear indication that something is not right. I want to write the drama in which everyone wins; where the lion gets to eat and the gazelle gets to live. But this sick feeling is one that I must learn to embrace because it is a sign that I am not yet home.

The part of my spirit that rebels against the pull of this planet longs to take flight, and yet I am held in place by a force greater than myself. Someday the Operator of this ride will give the "all clear" and say that it is safe for me to exit the ride. Someday the tension will all be washed away in a shower of angelic praises. Until then, I will stay put, knowing that when the floor gives way I won't be allowed to fall.

Excerpt taken from *Letting Go of Perfect* by Amy Spiegel (© 2012).

The Difference God Makes

Go around Zion, encircle it; count its towers, note its
ramparts; tour its citadels so that you can tell a future
generation: "This God, our God forever and ever—
He will always lead us." (Psalm 48:12–14 HCSB)

You and I have a lot of things to be thankful for and proud of—
not proud in a "look at me, aren't I something" kind of way, but
with a settled sense of accomplishment or at least a general happiness with how things are going.

Our families, for instance. Certainly all of us experience our hic-
cups and heartaches within the rub and pull of our family relationships, to varying degrees of severity. Few homes function quite as
smoothly and effortlessly as they sometimes appear from the outside. But while there may be kinks to work out, we can look at our
patient parents, or our maturing marriage, or our growing kids and
grandkids, and think, *This is good. This feels good. I like what I'm see-*
ing here.

Our physical homes and property. There's nothing wrong with
backing away from an all-day home improvement project in the late
hours of a Saturday afternoon and feeling glad for what we've done.
Or driving with the window down after washing our car to a gleam-
ing shine. We know they're just *things*, but there's honor in being
good stewards of them and keeping them fully functional, even in
making them beautiful.

Our jobs and careers. Do the math, and you'll discover that
while work is not supposed to outrank other superior priorities, we
do spend more waking hours at our full-time jobs than anywhere

else. So these people we work with, the things we accomplish together, the problems we solve, the customers we serve—we should be enthused by what our effort is achieving. We put so much of ourselves into these important tasks. When we *do* them well, and when they're making a difference, we ought to feel proud of that.

But people who aren't believers can have strong families, and nice homes, and good jobs and careers. What they *can't* do is walk around the circumference of these things and see the work of the Lord inside it.

Their kids may be exceptional, but have they been taught and experienced the Word of God as a regular part of their family life? Have they been faithfully prayed over, day after day? These people's homes may be splendid, their work may be fulfilling. But do they have friends who would say their lives were forever changed by a late-night conversation shared in that tastefully decorated den or kitchen? Do they have employees or coworkers who possess an eternal future now because of their godly influence and example?

"Go around Zion, encircle it; count its towers, note its ramparts; tour its citadels"—and see if you can say of these things that represent your life . . . see if they give evidence of God, not just evidence of you.

You can *really* feel good about that.

Excerpt taken from *100 Days in the Psalms* (© 2016).

I Admit It

Against You—You alone—I have sinned and done this
evil in Your sight. So You are right when You pass sentence;
You are blameless when You judge. (Psalm 51:4 HCSB)

In a perfect world, we would need no Psalm 51.

But ours is not a perfect world. And we are not perfect people. And until we one day become by God's grace an eternal citizen of a world that truly *is* perfect—in every possible way—we will need to find our repentant way to Psalm 51 often.

Its background, of course, is more well-known than perhaps any other psalm in the songbook. David had committed adultery with Bathsheba, a woman he'd espied and desired and had used his kingly power to persuade. Furthermore, he covered up his sin—first by bringing the woman's husband home from the battlefield; then when that didn't work, sending orders to expose the man to the enemy in a callous act resulting in his death.

David, like us, whenever we're unwilling to deal with our own sins, remained blinded to the raw extent of what he'd done. We don't want to see the evil in ourselves. We don't want to think we're capable of it. We certainly don't want to get caught, then be forced to pay for something that we've already excused away in our minds as not really being that big of a deal. And that's basically the story to which David was holding until Nathan the prophet arrived with a message: the story of a poor man, his little children, and their one little sheep—and of a rich man, unwilling to eat into his own abundance of livestock, who pilfered the poor family's pet so that he could put supper on the table for a traveling houseguest.

David's reaction seems a bit of an overreaction—an almost violent anger at the audacity of this fictitious rich man, revealing an oversensitive indignation at the actions of a man that so closely paralleled what David himself had done. When Nathan dropped the hammer by declaring, "You are the man!" (2 Sam. 12:7 HCSB)—*the rich man is YOU!*—everything came crashing down in a dust-spraying collapse of all David's plans and pretensions.

He was still on the throne, however, still the mightiest man in the land. He certainly possessed the credentials to sling Nathan right back out the door he came from. Instead, the king's response is riveting in its humility—and highly instructive to those of us still living imperfectly in an imperfect world.

"I have sinned against the LORD," he said (v. 13 HCSB).

It's me. I did it. I'm the one totally responsible for it.

And while nobody's condoning what any of us have done in sinning against our families, our friends, our employers, even ourselves, there's always hope for a man or woman who'll admit and come to terms with what they've done.

There may not be a way back. But this is the only way forward.

Excerpt taken from *100 Days in the Psalms* (© 2016).

Break My Heart

The sacrifice pleasing to God is a broken spirit. God, You will not despise a broken and humbled heart. (Psalm 51:17 HCSB)

Have you ever considered that any disinterest you may feel in serving and caring and getting your hands dirty might really be because you've never set your heart before Him and asked Him to break it, to make it more sensitive to the ailments of others? Most often we're asking Him to heal it, strengthen it, or restore it. But what kind of supernatural power are we choosing to avoid experiencing by not having a heart broken for the plights of those around us?

Jesus had one. A broken heart.

Throughout the Scriptures we see the portrait of a Man who didn't walk blindly down the dusty, ancient roads of His day, bypassing human devastation and need without a second glance. Rather, He paid close attention. He was moved with compassion. He stopped to care for those who were disenfranchised and distressed.

When He wasn't *extending* compassion, He was *talking* about compassion—telling stories, giving reminders, pointing people in that direction. Showing mercy toward others was an important part of the gospel He came to offer. He didn't turn a blind eye to people's physical needs in order to get to the "more important" spiritual one.

We are part of the church—His church—God's answer for the desperation of our time. If we only attend women's conferences, read encouraging books, listen to sermons, sing worship songs, and yet do little if anything to help others in a tangible way, we relegate our demonstration of His gospel to an impotent, watered-down, self-absorbed exercise. And while I hope you do all these things and benefit greatly from them, I also pray that you sense a little dissatisfaction that causes you to seek something more—something with an outward focus. He saved you for many reasons, but one of them is so that others can sense His compassion manifested toward them through you.

Jesus didn't just *preach* a gospel; He lived one. And now you are His hands and feet—hands that are for more than writing personal checks, feet that are for more than walking to church or to the mailbox so that someone else can be resourced to go. Sending help is honorable. Do it. People need it. But hiding beneath the cloak of giving keeps you from experiencing the benefits of being the helper God is commissioning you to be.

When Jesus felt empathy toward others, it wasn't a clichéd emotion. It was a deep, gut-wrenching reaction that, according to many commentators, would affect Him physically—the equivalent of having an uneasy stomach. How did He choose to respond to that? He didn't go home, hoping that a good nap would cause His sadness and irritation to wear off. He took His broken heart as a sign to do something, to act in accordance with the Father's will. He went. He served. He listened. He healed.

Excerpt taken from *The Resolution for Women* by Priscilla Shirer (© 2011).

The Fear of Death

My heart shudders within me; terrors of death
sweep over me. Fear and trembling grip me; horror
has overwhelmed me. (Psalm 55:4–5 HCSB)

G randma, can I ask you a really weird question?" She nodded
and adjusted her hearing aid.

"Are you ever afraid of dying?"

She smiled a little and shook her head from side to side.

She wasn't.

I asked her why and she told me that she had lived a beautiful life and it just didn't scare her. I stared at her in amazement because I wanted her faith. I wanted the freedom that came from not having to obsess about what might or might not happen.

I wanted to look at the ocean like it was beautiful and not something that could swallow me up. Yet fear of death still gripped me.

I prayed, I read Scripture, I asked the Lord to help me, and yet, I still lay awake at night in tears of desperation, ashamed at what I perceived as a lack of faith.

What I long to do is to wrap this up with a beautiful bow and tell you that the Lord has removed this fear from my life. Sadly, that isn't the case. I still struggle with fear of death. However, I now see it a little differently than I once did.

I think it's natural for us to fear death—both our own and the death of those we love. It is a horrific reality that sin exists. Satan delights in our sleepless nights and our doubts in God's sovereignty. We must continually turn it over to the Lord and surround ourselves with people who urge us to trust His goodness.

Like every other fear, Satan clings to the thought that we will be ashamed to tell others. Once I opened up to some women I trusted about this fear, I felt such great relief through their understanding and suggestions.

Fearing death is a part of life, and because "we do not have a high priest who is unable to sympathize with our weaknesses" (Heb. 4:15 NIV), we should feel safe going to Him with our concerns.

David, who was called a "man after God's own heart," experienced the fear of death as his best friend-turned-enemy sought to kill him.

Many times, like David, I have dreamed about what it would be like to flee from the storm to a safe place only to be reminded that the Lord is our refuge. He is the safe place I have spent so many days trying to create for myself.

It gives me peace to know that the Lord has given us examples in His Word of people who were faithful, devoted servants of Christ who had fear. What these examples teach us is that we have an opportunity to glorify God in how we respond to fear. David was still unsure of his future, and yet he turned his fear into an opportunity to trust. What a beautiful image of belief and peace in a moment that could have destroyed him.

Excerpt taken from *What Women Fear* by Angie Smith (© 2011).

The Pattern of Prayer

I complain and groan morning, noon, and night,
and He hears my voice. (Psalm 55:17 HCSB)

Practically speaking, there are several exciting lessons to learn in the prayer pattern expressed in this verse.

Personal Petition

Prayers must be personal, expressing individual need and heart's desire. The most personal prayers in Scripture present an outpouring through direct petition to God. Note Hannah who prayed and wept before the Lord, pleading for a child.

"Making a vow, she pleaded, 'LORD of Hosts, if You will take notice of Your servant's affliction, remember and not forget me, and give Your servant a son, I will give him to the LORD all the days of his life, and his hair will never be cut'" (1 Sam. 1:11 HCSB).

She expressed her heart's desire clearly and earnestly. We can do the same.

Confident Expectation

Prayer ought to be offered in faithful confidence. "But I call to God, and the LORD will save me" (Ps. 55:16 HCSB). Mary, chosen to be the mother of the Lord Jesus, prayed in quiet confidence: "May it be done to me according to your word" (Luke 1:38 HCSB). Despite the difficult days ahead, Mary then praised the Lord and waited for Him to meet her needs. You must trust the providence of God to fulfill even our most mundane necessities.

Grateful Testimony

Not only in this psalm, but in others as well, there is the encouragement to cry aloud unto the Lord. Anna's prayer of thanksgiving in the temple as she saw Messiah was voiced aloud so that all of those around her could hear her joyous testimony to the Lord.

> "At that very moment, she came up and began to thank God and to speak about Him to all who were looking forward to the redemption of Jerusalem." (Luke 2:38 HCSB)

Appointed Time

Prayer is offered throughout the day. Definite quiet times for communion with God the Father are set aside. Perhaps the evening prayer is a period for meditation and refreshment; the morning prayer, a time for strength and creativity in the new opportunities; and the noontime, a pause for dealing with that day's particular problems.

Daily Challenge

Prayer is also offered seasonally. For example, the fall has traditionally been a time of renewal and revival in churches across the land. The returning of children to school, the resuming of disciplined schedules after family vacations and leisure, the changing of the season—all these factors affect life and family. What an appropriate time to examine your relationship to the heavenly Father, to recommit yourself to the spiritual nurture of a daily devotional time, and to set the example for doing so before your children.

You will find your responsibilities more rewarding, your burdens lighter, your satisfactions more fulfilling, your lives more enriched and meaningful when you pray evening, morning, and at noon. You then keep the Lord close as you walk through your day, enjoying His presence continually and having His guidance consistently.

Excerpt taken from *A Woman Seeking God* by Dorothy Kelley Patterson (© 2013).

One for the Record Books

You Yourself have recorded my wanderings. Put my
tears in Your bottle. Are they not in Your records? Then
my enemies will retreat on the day when I call. This
I know: God is for me. (Psalm 56:8–9 HCSB)

We think it's nice and convenient (or maybe just really nosy) that our grocery store sends us coupon offers every month, targeted to our specific buying habits and patterns, including some habits we wish they *didn't* know, like our weekly weakness for a carton of ice cream.

But God has been keeping comprehensive records like these for way longer than any of us have been alive.

The prophetic Old Testament book of Malachi speaks about a "book of remembrance" that is kept in His presence (Mal. 3:16 HCSB). There were people in that day who were saying, "It is useless to serve God. What have we gained by keeping His requirements and walking mournfully before the LORD of Hosts?" (v. 14 HCSB). But God, the Scripture says, was making note of such things, keeping a record of "those who feared Yahweh and had high regard for His name" (v. 16 HCSB).

John's Revelation also talks about books being opened in heaven, including the "book of life," and how people will be "judged according to their works" by what is "written in the books" (Rev. 20:12 HCSB). But we also learn of something else being kept: "the prayers of the saints," existing in the form of incense contained in golden bowls (5:8 HCSB), its smoke fragrantly wafting upward from an angel's hand into "the presence of God" (8:4 HCSB).

So when David lifted another of his many prayers to the Lord—this one, cataloged for us as Psalm 56, being voiced during Saul's paranoid pursuit of him—he was totally convinced that "You Yourself have recorded my wanderings" and kept "my tears in Your bottle," as well as "in Your records." God's love for him, he realized, was so remarkably deep and complete that he could imagine Him almost scrapbooking their various interactions and keeping photographic memories of everything David had endured.

Perhaps you find this insight into God's nature a little too doting for your taste, as if surely He wouldn't allow Himself to appear so smitten with us that He treasures keepsakes of our relationship, like a silly adolescent. We should be the ones so taken and enamored with *Him*, you might say. *True.* But it's not any kind of neediness or codependence on His part that inspires Him to watch us and watch over us so devotedly. It's just that when He does anything, He does it completely. And while His care does have the effect of wrapping us all the way around with the confidence that "God is for me," it also just puts on infinite display the mind-blowing capabilities of His omniscience, omnipotence, and omnipresence.

What a wonder He is . . . that we never have to wonder if He's taking care of us.

Excerpt taken from *100 Days in the Psalms* (© 2016).

Slice and Dice

I am surrounded by lions; I lie down with those who
devour men. Their teeth are spears and arrows; their
tongues are sharp swords. (Psalm 57:4 HCSB)

A sharp-edged knife is an essential tool for cooking. One of my husband's recurring complaints has been the condition of our kitchen knives. He enjoys spending a Saturday or Sunday afternoon chopping and mixing exotic ingredients in order to sauté, baste, braise, or broil the latest dish featured on a television cooking show. However, the bargain-store set of knives we received as a wedding gift eighteen years ago "just aren't cutting it." (Pardon the pun.)

How can he achieve culinary excellence when his scallions and shallots are getting mulched instead of thinly sliced as the recipe says? His frustration reached such a point that one day I arrived home after running errands to find all but one knife in the garbage can. (Being the practical type, I rescued them.)

I've already purchased a set of heavy-duty professional chef knives made of stainless steel to give to him for our next anniversary. They lie in wait on black velvet in a glass-and-aluminum enclosed case. Just a few moments ago, I opened the case and lightly brushed my thumb against the edge of the largest knife. It's sharp. Very sharp. An edge like that is certain to cut. It'll be great for cooking!

Unfortunately, as we all know, a sharp knife also can be used as a weapon. The same edge can create or kill—it all depends on how it is used. The Hebrew word for mouth is often translated "edge." Like a knife, the tongue has a sharp, powerful edge that can either create or destroy. It can function as a helpful tool or a destructive weapon.

David knew firsthand that a wound inflicted by the tongue bleeds the spirit more severely than a wound inflicted by the sword bleeds the flesh. Have you ever felt like David? Have you ever felt wounded by the sharp edge of someone's tongue? I have. People have hurt me deeply with their words. But it's sobering for me to realize that my mouth carries the same edge as theirs. It has the same destructive potential. The Bible is replete with verses describing the destructive power of the tongue. Here's just a sample of the comparisons:

- Jeremiah 9:8—deadly arrow
- Proverbs 16:27—scorching fire
- Psalm 140:3—poison of vipers
- Job 5:21—lash/whip
- Proverbs 18:7—a snare

God wants us to be aware of the potential of our tongues—the potential for evil and for good. The Bible says if you live by the sword you will die by the sword (2 Sam. 12:10; Prov. 26:27). If you choose to use your tongue as a sword, your relationships will experience "perpetual calamity." On the other hand, if you choose to put your sword into its sheath (a mark of peace and friendship—Jer. 47:6), you will reap rich rewards (see Prov. 12:14).

Excerpt taken from *Conversation Peace* by Mary Kassian (© 2004).

Overwhelmed!

God, hear my cry, pay attention to my prayer. I call to You from the ends of the earth when my heart is without strength. Lead me to a rock that is high above me. (Psalm 61:1–2 HCSB)

Isaiah 24 refers to "the city of chaos" (v. 10 HCSB)—the condition of the earth when under judgment of God, when sin and error and selfish pride have brought on the reaped consequences of loss and destruction. "Every house is closed to entry. In the streets they cry for wine. All joy grows dark; earth's rejoicing goes into exile. Only desolation remains in the city; its gate has collapsed in ruins" (vv. 10–12 HCSB).

We don't know what caused David in Psalm 61 to declare himself as being "without strength." But we do know he'd found himself at "the ends of the earth"—perhaps in a "city of chaos" situation where no one could help him, where the darkness was closing in, where whatever joy he'd experienced in life felt far away and forgotten now, underneath this heavy, overriding sense of . . . let's call it "overwhelmed."

That's actually what the translators of the King James Version of the Bible called it. "Hear my cry, O God; attend unto my prayer. From the end of the earth will I cry unto thee, when my heart is overwhelmed" (Ps. 61:1–2 KJV). Sounds like these seventeenth-century theologians were more modern than we think. We still today endure a lot of weary moments when our heart cries out to God admitting we are "overwhelmed."

We are *over* it.

But just when we think everything is piling on top of us, we look up and see *one* thing above us that is not set to fall . . . because it is set there in stone. The "rock" that is "high above" us (Ps. 61:2 HCSB) is our "everlasting rock" (Isa. 26:4 HCSB).

In fact, in this chapter from Isaiah where the prophet refers to God as "everlasting rock"—only two chapters removed from where he was touring that "city of chaos"—we find him in *another* city, a "strong city," where "salvation is established as walls and ramparts" (Isa. 26:1 HCSB). "Open the gates," the prophet cries—those gates that before were falling off their hinges. "Open the gates so a righteous nation can come in, one that remains faithful" and can enjoy where God has called them to live (v. 2 HCSB). Chaos has ruled and had its day, giving us that "overwhelmed" feeling again. But "You," Lord, "will keep the mind that is dependent on You in perfect peace, for it is trusting in You." We can "trust in the LORD forever, for the LORD GOD is an everlasting rock!" (vv. 3–4 ESV).

"God, hear my cry; pay attention to my prayer. I call to You from the ends of the earth when my heart is without strength. Lead me to the rock that is high above me" (Ps. 61:1–2 HCSB).

Lead me to You.

And lead on.

Excerpt taken from *100 Days in the Psalms* (© 2016).

The Power of Purity

If I regard wickedness in my heart, the Lord
will not hear. (Psalm 66:18 NASB)

S*in has consequences.* Always has and always will. Keep this revelation fixed squarely in your mind. Because whether we like it or not, here's how the spiritual economy of life works for believers: Obedience to God garners intimacy and nearness, divine blessing and favor. Disobedience creates a sense of distance and loss, grief and regret. Always. Sometimes the consequences of caving to temptation are practical and tangible, changing your daily experience, drastically enough in certain cases to fundamentally affect the rest of your life. But no matter how immediately noticeable the cost, the ripple effects of sin always affect your connection with the Father. And this, *this,* is exactly what the enemy is hoping for. It's why he is so personalized and meticulous in his advances to tempt you.

Impurity weakens your praying—which in turn weakens your power. When our lives are not aligned with the teaching of Scripture and the transforming work of God's Spirit—when we're resisting His wise, loving instruction concerning our lifestyle and attitudes—our prayer closets start to feel like soundproof rooms. Our spiritual armor becomes little more than the plastic painted stuff they sell as a kit in the toy section of the Christian bookstore. The energy we expect our prayers to access and generate is momentarily choked off and shorted out. We've compromised the system. We've created a bottleneck. We're leaking oil, leaking power. We end up, in practical terms, living like the double-minded man in the New Testament book of James, who the Bible says "should not expect to receive anything from the Lord" because he's "unstable in all his ways" (James 1:7–8 HCSB).

It's not because God's hand is "so short that it cannot save; nor is His ear so dull that it cannot hear. But your iniquities have made a separation between you and your God, and your sins have hidden His face from you so that He does not hear" (Isa. 59:1–2 NASB). Separation. That's what sin creates. Which is why the enemy is dead set on crafting temptations for our lives. He knows that the "effectual fervent prayer" that James 5:16 (KJV) says "availeth much" contains parameters. Prayers that have power come from a person in pursuit of righteous living.

Yes, righteousness matters.

That's why you and I must deliberately strategize in prayer for the daily, ongoing protection of our purity. Prayer keeps us on guard, our spiritual radar sensitive to the enemy's ploys and clever decoys. Without this close contact with the Father, we become convinced that our careless behavior is "not so bad."

The devil's strategy is to make us believe impurity is normal—that if nobody's hurt it's no big deal. But if we were steadily engaged in fervent prayer—with *our* strategy counteracting *his* strategy—we'd see in a snap that unrighteousness is not "no big deal." It's a house of horrors. It is a *totally* upside-down way to live.

Excerpt taken from *Fervent* by Priscilla Shirer (© 2015).

The Nature of Things

*The day is Yours, also the night; You established the moon
and the sun. You set all the boundaries of the earth; You
made summer and winter. (Psalm 74:16–17 HCSB)*

In the beginning God created the heavens and the earth" (Gen.
1:1 HCSB)—darkness and light; earth and sky; land and sea; fruits
and veggies; sun and moon; fish and fowl; lions and tigers and
bears—(oh, my) and even us.

He made everything. Just the way He wanted.

Now this world, of course, is the only one we know. He created
us with a physiology that was able to acclimate to it little by little,
from the moment we arrived, so that we gradually picked up on
where things went, what they looked like, and how they operated.
This earth is our normal.

So while we may worry and wonder about many, many things
throughout the course of a day, there are tons of things we never,
ever think about. We never stop to question why they function as
they do.

We just accept, for example—colors. We don't try to go make
new ones. We just live with the ones we've got. But isn't it interesting, having learned the difference between "warm" colors and "cool"
colors, that the predominant colors in nature are green, blue, and
brown? Peaceful colors? Restful colors? Calming colors?

Why?

Just lucky how it lined up that way? I don't think so. God specifically chose the color palette that He wanted to wrap us in. And
He specifically made our minds and bodies so that we respond to

these colors with a general, particular mood and feel. They represent to us the peaceful nature and all-around provision of God . . . who could've chosen *any* colors for grass, sky, and dirt . . . or could've decided to make them different colors every day . . . or every third Tuesday . . . or not to even *have* Tuesdays.

See, God's choices are endless, and yet He chose . . . *these*. For a reason. For our sanity. For His own superior knowledge of what needed to happen, or else nothing would be able to work right.

And so when we wake up to the sunrise every morning and find to our delight that everything is still where we left it when we went to bed last evening, we should view these everyday miracles as fresh, new reasons to praise God for His wisdom, care, and attention to detail.

The day, the night; the moon and the sun; the boundaries of the earth; the uniqueness and distinction between summer and winter—all of these are gifts of necessity, variety, and creativity from the hand of our infinitely powerful and infinitely loving God. And if your world just happens to feel a little dull and boring today, or perhaps feels as though it's been turned completely upside-down, be grateful that He's fashioned it just the way He's given it.

Excerpt taken from *100 Days in the Psalms* (© 2016).

A New Fighting Position

They were to rise and tell their children
so that they might put their confidence in God
and not forget God's works,
but keep His commands.
Then they would not be like their fathers,
a stubborn and rebellious generation,
a generation whose heart was not loyal
and whose spirit was not faithful to God.
(Psalm 78:6–8 HCSB)

The family is one of the key axis points of God's purposes on earth. And *your* family, at the point of *your* sphere of influence, is a major component of what He is doing right here where you live. In order to make sure you're fully cooperating with Him and with the enormous opportunity embodied in your family structure and its people, they need you to not be on their backs, not be up in their faces, but be down on your knees.

Assume a new fighting position.

I think we've all resorted at one time or another to the roll-call system for covering our family in prayer. *Lord, bless my husband; Lord, bless my kids; be with my aunt and uncle in Ohio; be with my dad and his knee replacement rehab; be with my brother who's looking for work.* Quick. Easy. Over and done. Better than totally ignoring them perhaps, but hardly a satisfying confidence that you're going all out, participating mightily with God in their future, their provision, or their rescue.

"Beloved," the apostle John wrote, "I pray that in all respects you may prosper and be in good health, just as your soul prospers"

(3 John 2 NASB). "May He give you what your heart desires and fulfill your whole purpose" (Ps. 20:4 HCSB). The Scripture is full of eternal truths, made even more relevant when framed against the context of your family's life, specific needs, and dilemmas.

Homes, families, marriages, and children can all too easily become combat zones, which is the last thing in the world you foresaw when you pledged your life to your husband and brought home your child from the delivery room. And while you may not be able to control all discord and unwise choices within your family, you can engage in combat in the heavenlies, in prayer, in secret.

The enemy who's intent on disrupting the peace in your home doesn't flinch when you try to fix things on your own, but he does start worrying when you start avoiding the noise at the periphery and start praying, making some noise of your own, right outside the door to the devil's workshop.

For the sake of your family, take the fight into your *prayer* room rather than your *living* room. Use the promises and passages in Scripture to get started. Then take your vocal pleas to God instead of making your vocal presence such a common fixture around the house. Get ready to go to war for your family. And get ready to see some changes you've never seen happen before.

Excerpt taken from *Fervent* by Priscilla Shirer (© 2015).

He Led Them

He led them safely, and they were not afraid. (Psalm 78:53 HCSB)

Our oldest daughter, Audrey, has become a full-fledged horse girl. She's always on the back of her horse. Gypsy is a copper-colored quarter horse who's won her way into our hearts. I'm amazed every time I watch Audrey ride Gypsy. This girl who doesn't weigh 100 pounds soaking wet can maneuver her 800-pound horse with a rope tied on both ends to a small piece of metal in the horse's mouth. Even on more stubborn days, Gypsy only needs a swift nudge from a spur's edge to cooperate.

I'm not fooled though. There is a give and take happening. At any moment, Gypsy could refuse to be bossed around and send Audrey flying in the air. Yet, Audrey has gained Gypsy's trust. She has been faithful to feed her, groom her, and tend to her hooves when a rock is lodged in her shoe. Audrey has nuzzled her head into the crook of Gypsy's neck and scratched her in just the right place that sends her head back and nose up in sheer pleasure.

Despite over a year of consistent love and care, Gypsy still shows signs of insecurity when she's put in a new situation. The latest scenario was when we tried to load her into a trailer. We had placed a halter on Gypsy to lead her. Usually with the halter, she follows with no problem, making you believe the rope is what's forcing her to move with you. The ruse was up when she stopped just short of the ramp. No amount of tugging on that rope made her budge. After an hour of much coaxing, Gypsy loaded. Everyone broke into shouts and cries of relief. From then on, Audrey worked with her consistently, placing her feed in the bin inside the trailer. She proved to

Gypsy that walking into the trailer was safe and good, and that she could trust Audrey to lead her.

Once we've come to the place where we admit we're poor and needy and have humbled ourselves to cry out to God, He will lead us out of the desert. To be led implies there's following involved—a yielding of one's will to another. It's nice when those wills line up naturally, but stretching when they don't. Gypsy will gladly submit to Audrey's direction when she's bringing her back to the barn after a long trail ride. Gypsy knows relief is coming and heartily yields. When it comes to something new like the trailer, an abundance of assurance is required for her obedience.

Are we not unlike Gypsy? We're all in if the path seems pleasurable but the moment things get hard or the way is unfamiliar, we dig our heels (or hooves) into the sand and refuse to budge. Oh, but if we would trust Him to lead us all the way. If we would yield our wills to Him and know Him more deeply on the journey, knowing that relief is coming if we trust Him.

Excerpt taken from *Steadfast Love* by Lauren Chandler (© 2016).

Fast-Acting Relief

If only My people would listen to Me and Israel would follow
My ways, I would quickly subdue their enemies and turn
My hand against their foes. (Psalm 81:13–14 HCSB)

Take a closer look at the typical car commercial—you know, the ones where at some point the sleek auto is snaking around a curve between a mountain pass, spraying up fallen leaves from its roadside wake—and you'd be shocked how many individual film images these ad spots include, and how quickly they cycle from one to the next. It's a microcosm of the speed with which we tend to attack life and how we expect it to travel. Fast.

Or to use the psalmist's word . . . *quickly.*

Perhaps we should be more deliberate than a luxury car commercial in embracing hurry in certain aspects of our lives. God has always been willing and able to move in fast motion to bring about changes in people's circumstances. *We're* the ones who often drag our feet and put things off.

Let's use Jonah as an applicable example. We'd probably all agree that three days surrounded by the chalky digestive fluids of a huge fish would seem like an eternity. But if you were trapped like him in a situation of your own sinful making, and God spun the whole thing around and set you off with a second chance in only a few days' time, you'd likely be somewhere between relieved and ecstatic with how quickly He'd brought this reversal about.

One of the reasons why we get mired in our sins and don't initiate the bold, radical steps that could steer us clear of them is because we're not sure we're up for the long road out. And, yes, in many ways, the process of changing our habits and being transformed in our thinking does quite often take a lot of hard time to generate.

But there's a quickness to it as well—the noticeable brightness of renewal and feel-better blessings that God simply delights in delivering to us.

The prophet Hosea urged the people of Israel to "come, let us return to the LORD. For He has torn us, and He will heal us; He has wounded us, and He will bind up our wounds. He will revive us after two days, and on the third day He will raise us up so we can live in His presence" (Hos. 6:1–2 HCSB). There's obviously some Messianic foreshadowing and imagery there, but still . . . instead of always assuming we'll need a week or two of repenting before God will even *begin* wanting to hear from us again, "let us strive to know the LORD. His appearance is as sure as the dawn" (v. 3 HCSB). Why waste even another minute before we get up, get out, and get on with it?

God doesn't want you waiting around until you're good and sorry. He just wants to start subduing these enemies of yours, so . . . would today be soon enough?

Excerpt taken from *100 Days in the Psalms* (© 2016).

The Ultimate Promise

If they dishonor My statutes and do not keep My commands,
then I will call their rebellion to account with the rod, their
sin with blows. But I will not withdraw My faithful love from
him or betray My faithfulness. (Psalm 89:31–33 HCSB)

God's covenant with David went like this: "I took you from the pasture and from following the sheep to be ruler over My people Israel. I have been with you wherever you have gone" (2 Sam. 7:8–9 HCSB).

In addition, "when your time comes and you rest with your fathers, I will raise up after you your descendant, who will come from your body, and I will establish his kingdom" (v. 12 HCSB). If this son of David began to engage in sin and rebellion against God, he could expect his wings to be clipped till he learned to fly right. "But My faithful love will never leave him as I removed it from Saul. . . . Your house and kingdom will endure before Me forever, and your throne will be established forever" (vv. 15–16 HCSB).

God wasn't going to be caught off-guard by disobedience among those to whom He'd promised His total loyalty and protection. The strength and beauty of His covenant would not be based on how well people performed under it, but by how complete and unconditional His love would remain toward those He had claimed as His own.

We can read this covenant terminology today, extended by implication to us (since we are sons and daughters of the One who occupies David's throne forever), and we see all kinds of loopholes in this plan—loopholes that seem to work to our spiritual advantage. That's certainly how the opponents of grace articulated their views centuries later during Paul's day. "What should we say then? Should we continue in sin so that grace may multiply?" (Rom. 6:1 HCSB).

Have cake; eat too.

Yes, it would seem so, except that God knows He's the only One who can deliver any cake. And while those of us scanning the menu options cannot help but make some bad choices from time to time—and will pay for indulging in things that are not good for us—the Lord takes "no pleasure in the death of the wicked, but rather that the wicked person should turn from his way and live" (Ezek. 33:11 HCSB). So we who live under His covenant need not be looking for ways to sneak a second helping. His covenant comes with a desire to "walk in the light as He Himself is in the light" so that we can enjoy "fellowship with one another" through the blood of Jesus, which "cleanses us from all sin" (1 John 1:7 HCSB).

Yes, His covenant is certainly a good deal for us, but not because it gives us breathing room for enjoying a few spare sins here and there. It's a good deal because it leads us to the inescapable reality that His way is truly and indeed, in every way, the only way.

Excerpt taken from *100 Days in the Psalms* (© 2016).

The Safe Harbor

*The one who lives under the protection of the Most High
dwells in the shadow of the Almighty. (Psalm 91:1 HCSB)*

As Jesus had a mind to lead the disciples through the storm and to the other side, so the Lord leads us through the storm to a "desired haven." Whether we know it or not, our hearts pine for something in particular. Ecclesiastes 3:11 says that the Lord has put eternity into man's heart. There's a longing in every limited being for the limitless—for something outside ourselves. That Something, or Someone, designed us that way, and He is the only fulfillment of our soul's desire.

He is the object of our desire, and He is our safe haven, or harbor. In order for harbors to be efficient, they must have two important characteristics: depth and protection. The water must be deep enough to allow large ships to drop anchor, and it must be sheltered by prominent land features on several sides from stormy weather. These elements can be found naturally or are constructed artificially by dredging and building seawalls and jettys.

Likewise, when we hide ourselves "in the shelter of the Most High," He provides depth and protection (Ps. 91:1 ESV). His love is deep enough to swallow up anyone. No one is too much for Him. And for the curious and knowledge-thirsty, "Oh, the depth of the riches and wisdom and knowledge of God! How unsearchable are his judgments and how inscrutable his ways!" (Rom. 11:33 ESV). He is deep enough for our hardest questions—the whys and the why-nots.

We are only safe in Him.

"Even when I go through the darkest valley, I fear no danger, for You are with me; Your rod and Your staff—they comfort me" (Ps. 23:4 HCSB).

Psalm 23 reminds me that although I may walk through the deepest valleys with the darkest shadows, my soul is safe. There is no evil that can overcome me because the Lord is with me. I am comforted by the fact that regardless of what comes my way, whether the loss of my husband, or my children, or reputation, or home, or station in life, it will all be goodness and mercy toward me from the Lord of steadfast love. And one day, I will forever be safe in the house of the Lord.

Our desired haven is found in Christ—to be hidden in Him so that when He, who is my life, appears, then also I will appear with Him in glory (Col. 3:4).

The storms of life remind us that this is not all there is. There is a glory coming that we have yet to see fully. There is a healing of our souls that goes beyond any physical healing on earth. It's already begun but it's not all here yet. So we wait with eager expectation. We weather the storms with Him on the earth as the wind and waves whet our appetite for the coming glory. Our voices lift from the rain-beaten vessel, "Come, Lord Jesus, come!"

Excerpt taken from *Steadfast Love* by Lauren Chandler (© 2016).

Test Day

*Today, if you hear His voice: Do not harden your hearts
as at Meribah, as on that day at Massah in the wilderness
where your fathers tested Me; they tried Me, though
they had seen what I did. (Psalm 95:7–9 HCSB)*

We can only imagine how hot it was. And not having any water to drink was a serious hardship.

Most likely, though—based on other squabbles that came to light during their shove-off from the land of bondage—this little incident that occurred at a place Moses later named Massah and Meribah (meaning "tested" and "complained") was less about being thirsty and more about being contentious. God did graciously provide them water from the unlikely source of a rock along the roadside, but their pattern of testing Him hadn't gone unnoticed.

They'd eventually have forty years to think about it.

"For 40 years I was disgusted with that generation," the Lord is quoted as saying in Psalm 95. "I said, 'They are a people whose hearts go astray; they do not know My ways'" (v. 10 HCSB). So they forfeited their privilege of entering into His "rest" (v. 11 HCSB)—a long and prosperous life in the Promised Land. The milk-and-honey experience of Canaan would be delayed until the following generation, a knowing piece of discipline employed against a people who never quite learned to appreciate the gift they'd been given.

One can't help but wonder, though, how a single day could be important enough to become forty-years costly.

Maybe our best clue comes from the book of Hebrews, where this same passage from Psalm 95 reappears to teach another generation of followers the hard lessons of the past. The whole bit is here again—"Today, if you hear His voice" (Heb. 3:7 HCSB), followed by the reports of testing and complaining and the forty-year result of their going astray. Only this time, in an instructive nod toward future readers like us, the writer deposited some counsel that bears a "daily" solution.

"Watch out, brothers, so that there won't be in any of you an evil, unbelieving heart that departs from the living God. But encourage each other daily, while it is still called today, so that none of you is hardened by sin's deception" (vv. 12–13 HCSB).

A single day's sin is obviously a day too many. God deals with us, of course, in perfect awareness of our hearts. He alone understands both why and when the most fitting result of our sin should be either a long-term or short-term consequence. But what if those "days" when sin seemed so worth it could've been avoided by someone's encouragement to think before we spoke? And what if someone else's "day" of sin today could be rethought by a word of wise encouragement and counsel from us? Let's look for daily opportunities both to hand out and listen for the kind of trusted advice and inspiration that could save us all kind of trouble on the back end.

Excerpt taken from *100 Days in the Psalms* (© 2016).

Resolved!

I will be careful to live a blameless life—when will you come to help me? I will lead a life of integrity in my own home. I will refuse to look at anything vile and vulgar. . . . I will have nothing to do with them. (Psalm 101:2–3 NLT)

This was not the norm for the kings of ancient nations. Powerful and highly unaccountable, these monarchs felt free to live as they pleased anywhere they went, especially within the confines of their personal living quarters. Unchecked. Unbridled. No one had the right to tell them what to do. King David, however, wanted to be different, and he expressed several of the commitments he employed to help him achieve his goal—ones that we can make as well.

1. Have no tolerance for evil. "I will refuse to look at anything vile and vulgar," he wrote (v. 3 HCSB). He was unwilling for anything that went against the standards and statutes of God to be paraded before him as entertainment. He promised not to engage in any activity that could slowly, progressively cause him to be desensitized to sin.

2. Closely monitor the type of people you allow to influence you. "I hate all who deal crookedly; I will have nothing to do with them. I will reject perverse ideas and stay away from every evil" (vv. 3–4 HCSB). No one who was slanderous, proud, or lacking in integrity would be able to live in close relationship with him. He was not about to let their poor character and counsel become a loud, persistent voice in his head or discourage him from the upright path.

3. Recognize your need for divine help. "I will be careful to live a blameless life—when will you come to help me?" (v. 2 HCSB). David knew he could never keep the demands of this resolution in his own strength. Only with God's empowerment and encouragement did he stand a chance against the enemy's wiles and his own fleshly tendencies. Never expect that you can recalibrate the frequency settings on your life without lots and lots of God's help, grace, and shepherding.

These are extreme resolutions, but truth be told, I don't think I've ever met a woman of godly, admirable character—one who in my moments of clearest, most serious thinking I longed to pattern my life after—who was not a person of extreme action and resolutions. Those who enjoy the extra measure of God's blessing and favor, who truly navigate their lives well, are those who discipline themselves in ways that many of us would consider borderline ridiculous. But like David, they've found it necessary to be as extreme in one direction as the culture has chosen to be in the other.

By His power you can resolve.

By His strength you can walk blamelessly.

By His might you can expect to be a woman who pursues in the dark what she proclaims in the light.

Excerpt taken from *The Resolution for Women* by Priscilla Shirer (© 2011).

The In-Between

Our fathers in Egypt did not understand Your wonders; they did not remember Your abundant kindnesses, but rebelled by the sea, at the Red Sea. . . . They quickly forgot His works; they did not wait for His counsel . . . but grumbled in their tents; they did not listen to the voice of the LORD. (Psalm 106:7, 13, 25 NASB)

The Israelites were a forgetful people. And what they missed as a result of their forgetfulness were numerous opportunities to recognize what God had done, what He was presently doing, and what He was still yet to do. God can and does move on behalf of His people. These thirsty in-between times when you're trudging through a particularly rough or stagnant patch haven't fallen on you by mistake. He's making a way for His greatness to be seen, for His glory to be put on full display—a way for you to *experience* in real time what He promises to be when you're sitting on the pew, hoping it's true.

What are you asking God to do for you at this season of life? What would you say you most desire if you were able to verbalize it? What would be the most shocking, delightful outcome to whatever series of circumstances you're being called to walk through these days?

No, we can't demand that of God. He's not one who can be told what to do. But there's a world of difference between dictating and expecting. When we pray for what we most wish to happen, we can trust with absolute assurance that He will either act according to our prayer . . . or do something better. He'll either bless us with what we want, or He'll bless us with what we really need and change our hearts to desire what He's given. He alone knows what will get us most prepared for our next stage of abundant living, what will draw us nearest to Him in fellowship and intimacy, what will cause His glory to burst upon the stage of our lives with weighty significance, where everybody who wants to can see it. We can totally rely on Him to take us exactly where we need to go . . . if we'll only be willing to follow.

You simply can't go wrong approaching an in-between time with that kind of heart and spirit. So be encouraged. You can stand in the midst of uncertainty, trusting you're safe in your Father's arms. You can weather the slow and uneventful waiting, believing He's taking you somewhere significant. You can endure the pain, even if it keeps you up at night. And you can experience a foretaste of glory even with a mouthful of bitter pills to swallow. Why? Because He's got more in store for you than you can ever imagine.

Be watching. Be waiting. Believe in between.

> I will lift up my eyes to the mountains; from where shall my help come? My help comes from the LORD, who made heaven and earth. He will not allow your foot to slip; He who keeps you will not slumber. (Ps. 121:1–3 NASB)

Excerpt taken from *One in a Million* by Priscilla Shirer (© 2010).

Cry Out!

Then they cried out to the LORD in their trouble; He
rescued them from their distress. (Psalm 107:6 HCSB)

My parents weren't due to be home for another hour, plenty of time to whip up a cake. What's that you say? Instructions? Nah, I'm good. A few scoops of flour here, a dash of sugar there. A little bit of salt and whatever's in this small orange box in the fridge for good measure. Gotta make it wet somehow. I know, water! Stir with a whisk, pour into a pan, bake at 350 degrees for, I don't know, I'll just keep an eye on it.

The odor, er, aroma, wafted in the air, filling the kitchen. It had only been twenty minutes but it must be ready! Hands tucked into mitts, eyes eager for a baked delight, I removed the cake from the oven. To call this thing "cake" was generous. To call it edible was delusional.

For a hardly domesticated twelve-year-old, improvisational baking was a stretch. I had watched my mom bake melt-in-your-mouth pound cakes and throw together her own scrumptious versions of culinary staples, but I had yet to learn the art of following a recipe. Adhering to my instincts and striking out on my own produced terrible results. There are some things better to be done with help. Help from a well-tried, well-written method, or help from someone who knows what they're doing.

Finding one's own way out of the desert is like me finding my own way to bake a cake. You may not end up with a mouth full of bland mortar mix, but you will find yourself stuck. Psalm 107:4 says those who wandered in the desert found no way to a city to dwell in.

This means they at least tried. They may have seen light from the cities in the distance but failed to discover a road in. So how did they manage to get out?

They cried to the Lord. Not when they ceased feeling hungry, tired, thirsty, and hopeless, or when they managed to stiffen their upper lip and act like everything was fine, but right in the middle of their desert, right in the middle of their beaten-down sighing. Too often I feel as though I need to pull myself together in order to cry out to the Lord. If my circumstances aren't rosy, I can at least pretend I'll get through it somehow. That's not what we see here. They cried to Him *in their trouble*.

Pride often prevents me from admitting that I'm at the end of my rope, that I wasn't smart enough to figure it out by myself. This is a dangerous place to be. Pride will keep us wandering in our wastelands and wildernesses.

It takes humility to cry out to the Lord in our distress. Our crying out proves that we can't do it alone. It exposes us for what we are: poor and needy. Yet, we can rest in God's promise to respond. His tender care truly takes the cake.

Excerpt taken from *Steadfast Love* by Lauren Chandler (© 2016).

Let Them Give Thanks

"Let them give thanks to the LORD *for His faithful love and His wonderful works for all humanity. For He has satisfied the thirsty and filled the hungry with good things. (Psalm 107:8–9* HCSB*)*

My friend Lisa and her daughter, Gracie, had gone through a rough year. They moved out of a living arrangement that had become toxic. Although they were grateful to escape, their leaving was with much pain and sorrow. Lisa, in particular, felt alone. Then she met Pam.

Pam extended a lifeline to them—a place to live and community. She invited Lisa and Gracie to our church. They sat almost every Sunday morning for months beside Pam and her family. Lisa grew up knowing about God, but He had yet to become real to her.

We met Lisa through a mutual friend. My daughter, Audrey, had been taking horseback riding lessons from this friend, but she thought Lisa would be a better fit. She had the time and space to devote attention to Audrey's development as a rider. She knew we needed Lisa, and Lisa might need us. At that time I couldn't have imagined how much.

Audrey was spending large amounts of time with Lisa and becoming her protégé. We wanted to know who Lisa was—what was she really like? We opened our hearts and home to her and Gracie. Over the past two years they have become family. Lisa came to a saving knowledge of Christ. I got to stand with her in front of our church as she testified to God's faithfulness toward her. I've watched her struggle well, pour over God's Word, and be surrounded by people who love her. Once alone and on her own, now she belongs to a community who made God tangible.

Real, loving, biblical community does that. It puts flesh on the unseen. Men and women become the hands and feet of God. They sit across from us, look us in the eye, place a hand on our shoulder. They listen as we pour out our hearts. They pray with us. They pray for us when our words struggle to surface. They preach the gospel to us when we forget what it sounds like. They point us to Scripture and remind us of the Truth.

Those of us who know Christ have all been led out of the desert of unbelief and into fellowship with God and His people through faith in Christ. We know what it's like to wander and be warmly received. We remember the brass heavens, the mouthful of sand, the sighing, the lamenting. Though our deserts may have looked vastly different, we have been delivered by the same Lord with the same steadfast love.

Scripture calls us to declare it, to worship God for all He's done for us, to talk often of the needs only He could have satisfied. God receives our thanksgiving as worship and then tosses it back as a lifeline to the Lisa and Gracie's all around us.

Excerpt taken from *Steadfast Love* by Lauren Chandler (© 2016).

Hope in Every Storm

Then they cried out to the LORD in their trouble, and He brought them out of their distress. (Psalm 107:28 HCSB)

In every storm—Your Father gives you a life preserver—and it is always His Son.

In the face of every rising wave overwhelming you—it's always turning to God's face that overwhelms you with a rising grace.

In every great crisis—let it bring out the greatness of Christ in you. *Real prayer always has eyes on **Christ**, not the **crisis**.*

Psalm 107 speaks of four different kinds of people crying out.

- Home-seekers: *"Some wandered and were homeless."* Who isn't seeking a Home in a thousand lost and weary ways?
- Hero-seekers: *"Some sat in darkness and the deepest gloom, prisoners suffering in iron chains . . ."* Who isn't seeking a Hero to rescue from a dark suffering and save and literally set us free?
- Healer-seeker: *"Some became fools through their rebellious ways and suffered affliction because of their iniquities."* Who isn't seeking a Healer for hidden wounds?
- Hand-seeker: *"Others went out on the sea in ships . . . their courage melted away . . ."* Who isn't seeking a Hand to hold on to in the midst of the pounding waves and the ravenous storm and the frothing, drowning sea?

And it's Psalm 107's Home-seekers and Hero-seekers and Healer-seekers and Hand-Seekers—who find everything they seek in Him—Jesus—because Jesus is everything. In spite of different stories and different storms, all simply cried: *"Then they cried to the Lord in their trouble."* The way the children of God get the unwavering, steadfast love they need in their life—is to cry out for it.

Child—start praying. Feel the preserving encircling of Christ around you and start praying and praising and thanking and worshipping. Stand in the rising, twisting storm—and let Him gently wring an unforgettable worship from our hearts.

Sometimes what we're holding on to isn't really an anchor for our soul—but an idol for our destruction. Sometimes when it feels like God's breaking our anchor—He's really breaking our idols—*what we were holding on to more than we were holding on to Him.* Sometimes God allows all our anchors to break—*so we know the only unbreakable anchor we have is Him.*

Overwhelming waves can carry you into the open arms and overwhelming love of God.

Yes, that, *that*: When you don't know how to get out the other side—keep pressing into Christ's side.

> "... and he delivered them from their distress ...
> He sent out his word and healed them,
> and delivered them from their destruction.
> Then they were glad that the waters were quiet,
> and he brought them to their desired haven.
> Let them thank the Lord for his steadfast love ...
> Whoever is wise, let him heed these things and consider the great love of the Lord." (Ps. 107: 19–20, 30–31, 43 esv)

Excerpt taken from *Steadfast Love* by Lauren Chandler (© 2016).

Standing Steadfast

*Good will come to a man who lends generously and conducts
his business fairly. He will never be shaken. The righteous man
will be remembered forever. He will not fear bad news; his heart
is confident, trusting in the LORD. (Psalm 112:5–7 HCSB)*

The word *steadfast* is written all over the Bible. Paul used it to
describe the believer who's become totally convinced that what
God has said about the once intimidating, now toothless power of
death is absolutely true: "Death has been swallowed up in victory,"
so that "Death, where is your victory? Death, where is your sting?"
(1 Cor. 15:54–55 HCSB). Therefore, we've been given every reason
in the world for being "steadfast, immovable, always excelling in the
Lord's work, knowing that your labor in the Lord is not in vain"
(v. 58 HCSB).

He repeated this word when declaring to the Colossians the
incredible news—yes, you heard right; it's really true—that through
Christ, "He has reconciled you by His physical body through His
death, to present you holy, faultless, and blameless before Him"
(Col. 1:22 HCSB). Holy? *Me?* Faultless? *Me?* Blameless? *Me?*

You've obviously confused me with somebody else.

Nope. You can stay "steadfast" in believing this truth, thoroughly "grounded," "not shifted away" from this ironclad hope of
the gospel (v. 23 HCSB).

Anchored. Steady. Steadfast.

What an awesome place to be.

And according to Psalm 112, this unshaken, unruffled manner
of life is available to all who fear the Lord and take "great delight in

His commands" (v. 1 HCSB), those who put into living practice the wisdom that comes from being in a squared-up relationship with Him.

We'll experience blessed families. "His descendants will be powerful in the land; the generation of the upright will be blessed" (v. 2 HCSB). Not everything will be ideal, of course, but we'll be setting the table for peace to reign and be pervasive in our homes.

We'll enjoy abundant resources. "Wealth and riches are in his house" (v. 3 HCSB)—not only, or necessarily, the financial kind (although having ample money is nice), but simply the full-life feeling that comes when "light shines in the darkness" (v. 4 HCSB).

We can expect good things to happen. "Good will come to a man who lends generously and conducts his business fairly" (v. 5 HCSB). The upshot of being a gracious, compassionate, caring, high-character follower of Christ results in a lot of good things boomeranging back into our lives.

We won't fear the unexpected. "He will not fear bad news; his heart is confident, trusting in the LORD. His heart is assured; he will not fear. In the end he will look in triumph on his foes" (vv. 7–8 HCSB).

Taken together, it all leads to both an internal and external demeanor of not being "shaken"—confident in God, confident in the rightness of our behavior, confident in the honest way we deal with people, confident in the freedom we enjoy from not being controlled by worry, by fear, by money, by anything.

How would you like to be *steadfast?*

With God, we can!

Excerpt taken from *100 Days in the Psalms* (© 2016).

Eyes on the Prize

Not to us, Yahweh, not to us, but to Your name give glory because of Your faithful love, because of Your truth. (Psalm 115:1 HCSB)

I love the fact that when faced with a particularly difficult question from the kids, say, how many inches are in a mile, I can go online for a visit with my friend Mr. Google and have the answer. But there is a dark side to all this finger-tapping and that is knowing where to draw the line. Ina Garten might have time to make individual centerpieces, cocktails, and rack of lamb for ten, but I just need to know how to make dinner for ten in under an hour and for less than $20. Queen Homeschool might have the ability to supervise fourteen children in their Latin and Advanced Mathematics lessons while making soap out of goat's milk, but I just need to come up with an activity to keep my kids busy while I get my blog post done. I do not want to put down women who seem to have boundless amounts of energy and pull off perfection without a hitch. They are out there and many are genuine and lovely ladies. These superwomen and all their cornucopias of knowledge should be a tool that makes our lives better, not a baseball bat with which we beat ourselves over the head.

By recognizing we all occupy the same level plane, we have no need to elevate or tear down one another. If these women are believers, then they are aiming for the same goal and are on the same team. Our role might not be as high profile, but we are all working for God's glory. Our resentment probably says more about our desire to be glorified than it does about theirs.

Keeping the goal to glorify God with our lives, first and foremost in our minds, prevents us from unnecessarily eviscerating those around us and complaining about our role. It also helps us to practice discernment when processing influences and advice. Whether you bury yourself in the Bible or read the entire women's section of your local Christian bookstore, or both, you are going to mess up. It is not a lack of knowledge that causes you and I to fall short in life, it is lack of godliness. The apostle Paul says, "I have the desire to do what is good, but I cannot carry it out. For what I do is not the good I want to do; no, the evil I do not want to do—this I keep on doing" (Rom. 7:18–19 NIV).

The gospel isn't good news to us only when we are dead in sin and condemned before God. The gospel is the good news that leans down to pick us up when we fall into sin again. The gospel is the good news that washes off the mud of our transgressions daily. When I fail, I am not disproving the truth of the good news, only confirming my need for a Savior.

Excerpt taken from *Letting Go of Perfect* by Amy Spiegel (© 2012).

Idol Threats

*Those who make them are just like them, as are
all who trust in them. (Psalm 115:8 HCSB)*

We honestly don't think the termites can do that much damage. We honestly don't think our son will get into any trouble with those kids he hangs around. We honestly don't think our CPA would give us untrustworthy advice about that deduction.

We make some bad assumptions sometimes.

Like, we really don't think our idols can do much to hurt us. *Idols.* What a clumsy, archaic word for it anyway. Okay, so we're a little hooked on a certain TV series that, yes, can get pretty raunchy in spots. But the acting is so good, and the writing is so compelling and spot-on—it's just something we enjoy and look forward to. That's all. No big deal.

Okay, so we don't always do the best job of controlling our eating habits. We know that. We went through the phase where we didn't even bring the tempting snacks inside the house at all. As long as they weren't there, we figured, we couldn't go scavenge for them. But we've gotten a little lazy with that strategy lately. And on some nights, when the munchies hit . . .

We should see it coming by now. We should know what these seductions are capable of. We should know why they've earned the idolatry label . . . because we do sort of worship them. We move other things or people out of the way so we can enjoy them. We've been known to build our plans and schedules around them. Yes, we do sometimes realize that we shouldn't or can't afford to keep entertaining them as we do, and yet . . . they seem to have our will-power in a headlock.

On one hand, we see it objectively. It's just a habit, not a tyrant. It's not as though these idols of ours have the power to chain us down and force us to comply. They're an inanimate, invisible urge. Like the idols of Old Testament days, "they have mouths but cannot speak, eyes, but cannot see. They have ears but cannot hear, noses, but cannot smell. They have hands but cannot feel, feet, but cannot walk. They cannot make a sound with their throats" (Ps. 115:5–7 HCSB).

But.

They *can* do something that no voiceless, senseless, motionless thing should ever be able to do: they can make us as blind, deaf, and dumb as *they* are. They can harden our heart toward God making it stone-like, the same as how they just stand there, unfazed, immovable.

We may honestly not think they can really cause us problems, that we're always free to kick them out the door if we start developing a real issue. But the problem is, merely by making them, we become "just like them."

Deadened. Shut down. Walled off. Hard to move.

Let's see our idols for what they are . . . and for what we never, ever want to be.

Excerpt taken from *100 Days in the Psalms* (© 2016).

If That's Not Maddening

Rage seizes me because of the wicked who reject Your instruction. Your statutes are the theme of my song during my earthly life. (Psalm 119:53–54 HCSB)

Psalm 119 is a biblical giant. Located almost squarely in the center of your Bible, it covers *far* more real estate than any other chapter of Scripture. In fact, it's actually longer than quite a few entire *books* in the Bible.

We could make a lot of stops here.

That's because with few exceptions, each verse of this extended chapter includes some kind of synonym for the Word of God including *law* or *statutes* or *precepts, commands, ordinances*. While it's hard for our short attention spans to hang with it from start to finish, each little chunk or stanza is sure to leave you with a high, lofty view of Scripture. Which all of us need . . . because, as verses 53–54 say, the power of God's Word ought to incite some specific reactions from us.

Including *anger*.

Not that every loud protestor or activist is presenting a Christlike face for the cameras, obviously. But anger is a legitimate response of the believer to what we see taking place in our society and world. Not anger at individual people, but anger at how God's Word is being maligned and mistreated.

Rage is actually the hot-button word that's used. We know we see Jesus angry to the point of rage a few times in Scripture, most notably while ridding the temple in Jerusalem of those manipulative, profiteering religious professionals who were turning this "house of prayer" into a flea market. So while we like being nice guys and gals who don't raise much of a fuss, something's probably a little spiritually askew within us if we are never compelled to anger by what human injustice, abuse, oppression, and other godless actions daily inflict on others.

We see the news of it on television—the stories that grab the headlines and are chased all over the globe by the CNNs of the world. But have you ever noticed yourself becoming caught up in the bloody, smarmy details—sort of semi-entertained by the coverage and commentary and all—but not *enraged* by it? Not driven to your knees in prayer—for the victims, for the church's response, for an entire society growing numb to evil and hatred?

But that's just the more provocative, public fare. Are you sorrowfully angry at how our Enemy is deceiving Christian leaders and families into treating lightly the clear calls of Scripture on our lives? Are you ever moved to tears by the hardships being suffered by people you know, because of people in their lives who "reject" the Lord's discipline and instruction? And—here's the hardest hitting question—are you angry that one of the people who's too often rejecting His instruction is *you?*

"Rage seizes me." Doesn't strike us as sounding very biblical. But at certain times and places, it's among the most biblically proper responses to life that we ever make.

Excerpt taken from *100 Days in the Psalms* (© 2016).

A Safe Voyage

*Your word is a lamp for my feet and a light
on my path." (Psalm 119:105 HCSB)*

Once I was invited to go on the helm of a British Columbia ferry during its crossing from Vancouver to Swartz Bay. Three days before I boarded that ferry, a terrible accident occurred in Swartz Bay. The nineteen-thousand-ton passenger ferry, the *Spirit of Vancouver Island,* collided with a small yacht, the *Star Ruby*—killing one man and critically injuring a woman.

The captain of the ferry had spotted the *Star Ruby* and had repeatedly sounded the horn and attempted to make radio contact. He followed all the applicable maritime procedures. But for whatever reason, the captain of the *Star Ruby* didn't. The consequences of his neglect were fatal.

Before taking their vessels to sea, captains must be versed in standard maritime rules and procedures. They need to know who gets the right-of-way and how to pass other vessels. They need to know how to tack their sails and use their rudders to maneuver their boats effectively.

Governing agencies have formulated maritime rules so that each boater can have a safe voyage. Wise captains realize that regulations are for their benefit, not to unduly restrict them. Therefore, they esteem and appreciate the rules and are careful to follow them.

In the same way, God's standard is not meant to restrict us. James identifies it as "the perfect law that gives freedom" (James 1:25 NIV). Just as following maritime rules gives sailors the freedom to enjoy the sea, so following God's rules gives us the freedom to enjoy our lives. God has provided rules and procedures intended to make our voyage safe and enjoyable. They are recorded in the Bible and are known by various names, such as precepts, statutes, words, ordinances, laws, commands, or ways.

Read what David—the shepherd who became a king—had to say about God's regulations:

> "The law of the LORD is perfect, reviving the soul. The statutes of the LORD are trustworthy, making wise the simple. The precepts of the LORD are right, giving joy to the heart. The commands of the LORD are radiant, giving light to the eyes. The fear [respect] of the LORD is pure, enduring forever. The ordinances of the LORD are sure and altogether righteous. They are more precious than gold, than much pure gold; they are sweeter than honey, than honey from the comb. By them is your servant warned; in keeping them there is great reward." (Ps. 19:7–11 NIV)

David listed some benefits of following God's regulations. Did you catch them? The statutes of God:

- revive the soul,
- make the simple wise,
- give joy to the heart,
- and give light to the eyes.

They are:

- more precious than gold,
- and sweeter than honey.

They bring great reward. Now that doesn't sound like a God whose desire is to restrict us or put us in bondage, does it?

God's laws are for our protection and pleasure. It is within his boundaries that we experience the true freedom to set sail.

Excerpt taken from *Conversation Peace* by Mary Kassian (© 2004).

True Humility

*LORD, my heart is not proud; my eyes are not haughty. I do not
get involved with things too great or too difficult for me. Instead,
I have calmed and quieted myself like a little weaned child with
its mother; I am like a little child. (Psalm 131:1–2 HCSB)*

David's exploits at an early age had been enough to make him a
semi-celebrity among the Israelite masses. That slaying of
Goliath alone—I mean, that's enough to make you go viral.

He was somewhere between a young teen and a young man
when this brave act of heroism made his face recognizable nearly
everywhere he went. He "marched out with the army and was successful in everything Saul sent him to do. Saul put him in command
of the soldiers, which pleased all the people" (1 Sam. 18:5 HCSB).
When the troops were returning home amid reports of their victory
over Goliath and the Philistines, "the women came out from all the
cities of Israel . . . singing and dancing with tambourines," with
"shouts of joy," with welcome-home reverie. And "as they celebrated,
the women sang: 'Saul has killed his thousands, but David his tens
of thousands'" (vv. 6–7 HCSB). He was even upstaging the king himself in earning the crowd's jubilant adulation.

The Goliath thing, of course, was only the first in a long line of
victories that wove together into a larger-than-life legacy, rich
enough to put David on the throne. Perhaps no one before or since
could rival what David accomplished as both a warrior and a wor-
shiper, which led to an understandable swagger of arrogance and
ambition in his walking gait.

But at some point—through the impact of hard loss or hard knocks, through sin or through the aging of spiritual wisdom—he had seen the fallacy of thinking too highly of himself. He'd experienced enough private moments—when the crown was off, when he was in his underwear, times when he looked just like anybody else underneath all the hype, and he found a far superior, far more honest state of mind.

Humility.

"My heart is not proud; my eyes are not haughty."

This wasn't a false show of self-deprecation; it was an admission of what was true . . . and of the person he now knew he wanted to be.

Just quiet before the Lord. Accepting of what God asked and whatever it entailed. Not exerting the power and influence of a man in his position, but reverting to the simple trust of a child in relation to his mom. The emptiness that ultimately came from being so full of himself had inspired him to take it all the way—to empty himself of pride and pretense, and to live in humble, utter reliance on God.

This is not a place of *childish* denial, the abandoning of grown-up responsibility. It's instead a place of *childlike* acceptance that God is God, that I am not, and that any other mind-set is living a lie our arrogance cannot support.

Excerpt taken from *100 Days in the Psalms* (© 2016).

Say It Again

Give thanks to the LORD; for He is good. His love is eternal.
Give thanks to the God of gods. His love is eternal. Give thanks
to the Lord of lords. His love is eternal. (Psalm 136:1–3 HCSB)

Psalm 136 is unique among all the others in the way it's constructed. One look, and you can instantly tell it. All twenty-six of its verses begin with a statement of truth or fact or remembrance, followed every time by the same exact words of response: "His love is eternal."

This psalm was apparently composed as a praise song to be sung antiphonally between a worship leader and choir. It's back and forth, intended for bouncing the sound from every corner of the room. Praise is coming from everywhere. And it's continually driving home the rhythm of God's covenant.

His love is eternal. His love never ends.

The Hebrew term for this kind of love is the word *chesed*. To say it correctly, you start it in the back of your throat, gargling out the hard "ch-" sound, expressing the deep-down intensity of what it's meant to communicate. God's *chesed* love is His faithful, kind, and loyal love—constant in its quality and unconquerable in its essence. So when the psalm writer praises God for His natural wonders, for His deliverance of Israel from Egypt, for His victorious rout of Canaanite kings, and for His gift of the Promised Land to the vastly outnumbered nation of Israel, the clear implication is that this kind of faithfulness and covenant loyalty can be expected to continue throughout all generations. The track record is strong enough to support it, and the future contains nothing too large to threaten it.

Perhaps, though, this is one of those psalms that just kind of doesn't do it for you. You come away from it without quite being moved by the whole effect. It just feels rather choppy and clunky to read.

Then consider at some point making your own list of life experiences where God has demonstrated His unbreakable love and loyalty toward you, your family, your church, or a number of your friends. Consider composing your own song of praise that documents your history with Him—what He's done, what He's shown you, what He's saved you from, what He's given to you with ongoing regularity. His love is not only proven eternal by what He did during Bible days with the children of Israel and their well-preserved march through history. His love is also proven by its unique application to your own life—the faithful, covenant, *chesed* love that even now has gone to "prepare a place for you" (John 14:3 HCSB), so that you can continue to experience its unbreakable nature throughout the unbroken lengths of a heavenly eternity.

Praise God today with these words of honor and glory that simply cannot be stated enough. And your worship will only make the music louder and bigger and better with every single singing of it.

Excerpt taken from *100 Days in the Psalms* (© 2016).

Happy to Be You

*LORD, You have searched me and known me. You know when
I sit down and when I stand up; You understand my thoughts
from far away. You observe my travels and my rest; You are
aware of all my ways. Before a word is on my tongue, You know
all about it, LORD. You have encircled me; You have placed
Your hand on me. This extraordinary knowledge is beyond me.
It is lofty; I am unable to reach it. (Psalm 139:1–6 HCSB)*

Many of us spend so much of our lives wishing or pretending we were somebody different from who we are, we never get to experience the sheer freedom of just being ourselves. In some cases we've spent so many years and put so much effort into steering clear of our own uniqueness, we wouldn't know our true self if we bumped into her face-to-face.

But rediscovering and celebrating the *you* that God originally created is paramount for any woman who desires to live out her primary purpose.

You are the only *you* the world has. The only one we really need. The one who, according to Psalm 139, has been . . .

- examined by God.
- known by Him.
- seen by Him.
- protected by Him.
- followed by Him.
- blessed by Him.
- guided by Him.
- strengthened by Him.
- supported by Him.

- carefully created by Him.
- led by Him.

Have you ever really tried getting acquainted with this person who was important enough to God Himself to put this much time and attention into creating and supporting? When *you* strip away the facades and remove the veneers, when you take off any masks and remove any pretense or disguise, what's left is the authentic person who is precious in the sight of God Himself—fully capable and distinctively designed to achieve His purposes for her life.

You. Just the way *you* were meant to be.

So take time to uncover and reconnect with these, things that truly describe you: your gifts, talents, passions, eccentricities, dislikes, weaknesses, interests, and uniquenesses—in their rawest, most unspoiled form. Don't rush through this. Peeling back the stereotypes and labels, the misinterpretations and stigmas you've used (both knowingly and unknowingly) to define yourself will probably require some time and effort on your part. And choosing to move forward in authenticity will require even more.

Pinpoint what ways (if any) that you have neglected to use or celebrate these characteristics and become intentional about honoring your uniqueness in the future. Think what a wonderful gift this return to authenticity could be to you over the years, even over the next few weeks. Being able to live in genuine freedom, unburdened from the harried exhaustion of making impressions or trying to act like somebody you're not. No longer overcompensating for things that have kept you feeling like you don't measure up. Aligning yourself with God's will instead of constantly fighting His plans and always working at cross-purposes.

Accepting yourself.

Treasuring the value He's encased within you.

It's a resolution worth making.

Excerpt taken from *The Resolution for Women* by Priscilla Shirer (© 2012).

Where Can I Flee?

*Where can I go to escape Your Spirit? Where can I
flee from Your presence? (Psalm 139:7 HCSB)*

God's continuous presence is a soothing balm to the hurting, a
sweet relief for the broken and betrayed, a haven for those who
find themselves feeling strangely out of tune with the music of this
world. But to those living in disobedience, to those who don't want
to submit to their current circumstances and see what God might
want to accomplish through them, His presence is a scorching fire.
We duck our eyes to keep from coming face-to-face with Him. We
slip down a side hallway. We go the long way around.

We run. Sometimes in ways nobody else could notice.

But in running—even if it's the inside, unseen kind—we place
ourselves in the worst possible position we could be in. We stand
outside of God's will, outside of His blessing. Just like when we say,
"I know what the Bible says about that, but . . ." Oooo, be careful
when those words bubble up out of your heart. They mean the starting gun has fired, and a runner has taken off.

Remember when God said to Jonah, "Go to the great city of
Nineveh and preach against it" (Jonah 1:2 HCSB). From how the
Bible describes it, Jonah didn't appear to spend even one second
mulling it over. The word of the Lord came, Jonah hopped up in a
huff, and headed for the nearest shipyard. Like ourselves too often,
he wasn't willing to consider that something so apparently illogical
could be the precise will of God for him at that moment in time,
that doing anything less would not only result in a costly detour but
in missing out on the miracle God had planned.

We just cannot comprehend, as God can, why He has met us with this piece of conviction right now or placed us in the midst of this circumstance. So the determining factor we use in choosing obedience over disobedience—in choosing surrender over stubborn resistance—can never be our finite ability to understand His directives. Making sense of God's call is not a prerequisite for following it. His Word and His promises are enough.

Have you already packed your bags for Tarshish? Have you been trying as hard as you can to avoid being seen in the places where God's presence is most tangibly felt? Have you closed off any likelihood that this interruption might ultimately lead you to somewhere of divine importance? Are you trying to get as far away as possible from what He's called you to do, disengaging emotionally and energetically if not physically?

It's not too late to turn your ship around and sail back in the direction of His will. It might not make sense to everybody. It might not even make sense to you. But this I know for sure. In fact, I know it beyond any reasonable doubt. Heading back to the mainland of obedience will be the best decision of your life.

Excerpt taken from *Life Interrupted* by Priscilla Shirer (© 2011).

In Thought, Word, and Deed

If I say, "Surely the darkness will hide me, and the light around me will become night"—even the darkness is not dark to You. The night shines like the day; darkness and light are alike to You. (Psalm 139:11–12 HCSB)

Be aware of the progressive nature of sin. We've all experienced this. Read 2 Samuel 11:1–5 and note three progressive areas of sin.

Step 1: *David sinned in thought.* First of all, David saw the woman bathing and concluded she was very beautiful. Sight turned into desire. The seed of sin was first sown in his mind as he tarried on the rooftop, just as the seed of sin is first sown in our minds.

Step 2: *David sinned in word.* If we do not confess and repent the sin of the mind, it virtually always gives birth to the next stage. The meditation of David's mind turned into the conversation of his mouth. God knows that our meditations (the focus of our thoughts, what we think and rethink) will ultimately turn into conversations. That's why He tells us to meditate on Him and His Word!

Temptations rarely go from the mind to the deed. The second stop is usually the mouth. David saw Bathsheba and allowed himself to dwell on wrong desires (the participation of his mind), then he summoned someone and expressed his interest (the participation of his mouth). These two steps enticed a third.

Step 3: *David sinned in deed.* David flirted with adultery in thought and word, stopping at neither venue to repent and ask God for help. Action followed. David committed adultery and set in motion a hurricane of repercussions.

If wrong thoughts give way to wrong words, often giving way to wrong actions, we must learn to allow God to halt sin in the place where it begins—the thought life! We are wise to aggressively confess the sins of our thoughts! The sins of our thought lives are so numerous that their familiarity tends to make them less noticeable. Jealous thoughts, sudden lusts, quick criticisms, and harsh judgments may be fueled in our minds without any regard toward them as sin.

A heightened awareness of wrong thoughts will work greatly to our advantage. Getting in the habit of confessing sin in the thought life is not to remind us constantly what wretches we are, but to remind us what victors we are! Confessing wrong thoughts stops sin in the first stages, before it comes out of our mouths and then directs our actions.

If I allow God to halt sin before it takes one step out of the mind into word or deed, the only person hurt will be me. Once sin progresses from the mind to the mouth and deeds, we've involved others, and the repercussions and chastisements escalate.

Unchecked thoughts will usually progress. Our minds can't be "fairly pure." Purity comes with a radical attitude toward the thought life. God was looking out for our best interest when He commanded us to love Him with our whole minds!

Excerpt taken from *Portraits of Devotion* by Beth Moore (© 2014).

His Love Stands Firm

Let me experience Your faithful love in the morning,
for I trust in You. Reveal to me the way I should go
because I long for You. (Psalm 143:8 HCSB)

Of all the descriptions of the love of the Father, the most common is that his love is unfailing, faithful, and steadfast (Pss. 6:4; 13:5; 33:5; 36:7; 48:9; 90:14; 107:15; 130:7; 147:11). This means that the Father's love is consistent and dependable. We can take it to the bank. Psalm 89:2 (NIV) says that His love "stands firm."

Our earthly fathers are not perfect in their love. Even great dads have bad days. They can disappoint us through inconsistency, through undependability, or because of circumstances beyond their control. Their love can fail.

Think of all the things that can separate you from the love of your earthly father. You could include everything from obsession with work to divorce, from depression to death. Then compare those things to the words of Romans 8:38–39.

> For I am persuaded that not even death or life, angels or rulers, things present or things to come, hostile powers, height or depth, or any other created thing will have the power to separate us from the love of God that is in Christ Jesus our Lord! (HCSB)

Nothing can separate you from your heavenly Father. He will never fail you. He is totally dependable in every circumstance and at every time. His *love* will not fail you. Not ever.

A friend told me how angry she had been because she believed God let her down. Later she realized the Father simply did not do what she wanted Him to, when she wanted Him to do it. She said at the time she could see no good in her situation. But later, events showed her how fortunate she had been that God did not surrender to her selfish demands. Have you ever felt let down or disappointed by God the Father? According to Scripture (Rom. 8:38–39), the love of the Father will never fail us. In light of this, can you think of another reason for your disappointment?

David knew the agony and questions of pain. He wrote, "LORD, how long will You forget me? Forever? How long will You hide Your face from me? How long will I store up anxious concerns within me, agony in my mind every day? How long will my enemy dominate me?" (Ps. 13:1–2 HCSB).

But David had studied the love of God, and his confidence in the love of the Father was unshakable. Despite his questions, in his next breath he acknowledged the dependability of God's love. "But I have trusted in Your faithful love; my heart will rejoice in Your deliverance. I will sing to the LORD because He has treated me generously" (Ps. 13:5–6 HCSB).

Like David, you can be assured of the dependability of the Father's love, even in the midst of your pain and suffering. His love will not fail you. Not ever.

Excerpt taken from *In My Father's House* by Mary Kassian (© 2005).

Out of the Shadow of Death

Man is like a breath; his days are like a
passing shadow. (Psalm 144:4 HCSB)

The Lord not only brings us out of darkness, He brings us out of the shadow of death. Each of my kids has gone through a stage where they are mesmerized by their shadow. Usually, it's when they're at a toddling age. A summer sunset lures us to the driveway. We press bare feet on warm concrete, dancing to the hum of locusts. A faint figure synchronizes its steps with the child. He anxiously giggles picking one foot high off the ground and waving an arm above his head. It's like him but it's not him—a shadow.

Our chains of sin and fear are like death but not yet death. Make no mistake, unless the Lord delivers us from the chains of the rebellion of unbelief, we will die (spiritually and physically). But when He delivers us from the chains, we will feel like we've been brought back to life.

This sounds exciting and hopeful, and it is. However, the reality is that dead things can't feel. And feeling is entirely different from not feeling. (You know the feeling.) Like when your foot is wedged under your other leg sitting crisscross on the ground and you stand up to let the nerves reorient themselves, and it's all pins and needles, and you regret standing up? But if you hadn't, who knows if your foot would have fallen off right there on your living room floor and you wouldn't have known because you forgot it was even attached? Feeling after not feeling is like that. It hurts at first.

You aren't numbing the pain by setting up an impenetrable wall around your heart. You aren't tempering all feeling with a substance or relationship. You're finally willing to be undone without making it all right.

The feelings start taking over. You discover the height of joy but also the depth of disappointment. Your cold stone heart is replaced with warm flesh, susceptible to scarring. It's terrifying, like your entire being is coming awake after feeling only pins and needles for so long. But there's good news. Because of Christ, our hearts aren't just slightly more alert and awake. They are new. We don't just move out from the shadow of death, we move into the Promised Land.

> "I will give you a new heart and put a new spirit within you; I will remove your heart of stone and give you a heart of flesh. I will place My Spirit within you and cause you to follow My statutes and carefully observe My ordinances. Then you will live in the land that I gave your fathers; you will be My people, and I will be your God." (Ezek. 36:26–28 HCSB)

The new heart of flesh will beat wildly for Him. His Spirit will cause us to walk, not in rebellious chains, but in glorious obedience. He will be our God. Any trauma our new heart will take will only be what He allows for our good and His glory.

Excerpt taken from *Steadfast Love* by Lauren Chandler (© 2016).

Who He's Always Been

The LORD is gracious and compassionate, slow to anger and
great in faithful love. The LORD is good to everyone; His
compassion rests on all He has made. (Psalm 145:8–9 HCSB)

You might not recognize this statement as being almost the motto—God's calling card—throughout the entirety of the Old Testament. But if you want to take a little spin through Bible history, you'll see this statement (or a close variation of it) showing up in places all over the ancient world.

Exodus 34:6—God was presenting Moses with a duplicate set of tablets containing the Ten Commandments, after Moses had smashed the first pair in anger at the people's rebellion. Now meeting him again on Mount Sinai, defending His reason for forgiving the people, God introduced Himself as "a compassionate and gracious God, slow to anger and rich in faithful love and truth" (HCSB).

Numbers 14:18—This time Moses was the one doing the talking, in the Wilderness of Paran, after the spies had brought back an unfavorable report on the Promised Land. God said He was going to retaliate by destroying them, but Moses appealed to Him for mercy—the One who is "slow to anger and rich in faithful love, forgiving wrongdoing and rebellion" (HCSB).

Nehemiah 9:17—Following the success of Nehemiah's wall rebuilding project in Jerusalem, the religious leaders led the people in a national day of confession. The prayer that opened their ceremony recounted many scenes from Israel's past—living proof of the Lord's reputation as a "forgiving God, gracious and compassionate, slow to anger and rich in faithful love" (HCSB).

Joel 2:13—After a number of prophetic warnings concerning the people's rebellion, complete with locusts and withered fields and blazing fires and violent earthquakes, Joel's words from the Lord finally took a turn toward the better, inviting the people to repent: "Tear your hearts, not just your clothes, and return to the Lord your God. For He is gracious and compassionate, slow to anger, rich in faithful love, and He relents from sending disaster" (HCSB).

Jonah 4:2—The mercurial prophet had witnessed the massive scene of revival in Nineveh—a widespread awakening of repentance inspired by Jonah's preaching, though not exactly embraced by his heart. Angry at God for choosing to forgive these Ninevite scourges on the nation of Israel, Jonah said to Him, "I knew that You are a merciful and compassionate God, slow to become angry, rich in faithful love, and One who relents from sending disaster" (HCSB).

See what I mean? Even in the psalms, in addition to this passage from Psalm 145, similar wording appears in Psalm 86:15 ("You, Lord, are a compassionate and gracious God, slow to anger and rich in faithful love and truth" HCSB), as well as in Psalm 103:8 ("The Lord is compassionate and gracious, slow to anger and rich in faithful love" HCSB).

So when James instructed us to be "quick to hear, slow to speak, and slow to anger" (James 1:19 HCSB), he was just telling us to be like God . . . because that's who He's always been.

Excerpt taken from *100 Days in the Psalms* (© 2016).

Big and Small

*He heals the brokenhearted and binds up their
wounds. He counts the number of the stars; He gives
names to all of them. (Psalm 147:3–4 HCSB)*

God is great. God is good.

The reason why we can never run short of reasons for praising Him is because He fills up our lists at either end of the spectrum. When we feel as though we've praised Him for all the grand and glorious things we can think of—all the way to the stars and back, which He's counted and named and cataloged by location in the universe—we can then praise Him for things that no God this powerful should ever be expected to do—to care for the brokenhearted, to hear the cries of the helpless, to heal the wounds of the hurting.

He is God and is great at both extremes.

Psalm 147 yo-yos down the worship pike in this kid-in-a-candy-store fashion, as if saying, "Ooo! Look over here!"—then, "Ooo! Look over there!" He can do *this,* and He can do *that,* and—oh, and *this* and—yeah-yeah-yeah, *that too!*

"Our Lord is great, vast in power; His understanding is infinite" (v. 5 HCSB). There's the big stuff again; the big words. *Great. Vast. Power. Infinite.* But before the writer can totally lose himself in the grandeur of God's blue-sky greatness, he realizes he can never forget, too, how "the Lord helps the afflicted" (v. 6 HCSB), caring enough about the plight and suffering of the oppressed that He stands as their advocate against the wicked, caring for the weak in unseen ways.

"Sing to the LORD with thanksgiving; play the lyre to our God, who covers the sky with clouds, prepares rain for the earth, and causes grass to grow on the hills" (vv. 7–8 HCSB). Nobody else can do stuff like that—puff moisture-filled clouds through the jet stream, causing rain to fall across the thirsty hills and plains, making plants and crops be able to grow from the earth, producing food from seeds that replenish themselves with each year's yield. We act sometimes as though this is no big deal—clouds, rain, grass, the water cycle. We've known it since the third grade. But someone has to *do* that. Someone needed to think all that up. And the Someone who did, and does, and keeps doing it every day is the One we worship with our highest praise.

Yet His reason for proving Himself so big and capable is not to show off or to test drive His enormous skills for His own amazement. He does it to provide "the animals with their food, and the young ravens, what they cry for" (v. 9 HCSB). Watch a bird bathing itself in a roadside water puddle, and you might just say to yourself, "Oh. So *that's* what He leaves those there for."

God is great. God is good. And we have so very much to thank Him for . . . starting perhaps with our food, yes, but then going on from there . . . and literally going everywhere.

Excerpt taken from *100 Days in the Psalms* (© 2016).

Cause For Celebration

*Let them praise His name with dancing and make music
to Him with tambourine and lyre. (Psalm 149:3 HCSB)*

I don't go to a dancing kind of church. I mean, we raise our hands, we speak out loud a little, and we don't mind getting really happy about Jesus while we're at it, but we don't do much if any dancing in the aisles. None of this matters to Daniel, however, who takes his chosen place every Sunday without fail and enters into worship by doing what Daniel does. He dances. And frankly, I've often wondered where this ongoing urge of his comes from.

Well, recently I asked him. And was amazed what I found out.

Daniel was born to a mentally ill mother and was then adopted by his grandparents. But they lived in a tough, underprivileged area of town where trouble usually came looking for young kids, even if they weren't exactly looking for *it*. When his godly grandfather died, Daniel lost about the only thing that had been keeping him from falling even deeper into the drug culture that consumed his school and neighborhood. And one fateful day, in the midst of a drug deal gone horribly wrong, Daniel pulled the trigger on a gun that killed a person in cold blood. As a result, he was sentenced to spend every moment until his eighteenth birthday in the custody of the Texas Youth Commission, with his adult sentencing to follow at that time.

How he dreaded turning eighteen—with a much greater intensity than most people look forward to it—because while the youth correctional center was certainly no picnic, it was nothing like doing hard time in the state pen. Every day that inched closer to that monumental teenage milestone, his stomach turned one twist tighter.

His dread of the future grew meaner and nastier, more frightening to think about.

Little did he know, when he walked into that wood-paneled courtroom on his eighteenth birthday, that the change in his life was about to be for the better. *Way* better. The grandmother of his shooting victim had composed a handwritten letter to the authorities, asking the courts to "please give this young man a second chance." And the judge, moved by the compassion of a grieving grandma, gave a recommendation for leniency in Daniel's case. His sentence was suspended. He was free to walk out the door with nothing more than a parole period to serve.

"And I will dance in front of this church until the day I die," he told me, "because when you've been given a second chance, you've got something to dance about."

I'm reminded of Jonah 3:1, "Then the word of the LORD came to Jonah a second time" (HCSB). If a man vomited out of a fish after three days in its digestive tract has any strength left in his legs at all, I'm guessing Jonah did a bit of a jig along that sandy stretch of oceanfront when he got his.

Second chances call for a celebration. Let's dance!

Excerpt taken from *Life Interrupted* by Priscilla Shirer (© 2011).

The End of All Things

Let everything that breathes praise the LORD. (Psalm 150:6 HCSB)

The psalms end the way that each day, each season, each moment of life should end for us . . . with praise.

The psalms take us to the emotional bottom, to the heights of joy and celebration, and to just about every other experience of life in between. There aren't many places we go, even today, where the psalms haven't already been before.

But when it's all said and done, whether the mood seems ripe for it or not, praise is where life should take us. Praise is the end of all things.

For if we were somehow able to sit in God's seat today, seeing things as He alone can see them, they would look a lot different than they do from this end of the equation. The amount of perspective we're able to ascertain from our single moments in time, limited by the extent of our own knowledge and experience, is fairly slight. We know where we've been; we know where we are; we think we know where we're going. But even the past and present, having actually lived it already, being in the right-now process of it today—even *these* we can't interpret with total clarity, much less what is yet to come.

But God, through His indescribably generous grace and mercy, has cast Himself into relationship with us. Through our new life in Christ, He has placed His Spirit within us to expand our capabilities of understanding and spiritual perspective, as He guides and speaks and leads us by His gentle voice. Yet even still, our natural resistance, our learning curve, our human weaknesses and deficiencies—they prevent us from being able to grasp all the answers we seek or to completely understand the whys and how-comes behind the issues we face in our families, our nation, our world.

And as frustrating as this reality can be—feeling the uncertainty, yet not being able to solve it or explain it—our hope is in that place where God can totally see and understand. And if we could see what He sees—if we knew what He already understands—we would not be in despair.

We would be in praise!

So faith invites us to go where only God can live—except that through praise, we can actually live there too.

"In the heights" (Ps. 148:1 HCSB) . . .

"Above the heavens" (v. 4 HCSB) . . .

"In the assembly of the godly" (Ps. 149:1 HCSB) . . .

Where together we "celebrate" our Maker and "rejoice" with our King (v. 2 HCSB).

"For Yahweh takes pleasure in His people; He adorns the humble with salvation"—so "let the godly celebrate in triumphal glory; let them shout for joy on their beds" (vv. 4–5 HCSB).

Let us shout for joy in all seasons, praise Him for who He is and what He's doing, and know we're only beginning to see it all.

Excerpt taken from *100 Days in the Psalms* (© 2016).

Love and Hate

"How long, foolish ones, will you love ignorance?
How long will you mockers enjoy mocking and you
fools hate knowledge?" (Proverbs 1:22 HCSB)

The surprising, rather blunt assessment of those who don't actively pursue wisdom is that they "love ignorance" and "hate knowledge." But just because we put off cleaning the bathroom, does that mean we love mold and mildew? Just because we occasionally text and drive, does that mean we love breaking the law? Just because we rarely get our recommended servings of fruits and veggies every day, does that mean we love putting ourselves at higher risk of heart disease?

Well . . .

One of the things we can often find repellent about the proverbs is their abruptness, their sharp edge, their unflinching willingness to tell it like it is. We prefer our rebukes with a bit more understanding. We want room to explain why we didn't do exactly what we should've done. It's not like we weren't even trying at all.

Yet as Jesus would later say, in equally dissecting terms, "No one can be a slave of two masters, since either he will hate one and love the other, or be devoted to one and despise the other" (Matt. 6:24 HCSB). To not *love* wisdom—to not seek it, not hunger for it, not go out looking for it while everybody else is reading the sports page and the cereal box—is in essence to *hate* it.

Wisdom is not an opt-in/opt-out kind of thing.

"The one who follows instruction is on the path to life, but the one who rejects correction goes astray" (Prov. 10:17 HCSB). "Don't rebuke a mocker, or he will hate you; rebuke a wise man, and he will love you" (9:8 HCSB). Gray areas, yes, do exist in life, but oftentimes (more often than we think) we're only given two real choices. And to choose *one* is ultimately the arm's-length difference between life and death, love and hate, winning and losing.

So when bumping up against the proverbs, and finding them to feel rather hardline and critical for our tastes, we should use the experience to help us do a couple of things.

First, *be diagnostic.* Let our initial recoiling or our taking of offense be an indicator that something inside us is resisting what God's Word is showing us. For as the writer of Hebrews said, this Word is "sharper than any double-edged sword . . . able to judge the ideas and thoughts of the heart" (Heb. 4:12 HCSB).

Second, *be definitive.* Let's determine not to take a halfway approach to what we're learning, to stop depending on our ability to tap dance and improvise. Instead, let's take these stark contrasts as motivations for choosing hard and choosing well. For going all-in. For believing that if we stake our full claim on God's way of seeing things, we will see the truth of it taking shape as we go along in life.

Wisdom. We either love it . . . or we don't.

Excerpt taken from *100 Days in the Proverbs* (© 2016).

Follow the Chart

[Widsom's] ways are pleasant, and all her
paths, peaceful. (Proverbs 3:17 HCSB)

Charts are essentially maps. They show the navigator the layout of the territory. A nautical chart, for instance, cites the depth of the water, the major currents in the area, and the location of buoys and lighthouses.

A chart also shows the planned route and destination. The Bible charts a course for us on the journey of life. The instructions are clear; the directions are good. In the book of Proverbs, the Bible's route is identified as the "way of wisdom." Proverbs chapter 4 records what a wise father once told his son about following the way of wisdom:

> Listen, my son, accept what I say. . . . I guide you in the way of wisdom and lead you along straight paths. When you walk, your steps will not be hampered; when you run, you will not stumble. . . . Do not set foot on the path of the wicked or walk in the way of evil men. Avoid it, do not travel on it; turn from it and go on your way. . . . The way of the wicked is like deep darkness; they do not know what makes them stumble. . . . Above all else, guard your heart, for it is the wellspring of life. Put away perversity from your mouth; keep corrupt talk far from your lips. . . . Make level paths for your feet and take only ways that are firm. Do not swerve to the right or the left; keep your foot from evil. (Prov. 4:10–27 NIV)

In these verses, the way of wisdom is described as straight, unhampered, level, and firm. The path of foolishness is just the opposite. It's crooked, uneven, and treacherous. Those who travel this path don't have a clue why they are tripping up in life—"They do not know what makes them stumble."

Are you tripping up in life and wondering why? Notice how the father tells his son that the way we talk is a big factor in our failure or success. The father would be able to tell if his son was following the way of wisdom by observing the way the son used his mouth.

Later in the book of Proverbs, the father says, "My son, if your heart is wise, then my heart will be glad; my inmost being will rejoice when your lips speak what is right" (Prov. 23:15–16 NIV). The son's speech would be the primary indicator as to whether or not he was on course.

It's the same way with us. The words that come out of our mouths indicate whether or not we are on course with our lives. If we are steering our vessels the right way, our lips will speak what is right.

Do you gossip?

Slander?

Retaliate?

Are you sarcastic or critical?

Those who are wise recognize that "he who guards his lips guards his life" (Prov. 13:3 NIV). They actively seek to follow the Bible's navigational chart for speech.

Excerpt taken from *Conversation Peace* by Mary Kassian (© 2004).

Measuring Honesty

*When it is in your power, don't withhold good from
the one it belongs to. (Proverbs 3:27 HCSB)*

In ancient matters of commerce, before coins were commonly
used as means of exchange, the price of a purchase would often be
a prescribed weight of gold or silver or some other precious metal.
That will cost you two ounces, sir—or whatever the particular measurement might be. The person would then hand the merchant
what he thought to be the correct amount, and it would then be put
on the scale to determine the exact weight.

Scales were also used the other way, too—for measuring out the
quantity of an item that was being bought. A pound of wheat, a
pound of butter—whatever you might be picking up that day.
They'd put it on the scale, same as when you buy deli meat or a
handful of oranges from the grocery store, and the price would be
set accordingly.

Always room for an angle, though, right?

Can you spot the potential loophole in this system?

The scale was where some extra money could be made. The
scale was under the control of the seller. The scale—assumed to be
accurate—could in practice be adjusted so that it favored the shady
businessman.

And that's exactly what some did.

Shave off an eighth of an inch—an unnoticeable amount—from
the bottom of your one-pound measuring block, selling that pound
of flaxseed for *a bit less* than you said. Make the second block a hair
heavier, and the ounce of gold you received as trade for purchase was

actually *a bit more*. Spread the savings over time and the volume discounts could really add up.

And nobody's the wiser.

But, no, actually somebody's a real fool. And it's not the poor sucker just swindled by the shop owner. "Honest balances and scales are the LORD's; all the weights in the bag are His concern" (Prov. 16:11 HCSB). "Differing weights and varying measures—both are detestable to the LORD" (20:10 HCSB), "Dishonest scales are unfair" (20:23 HCSB). Cheating makes us a few bucks here and there, but our little bag of tricks is not as well-hidden in secret as we think. We're known in the eyes of the Lord. He sees what we're doing: holding back, hurting people.

That's why Proverbs tell us, "When it is in your power"—and it always is—"don't withhold good from the one it belongs to. Don't say to your neighbor, 'Go away! Come back later. I'll give it tomorrow'—when it is there with you" (3:27–28 HCSB). The small amounts we think we're saving by not treating others fairly in matters of finance are in reality costing us dearly by harming our relationship with God.

Be straight up. Offer a fair price. Make it all aboveboard. And if anybody's going to be cheated or lose a shade of margin in the trade, let it be you. Because you're the honest one. And that makes you the wise one.

Excerpt taken from *100 Days in the Proverbs* (© 2016).

Look Up!

*I am teaching you the way of wisdom; I am guiding
you on straight paths (Proverbs 4:11 HCSB)*

In the midst of all the craziness of writing my first book, I decided to take my kids camping. After all, there can never be too many stressful endeavors in one's life, right? Lots of it was awful and I will spare you the details. There were bright spots, however, and one of these was hiking.

This hike was marked "rugged" on the map, and those park rangers were not kidding. After a steep descent, we hiked along a rock-strewn creek bed, surrounded by breath-taking bluffs and ancient trees. There was no real trail so we had to pick our way over the rocks while trying to avoid falling into the creek. I spent half my time looking down in order to avoid tripping and the other half looking ahead, trying to figure out the best way to get where I was trying to go. If I spent too much time looking down, I would find myself way off track. If I spent too much time looking up, I would find myself stumbling over an unseen obstacle or standing in knee-deep water. Interestingly, the kids didn't seem to struggle with this at all. They just hopped from rock to rock and enjoyed the journey without thinking too far ahead. Sometimes they waded into the water on purpose and then made their way back to dry land. Sometimes they stopped on the rocks and rested for a while before moving forward.

That night as I lay in the tent listening to the sounds of my children's snoring mixed with the hiss of my ever-deflating air mattress, it struck me how this effort to balance looking down and looking ahead is a lot like life. Looking down is analogous to how I live when I shut out all outside influences and commitments and focus on what is right in front of me. My kids, my husband, my own thoughts. Straightening the house, paying the bills. I need this time in small doses, to keep my balance and not get overwhelmed with the vast possibilities that lie just outside my door and mind. But if I live this way for too long, it is easy for my thoughts to become "inbred." Without outside opinions and interactions, my tunnel vision can often lead to a dead end. I find myself stranded and needing to backtrack. That's why it is important to "look up" and get my bearings. I need the wisdom that only God can give to help me see the next step to take. Looking up helps me to remember where I am trying to go and what path is best to get me there.

Jesus' perfection and the pain He endured for my sake is the cornerstone on which my salvation is built. My mistakes and transgressions are shaped into something beautiful by the Master Craftsman's hands. They are the stones paving my way to paradise, and I wouldn't trade a single one.

Excerpt taken from *Letting Go of Perfect* by Amy Spiegel (© 2012).

Heart Health

Guard your heart above all else, for it is the
source of life. (Proverbs 4:23 HCSB)

There are some statements of Scripture that just say it all, sometimes in very few words. They seem to say, "If you only remember one thing, remember this." And that one thing changes
everything.

Proverbs 4:23 belongs firmly in that category of spiritual instruction. "Guard your heart above all else, for it is the source of life"
(HCSB).

The phrase "above all else" is more literally translated "more
than all guarding." Think of the things you guard with the most
ferocious intensity. Your time, perhaps. Your money. Your family.
Your job. Your marriage. There's nothing wrong with guarding any
of those important things. But while you're busy protecting your
home and valuables, are you perhaps leaving wide open the one
thing Scripture tells us to guard "above all else"?

The *heart*, in the language and lore of Hebrew history, is not the
squishy, weepy, gooey, romantic, feel-good part of our nature. It is
rather the location of knowledge, the inner source from which we
determine our actions. "As water reflects the face, so the heart reflects
the person" (Prov. 27:19 HCSB). "What comes out of the mouth
comes from the heart," Jesus said (Matt. 15:18 HCSB).

So your heart is . . . who you are. It's what you've taught and told
yourself to be. Solomon, in making his wide and various observations about life, said, "I saw, and took it to heart; I looked, and
received instruction" (Prov. 24:32 HCSB). He, like we, form our

worldview by what we hear and see—and seek—by what we allow to penetrate the walls of our beliefs about God, ourselves, our world, and others. If we had not been created by God as these marvels of divine design, we could keep all that knowledge tucked inside its own little island of facts and figures that didn't touch anything else. But the heart is more than a database; it is a developer of actions and decisions. The truths (or lies) that live inside us come out in how we live. Automatically. Unavoidably. "A good man produces good out of the good storeroom of his heart. An evil man produces evil out of the evil storeroom." Everything we do and say and think can be characterized as coming from "the overflow of the heart" (Luke 6:45 HCSB).

Back to that list of things we work to guard and protect—things we desire to use, bless, and treat with the utmost care, love, and integrity. The best way to use our time and money . . . the best way to bless our home, marriage, and family . . . the best way to perform our work with massive amounts of service and excellence . . . and surely, the best way to honor, worship, and live for God in every aspect of our lives . . . is to place primary emphasis on what we put *in* and keep *out* of our heart.

Be sure to put your guard up today.

Put It in Writing

*Tie them to your fingers; write them on the
tablet of your heart. (Proverbs 7:3 HCSB)*

A recent scientific study tested students' ability to recall and synthesize information from notes taken during college lectures. Among the more expected findings was that taking personal notes is more effective than merely reading handouts from the professor. The mere process of grappling with the material, forcing yourself to arrange it in whatever way you devise, apparently aids in your ability to retain it.

The more surprising discovery, however, was that taking notes with pen and paper is actually more effective than typing them into a laptop, even though keyboard entry allows for a greater volume of recorded words. The reasons behind this outcome are subject to interpretation, but among the conjectures is this: the slower, more cumbersome and tactile task of handwriting yields more time for the mind to connect with new information—our brains do a better job of understanding what we've both heard *and* written.

Writing it down. It matters.

The older we get, the more we learn this reality anyway. If we don't write something down, we're much less likely to remember it. Even if we write it down and *lose the list*, something about having taken the time to put it onto paper seems to cement it somewhere in our memory. Of course, we can't always remember why we got up and came into the living room just now. We can't remember where we laid the reading glasses that are now propped on top of our head. So perhaps our anecdotal observations aren't worth the, uh . . . aren't worth "the paper they're written on." But still, the written word is obviously powerful.

James instructed his New Testament readers that part of ridding themselves "of all moral filth and evil" was to "receive the implanted word, which is able to save you" (James 1:21 HCSB). That's how we can more consistently become "doers of the words and not hearers only" (v. 22 HCSB).

The prophet Jeremiah, in words that were picked up and repeated by the writer of Hebrews, quoted God as saying to His people, "This is the covenant I will make with the house of Israel . . . I will put My teaching within them and write it on their hearts" (Jer. 31:33 HCSB). "No longer will one teach his neighbor or his brother, saying, 'Know the LORD,' for they will all know Me, from the least to the greatest" (v. 34 HCSB) . . . because His Word is written inside them.

What, then, can we take from Solomon's encouragement to his children, telling them to tie his words of wisdom around their fingers, to write them "on the tablet of your heart"? We can ask God to show us whatever creative, constructive way He wants to provide us, so that His Word becomes a wraparound, inescapable presence within our field of vision and learning . . . because we don't just want to remember it; we want to *do* it.

And we'll put that in writing.

Excerpt taken from *100 Days in the Proverbs* (© 2016).

Adds Years to Your Life

For by Wisdom your days will be many, and years
will be added to your life. (Proverbs 9:11 HCSB)

All of us hope for a long, rich, full, happy, healthy life. We like to think that we're still looking ahead to many years of being able to grow and learn and deepen and experience new things.

Scripture instructs us, of course—as if the daily obituaries aren't proof enough—that our mortal lives are bookended by a certain date with death. More than 150,000 people actually, all over the world, will spend their last hours on the earth today. (Let that number sink in on you.) Besides that, we're told, as David said of God, "All my days were written in Your book and planned before a single one of them began" (Ps. 139:16 HCSB). We number our days because our days are numbered. Our time on this planet with our family and friends and puppy dogs and houseplants is not an endless amount.

But here's what perhaps is *not* so obvious: among the days written in God's book are those attributed to the way we apply His wisdom to the challenges and temptations of life. Wisdom is a life preserver. Wisdom is a life extender. Wisdom even allows us to cram enough extra joy, ebullience, fullness, and fruitfulness into certain days that they're actually almost *bigger* than simply one day—as though we've stolen several bonus hours that would otherwise have been lost to worrying, sleeping late, waiting on tonight's lottery numbers, or watching *Full House* reruns.

Solomon said wisdom "will bring you many days, a full life, and well-being" (Prov. 3:2 HCSB). "Long life is in her right hand; in her left, riches and honor. Her ways are pleasant, and all her paths, peaceful. She is a tree of life to those who embrace her, and those who hold on to her are happy" (vv. 16–18 HCSB).

"Listen, my son. Accept my words," he said, "and you will live many years. I am teaching you the way of wisdom; I am guiding you on straight paths" (4:10–11 HCSB). For as he imagines wisdom itself saying in some of his later discourses, "The one who finds me finds life and obtains favor from the LORD, but the one who misses me harms himself; all who hate me love death" (8:35–36 HCSB). "For by Wisdom your days will be many, and years will be added to your life" (9:11 HCSB). "The fear of the Lord prolongs life, but the years of the wicked are cut short" (10:27 HCSB). "Gray hair is a glorious crown; it is found in the way of righteousness" (16:31 HCSB).

So go on hoping for a long, prosperous life. God will be with you all the way. But just be confident that, no matter *how* many years He gives you before welcoming you home with Him forever, they will always be their best when you fill them full of wisdom.

Excerpt taken from *100 Days in the Proverbs* (© 2016).

Structurally Sound

The one who lives with integrity lives securely, but whoever perverts his ways will be found out. (Proverbs 10:9 HCSB)

I'd like you to consider a resolution, a commitment that is impossible to take lightly. Ready? Here it is.

I will not tolerate evil influences even in the most justifiable form, in myself or my home . . . *Even the most justifiable form.* That's the phrase that sort of cut beneath the skin. Caused a noticeable flinch. Involuntary. Ouch. Most women don't have trouble avoiding (or at least recognizing the problem with) the conspicuously evil things, the outright no-no's. It's those undercover, low-key matters, the ones that cloak themselves in the guise of entertainment—those are the ones that hook us. They're unobtrusive. Quiet. Too comfortable and familiar, really, to be asked to leave. Just there. Justifiable.

Yet when seen in the stark black and white of a resolution list like this, they strangely lose their cover and camouflage.

No doubt, this point of resolution calls for an intimate, personal, introspective look at what's going on in our hearts and homes. It touches on some of those allowances we make behind closed doors, in the quiet of our dens and living rooms, where laziness and leniency have been known to hang around after dinner and stay up into the wee hours. That's why, honestly, it often requires a resolution like this before we recognize that these things we've been sanctioning with our time and attention are a glaring contradiction to who we are and what we say we believe.

What starts with a sliver, becomes a river.

Obviously a lot of the lifestyle choices exhibited and lauded on *this* show or in *that* book are things we would never agree with in person, activities we would never engage in. And while it would be legalistic and impersonal to tell people exactly what types of shows they should or shouldn't watch, exactly what kinds of movies and books they should or shouldn't like, we all know the difference between valuing honest discourse and being entertained by sin. We know when we're not just observing the grittiness of real-life issues but are finding it personally provocative, enjoyable, almost (almost?) desirable. Instead of being repulsed by certain behaviors and grieved at the lies being foisted on our generation, we find ourselves more accepting of them, willing to watch and laugh, considering them suitable viewing with a side of popcorn.

And what does that make us but the hypocrites we never wanted to be. Discouraging one thing in public while finding it addictively exciting in private. This speaks to the essence of integrity.

Integrity means being the same underneath as we are on the outside. Unimpaired, whole, and sound. It's what the engineer is intent on achieving by designing a bridge that not only *looks* like it can handle the traffic flowing across it but is architecturally able to support the weight of it, day after day, year after year. *Structural integrity.*

That's what we're after.

Excerpt taken from *The Resolution for Women* by Priscilla Shirer (© 2011).

Shhhhh!

Too much talk leads to sin. Be sensible and keep your mouth shut. (Proverbs 10:19 NLT)

More than a decade ago, while living on the cusp of my wedding and marriage, I came across this insightful definition of *wisdom:*

(1) knowing what to say, and (2) not saying it.

Of all the things I'd read and heard through various newlywed books and bits of premarital advice, something about this one simple statement seemed to leap off the page and linger in the air, challenging me, convicting me, redirecting me. Even today—even right this minute—I am captured by both its brevity and perspicacity.

It still speaks to me. Telling me that wisdom is often revealed in silence.

Granted, this wasn't entirely new information. My own mother said something similar to me—or at least to the much mouthier version of me who shared this same body during my teenage years and often spoke without thinking, "You don't have to say everything that pops into your head," she said. But my mom, of course, wasn't the first to communicate that sage advice. Long before I was a teenager, certainly long before I became a wife, a man of great wisdom chronicled the following words into Scripture:

Too much talk leads to sin. Be sensible and keep your mouth shut. (Prov. 10:19 NLT)

Silence is our friend. Silence is our strength.

Obviously I'm not saying we should never speak up or should change our core personalities. It's just that we probably don't need any instructions on how to be better talkers. Let's be honest, we've pretty much got the talking part mastered, don't we? But understanding the wisdom and power of silence—the last thing we often consider when faced with a situation begging for an opinion, decision, or *anything* to break the ackward stillness—I'm guessing that's something worth talking about.

Silence is our way of growing deep, of discovering maturity, of exercising the kind of influence God has created us to have on others, as opposed to the destructive, discouraging alternative. "Knowing what to say" and "not saying it" at an inappropriate time puts us in a position where—when the time is right for expressing ourselves—our words can yield an extremely positive blessing.

A woman who is quick to listen is one who gathers up all the information before releasing her reaction. She resists the urge to spout off everything her mind formulates, choosing rather to give her solutions time to settle, to become properly shaped before being shared. When she speaks, her advice and assessments are sensible and sober. Those on the receiving end of her conversation realize they're hearing a response that hasn't been considered halfheartedly. They're primed to listen on the edge of their seats—eager, hungry, ready to hear—knowing that "the tongue of the righteous is pure silver" (Prov. 10:20 HCSB). Valuable, prized, precious and worthy.

This is wisdom.

This is power.

The blessing of silence. May we learn it, love it, and live according to it.

Excerpt taken from *The Resolution for Women* by Pricilla Shirer (© 2011).

Storm Warning

*When the whirlwind passes, the wicked are no more, but
the righteous are secure forever. (Proverbs 10:25 HCSB)*

L ife exists within a dangerous weather pattern.

And any day could bring another storm.

You've experienced them, of course—those moments when the
room darkens, the thunder rumbles, the lights flicker off and on.
Erratic strobes of lightning flash in the low-hanging clouds. The
wind starts to pick up, scooting chairs across the back deck, lifting
the plastic lids off the trash cans.

You wonder how bad it's likely to get. You didn't even realize
rain was in the forecast today. Snapping on the television, you notice
they're already giving it breaking-news coverage. Radar images and
storm-tracking technology show your area, your side of town—
practically the street where you live—dead in the crosshairs of a
potential swath of danger.

You're not ready. You aren't prepared. You don't even know
where your safe-place is supposed to be. *The basement? The bathroom? What do they always say—the lowest room in your house? Put as
many doors and walls as possible between yourself and the windows?*

Better act fast.

Because the whirlwind. It's coming.

It's always looming out there as a possibility.

Could be financial. Could be health-related. Could be a pressing demand that pops up out of the blue—the last thing you've got
time to handle at the moment. You thought this was going to be just
another day, the kind where you're able to stay in complete control

of your plans and your calendar. The kind where it doesn't matter whether your insurance covers this kind of loss or whether you've been habitual about backing up your computer files. It didn't matter until this crisis came up. Until the phone rang. Until your car broke down. Until a certain bill arrived in the mail. And now you don't know what to do . . . because not even your most interior closet is safe from a whirlwind such as this one.

Like the rest of the Bible, Proverbs never promises that life's tornado warnings won't arise. As Jesus said, rain falls "on the righteous and the unrighteous" (Matt. 5:45 HCSB). The difference is in how the storms appear. For while always serious and unwanted, they look different to those who've lived wisely, with steady character, with honesty, with righteousness, compared to those who've lived foolishly, cutting corners, who haven't made any contingency plans, who haven't allowed any margin for possible disruptions.

"The one who lives with integrity lives securely," the Proverbs says, "but whoever perverts his way will be found out" (10:9 HCSB). "The righteous will never be shaken" (10:30 HCSB). Those who live wisely, in fact, are told they needn't "fear sudden danger . . . for the LORD will be your confidence and will keep your foot from a snare" (3:25–26 HCSB).

"No disaster overcomes the righteous, but the wicked are full of misery" (12:21 HCSB). They never know what that whirlwind is likely to expose when it rolls through. "The righteousness of the blameless clears his path, but the wicked person will fall because of his wickedness" (Prov. 11:5 HCSB)

Dangerous weather patterns strip us of our own contingency plans. Our only true security can be found in the one true God.

Excerpt taken from *100 Days in the Proverbs* (© 2016).

Bumps on the Road

The righteousness of the blameless clears his path, but the wicked person will fall because of his wickedness. (Proverbs 11:5 HCSB)

Scientist, author, and musician Doug Larson is quoted as saying, "Wisdom is the quality that keeps you from getting into situations where you need it." Pretty astute observation, wouldn't you say? Most of the trouble we escape is not the kind we skirt away from, but rather the kind we never get in the middle of in the first place.

So let's walk this out a little and see where it takes us. One of the major categories featured in the proverbs is the matter of our words, our speech. How many problems would you estimate you've created or intensified for yourself by something you said? Maybe it wasn't a full-blown temper tantrum or a biting dig that cut into someone's sensitive nature. Maybe it was just a situation where you overcommitted to a task or church committee, and it's ended up being the *wrong* way for you to spend your limited amount of flexible time. You felt guilted into it, or obligated into doing a favor for someone, but it wasn't the wisest choice to make. You should never have taken it on. If only you hadn't spoken up when you did . . .

Another major thread in the proverbs are teachings about how to handle our money. Again, let's ask: How has a foolish financial mistake cost you far more than you ever imagined it would? Perhaps you committed to a certain purchase or a timeshare or some other business transaction, and you still *kick* yourself for not seeing the headaches that could happen. We can sacrifice so much equity in the peace department by being talked into something that didn't exactly feel right, or by allowing greed to drive an impulse that we're still making monthly payments on, perhaps long after the good or service is actively benefitting us. If only we'd been more careful with our money . . .

Life unfortunately provides way too many opportunities for these types of potholes to develop. You could easily enumerate the main ones you've encountered along your journey—foolish errors, sinful habits you refused to relinquish, people you dismissed as being too much of a bother, do-it-yourself endeavors that you really should've entrusted to a professional. We've lived, and hopefully learned, and hope not to make some of these same mistakes again.

So let's do it. Let's spend some extra prayer time today, asking God to keep driving these truths from His Word home in your heart? Recommit yourself to following the heart of these proverbs—surrendering yourself to His wise, sovereign Lordship—so that "when you walk, your steps will not be hindered; when you run, you will not stumble. Hold on to instruction; don't let go. Guard it, for it is your life" (Prov. 4:12–13 HCSB).

Let Him keep leading you to a life, to a road, with fewer orange cones and barrels to work around.

Self-Inflicted Wounds

The righteousness of the upright rescues them, but the treacherous are trapped by their own desires. (Proverbs 11:6 HCSB)

Doesn't take much review of the news these days before we're scared half out of our wits. Not that we're not so shortsighted to think long-ago times didn't possess their own form of doomsday fears, from Middle Age outbreaks of deadly plague to Cold War constructions of holed-up bomb shelters. But it's hard to imagine anything, at any period in history, quite holding the same candle of sinister danger as the era in which we're currently living.

Terrorism. Cyber attacks. Random acts of mass murder.

They're the nightly fare of our nightly news. And what with their regularity in the headlines, they appear to show no signs of waning in the foreseeable future.

So we do our best to protect ourselves from the havoc these scourges and others like them can create. We stock up on non-perishables in case of cutoffs to our food and drinking water supply. We invest in motion-activated security systems that alert the police to potential break-ins. We layer our computers with encrypted, protective software, giving us the impression that we're guarding our personal passwords and information from hackers and identity thieves.

But while all these precautions are probably well and good—to the point of representing real wisdom, circa twenty-first-century living—they don't really touch a particular brand of danger that's actually many times more likely of claiming us as its victim: the threat of sinful, stupid, self-inflicted consequences.

The first chapter of Proverbs says what everybody knows: "It is foolish to spread a net where any bird can see it" (v. 17 HCSB). The last place to hide the spare house key is under the mat or the flower pot, when everybody knows those are the first places to look. But too many of us—utilizing the same breakdown in logic—are carelessly negligent about some of the things we allow ourselves to do, support, and engage in. And because we turn a blind eye to the potential problems they create for us—relationally, spiritually, physically, emotionally—we hand them the very weapon to hurt us. We're like those who unwittingly "set an ambush to kill themselves; they attack their own lives" (v. 18 HCSB).

So instead of wringing our hands at the foreign-inspired terrors that always seem poised to break out wherever large crowds gather, let's maybe spend a little more time being sure we're not inadvertently (or all too obviously) taking dead aim on our own sanity and security ourselves, right here at home.

"The righteousness of the upright rescues them, but the treacherous are trapped by their own desires" (Prov. 11:6 HCSB). "A kind man benefits himself, but a cruel man brings disaster on himself" (11:17 HCSB). "Righteousness guards people of integrity, but wickedness undermines the sinner" (13:6 HCSB).

Don't let the person who causes you the most trouble and concern in life be the same person who uses your toothbrush.

Excerpt taken from *100 Days in the Proverbs* (© 2016).

Off Broadway

A gracious woman gains honor. (Proverbs 11:16 HCSB)

The other actors never signed up to participate. They are unknowingly living their lives in a role they never agreed to play and didn't realize they were expected to fill. But now the people who make up the regular cast of your life—husband, daughter, son, friend, parent—are enslaved by your expectations, held captive to roles you wrote for them without their consent. They'd like to be themselves, to experience the same freedom they find everywhere else. But here at home, going out of character can cost them dearly.

The crushed look on your face.

The stunned rejection in your response.

The disapproval resonating from your voice.

It's clear you'll not stand for anyone messing with this production, this script, this play of yours. They learn to live without their freedom, their authenticity, ultimately their joy.

Not so with the woman of grace.

She recognizes and admits that, yes, she has a predetermined plot line for her life and surroundings, a compilation of past experiences and make-believe notions. We've all done this to some degree—written out the script of our lives. We've brought our expectations into *this* relationship, into *this* situation, into *this* arrangement of circumstances. Now that we're here—now that this is our reality—our expectations have come through loud and clear, stark and startling, bold and bright.

And it's going to take a real woman of grace to slip out of the director's chair and release the people in her home from the fantasy world she's created.

Once we get really honest with ourselves, it's not so hard to see the damage our assumptions have caused. They are the flame smoldering underneath much of the conflict, tension, and dissent that resides in our home. So the woman resolved to live with grace, while not lowering her expectations, does intentionally recalibrate them. Rather than basing them on a fantasy delusion and forcing everyone else to fit in, she looks at her reality first and then shapes her expectations accordingly. She seeks to discern the true needs of her loved ones and then adapts her own view of things so that she can do what is best for them, nurturing an atmosphere in which they can genuinely flourish.

She gives grace.

One preacher described grace as an oil that lubricates friction and relieves tension. It is the WD-40 of life that eases rigidity and soothes the squeaky hinges. Grace is the smile that everyone you love is waiting to receive from you . . . so that they can finally be themselves around you.

It's time for this fantasy stage to fade to black. The lights and glamour just aren't ours to command anymore. Who wants them? We want authenticity more than scripted story lines. We desire genuine relationships and a relaxed atmosphere instead of all these painted faces and nervously protected conversations. We want life— *real life*—showered by a powerful, potent, palatable peace.

A woman resolved to grace can have exactly that.

Excerpt taken from *The Resolution for Women* by Priscilla Shirer (© 2011).

Cheer Us On

Anxiety in a man's heart weighs it down, but a good word cheers it up. (Proverbs 12:25 HCSB)

Anxious days. Anxious nights.

They're hard to keep living through.

And while the situations that cause them aren't likely to quit coming around, always threatening us with new rounds of worry and concern, we can certainly do *one* thing to make them a little more manageable.

We can stop trying to handle them alone.

This modern life that puts the world in our hand and independence at a premium has done a disruptive number on our peace of mind. We've pulled away from needing and relying on other people. Maybe there was something a little weird or intrusive about knocking on our neighbor's door to ask if we could borrow an egg, an onion, or a cup of sugar. But trading a sense of community in exchange for being able to go get our own dinner ingredients with a quick, impersonal purchase at the supermarket hasn't really served us well. We're just more worried, more disjointed, more harried, more dysfunctional.

More anxious.

We still need each other.

Solomon was dead-on when he remarked how "anxiety in a man's heart weighs it down." Based on the style of these written proverbs, he could've just stopped with this depressing observation. Anxiety, heaviness—yes, it leaves us feeling bogged down. But he curved this hurting lesson into a smile with the second part of his saying—how a "good word" can shine a perspective of cheer into even the heaviest heart.

The Bible is a book about community. The gospel is a story of community. The church is a living expression of community. No one should be left out or suffering alone where there's this community.

We've reduced Christian living down to quiet times and personal prayer and Bible reading—all of which is well and good, vitally important. But we've lost some of David's passion for rejoicing "with those who said to me, 'Let us go to the house of the LORD'" (Ps. 122:1 HCSB). We've lost the excitement of those early believers who "devoted themselves to meeting together in the temple complex, and broke bread from house to house," experiencing life alongside one another "with a joyful and humble attitude" (Acts 2:46 HCSB). We've lost the personal connection of John, who said he loved writing to encourage his fellow brothers and sisters in their Christian faith, but really, "I don't want to do so with paper and ink. Instead, I hope to be with you and talk face to face so that our joy may be complete" (2 John 12 HCSB)—so they could give a "good word" to each other.

Just wondering here if we'd be suffering with quite so much anxiety if we were committed to being a living word of cheer and encouragement to the people around us . . . and them to us. Solomon would certainly agree with that assessment.

Wonder what we could do about it?

Excerpt taken from *100 Days in the Proverbs* (© 2016).

Serving Up Gratitude

A lazy man doesn't roast his game, but to a diligent man, his wealth is precious. (Proverbs 12:27 HCSB)

You don't need to be a raving environmentalist to recognize how much waste and food spoilage occurs in the average American household. We buy more than we need; we pass up the healthy options in the fridge for the processed packages in the pantry; the kids don't eat what's on their plates; then we toss it all out with Saturday's garbage and go restock from the grocery again. Rough estimates of food waste are listed as high as 30 percent. Pretty shocking.

While a bit of overreaction may be in play on this subject, there's perhaps also a spiritual lesson involved: an appreciation and value for what God has given.

"A lazy man," Solomon said in Proverbs 12:27 (HCSB), "doesn't roast his game"—perhaps because he doesn't have the patience to cook it all the way through, or perhaps because he just never got around to preparing what he brought home from hunting. All that cleaning, preparation, waiting for the fire to get hot, and cleaning the dishes afterward . . . he might rather go to bed hungry than go to so much trouble.

A similar proverb says it another way: "The slacker buries his hand in the bowl; he is too weary to bring it to his mouth" (26:15 HCSB). The sustenance he needs is right there. It's just not worth moving a muscle to get it.

"But to a diligent man, his wealth is precious." He knows what goes into making a hundred dollars and how thankful he is to God for providing these precious resources—gifts from His loving, generous hand. He knows time and sacrifice are always involved in taking a raw piece of meat from the cellar to the table. He realizes it can be a laborious process. But he deems his bounty as a blessing to be stewarded, not waste to be discarded.

So it's more than just the food involved. It's more than just the outdoorsman's integrity of not killing things merely to be killing them, making sure each deer, turkey, and waterfowl taken from the wild is later set down as a meal before a hungry stomach. This lesson from Proverbs is also about the lost spiritual art of seeing worth in what we possess and maximizing its use. Not letting our hearts become numbed to this throwaway mentality that presumes God's blessings rather than remaining grateful for them.

Jesus said, "Whoever is faithful in very little is also faithful in much, and whoever is unrighteous in very little is also unrighteous in much. So if you have not been faithful with the unrighteous money, who will trust you with what is genuine? And if you have not been faithful with what belongs to someone else, who will give you what is your own?" (Luke 16:10–12 HCSB).

In what way might a lesson such as this one apply to you today?

Excerpt taken from *100 Days in the Proverbs* (© 2016).

Hope

*Delayed hope makes the heart sick, but fulfilled
desire is a tree of life. (Proverbs 13:12 HCSB)*

Without hope, we die.

Hope is what distinguishes us as believers in Christ. By obtaining "access through Him by faith into this grace in which we stand," we are able to "rejoice in the hope of the glory of God" (Rom. 5:2 HCSB)—a hope that "will not disappoint us, because God's love has been poured out in our hearts through the Holy Spirit who was given to us" (v. 5 HCSB). That's why Paul could confidently pray for the church, asking that "the God of hope fill you with all joy and peace as you believe in Him so that you may overflow with hope by the power of the Holy Spirit" (Rom. 15:13 HCSB). Even when we suffer loss and pain, even when we hurt and grieve, we do not "grieve like the rest, who have no hope" (1 Thess. 4:13 HCSB).

Our "faith and hope are in God" (1 Pet. 1:21 HCSB).

But God, in His dealings with us, often appeals to the exercise of our discipline, causing us to wait for a desired outcome to appear on the horizon. Sometimes these delays are the result of our own harbored sins, pockets of rebellion against God's rule in our lives. We're stuck and can't go forward until we actively repent and remove them from our lives, laying them aside forever. At other times, the waiting may simply be God's way of developing trust in our hearts, using the long days, weeks, and months to toughen our faith and build our spiritual core around total confidence in Him.

But either way, the presenting feeling at the moment can be what Solomon described as *heartsickness.* "Delayed hope makes the heart sick." We all know exactly what he means. And if it weren't for the fact that "in this hope we were saved" (Rom. 8:24 HCSB)—the hope that God is restoring our dying, suffering hearts and souls into ones that will one day be free of all pain and night and grief and sorrow—we might as well curl up inside our saddened, sickened hearts and waste away.

But in eternal, God-promised reality, "fulfilled desire" is what's in store for us as His children. It may take a long time, much longer than we think we can hold out. But as people with Bible-based proof of our confidence in Him, the hope that accompanies our waiting— the "hope of the righteous"—can be "joy" " (Prov. 10:28 HCSB).

If you're in a waiting place today, your *feelings* may be telling you to give up. You may not feel like doing much of anything—not eating, not smiling, not caring anymore. But Solomon would tell you to eat the "honey" of hope, "for it is good" and "sweet to your palate; realize that wisdom is the same for you. If you find it, you will have a future, and your hope will never fade" (24:13–14 HCSB).

Excerpt taken from *100 Days in the Proverbs* (© 2016).

Fountain of Life

*A wise man's instruction is a fountain of life, turning people
away from the snares of death. (Proverbs 13:14 HCSB)*

Solomon knew what we needed to hear. But aside from all the
things we're told to avoid or stop doing, Proverbs also offers a
refreshing portrait of what wisdom can cause you to become.

A fountain of life.

Perhaps by the time you've made it through the day, you've
heard enough complaints and aggravations to last you till next week.
Customers unhappy with one thing or another. A spouse who's
unloaded his or her frustrations with some below-the-belt jabs,
pokes, and nags. Kids who are upset by what they perceive as injustice and unfairness in how you've handled things between themselves and their brothers or sisters. Add to those the audio sequences
playing on a loop inside your head, reminding you how unworthy
you are, how weak you are, how unlikable you are, how hopeless
everything is. Plus, from the news reports to the talk shows to the
overheard conversations and opinions of others, a lot of deadening
lies and worries can land in your lap as the result of what you've
heard.

It's a fire hose. It's a jet of scalding steam. It's an acid bath, a
drippy faucet, a downpour, a steady drain.

It's anything but a fountain.

Maybe you, too—having borne the brunt of all this stinging displeasure and unhappiness—have done your fair share of dishing out
the dirty dishwater yourself. "A gentle answer turns away anger," we
know from one of the more well-known proverbs (Prov. 15:1 HCSB).

But a quick, biting, retaliatory answer can often be the one that feels best coming out. In the end, though, all our exasperated spouting only creates more messes to clean up, and we're left with nothing but apologizing as our only method for getting past what we said.

Wisdom, though, is your opportunity to adjust the spin cycle. When your mouth is trained and instructed by wisdom, you become a source of cool, clean water to people who are as parched as you from hearing such a steady diet of tripe and trivia. "The mouth of the righteous is a fountain of life" (Prov. 10:11 HCSB). "The words of a man's mouth are deep waters, a flowing river, a fountain of wisdom" (18:4 HCSB).

Me? A fount of wisdom? I don't think so.

Yeah, but "the fear of the LORD is a fountain of life" (14:27 HCSB). "Insight is a fountain of life for its possessor" (16:22 HCSB). The very things you're becoming committed to seeking as a man or woman pursuing wisdom—they can't help but begin coming out in your language, your advice, your tone of voice, even in your appropriate silences. And that makes your presence a welcome, sought-after commodity among your friends, your family—everyone who's blessed by the God-honoring, eternity-minded joy and compassion your words convey.

Be a fountain for someone today. Heaven knows they can use a taste of it.

Excerpt taken from *100 Days in the Proverbs* (© 2016).

Easy

A mocker seeks wisdom and doesn't find it, but knowledge comes easily to the perceptive. (Proverbs 14:6 HCSB)

A mocker seeks wisdom."

He does? Doesn't sound like most of the other proverbs we read. Mockers are the ones who *hate* wisdom, *despise* wisdom, who have absolutely no *use* for wisdom. But they aren't so dim-witted not to recognize sometimes when they've gotten themselves trapped between a thorn bush and a barking dog, times when they launch up a "help me!" prayer, desperate for some way out of this impossible situation.

That's a mocker seeking wisdom—as a last-gasp, life-or-death resort.

"But knowledge comes easily to the perceptive." Boy, is that not an unexpected breath of fresh air to hear from the proverbs. "Knowledge comes easily." That's the very course description we've been looking for.

Probably the best way for us to understand this statement is by thinking of someone who is highly skilled at a particular craft. Maybe they're an expert fisherman, able to reach into that tangled tackle box and lift out a precise shape and color of lure, knowing it'll give them the best chance of landing the type of fish they're hunting in these waters under these conditions. And when they drop it in, and soon are reeling in a nice big one, they grab that wriggly fish by the tail and mouth, not tensing up around those sharp, pointy fins the way you or I might, half-afraid of even touching the thing. They laugh and hold him out for us to see, then toss him back over the side—a lot more intrigued by the sport of catching him than actually cleaning and eating him.

They make it look easy.

Or maybe it's an actress who's played all kinds of roles on stage and screen. If you've ever been on-set or watched a behind-the-scenes piece on how movies are made, you realize the vast difference between the finished product we see in the theaters and the chaotic maze of activity that's actually happening during filming. Cameras and microphones. Thick cables snaking across the ground. Dozens of people standing around, performing various essential roles. You see short bursts of action, then retakes and shots at different angles. When actors say they're almost as unsure of what to expect when they see the movie for the first time themselves as someone who's not actually been there the whole time, you understand why. And yet they're able to play their characters so naturally, so flawlessly, so unaffectedly, even with all that distracting stuff going on all around them.

They just make it look easy.

Well, so do those who have made their craft the pursuit of wisdom. Sure, they started out as amateurs, like all of us do. But after a few months, after a year, after five years, ten . . . wisdom is just what they do. Being wise is just who they are. It comes easily to them now.

The same thing can happen to you.

Actions Have Consequences

*The disloyal one will get what his conduct deserves, and a
good man, what his deeds deserve. (Proverbs 14:14 HCSB)*

There are some foundational, yet overarching truths that bubble
up from the book of Proverbs. This is one of them: *actions have
consequences.*

A half-baked theology of the gospel can lead us to believe that
God has provided us an incredible workaround of this baseline
truth. Our sinful identity and actions deserve death—how true—
and yet He has amazed us with life. We must somehow be a little
exempt from everything this horribly confining statement entails.

No. Our actions *have* had consequences. They cost the life of
the Son of God. I know we've heard this teaching for so long that we
can't quite let it hit us with as much full-force impact as if we were
encountering it for the first time. But let's pause for a second and
contemplate what this means. Our sin was so desperately wicked,
foul, and profane that the only solution to it was for Christ, the Son
of God, *God Himself*—feel the immensity of this fact—to submit
Himself to the degradation of an earthly life and the torment of an
actual death. *God died.* For you. For me.

I'd say those are some consequences.

Can't *get* any bigger consequences than those.

Our sins, you understand, didn't just get tossed into the do-over
pile; they were thrown piece-by-sickening-piece onto the back of
our Lord until He was shrouded in all their guilt, stench, and shame.
Our sins are not gone from us because God threw them out; they
are gone because Jesus paid for them. *D-e-a-r-l-y.* Only because He

willingly chose this plan have our sins been "removed" from us "as far as the east is from the west" (Ps. 103:12 HCSB).

Now, yes, these sins He paid for—thankfully they do include even every sin we're yet to commit. His atonement for them keeps paying forward. But each time we yield to sin's allure, we must remember how even the weight of this new one, this little one, sagged onto Christ at Calvary. Our actions *keep* having consequences.

So let's bring this reality back into view, even for us as believers. Let's recognize that even forgiven sin still comes with a cost. Best of all, let's use this spiritual knowledge to motivate us toward ever greater surrender to Him, empowered by His Holy Spirit to "walk in a new way of life" (Rom. 6:4 HCSB).

It's actually God's grace that, when you think about it, has left in place this action-consequence connection for us to keep experiencing in life—so that we are not lured to sleep and forget what's been done to rescue us. So the next time a consequence sparks you to cry out for forgiveness and commit anew to repentance, thank Him for not abandoning us to live in lies. Thank Him for keeping us grounded in truth . . . where our sins go to die.

Excerpt taken from *100 Days in the Proverbs* (© 2016).

Making Plans

Don't those who plan evil go astray? But those who plan good
find loyalty and faithfulness." (Proverbs 14:22 HCSB)

Plan your work, and work your plan.

Not sure who first said those words, but they've been absorbed by now so pervasively into business parlance that they've likely eluded all statutes of limitations on copyright. We all just claim them as ours now.

Plan your work, and work your plan. Lay out your ideas, sift and sort among what sounds right and what doesn't, bake them all down into a deliberate call to action, and then execute and follow through on what you've said you'd do.

We can actually err on either side of this equation, defeating the purpose of the entire exercise. Some of us, for example, sort of eat up the planning aspect. We feel utterly energized after compiling our color-coded markings, our targeted bullet points, our alliterated keywords, and our evenly spaced goal measurements. The problem is that life doesn't flow quite as smoothly and rhythmically as our plans try to force it into. And if we miss the first benchmark by a percentage of incompletion, necessitating a doubling of efforts the following week in a crash attempt at catching up, the process starts to shudder and shed auto parts, and finally crumbles into a heap of frustration. We can't seem to adjust. We just . . . quit.

The more common scenario, however, follows the "don't just stand there, do something" part of our natures, which has never met a packing list or set of instructions that couldn't be left in the box before launching into the assembly phase of a new bookcase or bicycle. *Planning is for sissies; thinking ahead is a waste of time.* But good luck finishing the job without a few nuts and bolts left over that didn't end up having a noticeable hole anywhere to fit into.

Planning. It's essential.

It is wisdom at work.

"The plans of the diligent certainly lead to profit, but anyone who is reckless certainly becomes poor" (Prov. 21:5 HCSB). God Himself is a planner. The purpose and meaning we enjoy in our lives is because we are living out the plan He has put in place for us. The reason our world functions as well as it does—and don't laugh, it could function a *whole* lot worse, just imagine—is because God made plans for the biological, scientific, atmospheric laws and requirements that are essential for life on this planet. He is working His plan every day, or else nothing would've survived from the moment His creation began.

If you today are feeling the pressure of too many things to do and never enough time to do them, or you're entering into a new phase of work or family life that you're eager to start exploring . . . do the biggest favor ever for your six-months-from-now self. Help make his or her life more consistently profitable, useful, and confident. *Make a plan.*

It'll make your life a little easier.

One Little Word

A gentle answer turns away anger, but a harsh
word stirs up wrath. (Proverbs 15:1 HCSB)

We like being right, and we want other people to agree that we are. That's why one of the hardest things to do in life is to resist the urge to flaunt that rightness. To win the argument. To send the other person away with his head hung in shame. We feel like our sentiments deserve the right to be heard, then understood, then agreed with and acted upon. And so we talk, and discuss, and quit listening, and run the other person down. Into the ground. Into submission.

Those on the periphery steer clear, tiptoeing around the edges of the tension, trying their best to evade commotion in a home that's supposed to be their resting place. They feel marginalized and excluded, wondering how this is all going to work out.

All because everyone wants to be right.

But it won't be right. Not until someone is bold enough, confident enough, courageous enough—*gracious* enough—to kindly, lovingly, carefully acquiesce and say . . .

"Okay."

To finish it. Once and for all. Not because their demands were met or their preferences catered to but because they prefer peace to madness. They desire restoration above discord. They want a home that feels full, not depleted and empty—a hollow shell that echoes long and hard with the loud racket and chaos of a fiery argument, then turns cold and icy, bristling from the biting sting of silent treatments.

One little okay makes the difference.

Now this is not some new age philosophy. It's an ancient, scriptural sliver of venerated wisdom.

Truly the wise woman doesn't always seek to be heard or validated but sometimes—in order to protect and preserve relationships, in order to invite peace back into her home—chooses a soft, delicate, gentle response in place of one that's sharp and explosive, harmful and wounding. She is resolved not to tend the fire of quarrelsome conversations, knowing she'll only be covered in its ashes long after the embers have burned out. She sees through the veneer of out-of-control temperaments and off-kilter comments, down to the reality of the circumstance, recognizing that the thing she's making such a big fuss over is likely pretty small and insignificant in the grand scheme. She's not about to lose the battle of her home over a tiny skirmish on a miniscule hill. She doesn't stir the pot of people's emotions just for the satisfaction of watching them cave under the mounting pressure. She is patient. She brings calm to the storm.

And that's what makes her a picture of wisdom. And grace. She isn't caving or being run over. Neither is she cocky or arrogant with her okay dismissal. There's no air of sarcasm in her comment. No sinister smirk on her face. She's just strong. God has produced enough courage in her to prefer the long-lasting sweetness of deference over the small, fleeting, unsatisfying victory of winning this momentary battle.

Excerpt taken from *The Resolution for Women* by Priscilla Shirer (© 2011).

Good, Bad, Better

Better a little with the fear of the LORD than great
treasure with turmoil. (Proverbs 15:16 HCSB)

One of the common teaching methods employed in the proverbs is the use of *contrast*—comparing a positive against a negative, a desired outcome against an undesired outcome, a statement of blessing against a warning of loss or failure. And it's all very effective, even if appearing at times to be somewhat overly simplistic. Because while life is obviously complicated, layered with all kinds of intricacy and nuance, much of it does revert back to basic things. Basic options. Basic choices. Choose this; not that.

Like *contentment*, for example.

Whenever contentment becomes lost behind a thick gauze of jealousy, worry, second-guessing, or bitterness, we can come up with all kinds of reasons for why it's not really a valid experience for us. We say, *Who could be content with these types of problems? With this level of debt? With this size house, yard, kitchen? Who can stay content when their unemployment benefits are running out, when none of those promising new job opportunities have resulted in the decency of a returned phone call? Who can be content knowing their child is facing surgery for a condition that may or may not respond to treatment? Who can find contentment as long as their marriage flounders, as long as their child continues to rebel, find trouble, and show no signs of listening to reason?*

Yes, you're right. Those are all understandable reasons for being discontent. Not hard to see where you're coming from. In fact, it's hard to imagine we'd handle it any differently if the same shoe were on our foot.

And yet contentment—as made available to us through the Holy Spirit—is not dependent on our current living conditions. As Paul memorably said, "I have learned to be content in whatever circumstances I am. I know both how to have a little, and I know how to have a lot. In any and all circumstances I have learned the secret of being content . . . through Him who strengthens me" (Phil. 4:11–13 HCSB).

It's a choice. An up-or-down, contrasting choice.

And according to the proverbs, it is always the *better* choice. "Better a little with the fear of the LORD than great treasure with turmoil" (Prov. 15:16 HCSB). "Better a meal of vegetables where there is love than a fattened ox with hatred" (15:17 HCSB). "Better a little with righteousness than great income with injustice" (16:8 HCSB). "Better a dry crust with peace than a house full of feasting with strife" (17:1 HCSB).

We could all probably imagine a state of affairs preferable to the one in which we find ourselves. But we could also, by the resurrection power of Christ, choose grateful contentment in the midst of it. Not self-talk. Not denial. Not mind games and techniques that try not to notice reality. But rather a godly, trusting, insightfully aware commitment to making bad situations a little better . . .

By choosing contentment.

Excerpt taken from *100 Days in the Proverbs* (© 2016).

The Fear of the Lord

The fear of the LORD is instruction in wisdom, and humility comes before honor. (Proverbs 15:33 ESV)

What we see throughout the book of Proverbs is the link between fear, obedience, and wisdom.

What is the evidence of our fear? Obedience.

What is the benefit of our obedience? Wisdom.

The fear of the Lord is the beginning of wisdom. When we fear Him the way we should, we stand in full recognition of His deity and authority over us. If we truly understand our position, we act in accordance with His commands.

I remember a time growing up when I was scared to come home and tell my dad I had lied.

But apparently I wasn't too scared to disobey him in the first place.

I should be so fearful of disobedience that I don't do the thing He tells me not to.

The litmus test for our fear of God is pretty simple.

How well do you obey Him?

In light of the fact that we all find ourselves in the "less-than-perfect" boat, I would hasten to say your record could have been better. I know mine could have been.

After I was grounded for a few weeks, my dad handed the keys back to me and told me I could go to a friend's house. He was very specific about the fact that this did not include (1) going downtown, (2) lying, and (3) a speeding ticket. I understood his request and I promised him I would do what he asked me to do.

I did.

And in an "I know the human example isn't the same as God but it serves as a good illustration" kind of way, I *practiced* fearing him.

And here's the cool part.

Later that night my dad sat me down and told me I could have a new car of my choosing and also that I no longer had a curfew.

Actually, that part really was hypothetical.

And if your expectation in fearing God is that you will be rewarded in the way you choose, let me give you a heads-up. You're probably going to be disappointed.

That is, unless you start to see that as your wisdom increases, so does your desire to please God. You will start to see (even if it's blurry) that what you see as punishment is actually a manner of teaching you to walk closer to Him. And as you move closer and closer, through many trials and temptations, you will find that true wisdom comes from aligning your will with God's.

You will experience the joy of knowing that you are living in accordance with what God Himself has deemed as best for you, and what you saw as setbacks will now take on a new life as blessings.

The more I fear God, the less I fear everything else.

I believe that true peace and true healing come from wisdom. Which comes from obedience. Which comes from, you guessed it, fear of the Lord.

Excerpt taken from *What Women Fear* by Angie Smith (© 2011).

A Welcome Interruption

A man's heart plans his way, but the LORD
directs his steps. (Proverbs 16:9 NKJV)

Think of it. Almost every person in the Bible whose story made a lasting mark faced a sizable interruption in his or her life. They each stood at a crossroad, forced to decide if they would yield to divine intervention or continue ahead on their own path. Beforehand they were just a name on a page. But after it happened, that's when they truly became historic and inspiring.

- *Noah* was interrupted. Snatched out of comfortable obscurity, he was called by God to build an enormous floating structure he'd never seen or even heard of before. A man who would've otherwise fallen dead and lost among the annals of history became a name still equated with unquestioning faith and rugged obedience.

- *Abraham* was interrupted. Commanded by God to leave his family and friends behind, he embarked on an adventurous journey with few GPS directions but one that ultimately led to the establishment of God's covenant with His chosen people.

- *Sarah* was interrupted. I can only imagine Sarah's shock in hearing that she would give birth to her first son at the ripe old age of ninety. Today, this woman who laughed out loud in disbelief at God's interruption leaves behind her legacy as one of the "holy women" of old "who hoped in God" (1 Pet. 3:5 NASB).

- *Moses* was interrupted. He was just tending sheep in the Sinai desert, when he was shocked to see the smoke signal of

God's presence show up, calling him from tending one flock to leading another (human) one. A wasted, tragic life turned into God's instrument for delivering His people from more than four hundred years of bondage.

- *Joseph* was interrupted. A simple day spent hanging out with his brothers ended up with his being tossed into a pit, left for dead, then sold to traveling slave traders bound for Egypt. Only God could write a story that would take him to the heights of leadership there, rising into position to rescue his forlorn family from a wasting famine.

- *Christ's disciples* were each interrupted. They were commissioned away from their normal duties, demands, occupations, and relationships in order to throw themselves headlong into following Christ as His closest companions. It would mean persecution and death for all of them yet also the opportunity to walk in intimate fellowship with the Master, inspiring millions more of us to want what they had, to know Jesus at all costs.

- *Mary*, perhaps most of all, was interrupted. She was just making some simple wedding preparations when an angel stopped by to visit, saying, "I've got different plans for you, plans that will make you a personal part of the one defining event in all of human history.

Your life and your interruptions have been superintended by the same God who intervened in the Davids and Esthers and Pauls and Jonahs of Scripture. Not every interruption was pleasant, of course. Few if any of them, even the good ones, came without extraordinary challenges. And yet that's what put these people into position for God to tell a story through them they could never have told before.

Excerpt taken from *Life Interrupted* by Priscilla Shirer (© 2011).

A Vulnerable Faith

*Pride comes before destruction, and an arrogant
spirit before a fall. (Proverbs 16:18 HCSB)*

O ur struggle for sovereignty is a big part of the reason why God
warns us so strongly against pride in His Word. It is a barrier
between us and Him.

Pride says, "I don't need You, God." It whispers, "I can do this
on my own." That's pride's arrogant side. But pride can be schizo-
phrenic. The insecure side of pride tells us to pull an Adam and Eve,
to hide from God because if He really knew us, He would
disapprove.

We know that God sees us completely. We can read in His Word
that there really is no hiding from Him, and yet, we still try to come
to Him all wrapped up in a perfect bow. Our prayers are shallow
and filled with Christian catch phrases instead of gut-wrenchingly
honest confessions about our deep flaws and needs.

Adam and Eve were unwillingly vulnerable. Suddenly side-
swiped by their own imperfections, they ran into the bushes to hide.
God was not surprised by their imperfections. He went looking for
them in their messed up state and seized the opportunity to lovingly
connect. Chances are, if you're not vulnerable with the people in
your world, you may be hiding (or rather attempting to hide) the
real you from God too.

When we try to build a relationship with the Lord on the same
projection of false perfection we use with our friends and family, we
get the same result—distance, isolation, and loneliness. The poster
children for this reality would be the Israelites. If God and His

people could list their relationship status in the Old Testament, it would definitely say, "It's complicated." Due to the Israelites' cycle of rebellion, their relationship with God was on-again, off-again. No doubt, this led to seasons of distance and isolation. But that was never God's choice. He does not change. He does not retreat from us. When distance and isolation creep into our relationship with Him, it is always our choice, not God's.

I've said all along that the answer to our loneliness is twofold. Just like Adam, we are hardwired for intimacy with each other *and* we are hardwired for intimacy with the Lord. Both require us to be vulnerable and to open-handedly display how broken we truly are.

There are lots and lots (and lots) of warnings against pride in the Bible. With so many warnings, we would do well to take heed. But what if the punishment for pride isn't fire and brimstone, but a lonely life? What if the fall the psalmist predicted is descriptive of the kind of life that comes when we exhaust our energy preserving the image of perfection? What if vulnerability is the secret to escaping the inevitable land mines of life with minimal harm?

Yes, it's true that vulnerability can be painful. There are times when it makes it feel like we are at the helm of a sinking ship. But when it comes to connectedness to God and others, it seems that vulnerability is also our life raft.

Excerpt taken from *Connected* by Erin Davis (© 2016).

Gossips

Whoever conceals an offense promotes love, but whoever gossips about it separates friends. (Proverbs 17:9 HCSB)

The gossip reflex.

How's yours?

Does a piece of information you've learned about someone stand a chance of being kept within your own two ears? Or would past history indicate that, if given a certain mix of conversation settings, you won't be able to keep from letting *them* know what *you* know about someone *they* know.

We don't need to go any further than this single sentence before we're each nodding our head in agreement that, yes, we know gossip is wrong. We know we shouldn't do it. So why does it burn such a hole in our sense of restraint? Why do we have such a difficult time not being the one to break a story, declaring ourselves one of the first to know. Even if we're hearing "the dirt" for the first time, why do we lap it up with such tell-me-more interest?

Well, since we're obviously so fascinated with words, let's not glance past the ones Solomon used to describe the words of a gossip. They are *malicious* ("A wicked person listens to malicious talk"— Prov. 17:4a HCSB). They are *destructive* ("A liar pays attention to a destructive tongue"—17:4b HCSB). They are instigators of conflict ("A contrary man spreads conflict"—16:28a HCSB). They are capable of causing *separation* in relationships ("A gossip separates close friends"—16:28b HCSB).

These aren't just harmless little tidbits we're whispering under our breath, hunched over the lunch table to be sure we're getting every last strain and syllable. These are damage reports. These are unsheathed weapons. These are the matches of personal injury that we have no business playing with.

The proverbs take a dim view of what's done in the darkness, tucked away from others' notice. We are called as Christians to be brave and direct—caring enough about others to let them answer accusations or innuendo for themselves, not wanting to do anything that might contribute to a breakdown in unity among the family.

So let's put these admonitions of Solomon's into our pocket, and then pull them out the next time we're tempted either to pass along secondhand news or to push up our chair more closely to hear it. "A gossip goes around revealing a secret, but a trustworthy person keeps a confidence" (11:13 HCSB). "A gossip's words are like choice food that goes down to one's innermost being" (18:8 HCSB). "The one who reveals secrets is a constant gossip; avoid someone with a big mouth" (20:19 HCSB). For "without wood, fire goes out; without a gossip, conflict dies down" (26:20 HCSB).

As much of a thrill as we might get from sharing gossip or being around a gossipy situation, we'd find it a lot more gratifying if people knew we could be trusted with the hurts and issues of their hearts. Then we'd be able to use this kind of information to *help* them, not make sport of them.

Excerpt taken from *100 Days in the Proverbs* (© 2016).

What Would You Do?

*Why does a fool have money in his hand with no
intention of buying wisdom? (Proverbs 17:16 HCSB)*

If you were surprised by your boss with an incentive bonus of ten
thousand dollars due to be included in your next paycheck, what
would you plan on doing with it?

Or if you could suspend every obligation on your calendar next
week, do whatever you wanted from Sunday morning to Saturday
night—sky's the limit—what would you decide to do first? And second? Third? Where would you go? Who would you go with?

And seriously, if you don't have time to answer these questions
right now (which you probably don't), that's okay. But please make
a note to contemplate them when you're in the shower tomorrow or
navigating your commute to work. Because while none of these
things is likely to occur right away, they're really not so far-fetched
in terms of how often we sort of wish for them, right? But if you did
happen to get them—some extra money ("Oh, what I wouldn't give
for some extra money right now!")—some extra vacation time ("Oh,
what I wouldn't give for a vacation break right now!")—how confident are you that you'd do something wise with them?

"Wise? Oh. I assume that means saving the money. I assume
that means staying home to paint the living room and clean out the
garage."

No, not necessarily. But if we wouldn't really know where to
begin or how to prioritize our answers to questions like these, then
why should God ever bother to answer our prayers for them—for
additional resources, for relief from our maddening schedule, for

whatever's the latest thing we've cried to Him for help with? If He gave it, what would we do with it?

See, a fool's real problem is not that he doesn't have enough money. It's that if he had it, he'd waste it. He'd blow it. A fool's real problem, no matter how hard he gripes and complains about it, is not that he doesn't have enough time. It's that if time were handed to him on a silver platter, he wouldn't make good use of it . . . even if making the best use of it genuinely meant kicking back and doing nothing but resting for a few days.

"Hope placed in wealth vanishes," the proverb says (11:7 HCSB). "The one who loves pleasure will become a poor man; whoever loves wine and oil will not get rich" (21:17 HCSB), even if a lot of money and cash flow has been involved in the process. If we're serious about pursuing wisdom, we should probably be able to have a fairly quick, prepared answer to what we'd do with even a *hundred* unexpected dollars in our bank account, with even an *hour* of unexpected free time on a Monday night.

So think about it. Think wisely about it. Then when it comes, you'll know what to do. And it won't be something foolish.

Excerpt taken from *100 Days in the Proverbs* (© 2016).

Care Beyond Compare

A friend loves at all times, and a brother is born
for a difficult time. (Proverbs 17:17 HCSB)

We are comparison shoppers.

To much of the inhabited world, the amount of property, possessions, and quality of life we enjoy would be decadent beyond imagination. And yet to us, it's our stupid old car with the 150,000 miles on it; our little old house that could really use another bedroom and a half-bath to make it half-livable; our dumb old city that doesn't have a single In-N-Out Burger in it. Anywhere.

We compare. Instead of being content.

And that's foolish.

But it can actually get even worse. We know we're in the advanced stages of foolishness when we're not only bummed by what we perceive as our comparative lacks and disadvantages, but we're also enjoying seeing other people who are having perhaps an even harder time of it than we are.

"The one who mocks the poor insults his Maker, and one who rejoices over calamity will not go unpunished" (Prov. 17:5 HCSB). "Don't gloat when your enemy falls, and don't let your heart rejoice when he stumbles" (24:17 HCSB). Other people's pain and misfortune should be hard for us to watch. We should never find anything that's even thinly satisfying in the suffering or poverty of another person.

None of us want to admit to this fallacy, yet we know we've felt it before, rising up within us. And while we may not be able to stop the initial flash of thinking it, we can certainly be wise enough to stop it in its tracks, using the opportunity to grow our compassion for others and expand the reach of our love and prayer.

One way to enhance this change of heart is by realizing, when looking into the eyes of another person—even if just passing a stranger on the street—that we are seeing an individual uniquely created in the mind of God. While we may not know much about them, *He* has known them intimately from before they entered the earth. He's been there throughout their childhood; He's comforted them through crisis; He's been devoted for a lifetime to drawing them toward Himself as the answer to their every question, cry, and sense of confusion. *He loves them.*

Though we may feel ourselves to be on such a first-name basis with Him—which we are, by His grace—we are no more worthy of His attention than anyone else. This person, this human form, this collection of mind, soul, and body walking past us, with all their hurts and insecurities, is a remarkable work of Almighty God. And we honor *Him* by honoring *them*, by treating them with respect and dignity, not with a superior check of their scuffed shoes and appearance.

A friend loves "at all times." We are here to help others through "a difficult time." People are not a backdrop for comparing scores; they are living opportunities for caring with the heart of Christ.

Excerpt taken from *100 Days in the Proverbs* (© 2016).

282

True Friends

A man with many friends may be harmed, but there is a friend who stays closer than a brother. (Proverbs 18:24 HCSB)

Can anyone have too many friends? According to the proverbs, maybe so.

Perhaps it's not the *number* of friends that's at issue, as much as how this person calculates what an actual friend is. You've heard people say: "Him? *Sure,* I know him. He's a good friend of mine." Oh, really? You might want to reconsider that assumption . . . because out of all those "good friends" who may appear in your contact list, you might not wind up with even one who would drive you to pick up your car from the repair shop, or help you move to a new apartment next weekend, or come over to help you pour concrete for some fence posts you're hoping to set before the weather gets too hot. Does that mean these friends are *harming* you? No. Not *harming* you. But they're probably not *helping* you much either.

Helpful friends are usually not too numerous.

But they're the only ones truly worthy of the title.

Not even *family* can serve the same function some of these friends can. You may accidentally have cut your hand badly trying to slice up some salad vegetables for dinner. You may have taken a nasty spill off the ladder while you were attempting to clean out the gutters. Your nearest family member—though loving you as much as they do—may live clear across town, or in Nebraska, or somewhere that would take them at least half a day to reach you. This means your best friend in that moment is not your dad or your big brother or the favorite cousin you've stayed particularly close with, but likely the guy who's next door or the woman who saw what happened from her front yard. "Better a neighbor nearby than a brother far away" (Prov. 27:10 HCSB).

We could all just benefit from understanding what genuinely qualifies as a friend—not only so we can have the kind of friends we need, but also so we can be that kind of friend to at least a firm handful of other people. Friendships have perhaps become so casual in our culture because we know some of them more through their online presence than from actual interaction. The lines of authentic relationship have blurred a bit since we've started being able to keep up with their various comings and goings from the artificial closeness of our smartphones.

But this "friend who stays closer than a brother"—how many of *those* would you say you possess? And how many people would be able to say you fit that description in their lives as well?

"A man with many friends may be" kidding himself as to where he stands with them. But a person with real friends—a person who *is* a real friend—knows the ones who truly help him stand taller.

Excerpt taken from *100 Days in the Proverbs* (© 2016).

A Good Name

A good name is to be chosen over great wealth; favor is
better than silver and gold. (Proverbs 22:1 HCSB)

S adly, those who understand best the value of a "good name" are those who no longer have one.

It seemed so unquestioned, so automatic. Everybody thought so highly of them. They didn't even do what they did, or live the life they led, necessarily to promote it. A good reputation just sort of came with the territory. People in the community had generally held good impressions of their parents through the years. The family name was one that carried a lot of unspoken clout. Being well-regarded was simply all they'd ever known.

Until they weren't.

Until *it* happened. Until the truth came out.

And now they're known for something else. Something painful to discuss. Something that's been costly to their marriage, and family, and children, and parents. Something that means they can't walk with the same carriage of freedom they once enjoyed. Something that will take some time to recover from. Something they now read in the eyes of others, even if it's not always there, or at least not to the extent they fear.

A shaky reputation is a hard thing to hold steady.

Wisdom helps us realize this fact from the outset, while our good name is still clean and untarnished. Wisdom knows to position this commodity among our most valuable possessions, where we guard it with the same care and keeping as we might our social security number or our banking account information. We don't want to do anything that would look badly on our character or judgment. Though people are always capable of misunderstanding us or our motives, we work hard to keep our integrity intact so that no accusation or insinuation against us can ever sprout long enough legs to get away with.

That's not just good Christian living, not just good business, it's "good sense"—the kind that "wins favor" (Prov. 13:15 HCSB). It's how the wise "inherit honor" (3:35 HCSB) and are "praised" for their "insight" (12:8 HCSB).

"The good person obtains favor from the LORD, but He condemns a man who schemes" (12:2 HCSB). "The remembrance of the righteous is a blessing, but the name of the wicked will rot" (10:7 HCSB). "When a man's ways please the LORD, He makes even his enemies to be at peace with him" (16:7 HCSB). "Many a man proclaims his own loyalty, but who can find a trustworthy man?" (20:6 HCSB).

A good name is something more highly valuable than any level of stock option or pay raise. "A good name is to be chosen over great wealth; favor is better than silver or gold."

Never risk your reputation—not for any amount of advantage in any area of life. Your good name may not be something you can redeem for cash, but plenty of people know it can't be bought when it's gone. Guard it well. And know its worth.

Excerpt taken from *100 Days in the Proverbs* (© 2016).

Indebted

*The rich rule over the poor, and the borrower is a
slave to the lender. (Proverbs 22:7 HCSB)*

Debt.

Depending on what kind of financial advice you're around, you'll hear various degrees of opinion on the subject of borrowing money. Some experts are adamantly opposed to carrying debt of any kind, with the lone exception perhaps of mortgage debt on your primary house, since few people are flush enough to come out of their pocket with several hundred thousand dollars.

Others, however, have no problem with incurring a measure of debt along the way, within cautious limits, both as a way of investing in yourself and establishing a good credit history. Still others, of course—the riskier ones—believe situations can arise in which "striking while the iron is hot" is more than advantageous enough to offset the cost of incurring debt service, rather than missing an opportunity that may never come back around again. Who wants to be sitting there, they say, at forty-five or fifty, finally able to afford entry into a business they always dreamed of owning and operating, when they could've been up and running for years by now, perhaps even thriving enough to be debt-free by now?

So the perspectives can run the gamut. Each proponent makes his or her claims and can tell all the success stories that support their view. They can paint the subject of debt in whatever shade and color they've discovered it to project throughout their many years of experience.

What they *can't* do is keep from making the borrower "a slave to the lender."

That's just the way it is.

In biblical times, this slavery aspect could be absolutely literal. The woman whose story appears in 2 Kings 4—widow of one of Israel's prophets—explained her plight to Elisha in these exact terms. Her husband, a God-fearing man, was dead, and "now the creditor is coming to take my two children as his slaves" (v. 1 HCSB). So the miracle that God worked through Elisha, where she borrowed empty jars from all her neighbors and kept pouring oil from her own meager jar until all the others were full, truly saved this family from becoming bought as bondservants.

But the spiritual, emotional, relational facet of being held under the enslavement of debt is something we've all likely experienced. May even be experiencing its heaviness right this minute. We'll leave it to the financial pros and strategists to help show us some of the common sense, sacrificial methods for moving ourselves to a better position. But while we're working out those hard details, let's at least do this: Let's keep our sense of enslavement confined to this one area—temporarily—not allowing its drain to lead us into behaviors and mind-sets that enslave us even further to sin, worry, addictions, and other tyrants.

Freedom is our inheritance as adopted children of the Father— freedom in every area of life. Let's start where we can, and then move outward from there . . . until we're experiencing freedom everywhere.

Excerpt taken from *100 Days in the Proverbs* (© 2016).

Silent Strength

A ruler can be persuaded through patience, and a gentle tongue can break a bone. (Proverbs 25:15 HCSB)

Patience is powerful. And no words are stronger sometimes than silence.

Christians often appear to be no different than other people in the world—which, on one hand, is the way it *should* be. Outside of what Christ has done to redeem us through our faith in His sacrifice, we are certainly no more special than anybody else. But *because* of Jesus' forgiveness of our sins, and because of the Holy Spirit's power within us, enabling us to live a godly life, we should be *drastically* different from those who are still muddling along without resurrection life inside them.

And one of those distinguishing marks—one of the featured "fruit of the Spirit" from Galatians 5—is *patience*. We should be steadily growing in patience.

"A patient person shows great understanding, but a quick-tempered one promotes foolishness" (Prov. 14:29 HCSB). "A hot-tempered man stirs up conflict, but a man slow to anger calms strife" (15:18 HCSB). "The intelligent person restrains his words, and one who keeps a cool head is a man of understanding" (17:27 HCSB). All of which is exactly what we would expect Solomon to say.

But two of his proverbs are a bit more descriptive than these. And the next time you find yourself in a pressurized moment where your patience is being seriously challenged, these would be good ones to have on the tip of your tongue.

First, the one at the top of today's reading: "A ruler can be persuaded through patience, and a gentle tongue can break a bone." Picture an ancient monarch, feisty and full of rash directives—the same kind of strike-first intensity that perhaps put him on the throne to begin with. One of his advisors had been trying to get through to him on a matter of policy, to which the ruler has not been *at all* inclined to listen. On more than one occasion, he has slammed his fist on the meeting table, demanding this aide to change his views or face the consequences. Yet with quiet, steady, respectful persistence, this official has continued returning to express his firm beliefs. And one night, with an air of sensibility wafting through the royal residence, the king slumped back in his chair, crossed his arms across his chest, and said, with a sigh, "You're right. You've convinced me." Patience had broken through.

Or this one: "Patience is better than power, and controlling one's temper, than capturing a city" (16:32 HCSB). Few things were more noble and worthy of acclaim to an ancient soldier than participating in the fall of a rival enemy. But the planning and valor involved in storming a neighboring city are nothing compared to the strength of will required in remaining patient and self-controlled in a heated moment.

Patience can move the throne.

Patience proves your strength of character.

Patience reveals the powerful presence of God in you.

Excerpt taken from *100 Days in the Proverbs* (© 2016).

Not So Naïve

*Trusting an unreliable person in a difficult time is like a
rotten tooth or a faltering foot. (Proverbs 25:19 HCSB)*

If you ever think you're too small and unimportant to make much
of an impact or difference, try experiencing a toothache. Or a
broken toe . . . even your little piggy one. These parts that are easily
taken for granted, comprising relatively insignificant areas of real
estate in our anatomy, can shut the whole rest of our body down.
Writhing on the sofa, barely able to walk, hundreds of dollars in
dental work.

If you've ever had the pleasure of either condition, you're familiar with the amount of pain and discomfort involved. Can you recall
it even now? If you can close your eyes this moment and remember
the throbbing sensation, take this opportunity to put that mental
imagery to good use. Keep it in mind when dealing with a relational
malady that for whatever reason tends to inflict Christians more
naturally than nonbelievers.

The greenness of gullibility.

Jesus instructed His disciples to use their smarts when they went
out on their first ministry journey as His followers. He had told
them to go door to door, fanning out two-by-two across the coun-
tryside, taking His Kingdom message to people who would receive
their words with responses ranging from ready acceptance and welcoming relief, to dismissive indifference and occasional outrage.

"Look," He said, "I'm sending you out like sheep among wolves."
*Not everybody is going to like what you're saying and who you're repre-
senting.* "Therefore be as shrewd as serpents and as harmless as

doves." And since some people will want to "hand you over to san-hedrins and flog you in their synagogues, beware of them" (Matt. 10:16–17 HCSB). Like the police sergeant doling out assignments to officers on the 1980s TV drama *Hill Street Blues*, Jesus' words were a "hey, let's be careful out there." Keep your head on a swivel.

This is the advice of wise Solomon as well: be careful who you trust. Don't believe everything you hear. Think before you head off in a particular direction or before you swallow down a piece of sorta-right-sounding theological counsel.

Discernment was his good word for it. "Wisdom resides in the heart of the discerning" (Prov. 14:33 HCSB). "The mind of the discerning acquires knowledge, and the ear of the wise seeks it" (18:15 HCSB). The path of the discerning "leads upward, so that he may avoid going down to Sheol" (15:24 HCSB). "Anyone with a wise heart is called discerning" (16:21 HCSB).

It's not the same as being the crotchety old-man next-door neighbor, or the stone-faced negotiator looking to squeeze out every possible dime of commission. But wisdom strikes a protective balance between closed doors and wide-open, whatever-you-say mindlessness.

Spare yourself a completely avoidable ordeal with a spiritual walking boot or a root canal. Take the wise time to evaluate who and what you can trust, and you'll feel a whole lot better in the long run.

Excerpt taken from *100 Days in the Proverbs* (© 2016).

Praise Potential

Let another praise you, and not your own mouth—a
stranger and not your own lips. (Proverbs 27:2 HCSB)

First hunches would tell you there's no comparison: the hardest thing for people to handle is adversity and hardship. But one of the greatest challenges to our hearts, oddly enough, is not the introduction of criticism, crisis, or chaos.

It's a compliment.

"Praise."

Part of the proof for how much "life and death" is in "the power of the tongue" (Prov. 18:21 HCSB) is what our mind does with a word of affirmation that's given to us. Sure, those ugly, shaming, condemning words—"death" words—can deposit themselves deeply into our mental tissue. We can hear them again and again, still rattling around inside our heads, many years after they were first spoken. But words of "life"—congratulatory words, loving words, words that tell us how amazingly talented or kind or exemplary or inspirational we are . . .

Boy, we can bring those back out for tasting and savoring all the way home.

Nothing wrong with that, really. As long as we know what to do with them. Corrie ten Boom, the Holocaust survivor whose story touched millions through her autobiographical account, *The Hiding Place*, once shared her strategy for dealing with the many accolades she received from her writing and speaking engagements. She told of how, at the end of an evening's appearance, after visiting with those who'd come to meet and hear her, she would go back to the place where she was staying; she would mentally gather up all the bits of adulation she'd received; and she would imagine them being a full, rich, sweet-smelling bouquet of gorgeous flowers. Then she would lift them invisibly in her hands before God in worship, saying, "Here, Lord, these belong to You."

The inherent danger that comes from being bragged upon, even appropriately so, is that our enemy will latch onto *anything* he can to destroy us or create distance between ourselves and Christ. And words of praise, ironically enough, are attractive to him because they hold the potential for inflating our *pride*—what C. S. Lewis called "the mother hen under which all other sins are hatched."

That's why Solomon said, "It is not good to eat too much honey or to seek glory after glory" (Prov. 25:27 HCSB). "A crucible for silver, and a smelter for gold, and a man for the words of his praise" (27:21 HCSB). In other words, "praise" is the hot oven where our true hearts are revealed. This is true whether we selfishly live our lives in hopes of earning respect and approval, or whether we serve faithfully for pure reasons, out of grateful worship to God and for the genuine benefit of others.

A similar proverb says it another way: "A crucible for silver, and a smelter for gold, and the LORD is the tester of hearts" (17:3 HCSB). What kind of test results were kicked out when you received your most recent nice compliment?

Excerpt taken from *100 Days in the Proverbs* (© 2016).

A Friendship Makeover

Iron sharpens iron, and one man sharpens
another. (Proverbs 27:17 HCSB)

It's amazing to see fashion disasters transformed into fashionistas. Life as a believer is a bit like that. We start out as a moral disaster and in the end are changed into something beautiful. Only our process is a very slow one. Sometimes we think we know what looks good on us, but in reality it is very unflattering. Rather than playing up our strengths, the old familiar habits or things we most long for highlight our flaws. You might say we want a makeover, but unless we are willing to put ourselves in the hands of the Designer, we will never be transformed.

Our views on friendship can be one such "problem area." We might try to disguise our longing for affirmation by dressing it up in language about the "body of Christ" when what we really are looking for is a place where we feel completely comfortable. We may say we want an outfit that is right for us, but the truth is we want to wear our sweatpants and look good too. We are not looking for community; we are looking for an entourage.

We should have to put up with friends sometimes as a way of practicing the discipline of patience. We should also remember that they probably find us just as annoying sometimes and in that way practice the discipline of humility. It is through human relationships that so much of our sanctification takes place. If we remember that all of our friends' irritating habits are from the hand of God, then as our friends grate on our nerves or challenge us to reconsider certain positions, it is God's way of polishing us into perfection.

If we need an example of someone who chose His friends in order to learn greater patience, we need look no further than Jesus. If I am tempted to choose sweatpants friends who are comfortable and easy to be around, Jesus chose camel-hair friends, friends who get under your skin and are very irritating. The disciples were not exactly prestige friends, and I'm sure they weren't in the elite carpool. Christ had something to offer them, not the other way around. He chose friends who needed a friend. He could have chosen just to hang out at the temple with the leaders and thinkers of the day. He and John the Baptist could have gone on a revival tour together. Certainly Jesus spoke to large crowds and interacted with people of influence and power. But in the end, the man who changed the world forever did so through relationships. He cared little for appearances and focused on all of His friends' needs, while I too often see friends as means to an end, accessories I can pull out to make myself look better. What would my friendships look like if I thought of them as Jesus did rather than as commodities bringing me greater satisfaction and comfort in life?

Excerpt taken from *Letting Go of Perfect* by Amy Spiegel (© 2012).

Say What You Mean

*One who rebukes a person will later find more favor than
one who flatters with his tongue. (Proverbs 28:23 HCSB)*

God has made each of us with our own unique temperament and
demeanor. Some of us are more the loud, chatty type, communicating through a combination of flailing words, hands, gestures,
and facial expressions. Some of us are much more the strong, *silent*
type, reticent to jump into the middle of a conversation with our
own opinions, content to keep our thoughts and ideas to ourselves.

And all of that is good. There's no right or wrong to either
extreme or to anyplace along the vocal spectrum where any of us
might plot our natural tendencies.

But when we do speak, are we speaking truth? Not just truth,
but have we developed any patterns where we use our words—even
if we don't say a whole lot of them—to manipulate people to do
what we want done for us?

Solomon, as we know, was way into truth-telling. As *all* of us
should be. But he wisely dug down beneath the surface of the words
we say (and hear), and found a level of lying that was equally dangerous and deplorable, even if not quite as easy to spot and recognize. It might be characterized best as *flattery* or *deception*, but it's
basically the kind of language where a person is saying *one* thing,
while on the inside they're believing another.

They don't say what they mean; they say what they think you
want to hear.

They don't say what they feel; they say what the temperature of
the room calls for.

They don't say what *you* need either; they say whatever *they* need to stay popular with you.

Know anybody like that? Ever seen one of them in your bathroom mirror? These are the kinds of speech patterns that prevent real work from being accomplished because people aren't being honest in pointing out potential flaws in a business plan or marketing strategy. They're the kind that can stockpile problems in marriage or other relationships because the other person had always assumed you actually felt the way you said you did . . . when obviously now you didn't. They're the kind that spoil children and allow other unhealthy conditions to continue because no one has the courage to say what actually needs to be said.

"Smooth lips with an evil heart are like glaze on an earthen vessel" (Prov. 26:23 HCSB)—an attempt at shining up one's own reputation or trying to take advantage of another by painting things in a false but favorable light. "When he speaks graciously, don't believe him, for there are seven abominations in his heart. Though his hatred is concealed by deception, his evil will be revealed in the assembly" (vv. 25–26 HCSB).

So talk all you want or as *little* as you want. But just be sure, when you say what you say, that you're saying what you mean—saying what needs to be said.

Excerpt taken from *100 Days in the Proverbs* (© 2016).

Trusting God's Word

*Every word of God proves true; he is a shield to those
who take refuge in him. (Proverbs 30:5 ESV)*

D id God really say?" It's the same question the serpent asked Eve
in the garden as he tempted her to taste the fruit God had
expressly forbidden. With one bite, Eve quickly discovered that
God's Word had been true, and the fruit had been off limits for her
good.

In the shadow of Eve's sin and often because of our own, some
people do not obey God's Word because they do not believe it to be
God's Word. They reject the Word because they see no authority
behind it.

Imagine this scene. A group of schoolchildren are enjoying
recess time on the playground. The teacher sits quietly on the bench
near the swing set. When it's time to go back to class, she tells one of
the students to call the others inside. If the children are having a
wonderful time, some of them will question the source of their
classmate's message.

"Who said we have to go in now?" they ask.

"The teacher said so!" comes the reply.

"Did the teacher really say we have to leave now? How do we
know? Maybe you're just making this up to make sure you get a turn
on the swing" they persist. Their desire to stay on the playground
will cause them to question the authority of the messenger.
Playgrounds can be rough!

In a similar manner, the serpent planted a seed of doubt in Eve's
mind regarding the source of authority: "Did God really say that?"

He knew that if she doubted the source of the command, she would disregard it.

"Did God really say?" the serpent asked. Eve responded rightly repeating God's command, but adding a misguided footnote.

> The woman said to the serpent, "We may eat the fruit from the trees in the garden. But about the fruit of the tree in the middle of the garden, God said, 'You must not eat it or touch it, or you will die.'" (Gen. 3:2–3 HCSB)

In Genesis 2:16–17, God explicitly commanded Adam not to eat of the tree of the knowledge of good and evil. (He never mentioned not touching it). The serpent's question undermined the holy authority of God and maligned the loving character of God. God's Word had not restricted Adam and Eve uncaringly; rather, His command offered amazingly abundant choices. In the garden, the man and woman had endless opportunities for obeying God by eating the fruit from any of the other trees. There was only one solitary possibility for disobedience. But it was at the point of the restriction that the serpent made his crafty attack.

Scripture warns us that our enemy is "cunning" yet he may not be too creative. He continues to attack God's children by nudging us to question the authority of Scripture and the truth found in God's Word.

Excerpt taken from *90 Days with the God Who Speaks* (© 2017).

Good Enough

Give me neither poverty nor wealth; feed me with the food
I need. Otherwise, I might have too much and deny You,
saying, "Who is the LORD?" or I might have nothing and steal,
profaning the name of my God. (Proverbs 30:8–9 HCSB)

Think of that memorable scene in the Christmas classic *It's a Wonderful Life*, when George and his new wife have just gotten married, but as they're driving off on the way to their honeymoon, they pass a cluster of people trying to crowd into his financial institution. A crisis moment has caused a run on the bank, and those whose shares are invested in Bailey's Building and Loan are demanding immediate cash payouts.

George is doing his best to accommodate their desperation with the two thousand dollars he and his new bride had been planning to spend on their trip—basically all the money they had. Some customers are pressing to be given every last penny in their account, while others—seeing as how he's floating these loans with his own personal funds—ask for lesser amounts, like twenty dollars, just enough to get by for a while.

These wise, tender verses from Proverbs 30 sort of feel like that little lady in this scene, standing meekly at the counter, when George asks, "All right, Miss Davis, how much do you need?"

A little pause. Let's see, "Can I have $17.50?"

Not too much, not too little.

Priceless.

And the same way he leans in to kiss her so appreciatively on the cheek—this must be just a little reflective of how God feels to hear such perceptive prayers coming from wise, insightful hearts.

"I trust You, Lord, not to abandon us. You've promised we will always have our needs met, that You will never leave us or forsake us. But, Lord, I'm not asking You for more than we need. I'd never want to be so rich that I'd be tempted to think I'd done something special, that I was too big now to still need You like I do.

"So meet our needs, Lord, please—as I know You'll be faithful to do. Prove again to us, and to all who see and know us, the certainty of Your faithfulness. But protect me from anything that would lead me into pride and self-reliance. I'd rather have less and have You, than have more and have only me."

Think God would honor and bless that prayer?

The loud, well-tailored appeals of the TV preachers, proclaiming that God's people deserve the best of everything—they make their point. Surely there's a measure of truth in what they say. But give me the man or woman Jesus described, who "when you have done all that you were commanded, you should say, 'We are good-for-nothing slaves; we've only done our duty'" (Luke 17:10 HCSB).

"Thanks for just letting me be here. And for letting me be Yours."

As long as we've got that, we should be able to call it good.

Excerpt taken from *100 Days in the Proverbs* (© 2016).

She's Amazing

Her sons rise up and call her blessed. Her husband also praises her: "Many women are capable, but you surpass them all!" (Proverbs 31:28–29 HCSB)

A number of years ago, the Southern Baptist Convention, during their annual national gathering, adopted by show of hands a declaration of biblical doctrine on the subject of marriage and family. The 250-word statement was most widely noted for a sentence that included the phrase, "A wife is to submit herself graciously to the servant leadership of her husband," reflecting the passage from Ephesians 5 that equates this marriage model to how the church submits to the headship of Christ.

As you can imagine, it created quite the ruckus.

Many women, it must accurately be told, were wholly supportive of the measure. They rightly and often articulately explained that the "submission" of wives to their husbands did not mean rolling over and playing dead, as though their man were infallible. They obviously still maintained the right to a strong voice within their marriage relationship. But certain opponents took extreme offense at the resolution, considering it demeaning of women, as if basically declaring them inferior and subservient to men.

It was to be expected. These folks were not the first to consider the Bible a slap in the face of women's progress, an archaic champion of the "barefoot and pregnant," broodmare expectations of past ages. But to those who misunderstand the God-ordained blessing of a marriage where a husband cares for his wife "just as Christ loved the church and gave Himself for her" (Eph. 5:25 HCSB)—or who find the Bible an offensive rag against the inherent worth and dignity of women—does its glorious tribute to the wife and mother known as the Proverbs 31 woman mean nothing?

This selection of Proverbs was written during a time in world culture when *truly* women were demeaned as substandard. Some were loved and doted on, yes. Most, however, were prized mainly for their water-carrying output. Yet look—here's this extended piece of biblical coverage, praising the exemplary qualities of a woman: her character, her intelligence, her initiative, her industry, her negotiating skills, her diligence, her compassion, her loving generosity.

We're left concluding that the loud knock against the Bible's stance on women is primarily a cherry-picking bias from those who are already conditioned to find problems with it. For to hear the writer of this final chapter of the proverbs tell it, she is one of the most incredible people he knows.

"Charm is deceptive and beauty is fleeting, but a woman who fears the LORD will be praised. Give her the reward of her labor, and let her works praise her at the city gates" (Prov. 31:30–31 HCSB).

That's a statement, I think, *all* of us can agree with.

Excerpt taken from *100 Days in the Proverbs* (© 2016).

P-31 Myth Busters

*Charm is deceptive, and beauty is fleeting; but a woman
who fears the LORD is to be praised. (Proverbs 31:30 NIV)*

The Proverbs 31 woman was not an actual, real woman. For so
many years I'd felt intimidated by this woman, only to discover
she wasn't one living, breathing woman, but a compilation of virtuous qualities women should strive to have.

Once I began to unpack the Proverbs 31 passage, it became evident that the stereotype of the Proverbs 31 woman is not only lacking but also inaccurate. The passage does not describe a
mild-mannered church lady whose primary purpose is to be a house-
keeper and helpmate to her spouse. I'm certainly not knocking those
qualities, but we've gotten way off track with portrayals that limit her
to this role only. One Bible commentary notes, ". . . the noble wife of
this chapter supervised a staff of workers (v. 27 NIV). She served as
buyer for her enterprises (v. 13). She sold what her staff produced
(vv. 18–24), and she invested her profits (v. 16). She had the freedom
to give to help the needy (v. 20). She was respected for her wisdom
and responsibility (vv. 14–15, 26–31).[1] Each of these is a "business"
function, and while the woman's activities were linked to her home
and family, the biblical picture of the woman's role is far from only
the "must-stay-home-and-care-for-the-kids" model.

Why are these qualities rarely addressed when we hear about the
Proverbs 31 woman? This is no Bible-totin' June Cleaver, friends. In
fact, the Hebrew word for "noble" in verse 10 is *chayil* (khah´-yil),
which means "a force, whether of men, means or other resources; an
army, wealth, virtue, valor, strength; band of men (soldiers),

company, host, might, power, riches, strength, strong."[2] This woman was a force to be reckoned with and it was this brand of virtue that made her a rare find with, "worth far more than rubies" (v. 10 NIV). Whether or not she works full-time, part-time, or is a stay-at-home mother is irrelevant as long as she is fiercely devoted to her God, her husband, and her children—in that order.

At the core of the virtuous woman's devotion is her relationship with the Lord. It trumps every other quality on the list. The virtuous woman serves her family because she first serves God. She is strong for the task because she draws her strength from God. She ministers to the poor out of an overflow of what God gives her. She is efficient because she views her work as a divine calling rather than a job. She can laugh at the days to come because she finds her joy in the Lord (and knows that the future belongs to Him anyway!).

This woman is no weak-willed doormat, so be careful about believing stereotypes that may portray her in that fashion. They don't tell the whole story. She is a mighty force who is vigilant in her devotion to God and family.

Excerpt taken from *Everafter* by Vicki Courtney (© 2013).

1. L. O. Richards, *The Bible Readers Companion* (Wheaton: Victor Books, 1991), 394, electronic edition.
2. J. Strong, S.T.D., LL.D. *A Concise Dictionary of the Words in the Greek Testament and The Hebrew Bible* (Bellingham, WA: Logos Research Systems, Inc., 2009).

Circle the Bandwagons

"History merely repeats itself. It has all been done before.
Nothing under the sun is truly new." (Ecclesiastes 1:9 NLT)

Ask the average mother what her deepest desire is for her children, and you will likely hear an answer that contains the words *happy* and *healthy*. Ask a Christian mother and she will likely add a tagline about "loving Jesus." Mothers feel a deep sense of responsibility when it comes to the future happiness, success, health, and spiritual well-being of their children. Because of our deep desire to see our children prosper, we are easy prey to parenting trends, books, and products that promise to give our children a guaranteed edge in the game of life. While you're at it, let's go ahead and add grandmothers to that list as well. While on a recent trip to Costco, I caved in and bought my grandson a value pack of toys, and as you might have guessed, he ended up preferring the boxes the toys came in over the toys themselves.

Scripture warns of this tendency in 2 Timothy 3:6–7 when it advises Christians to be on the lookout for those "who creep into households and capture weak women, burdened with sins and led astray by various passions, always learning and never able to arrive at a knowledge of the truth" (ESV). The context of this passage is speaking about the last days, which none of us can truly know is now or not, but ultimately the principle to be on guard against such things is one that is always applicable.

There will always be those in the faith who would rather subscribe to someone else's teaching than go directly to God's Word for the answers. For this reason, we need to learn to be critical thinkers and, more importantly, avid students of God's Word. Many spiritual bandwagons begin as sincere, God-centered movements led by sincere, God-fearing individuals. However, it's easy to take a turn off the main road and begin to look to a leader for answers rather than running straight to the Source for questions. As followers of Jesus, we always need to ask, "What does God's Word really say about this?"

The truth is, there will always be another bandwagon waiting around the corner. Some may be worth our time, while others will do nothing more than distract us from more important matters—eternal matters. Ecclesiastes 1:9 reminds us of the futility of parenting bandwagons. When we hop on a bandwagon, we need to remember that it's not a solo experience. We sign our entire family up for the ride. For this reason, we need to be careful about what we pour our time and passion into and be leery of extremes. You've heard the saying, "All things in moderation," and the same is true for many of the parenting bandwagons we are quick to hop on. Moderation is the key. And making sure you know when it's time to hop off the bandwagon.

Excerpt taken from *Everafter* by Vicki Courtney (© 2013).

Polar Opposites

There is an occasion for everything, and a time for every activity under heaven. (Ecclesiastes 3:1 HCSB)

In Ecclesiastes 3:2–8, God expresses His purposes via a series of contrasts. Multiples of seven indicate completeness, and these verses contain fourteen pairs of opposites. This interesting literary device, called *merism*, is one in which polar opposites are used so that each cancels out the other to suggest totality. Life and death present the whole view since death is a passage to life (see Ps. 78:3–4). Planting and harvest are both necessary to cultivate growth.

Killing and healing are but confirmations that life is a mixture of battlefields and first-aid stations. Breaking down and building up suggest that God pulls down and destroys as a means of building just as the demolition crews must destroy the old edifice before constructing the new.

Both weeping and laughter can be used by God to get your attention, but few would dispute that suffering is His most effective tool.

Mourning and dancing, casting away and gathering, embracing and standing apart are all descriptions of the reactions of the human family. There are times to affirm others and thank them for their encouragement, and there are times when caring confrontation and constructive criticism are needed.

Gaining and losing suggest that you may have to deprive yourself of some things in order to secure more important goals. Keeping and throwing away refer to the necessity of identifying what is of value to keep while being willing to cast out things no longer useful. Beleaguered sailors were willing to throw away supplies and equipment in order to save their sailing vessels (see Jonah 1:5; Acts 27:18–19, 38).

Rending and sewing suggest the need for mending after garments have been torn as a sign of mourning (Gen. 37:34). Repentance requires tearing away in order to build anew.

Being silent is contrasted with speaking. Speech is tempered because of the conviction that a time to speak will come (see Job 2:11–13). On the one hand there are times when it is wise, considerate, and loving to be quiet; on the other hand, there is a day for declaring one's convictions boldly whatever the cost (see Prov. 15:23).

Loving and hating form a couplet difficult to understand. The Lord may choose to cause the world to love His people, but He may also lift His protective hand and give them over to the world's hatred. In response to every season of correction comes a time for refreshing, namely, those "showers of blessings."

Peace and war also challenge the Christian. When tyranny threatens just as in the case of Esther and her people, whose destruction was sought by the wicked Haman, war may be a necessary self-defense (Esther 9:1–2).

Surrender, submit, and serenely wait on God. Let God exalt *in His season,* whether through prosperity or misfortune. Live for the present moment; cheerfully enjoy its pleasures (Eccles. 3:11). Everything comes as God foreordained and in His own good time (v. 15).

Excerpt taken from *A Woman Seeking God* by Dorothy Kelley Patterson (© 2013).

A Time for Everything

There is an occasion for everything,
and a time for every activity under heaven . . .
a time to weep and a time to laugh;
a time to mourn and a time to dance.
(Ecclesiastes 3:1, 4 HCSB)

There is absolutely nothing wrong with mourning the last-evers, assuming of course, the mourning is balanced with a celebration of the first-evers that will follow. In fact, I'd argue that shedding a few tears is a healthy way to express the closure of a meaningful and important chapter of your life.

Celebrate the first-evers, but also give yourself permission to mourn the last-evers. In doing so, you acknowledge the reality that your children will only be in your care for a season. I worry far more about the mothers who ignore this reality, opting instead for ignorance or denial. They will likely find themselves in a world of hurt when the day arrives to say good-bye on the steps of their child's dorm.

Trust me, it won't be pretty. I know it's uncomfortable and even sad for many of you to think about that moment when you'll have to say goodbye to your child, but it helps keep our ultimate purpose as mothers in the proper perspective. Our calling from God is a short-term assignment. We are stewards of the moments we have been given to parent them, and that role changes dramatically over the years.

If I had a nickel for every time an older mom offered the sage advice to, "Enjoy your children—it goes by in a blink," I'd be a wealthy woman. I couldn't comprehend the "blink" part when time seemed to crawl during the exhausting preschool chapter of motherhood. When my kids were young and dependent on me in every area of their lives, I couldn't imagine a day when I would no longer change a diaper, pack a diaper bag, schedule my errands around nap times, or awaken in the middle of the night to a tiny sniffle heard on a baby monitor. But that moment did arrive. And the next one and the next. The clock kept ticking, and eventually I became the mother who told mothers with younger children that it all goes by in a blink.

Ecclesiastes 3:6 reminds us there is "a right time to hold on and another to let go" *(The Message)*. Obviously, we hold on tight to our children in the early years when they are dependent on us for their protection and wellbeing. By the time our children leave the nest, we need to know how to let go physically, emotionally, and even spiritually. In order to do that, we must learn to let go gradually as they progress from infant to young adult. It's easier said than done. And it can be painful. When we loosen our grip, we are able to gently take their hand out of our own and place it directly into the hand of God.

Excerpt taken from *Everafter* by Vicki Courtney (© 2013).

The Gift of Emotion

A time to weep and a time to laugh; a time to mourn
and a time to dance. (Ecclesiastes 3:4 HCSB)

God created us in His image. It's why some people are so endlessly creative and innovative, because God is the Creator, the Innovator. It's why some people are so brilliantly detail oriented, because they are reflections of a God who thought up organic chemistry and the quadratic equation and built an orderly universe. It's why every single one of us needs community, because He (as Father, Son, and Holy Spirit) exists for eternity in community.

Our emotions are reflections of the very heart of God.

God loves.

God hates.

God gets angry.

God feels regret.

God feels compassion.

God feels pity.

God feels grief and sadness.

God feels joy.

God feels longing.

God feels hurt.

God feels jealous.

God feels delight.

God *feels*.

And our God Who Feels placed within each of us a soul capable of strong, furious, overwhelming emotion.

As humans, we have the ability to be racked with sobs, to yearn and ache and howl inside. We can love so intensely that our chests leap and throb and ache. We can feel joy so deeply that the only sensation to which we can liken it is flying. The point is, we feel things, and our feelings move us—they affect us.

Our feelings are so instinctive that we sometimes get to be surprised by our own emotions. It's why we burst into spontaneous laughter, because we don't choose the joy as much as joy happens to us; it bubbles up from somewhere deep inside. It's why we gasp, squeal, sigh, and moan—because those noises are as immediate as the emotions that prompt them; we utter them before we have the chance to attach words to what is happening inside of us.

God knitted us this way, and I believe that it gives Him great pleasure. God doesn't shun human emotion; He doesn't tell us to suck it up or to get over it. No, God responds to human emotion. His heart is moved by our desperation. The prodigal's shame and humility caused the father to run to him (Luke 15:11–31). Hannah's emptiness and sorrow prompted God to give her a son (1 Sam. 1). The bleeding woman's hopelessness and desperation moved Jesus to heal her (Matt. 9:20–22). The Israelites' contrition caused God to restore them—over and over again. Gideon's fear caused God to affirm and encourage him. God rewarded King David's joyous, flamboyant, get-your-groove-on worship of Him, and punished Michal for her snooty disapproval (2 Sam. 6:12–23). Throughout history God is not only emoting, but responding to His people's emotions with expressions of grace so divine that they could only come from a loving, feeling God.

The life of a follower of Christ is a roller coaster filled to the brim with high highs and low lows. God gives us huge burdens, entrusts to us huge hurts, and requires of us huge sacrifices. He also lavishes joy, peace, and love without measure.

Excerpt taken from *Enough* by Kate Connor (© 2014).

Loneliness vs. Being Alone

Two are better than one because they have a good
reward for their efforts. (Ecclesiastes 4:9 HCSB)

Although Adam was the only human being on the face of the entire planet, he was not alone. God Himself talked to Adam (Gen. 2:16). There was an intimacy present between the Creator and His creation from the very beginning. God provided everything Adam needed and was Himself a companion to him—yet something was off.

In Genesis 2:19–20, God parades a menagerie of creatures before Adam, who is given the unique and exciting privilege of naming every animal that God had formed. He was surrounded by beasts and birds, furry creatures to snuggle and slimy things to admire from afar. But it seems that the animal parade was really an object lesson in understanding God's plan for relationships. Before He brought a single animal to Adam, God said, "It is not good that the man should be alone; I will make him a helper fit for him" (Gen. 2:18 ESV).

As another sign of the intimacy between Adam and God, God graciously considered Adam's solitude. We have no indication that Adam complained about feeling lonely. He didn't ask God for more than He already had. But God knew that Adam needed a companion—and I don't think God's plan was ever for the animals to fill this void in Adam's heart.

"Maybe the lion will be a good mate. Nope. Too carnivorous. Perhaps the spider will keep Adam from being lonely. Ah. Too creepy? I guess you're right. Maybe a fish will do. But alas it needs to be in the water all the time and I didn't equip Adam with gills . . ."

Adam's naming of the animals was not a matching game gone wrong. Verse 20 says, "The man gave names to all livestock and to the birds of the heavens and to every beast of the field. But for Adam there was not found a helper fit for him" (ESV).

God knew that the animals could not fill the void in Adam's life, but Adam didn't. Adam was surrounded, and yet no matter how hard he tried, he could not find a creature that "got him." No one was enough like him.

"Though there was an upper world of angels and a lower world of brutes, and he between them, yet there being none of the same nature and rank of beings with himself not that he could converse familiarly with, he might be truly said to be alone."[1]

When God surveyed all that He had made only one thing displeased Him. Only one part of all of creation received His stamp of disapproval that it was "not good." It was Adam's loneliness. What God says of Adam, Solomon says of all men: "Two are better than one, because they have a good reward for their toil" (Eccles. 4:9 ESV). Our relationships matter to God.

Excerpt taken from *Connected* by Erin Davis (© 2016).

1. Matthew Henry, *Genesis*, Matthew Henry Commentary on the Whole Bible, accessed September 12, 2013, http://www.biblestudytools.com/commentaries/matthew-henry-complete/genesis/2.html.

A Solid Foundation

Enjoy what you have rather than desiring what you don't
have. Just dreaming about nice things is meaningless—
like chasing the wind. (Ecclesiastes 6:9 NLT)

Homes are only meant to provide shelter from the outside elements. A foundation of faith can be built in any home where a willing heart is present. A physical place to hang pictures on the wall and call our own is a bonus. Here is a frightening question to ponder: if our homes were to be suddenly destroyed by fire or storm, would we still have everything we need? Note that I said *need* and not *want* because there is a great distinction between the two. Many who have lost their homes have learned the hard way that there is a big difference between perceived needs and actual needs. If faced with the choice of physical shelter or the one true shelter from the storms of life, which would you choose?

I'd rather live in a homeless shelter with Jesus than a mansion where He is not present. For where your treasure is, there your heart will be also. Dream homes exist in every neighborhood and all price ranges. Dream homes shelter flawed people who are more concerned with remodeling their hearts than their kitchens. They are safe havens to confess shortcomings rather than pretending they don't exist. Dream homes see their fair share of tears and heartaches, but the tears and heartaches are never faced alone. My children had the privilege of growing up in a dream home because their mother realized the difference between a dream house and a dream home before it was too late.

Even so, I will always struggle on some level with castle envy. I'll flip through the pages of a design magazine and, inevitably, want to replace my garage doors, redo the master bath, and replace the wood spindles on my staircase with iron ones. You get the picture. I know my limits, and thumbing through an entire magazine can launch me into a full-blown episode of castle envy. Better to reach for my *One Year Bible* instead.

When I opened my Bible to the designated reading for the day, would you believe it was out of Ecclesiastes? You might remember Ecclesiastes—a book written by King Solomon and his quest for the meaning of life. In my daily reading, I read that King Solomon "denied [him]self no pleasure" (2:10 NLT) and that as part of his quest, he "tried to find meaning by building huge homes" (2:4 NLT). In the end, he concluded that "it was all so meaningless—like chasing the wind" (2:11 NLT). I'm pretty sure God staged an intervention of sorts to remind me of some important truths that I need to meditate on often. Dream homes come and go, but godly legacies are built on a foundation of faith.

Excerpt taken from *Everafter* by Vicki Courtney (© 2013).

Holy, Holy, Holy!

*"In the year that King Uzziah died I saw the Lord
sitting upon a throne, high and lifted up; and the train
of his robe filled the temple." (Isaiah 6:1 ESV)*

In some sense, we all have to have an "Isaiah chapter 6" experience if we're to claim we are His.

When Isaiah walked into the temple that day, he was in mourning. He was faced with a devastating loss and the uncertainty of his new role in the wake of the king's death. Hungry for instruction and longing for comfort, it's safe to say that while Isaiah didn't get exactly what he came for, he got exactly what he needed.

He doesn't waste his words, confidently retelling his experience, unconcerned with how it will be received by others. No apologizing, just stating the facts, complete with a description of the seraphim (angels) above God, one calling to another and saying, "Holy, holy, holy is the LORD of hosts; the whole earth is full of his glory!" (Isa. 6:3 ESV).

The temple itself began to physically shake and fill with smoke in response to God's presence, and in the midst of it we hear the voice of Isaiah crying out as he is overcome by the realization of his own unworthiness.

"Woe is me! For I am lost; for I am a man of unclean lips, and I dwell in the midst of a people of unclean lips; for my eyes have seen the King, the LORD of hosts!" (v. 5 ESV).

As God reveals Himself, we can't help but see who we are in light of Him.

He'd gone into the temple to find a respite from his sorrow and instead he came face-to-face with a reality much more traumatic than any earthly burden.

Stricken by his own condition, his response shows humility at its most basic and necessary form: *I am not God. But my goodness . . . You are. Have mercy on me, Lord, I am lost.*

Was God raging? Was He terrifying Isaiah, shaking His holy fists and screaming until His prophet acknowledged he was a weak and insignificant minion? *Is there any part of you that has interpreted Christianity this way?*

If there is, look again at this scene and allow the Lord to speak into all the other areas where you've struggled with seeing God's anger as more urgent than His love.

Isaiah didn't say he was afraid because God was frightening him.

In fact, God hadn't done a single thing outside of being present. That alone was enough to show the prophet who he was in light of God's tremendous love and holy mercy. Isaiah's response helps me understand what exists underneath a majority of my misconceptions about God.

I don't believe it was God's anger that bent Isaiah's knees; it was His *love*. Can you see the difference? We aren't forced to the ground, terror-stricken by a ruthless and cruel God. We bow low in His presence because we see how devastatingly beautiful it is to be loved by Love Himself.

Excerpt taken from *Chasing God* by Angie Smith (© 2014).

"Seeing" God

And one called to another: Holy, holy, holy is the LORD of Hosts; His glory fills the whole earth." (Isaiah 6:3 HCSB)

To rightly fear God, we must rightly see Him.

The Lord has incommunicable attributes—parts of His character that we do not share with Him. Although we are made in His image, there are some aspects of who He is that we cannot and will not replicate (1 Tim. 6:15–16).

He is independent. He doesn't need us nor anything He has made. We are utterly dependent creatures. We need air to breathe—and not just any gas, but a specific element, oxygen. We need food. We need human interaction. Our needs are practically endless.

The Lord is immutable. He does not change. Praise His name that we are not immutable! If this were the case, I would always be selfish, self-centered, self-seeking, jealous, envious, discontent, and immature in every way! By His grace, though, He is changing me—conforming me into the image of His beloved Son (Rom. 8:29).

God has no beginning and no end. He is eternal. I am a blip on the radar. Our lives are but a breath. Although we are promised everlasting life if we trust in Him, we each had a beginning.

He is omnipresent. There's nowhere that He's not. Whether the heights or the depths, He is there (Ps. 139:8).

God is holy. There's a scene in Scripture that displays this trait beautifully.

Isaiah was a prophet of the Most High God. Though he was chosen by God, he wasn't exactly loved and admired by the people.

The Lord was gracious to give him a vibrant vision that, I would imagine, provided comfort on darker days.

In Isaiah 6, the prophet details what he saw. It says that he saw the Lord sitting upon His throne, high and lifted up. Didn't 1 Timothy 6:16 say that no one has seen Him? How is this possible? Since both texts are canonized Scripture, I can trust that both are true. So there has to be something else going on here. Isaiah must be seeing a portion of who God is, and 1 Timothy is referring to the whole of who God is. Isaiah is seeing what the Lord has allowed him to see. In particular, He is letting Isaiah see His sovereignty (as He is seated on a throne, high and lifted up) and His holiness. This is confirmed when the angels surrounding Him break into song:

The sight of God's holiness indicted Isaiah and exposed his inadequacy. Who was he in light of the King, the Lord of hosts? All earthly wisdom was burned up by God's presence. The fear of the Lord sprouted in Isaiah's heart. He beheld God in His holiness, in His perfection, and it laid him open. He knew that he couldn't measure up on his own—nor could anyone else. He was frozen in fear because he knew he was completely powerless to do anything. The beginning of wisdom is coming to the end of ourselves.

Excerpt taken from *Steadfast Love* by Lauren Chandler (© 2016).

A Seed Worth Growing

"And I heard the voice of the Lord saying, 'Whom shall I send, and who will go for us?'" (Isaiah 6:8 ESV)

God's voice echoes throughout the temple, and Isaiah is so in awe of the Lord that he can barely wait for the question to be posed before he answers emphatically, "Here I am! Send me" (Isa. 6:8 ESV).

God has given us each a unique charge—a calling in life that will involve aspects we don't enjoy. In Isaiah's case, he knew this meant he was going to be a man who was frequently dismissed, and likely worse. But it pales in comparison to the mercy that has captured him, and instead of being fearful, he is eager to begin his journey.

Three words uttered in response to our awareness of a holy God who has accepted us, made us righteous, and rescued us from the clutches of death. With full knowledge that what is up ahead will likely be difficult, we cannot help but join in Isaiah's hearty acceptance of God's will for our lives.

Immediately the Lord gave Isaiah his mission: "Go, and say to this people . . ." (v. 9 ESV).

He didn't paint an optimistic picture of how they would respond to the call to repentance, either. He essentially told Isaiah that they weren't going to listen to him, and that they were going to continue to ignore God.

God was giving Isaiah a call to obedience.

He's speaking to us as well.

Our call is to obey Him, but that doesn't mean we won't ever doubt or ask Him to clarify our task; we say it in a thousand different ways, but the question remains the same: *How long, O Lord?*

God assured Isaiah that although he wouldn't see a revival of the people, a "holy seed" would remain. The land will be ravaged and it will look hopeless for a while, but there is a remnant that will follow the true gospel (v. 13).

This seed represents those who have been set apart by His grace, and no drought or famine can prevent it from growing in likeness to Him. We have been "born again, not of perishable seed but of imperishable, through the living and abiding word of God" (1 Pet. 1:23 ESV). A seed He saw as worth growing. We see with new eyes the cost of what He has planted.

A blood-soaked crown of thorns piercing Him as they ridiculed His claims of sovereignty. We stand in the shadow of a cross on Calvary, and though we look there no more to find Him, we should take care to never forget what held Him there.

Love.

His wounds have healed you; His cross lowered in death to raise you to life.

I have seen enough of Him to believe it is so, and my mouth calls out before my mind dares to object:

Here am I, the beloved of Christ . . .

Send me, Lord, for I know no other way to love You in return.

Excerpt taken from *Chasing God* by Angie Smith (© 2014).

Friend of God

Therefore the LORD is waiting to show you mercy, and is rising up to show you compassion, for the LORD is a just God. All who wait patiently for Him are happy. (Isaiah 30:18 HCSB)

Adam and Eve, unblemished with sin, were friends of the Father. The Lord God walked with them and talked with them face-to-face (Gen. 3:8).

When Adam and Eve sinned, humanity's fellowship with God was broken. Sinful man could not stand in the presence of a holy God. It was impossible. Not even Moses was allowed to look into God's face, for to do so would mean certain death (Exod. 33:19–23).

- Sin created a barrier in the relationship between God and humans. However, despite the barrier, the inclination of the Father's heart was still toward friendship. The Lord spoke to Moses "as a man speaks with his friend" (Exod. 33:11).
- He called Abraham "friend" (Isa. 41:8; James 2:23).
- King Solomon recognized Him as the "friend who stays closer than a brother" (Prov. 18:24).

The Father's desire for fellowship and friendship with His children is most evident in the life of Jesus. Jesus called His disciples "friends." The religious leaders sarcastically called Jesus the "friend of tax collectors and sinners" to criticize His friendly relationship with those who were social outcasts (Luke 7:34).

Jesus laid down His life so that we could be friends with His Father. But there are conditions to friendship with God, for friendship with God is not like human friendship. We are not God's equals, nor are we His peers. The Father longs for us to be His friends, but our friendship with Him is, of necessity, on His terms. He alone knows what makes friendship between divinity and humans possible.

John 15:9–15 emphasizes several aspects of friendship with God. It tells us that Jesus demonstrated the greatness of the Father's love when He laid down His life for His friends (v. 13) and that we are friends of God if we do what He commands (v. 14). Servants do not know their Master's business, but Jesus revealed the Father's heart to us. Therefore, we are no longer called "servants," but are called friends (v. 15).

Why would the Father want us to be His friends? It is not as though he lacks anything or would gain anything by our friendship (Acts 17:25). What is His motivation? We find an answer in 2 Corinthians 1:3. Paul refers to God as "the Father of compassion" (NIV).

Compassion is a tender emotion that arises from observing the unfortunate circumstances of another, accompanied by a desire to help and be involved. The Father wants to be our friend, not because it will benefit him but because He is a God of compassion. He sees our circumstance, and He is moved with tender emotion.

Compassion describes the Father's basic attitude toward you. He has a predisposition toward your well-being. You never have to wonder whether the Father wants the best for you, His friend.

Excerpt taken from *In My Father's House* by Mary Kassian (© 2005).

The Truth Remains

"The grass withers, the flowers fade, but the word of our God remains forever." (Isaiah 40:8 HCSB)

Jesus knew exactly how temporary the things of this world are. He was "with God in the beginning," after all, and "all things were created through Him" (John 1:2–3 HCSB). Even so, "He emptied Himself . . . taking on the likeness of men," the Creator becoming like one of His created for the sake of reconciling them eternally to Himself (Phil. 2:7 HCSB). He was Emmanuel, God truly with us.

The Son of God came to earth to die in our stead. Who would have blamed Him for biding His time until the end? But that's not who Jesus was. Ignoring the world around Him would not have brought glory to His Father.

And ignoring the people around Him was not in His nature—a nature defined by love and holiness, justice and grace. Instead of keeping His distance, the Son of God did the opposite: He fully entered in.

Jesus attended weddings and cooked breakfast. He started conversations with strangers and fed hungry crowds. He embraced lepers and healed the hurting. He took notice of widows and sat orphans on His knee. He wept with His friends and He loved His mama.

Jesus knew precisely what would and wouldn't last, and He chose to be all here. He chose to be fully present, out of obedience to His Father and love for His people. As followers of Christ, we are called to do the same.

The knowledge that this world is temporary, and the affirmation that only God and His Word are eternal, is not a license to give up on life as we know it. It's not our permission slip to care only about the everlasting life while harboring indifference toward this passing one. No, this knowledge is both an invitation and a mandate to dig in deeper—to live our earthly lives in earnest, in light of eternity.

God's Truth gives our temporary lives eternal significance. It speaks forgiveness over our sin, hope over our despair, worth over our shame, and life over our death. In its light, everything matters. And at the same time, nothing else does.

In the surety of God's love, we can let up on the reins of our everyday and enjoy the panoramic view of His covenant faithfulness, stretching as far as the eye can see. And we also have the freedom to lean in close to engage a friend's specific joy, panic, or pain, knowing that our infinite God cares for even the finite details of His children's lives.

When the temporary has passed away and every finite thing has returned to dust, we'll be left standing face-to-face with the Permanent One. We won't wonder if it was worth it to sacrifice our comforts for the sake of others. We'll know. We won't worry about climbing those mountains made of self and stuff. They'll be gone. We won't question the trustworthiness of our covenant-making Creator and His every word. We'll see it all clearly.

Excerpt taken from *She Reads Truth* by Raechel Myers and Amanda Bible Williams (© 2016).

Eagles Wings

But those who trust in the LORD will renew their strength;
they will soar on wings like eagles; they will run and not grow
weary; they will walk and not faint. (Isaiah 40:31 HCSB)

Eagles are large, powerful birds. They build their eyries (nests) in the tops of tall trees or cliffs. To teach a young eaglet to fly, the parent will coax it's offspring to come out on a limb and then will push it off. If this approach fails, the parent will stir the nest and throw the eaglet out. The eaglet, not yet knowing how to fly, hopelessly plunges downward. The parent quickly swoops down under the eaglet and flaps its powerful wings. The eaglet does not see the parent, but the updraft of air created by the parent's wings pushes the little eaglet up, enabling it to fly.

What a powerful and precious picture of how God responds to us, His children.

About three months after the children of Israel had come out of Egypt, they were camped in the wilderness of Sinai, beside the mountain of Sinai. There, God told Moses, "You have seen what I did to the Egyptians, and how I bore you on eagles' wings and brought you to Myself" (Exod. 19:4 NKJV).

In the same way an eagle teaches her eaglet to fly, the Father bore the Israelites "on eagles' wings." They did not see His support when they were suffering under their increased workload as slaves (Exod. 5:20–22). Nor did they see Him when they felt they would die, trapped by the Egyptian army (Exod. 14:11). Again, they must have felt like they were in a free fall without God's love and care as they worried they would die from hunger in the desert

(Exod. 14:10–12; 16:3). But the Father was continually upholding them. Like an eagle unseen, He was supporting them with his strength and His power, enabling them to fly.

Read what the Father said through the prophet Isaiah:

> Listen to Me, O house of Jacob, and all the remnant of the house of Israel, who have been upheld by Me from birth, who have been carried from the womb. (Isa. 46:3 NKJV)

Go back and read the verse again, looking for every action of the Father.

Upheld.

Carried.

Did you take note of how long the Father promised to support His children? God upholds you from the time you are born until the time you are old. He supports you with His mighty wings. Even if you do not perceive His presence, He is bearing you on eagle's wings, enabling you to fly. Though life can certainly be turbulent, you are never in a free fall. You may not feel God's presence. You may not clearly see His hand. Yet, God is ever near you. Just as He carried the Israelites out of captivity, through the wilderness, and into the Promised Land, even though at times they could not see Him, He will carry you.

Look up toward Him and soar!

Excerpt taken from *In My Father's House* by Mary Kassian (© 2005).

Our God Is Fearless

Don't be afraid, for I am with you. Don't be discouraged, for I am your God. I will strengthen you and help you. I will hold you up with my victorious right hand. (Isaiah 41:10 NLT)

Do. Not. Be. Afraid.

This issue of fear is so well-known and important to God that more than three hundred times in Scripture He tells His people—in one form or another—not to be afraid. "Fear not." "Be ye not afraid." "Do not fear." Look it up. It's everywhere. You know those times when you're searching high and low for just one verse to tell you what God wants you to do? Well, here's three hundred of them. And they're all saying the same thing: "Don't be afraid."

It's the enemy telling you, "Be *very* afraid."

Is that the kind of junk he's been feeding you lately? Twenty million reasons why you can't? Can't kick the habit? Can't stand up and lead a Bible study? Can't help start that inner-city ministry? Not qualified enough for that job? Can't do *this,* could *never* do that, be crazy to even *think* about doing that *other* thing?

Why not? Might take too much time? Not to mention the pressure? The germs? Do I really want to risk the rejection of being told no? Don't I realize what I'd be giving up in terms of security and salary and insurance benefits? What would people think if I did something so audacious, something out of my normal routine and pattern? Wouldn't I just be opening myself up to criticism and catty comments? What about my food allergies, my fear of flying, all my other various intolerances?

Are those the kind of speed bumps and roadblocks he's been laying in front of you, seemingly all your life? He's just full of it. Full of excuses. Invested in cramming you full of fear. Why? Because fear is the antithesis of faith. And faith is what allows you to step foot on the soil of your destiny.

Hear me out, and hear me good. I'm about to write a long, run-on sentence, but I want you hanging on every word: If God has given you clear direction, like He gave the children of Israel—direction that's confirmed by His written Word and by the sounding board of wise, godly counsel—and your only real reason for resisting Him is because you're *afraid* of what following Him down this path might mean or cost or entail, then you're not only on the threshold of being disobedient, you're about to miss an opportunity to give God some fresh, new glory by doing what He's wanting to do through you, which is the true impetus behind His invitation for you to join Him on this scary adventure in the first place.

In fervent prayer, we discover something: Our God is fearless. And because *He* is fearless, we can be fearless too. When His presence is with us and going before us, no Red Sea should faze us or give us pause.

So despite your hesitation, say yes.

Walk on. Have faith. Fear not.

Excerpt taken from *Fervent* by Priscilla Shirer (© 2015).

To the Weary

*But Jacob, you have not called on Me, because, Israel,
you have become weary of Me. (Isaiah 43:22 HCSB)*

What makes women weary?
Most women think that question has a thousand answers"

- babies with the earache,
- preschoolers with unbounded energy,
- sons and daughters who would rather fight to hold every boundary than to give an inch for peace
- teenagers whose rooms should qualify for federal disaster funds,
- husbands who don't help at home,
- employers who think a woman has only one full-time job
- schools, churches, and community organizations that are happy to overload their one and only volunteer . . .

Add infinitum.

However, these countless surface pressures point to some underlying enemies that lie in wait to catch their feminine prey. *Weariness can come from confusion*—confusion that issues forth in using your energies wrongfully, confusion in discerning the counsel emanating from many sources, confusion in determining which direction to go. Confusion is best defeated by special care in discernment. The book of Proverbs promises that godly counsel is available (Prov. 15:22), while the book of Isaiah warns about the worldly counsel that hinders your seeking the right help (Isa. 47:12–14). God offers protection in providing a sure means of avoiding this debilitating confusion: "Many plans are in a man's heart, but the LORD's decree will prevail" (Prov. 19:21 HCSB).

Godly counsel is never self-centered; it is not doing things your own way, according to your own feelings, thoughts, and desires (Isa. 57:10). Rather, godly counsel, of course, is God-centered; it is doing things God's way regardless of what you think, feel, or want. Only God's Word can provide this spiritual counsel (Ps. 119:9–11, 24).

Weariness is also the result of foolishness (Eccl. 10:15). A fool is often called an "idiot," which is derived from a Greek root meaning more literally "one's own." A fool insists upon having his own way (Prov. 12:15).

Weariness is the result of an attitude of self-pity, resulting from a bitterness of soul (Job 10:1; Pss. 6:6; 69:3). When you take your eyes off the Lord and forget His benefits to you, you are leaving yourself vulnerable to weariness, which begins with a tired body but soon marches deep within to sap the soul and spirit. Now, here is the heart of the matter: Weariness is an attitude toward God.

God has promised to satiate the weary soul and replenish the sorrowful soul (Jer. 31:25). Nevertheless, He will wait for you to seek Him and find the satisfaction and comfort that only He can give. The farmer does not wait for God to plow and sow his field; but having plowed and sown, he waits for God to bestow the blessing of harvest.

You can be "bone-tired" but not weary. You can experience fatigue but not with despair. Your body can be operating on low while your spirit and attitude are high. Being tired is a human affliction and God's tool for discipline and growth.

You are never too tired for God to refresh; you are never too old for God to renew.

Excerpt taken from *A Woman Seeking God* by Dorothy Kelley Patterson (© 2013).

Walking the Narrow Place

*But He was pierced because of our transgressions, crushed
because of our iniquities; punishment for our peace was on
Him, and we are healed by His wounds. (Isaiah 53:5 HCSB)*

At a time when our family was facing a season of suffering and
loss, we took many opportunities to read Bible stories to our
girls, illustrating the ways God had come through for His people in
miraculous ways. We also talked extensively about the times that He
didn't. I really believe the Lord spoke to them in ways we will never
fully understand because sometimes their insights were so far beyond
their ages that the only possible explanation was that the Holy Spirit
had granted them wisdom.

One night we were reading the story of Abraham and Isaac in
our favorite children's Bible, and all three of them were riveted. We
got to the part where Abraham raises his knife while Isaac lies
motionless, tied up in rope that his father's hands have wrapped
around him. The girls always hold their breath just before God says,
"Stop!" They know the outcome because we have read it to them
many times, but their expressions always stay the same until the
moment when he is loosened and set free.

I couldn't stop thinking about it.

It was his son.

His hands.

His rope.

And yet it was never His at all.

When people talked to me about what I was going through,
they often used the word *trial*. I think it was the right word. In the

thousands of years since Abraham and Isaac, the rules have not changed. We listen, we praise, we walk in the direction of God's voice, and we obey.

It's that simple.

Sometimes that means we get to unbind and celebrate.

Sometimes it means we don't.

I looked up the original Hebrew word for *trial* in one of my big fancy books. I hope that as you read these words, you will know the way He quieted me in that moment.

> TRIAL (Old Testament) noun: from the Hebrew word *sara* which comes from the root *srh*, which means, "to bind, tie up, restrict." Thus, the noun comes to denote **a narrow place in life where one is bound or restricted . . .**

I carried this image with me for days, saturating myself in the truth that I discovered about what it means to be walking where I was. As we walked this "narrow place," I was reminded of the power of being still and submitting to the God I trusted more than I ever thought I could. During these days I walked moment by moment with the God of the universe.

The God who chose Abraham.

The God who chose me.

I couldn't think of anyone I would feel safer with because, of course, the difficult, terrible, beautiful truth is that He Himself is not unfamiliar with the binding.

I bore my wounds tenderly, with worship ever on my lips because He did the same for me.

Excerpt taken from *I Will Carry You* by Angie Smith (© 2010).

Higher Thoughts

*For as heaven is higher than earth, so My ways
are higher than your ways, and My thoughts
than your thoughts. (Isaiah 55:9 HCSB)*

Significance. Each of us is searching for it. The woman I met who was devastated after being passed over for a promotion (again)—she's looking for it. Monica, the waitress at Planet Hollywood bemoaning her broken heart over her barely there boyfriend, is looking for it. The homemaker I was talking to recently is looking for it—the feeling of significance that's often swept away underneath the never-ending pile of laundry. Deep down we're *all* looking for it. We all want to matter. As believers in the Lord Jesus, we each want to know that God has called us to make some kind of difference, something that gives us a level of value and significance in the big picture.

And wouldn't you know it, the interrupted life is the cure for that search.

I'm serious. When God speaks, when He intervenes, when He permits a circumstance to rise up around you, it is your opportunity to write a story that people may still be talking about many years from now. Like those holy heroes of old from Scripture, your story of divine intervention—the one that brought you to your knees in frustration—could be the very thing that lifts others' eyebrows in wonder and amazement, the one that causes them to see the sparkle of substance, significance, and impact in your life. This could be the part of your story that encourages another to make their own decision to follow hard after God.

So just go with it. Follow Him—impossible as it may seem. You may not grasp what He's got in mind for this, but if you'll follow where He's leading, you will walk yourself right out onto the stage He has set for you. You will locate a significance bigger than you are because it's not based on your own smarts and planning and goal strategies but rather on your utter submission to the Father's eternal, all-wise plans—plans that are "higher than your ways" (Isa. 55:9 NASB), beyond anything you could "ask or think" or imagine (Eph. 3:20 NASB).

Oh, I know it can be extremely challenging sometimes.

Gut-wrenching and intense. Perhaps you've never faced anything this daunting before, a situation that asks so much of you or hurts in such deep places. But with the Red Sea in front of you and Pharaoh's armies barreling down close behind, you get to find out what the Lord can really do. He's put you in a tough spot so you'll get to see just how incredibly strong and sufficient your God is.

And others will see it too.

Your life is God's story being told and His character being displayed. So how does it read? What does it tell others about the God you serve? Will you dare to believe there's a message in this mess? It's quite possibly the best story some people will ever read.

Excerpt taken from *Life Interrupted* by Priscilla Shirer (© 2011).

What We Need

The heart is deceitful above all things. (Jeremiah 17:9 ESV)

The heart will lie like a dog. It can make you think you're going to live happily ever after with a guy who hasn't been happy a single day since you met him. It can make you chase a dream of fame until it turns into your worst nightmare. It says that how you feel right now is how you'll feel forever. It argues that life is not worth the effort and your family would be better off without you. A deceptive heart can convince you that you were meant for somebody else's husband and that thirty minutes of wonderful is worth three decades of regret.

A deceitful heart can rationalize that God still gets great glory from a great story you've mostly made up. It says going to church means you're going to heaven. It tells you there's no real harm in pornography because nobody's getting hurt and prostitution is victimless so who really cares. It promises you that you're not the kind to get addicted. It says that being with somebody, no matter how destructive or dysfunctional, always beats being alone and, if enough money is in it, you can put up with anything.

Until you can't.

Nothing is more depressing than realizing we no longer desire what we thought we wanted. No death feels deader than the death of desire. If we don't know what we want, we don't know who we are. That's when some of us finally slink over to Jesus because, if we're going to be dead to desire anyway, we figure we might as well be religious. The fact that Jesus is willing to show up in beauty where we'd surrendered to duty is a testament to His jaw-dropping grace.

He'll put up with any motive if it'll stick us on the path where we'll bump into His presence.

But then something completely unexpected happens. He awakens desire, calling it forth from the dead. You start feeling more than you've ever felt in your life. But, oddly, these aren't the old desires. It's not that they're nowhere in there. It's that they're squashed by something weightier and shushed by something louder and paled by something brighter.

Desperation can do the same thing if it leads us to collapse in a heap at the feet of Jesus. Life becomes so excruciating that we finally want what we need. In that precise surrender we discover that what we need is what we want more than anything else in this world. Next to the redemption of our very souls, nothing is more glorious and miraculous than the redemption of our desires. Never think for a moment that Jesus cannot heal a messed up heart. He'll pick up the pieces of your broken heart to refashion them into a mosaic of startling beauty and sufficient humility. We fall out of a lesser love by falling into one greater. Life-breathing love is the only thing lethal enough to kill murderous desire.

Excerpt taken from *Audacious* by Beth Moore (© 2015).

Knowing God's Love Language

*The LORD appeared to him from far away. I have loved
you with an everlasting love; therefore I have continued
my faithfulness to you. (Jeremiah 31:3 ESV)*

Perhaps you already know that love languages are the different
ways we express our love for one another. Love can be expressed
through words, by serving or doing things for the loved one, by
spending time with the loved one, by giving gifts, and/or by physical displays of affection. People express and receive love primarily
through their own basic love language. For example, although I
express my love for others in all five ways, the primary way I express
love is through service. If I really want to show people I love them, I
do something for them.

My son is different from me. The primary way he expresses his
love is through giving. He gives me pieces of gum, a feather, loose
change, little trinkets and baubles he finds on his way home, or
whatever he has in his pockets. Giving is the primary way he
expresses his love, and it is also the expression of love that is the
most significant to him. He is overwhelmed if I come home with a
little gift for him from the dollar store—not because he craves the
gift but because for him the act of giving is the expression of love
that means the most.

Understanding the love languages expressed by the various
members of my family has helped me to understand and appreciate
their expressions of love for me and communicate my love for them
in the way that is most meaningful. I know beyond a shadow of a

doubt that they love me, and they know beyond a shadow of a doubt that I love them.

How does this relate to the love of God? We know God the Father loves us. This is a fact we affirm on an intellectual basis. But do we know and understand and sense the Father's love in our lives on a daily basis? Do we recognize and understand our Father God's language of love?

King David was one man who really knew the heart of the Father (1 Sam. 13:14; Acts 13:22). His psalms are overflowing with accolades to God's heart of love. He wrote, "I will sing of the steadfast love of the LORD forever" (Ps. 89:1 ESV) and "Your steadfast love is better than life" (Ps. 63:3 ESV).

David was convinced beyond a shadow of a doubt that Father God loved him. It was the thought that was continually on his mind (Ps. 26:3). But how could David be so sure?

David's secret was that he meditated, studied, and contemplated God's actions. From this he understood the love of God. It was David who said, "Great are the works of the LORD, studied by all who delight in them" (Ps. 111:2 ESV). David was a great lover of God because he studied the great acts of God and thus understood the great love of God.

Excerpt taken from *In My Father's House* by Mary Kassian (© 2005).

Brag About It

*Oh, Lord GOD! You Yourself made the heavens and earth
by Your great power and with Your outstretched arm.
Nothing is too difficult for You! (Jeremiah 32:17 HCSB)*

This morning at the breakfast table, I reminded my children that their father's two-year term as president of his professional college would soon be ending. "That's too bad," sighed my son Matthew. "I really liked telling all my friends that Dad was the president."

Children love to brag about their fathers. Rare is the child who has not boasted about his or her father's abilities.

"My dad is so smart."

"My dad can run fast."

"My dad is strong."

Our heavenly Father is strong and powerful. One of his names, *Yahweh Sabaoth* reflects that fact. *Sabaoth* means "almighty." Might is the ability or power to do or accomplish. It means effective power and strength.

In Psalm 68:34, David tells us to "ascribe strength" to God. Likewise, in Psalm 29:1, David encourages us to "ascribe . . . glory and strength" to Him. I appreciate the reminder to give credit where credit is due. To *ascribe* means "to attribute to; to give credit." Ascribing strength to the Father, proclaiming the power of God, means that we see and acknowledge His great strength and mighty power.

David delighted in God the Father's strength in much the same manner as my children boast about how strong their dad is.

"Who is mighty like You, O LORD? . . . You have a mighty arm; strong is Your hand, and high is Your right hand" (Ps. 89:8, 13 NKJV).

Who is like you, LORD God Almighty? You, LORD, are mighty, and your faithfulness surrounds you.

> The LORD is robed in majesty and is armed with strength. (Ps. 93:1 NIV)

In the Psalms, David often reflected upon the great strength of the Lord. He saw God's strength evident in all creation: wild and domestic animals, thunderous waterfalls, towering forests, expansive deserts, lofty mountains, stars. But David also saw the strength of God in the fearful destructive power of floods, tornadoes, earthquakes, fire, hurricanes, fierce lightning, and thunder. According to David, the Father is so strong that the mere sound of his voice can initiate massive natural devastation. The following paraphrase from the Living Bible illustrates how strong God the Father is:

> "Praise the Lord, you angels of his; praise his glory and his strength. . . .
>
> The voice of the Lord echoes from the clouds. The God of glory thunders through the skies. So powerful is his voice; so full of majesty. It breaks down the cedars. It splits the giant trees of Lebanon. It shakes Mount Lebanon and Mount Sirion. They leap and skip before him like young calves! The voice of the Lord thunders through the lightning. It resounds through the deserts and shakes the wilderness of Kadesh. The voice of the Lord spins and topples the mighty oaks. It strips the forests bare. They whirl and sway beneath the blast. But in his temple all are praising, "Glory, glory to the Lord."
>
> At the Flood, the Lord showed his control of all creation. Now he continues to unveil his power. He will give his people strength. He will bless them with peace." (Ps. 29:1, 3–11 TLB)

Excerpt taken from *In My Father's House* by Mary Kassian (© 2005).

Faith Revived

Great is his faithfulness; his mercies begin afresh
each morning. (Lamentations 3:23 NLT)

*F*irst, God doesn't live in the past. Because God—your God—exists outside of time. To Him, the past that so haunts and hamstrings you, the past that so ruffles and frustrates you, is not in the past at all. In prayer, you are alone with a God who sees you only as you *are* and have always *been* since that beautiful moment when you placed faith in Him—holy, righteous, and blameless; past, present, and future. He forgives your guilt, removes your shame, and declares His work an established, all-the-time fact. Prayer does a complete end run around Satan's pitiful accusations, ushering us into an eternal realm with God where "the past" doesn't even compute.

And second, we only live by grace anyway. All that stuff Satan tries hanging over our head—those forgiven failings of ours are no longer reasons for shame but are now monuments to the totally amazing grace of God. I mean, just *look* at what He is able to forgive. Even this. Even that. *Yes, devil, even THAT! Isn't God incredible? That He could forgive even that?!*

The glory our God receives, and will eternally receive, from having saved our souls doesn't come from all the good things we do for Him. His glory comes from creating people of purity and spiritual passion who once did things like *that*. Like *we've* done. Like *you've* done. Like *I've* done.

So talk it up, devil. Because as high as you choose to ratchet it up, you're only showing off "the breadth and length and height and depth" (Eph. 3:18 NASB) of the love of Christ extended toward me!

Satan can be the "accuser of [the] brethren" all he wants to be (Rev. 12:10 NASB), but he can't change what the cross has done to throw all his accusations out of court—every last one of them—on an undeniably divine technicality.

Again, one of the qualities that makes the gospel so real and so great is that it doesn't eliminate our past but just so thoroughly deals with it. God forgives it. He changes it. He transforms all that mess into this huge mountain of grace that only takes us higher and closer to Him. So now, instead of being a reason for endless shame, guilt, and regret, our past is a reason for endless worship and free-flowing testimony.

And for continual, grateful, heartfelt prayer.

The truth is, there is not one of us—not one—who can't stare back into our past and wish a hundred times we'd done a hundred things differently. We're not perfect. We all struggle. We can tell from the fatigue we feel and the stiffness in our spiritual joints that we haven't always taken good care of ourselves. But prayer wakes us up with new mercies from God. Prayer is how we start to stretch and feel limber again, feel loose, ready to take on the world, our whole being fresh with energy and blood-pumping faith.

Excerpt taken from *Fervent* by Priscilla Shirer (© 2015).

Against the Grain

Nebuchadnezzar, we don't need to give you an answer to this question, If the God we serve exists, then He can rescue us from the furnace of blazing fire, and He can rescue us from the power of you, the king. (Daniel 3:16–17 HCSB)

In high school my socks were often purposefully mismatched, I wore jewelry made from silverware, and founded the Ecology Club years before it was cool to go green. Back then, it felt cool to be different. Now, however, the ways in which I am different feel less like being a free spirit and more like being a stick in the mud. Being different feels old-fashioned rather than forward thinking. Still there are times when our faith calls us to look behind us for wisdom rather than look around us for approval.

The Bible gives us good examples to follow when it comes to being countercultural. In the first chapter of Daniel, we are told that "Daniel resolved not to defile himself with the royal food and wine, and he asked the chief official for permission not to defile himself this way" (Dan. 1:8 NIV). Just imagine how popular this made Daniel with the guys. We, of course, see this as the first step in Daniel's long journey of courage. But at the time some of his friends were probably doing the Israelite version of eye-rolling. "What is Daniel trying to prove, anyway? We have lost our homeland. Why can't we just make the best of living in exile?" The difference between these two sets of people—Daniel and his fellow vegetarian teetotal-ers and those who capitulated to the ways of Babylon—was that the first group didn't *want* to feel at home among the pagans. They knew that being God's chosen people had nothing to do with geography and everything to do with their relationship to God and from that relationship flows their obedience. Daniel set himself apart not out of contempt for those around him or a desire to appear superior but rather out of a heart that looked heavenward for approval.

When we truly set our eyes on heaven, it will put us at odds with the culture around us, but if we do so in humility and faith we ultimately have nothing to fear. God may have mercy on us and choose to soften the hearts of our neighbors to the righteousness of our cause, as He did with Daniel. But then again, He may choose to test our resolve and purify us with the fire of persecution as He did Daniel's homeboys Shadrach, Meshach, and Abednego. These three showed the same kind of courage in the face of death. They chose to obey no matter what the outcome, and we should follow their example. It may mean that we attract people to ourselves in some unexpected ways, or it may mean that no one wants to sit with us at lunchtime but either way we are not really alone.

Excerpt taken from *Letting Go of Perfect* by Amy Spiegel (© 2012).

Behind Closed Doors

When Daniel learned that the document had been signed,
he went into his house. The windows in its upper room
opened toward Jerusalem, and three times a day he got
down on his knees, prayed, and gave thanks to his God,
just as he had done before. (Daniel 6:10 HCSB)

Sooner or later, for all of us, the inevitable pressures of life will reveal the truth of what's inside. Sure, external strength alone can be enough to handle some of the simpler, less demanding situations, but when the stress builds to a certain weight and downward force, the person lacking depth of integrity will snap.

When we come across a person who defies this depressing trend, we should come closer to observe. Look and learn.

Enter the prophet Daniel.

When he and his talented young friends, along with around ten thousand other Hebrews, were captured by King Nebuchadnezzar and hauled away to Babylon in 605 BC, they were threatened on numerous occasions to change their lifestyle to suit the new surroundings, to become something different from what they knew they'd been commissioned to do as followers of Israel's God.

Yet even in this new reality, Daniel refused to compromise his standards of holiness. And because no one could help but notice the superior intellect God had given him—surpassing that of even the king's most capable wise men and appointed officials—Daniel was swiftly promoted through the Babylonian ranks into positions of royal influence and service.

When the Persian Empire gained control over Babylon, toppling the power structure, Daniel was faced with the prospect of losing his prestigious career and promising outlook. Unless he wanted to risk the newfound stature he'd grown accustomed to, this might be a good time to make at least a few strategic, acceptable compromises away from the values of his upbringing.

He didn't have to wait long for the chance. When a jealous, conniving brood of officials sought to trap him by convincing King Darius to sign a decree commanding that everyone, for thirty days, direct their prayers and petitions only to the king and to no other god—punishable by death in the lions' den—Daniel had to choose. He could lower his standards temporarily, for a month. He could do his real praying in private, not out where everybody else could see it. Lead a double life to save his singular position.

But instead . . .

He didn't reformat his convictions to remain popular and accepted. He didn't hide his reverence to keep from being found out by others. He didn't alter his schedule to fold into the new dictates of the king's decree.

Rather, Daniel remained the same person behind closed doors (and open windows) as he claimed to be on the other side. Even when faced with the ultimate test—the extreme, lip-smacking pressure of the lions' den—he didn't crumble under the stress and strain. He was able to stand courageous in the face of daunting circumstances because he was "found innocent" before the Lord (Dan. 6:22 HCSB).

His integrity saved him.

Excerpt taken from *The Resolution for Women* by Priscilla Shirer (© 2011).

Remember Whose You Are

Therefore, I am going to persuade her, lead her to the wilderness, and speak tenderly to her. There I will give her vineyards back to her and make the Valley of Achor into a gateway of hope. There she will respond as she did in the days of her youth, as in the day she came out of the land of Egypt. (Hosea 2:14–15 HCSB)

The book of Hosea offers a heartbreaking glimpse into the reality of Israel's rebellion against God, like an adulterous wife who refuses the steadfast affection of her one true love. It also portrays the love and patience of the God who pursues His people, though they've done nothing but push Him away.

The covenant love of our heavenly Father toward His people is so great that our former, false loves become a forgotten memory. Our idols evaporate when exposed to the affection of our truest Love, like a morning mist that hovers over the water only to be dissolved in the light of noonday sun.

> For I will remove the names of the Baals from her mouth; they will no longer be remembered by their names. (Hosea 2:17 HCSB)

We can stop chasing lesser affections, stop trying to make ourselves worthy of love. Jesus has declared us worthy. The matter has been settled.

> "He made the One who did not know sin to be sin for us, so that we might become the righteousness of God in Him." (2 Cor. 5:21 HCSB)

The one true and holy God does not love us because we love Him. He loves us first (1 John 4:19).

He doesn't demand perfection from us, then stand, arms crossed and toe tapping, to see how we'll mess it up this time. He is patient with us, desiring for all to come to the knowledge of Him (2 Pet. 3:9; Isa. 30:18).

He made His covenant with us at the very beginning, choosing His Son to be our Savior before the foundation of the earth (1 Pet. 1:20).

In other words, God's covenant to us is not dependent on us. Not even a little bit. His guarantee is permanent, even when nothing we can muster in response is.

His love for me was sealed before He created me (Eph. 1:4–6). His love for you was set in eternal motion before you were knit together in your mother's womb (Ps. 139:13). It has been in place and upheld throughout every moment of every day of every year of our lives, generation after generation. How could it possibly depend on us?

God's covenant is true, even when we look elsewhere for love and acceptance. His covenant has been true every time you've acted out of fear and doubt. It is still true, no matter the circumstances we face or the hurt we hold in our hearts. Even when the temporary feels painfully permanent, His covenant is true.

Remember whose you are.

Excerpt taken from *She Reads Truth* by Raechel Myers and Amanda Bible Williams (© 2016).

Divine Interventions

*The word of the LORD came to Jonah son
of Amittai. (Jonah 1:1 HCSB)*

S ure, your plan was great. But there's no telling how unimagin-
ably fantastic the destination is that He's trying to get you to
follow Him toward.

Now let me pause here to say something important. By changing our terminology to call this a "divine intervention," I'm not saying God has necessarily caused it to happen. If your mate has left
you and filed for divorce, this is obviously not what the Lord
intended for your marriage. But be sure of this: God has seen it and
known about it. He has allowed this stabbing pain to enter your life
for some reason known only to His holy providence. And though
you cannot understand it or make any sense of why this is occur-
ring, you're being asked whether or not you will trust God even in
the midst of this lousy set of circumstances and surrender to what
He has allowed.

Perhaps your husband's work is such that the possibility of relo-
cating every few years is more likely than not. If you only choose to
view this as an interruption, you'll grow paralyzed with frustration.
But if you see it as a divine intervention, then your eyes will be
opened to the new opportunities open to you with each move.

Perhaps the makeup of your predominantly single-race neighborhood and part of town has begun changing to include more
immigrants and nationalities. If you and your church despise this
interruption to your settled routines and expectations, you'll no
doubt miss out on reaching the people whom God has sent you to.

But if you see it as a divine intervention, then you'll most likely realize the grand scope of God's will for your ministry.

Perhaps you only have to deal with your troubled in-laws on the rarest of occasions, but they've mentioned they'd like to come spend Thanksgiving with you this year. If you can't get over being steamed at this interruption to your plans, you'll spend your entire holiday wishing you were somewhere else. But if you see it as a divine intervention, . . . well, you may still wish you were somewhere else, but at least you could become aware of the underlying opportunity God is giving you on this "festive" occasion.

Your response at moments like these indicates whether you're going to yield to Him completely or take off like Jonah in another direction of your own choosing, ending up in an even worse place than you're in now.

If you find yourself balking at what God is asking of you today—a new responsibility, an added burden, a frightening unknown, an uncomfortable conversation to be had—it's an indication of the importance you place on Him and His will.

It's easy to say that His plans are your most essential endeavors. It's entirely another thing to live like it, to participate with Him even when what He's inviting you to do is something you don't understand and may never have chosen.

Excerpt taken from *Life Interrupted* by Priscilla Shirer (© 2011).

Life Interrupted

However, Jonah got up to flee to Tarshish from the LORD's presence. He went down to Joppa and found a ship going to Tarshish. He paid the fare and went down into it to go with them to Tarshish, from the LORD's presence. (Jonah 1:3 HCSB)

We've all been Jonah before, haven't we? We've gotten irritated. We've wanted to duck out. We've wished God would go pick on someone else for a change. So something important is still missing inside. Something is keeping us from living out what we say we believe about Him—that we can trust Him even when we don't understand, that He won't lead us astray, that His will is more important than ours.

Why do we still run from Him and His plans?

I know I don't want to let one more interruption send me off frantically dodging God's will and missing out on what He's wanting to accomplish in me and through me. I want my life to radiate what happens when God has a person's heart at His full control, when every event or circumstance is simply another avenue to know Him better and show forth His glory.

That's what Jonah's story is really all about. It's not just about the big fish—not just Jonah and "the whale." The main character in Jonah's story is God. Every single chapter—in fact, every single verse—speaks of the grandeur of God, the grace of God, the sovereignty of God, the beckoning of God, the discipline of God. Everywhere you look in this tiny piece of ancient historical literature, God is there. He's *always* there. He is right in the middle of every interruption.

So if you're feeling the pinch of the interrupted life, guess what? God is right here in the middle of yours too. This interruption— whatever it is, no matter how big or small—represents your next best chance to see Him take center stage, to show you what He can do when the unexpected only makes you more expectant than ever.

Like you I've run from change. I've run from life's surprises. Sometimes I've run just to keep moving when I didn't know what else to do. But I've run into a problem. Because in running toward what I thought was better, safer, more pleasurable, more fulfilling, less painful, less complicated, or less confining, I've actually been running from God, from His will, and from His blessing.

And I'm tired of running. Aren't you?

What if we *knew* this interrupted life was less about the problem and more about the process? What if we *knew* this roadblock or aggravation hadn't caught God by surprise even if it's come as a shock to us? What if we *knew* that the direction He was taking us provided opportunities we'd always dreamed about, even if they didn't look exactly the way we thought they would? What if we *knew*, by not getting what we want, God was ultimately giving us something better?

Excerpt taken from *Life Interrupted* by Priscilla Shirer (© 2011).

The Perfect Storm

Then the LORD hurled a violent wind on the sea, and
such a violent storm arose on the sea that the ship
threatened to break apart. (Jonah 1:4 HCSB)

Have you ever fled to "Tarshish"—someplace that feels much more exciting and inviting than doing God's will? Ever decided you'd had enough of what God expected of you and were headed off to do what you wanted for a change? Ever decided to check out emotionally on your marriage and children and quit being burdened about whether or not everybody's getting what they need from you?

Doesn't keep you happy and laid-back for long, does it?

That's because no matter how remote and relaxing, nothing fills the void of abandoned purpose. Nothing feels the same anymore when you're running from God. The freedoms that appealed to Jonah most about Tarshish would eventually become empty promises, then worse—dark, heavy regrets that would mock him the rest of his life. In Jonah 1 we find Jonah sound asleep as a storm rages around him. He didn't recognize the hopelessness he was heading for. But God certainly did and He graciously refused to let Jonah's deep sleep prevent him from experiencing His will. We've all been in storms. And then we've all been in . . . *storms!* You know, the ones where 1:00 in the afternoon looks like the middle of the night— lightning strikes, booming thunder, screaming winds, pouring rain. Jonah's storm came with that kind of fury . . . and then some.

God had already intervened in Jonah's life, inviting him to be involved in a mighty miracle of national repentance at Nineveh. And now—with Jonah thinking he'd pretty much put the kibosh on that—God intervened again. What had likely been tried as a gentle stirring in the prophet's spirit now came with thunder and lightning and the real prospect of shipwreck and death.

The perfect storm.

Because if not for *this* storm—at this particularly high level of volume and intensity—Jonah might've stayed below deck undisturbed all the way to his chosen getaway in Tarshish. God, however, couldn't bear to see this happen. Couldn't stand by while Jonah ruined his life. Couldn't remain silent while a precious child of the King took himself not only out of God's will but out from under God's blessing.

That's why He sent the storm. Not to *take* his life but to return it more fully to him.

Thank God for the storm.

When we're in the midst of a crisis—the loss seems too severe, the pain is too strong, the setback feels too final and irreversible. It's all so terribly depressing. And yet God has certainly succeeded at getting our attention, hasn't He? Anything less turbulent might not have been enough, but now He's radically changed our perspective. And in the days and years that follow, we may look back with stunned relief at how close we came to sailing off the deep end . . . if not for His stormy intervention.

Excerpt taken from *Life Interrupted* by Priscilla Shirer (© 2011).

A Divine Storm

Then they said to him, "Tell us who is to blame for this trouble we're in. What is your business and where are you from? What is your country and what people are you from?" (Jonah 1:8 HCSB)

Five questions, like weighty boulders, all being hurled at Jonah in quick succession. He probably couldn't even think fast enough to take them all in.

Yet, no doubt, the significance of these questions penetrated Jonah's heart and head. The reality of who he was, where he was from, and what he was doing must have felt like a searing weight on his rebellious conscience as the truth began dawning on him again. He could only muster enough courage to whisper from the depths of his weakened, anxious soul, "I am a Hebrew, and I fear the LORD God of heaven" (Jonah 1:9 NASB).

In declaring himself a Hebrew, Jonah couldn't help but be reminded of his connection to the one true God. This seemed to cause the ministry of God's Spirit to wash over him. His heart was overwhelmed with conviction, and he could do nothing less than proceed to spill out a laundry list of adjectives to describe the God who governs His people—the God who governed this runaway prophet, even on the sea-lane to Tarshish.

"I fear the LORD . . ."

". . . the LORD God . . ."

". . . the LORD God of heaven . . ."

The God who made the sea.

Oh, and the dry land too.

Jonah may not have been fully remorseful yet (it's clear from Jonah 4:2 that he was still hoping Nineveh would be destroyed), yet a divine storm had begun raging within him, even while the storm outside continued to rage on at sea. His journey out of danger was far, far from over. But be sure of this: *it had begun*. The change in Jonah's path from the road of rebellion to the pathway of penitence was underway.

And it all began with those first piercing questions.

Are you listening? Do you hear God's Spirit raising questions deep within you? Are there a few divine inquiries swimming around in your heart that seem to pop up at the oddest times—while you're stuck in traffic, cooking dinner, folding clothes, having a meeting? Are they dredging up some revealing answers about where you are and what you've been doing? Is He making it quite clear that what you've been hiding from others—perhaps even hiding from yourself—is not hidden at all before "the eyes of Him with whom we have to do" (Heb. 4:13 NASB)?

Don't ignore the Spirit's attempts to engage you, my friend. The conviction, the stirring, is the call of your Father, drawing you back to Himself, inviting you to put an end to your running, to start what needs to happen for things to get turned back around. Answer these—submit to these—and you'll be on the right track to healing and wholeness.

Excerpt taken from *Life Interrupted* by Priscilla Shirer (© 2011).

Grace Under Pressure

*Jonah prayed to the LORD his God from
inside the fish. (Jonah 2:1 HCSB)*

Jonah would have died, you know? Sure, three miserable days in a reeking aquarium of consequences must have scared the poor guy to death. At the time it may have seemed to him as though nothing could be worse than being buried alive in a fish's belly. But we can honestly say that if not for this big boy coming along when he did, Jonah would've died in the open water. He wouldn't have lived to see another day.

So this fish, as it turns out, had a name.

It was a fish called Grace.

We can sort of imagine how his pitch-black prison illuminated his past mistakes in all their stark, haunting reality, making it hurt for him to look at. Perhaps, quite honestly, he hadn't fully realized at the time how serious an offense it had been to resist God's call to Nineveh.

Sometimes it takes something as dire and dramatic as getting caught in a fish's belly to bring the gravity of our decisions to light.

It's a registered letter from the IRS, declaring that your tax return has been pulled for auditing—and you know you overstated your deductions by a good $10,000.

Caught.

It's the text message your spouse found on your cell phone that disclosed the secret sin you'd been hiding—maybe a touchy-feely, flirtatious relationship you've never been willing to put the brakes on.

Caught.

It's being told over lunch by a caring, concerned friend that she's noticed a real harshness and bitterness about you that wasn't there before. She just wonders if something's wrong you haven't told her. You really thought you'd done a better job of covering it.

Caught.

It's the ugly email that accidentally gets routed to the person you made the snide comment about.

Caught.

It's the lie you told to avoid keeping a commitment, before being spotted somewhere doing something else.

Caught.

It's the fish's belly God appoints for his beloved "Jonahs." Oh, the panic, the shame, the heart-racing reality when you're caught red-handed. You feel like you're not going to make it through this now that everything's out in the open, now that everything's come undone.

On the contrary, my friend, you're going to make it through this drama specifically *because* everything's come undone. This fish is designed to keep you from going under once and for all. Had God not allowed you to get caught, you would've eventually drowned for sure. But this uncomfortable outcome He's allowed is giving you a chance to catch your breath, come to your senses, and become more completely His.

It turns out, a fish's belly is really a conducive place for someone to take all the time needed to get all these things straightened out. Enough time even for repentance to occur. It certainly was for Jonah.

Excerpt taken from *Life Interrupted* by Priscilla Shirer (© 2011).

Second Chances

*Then the word of the LORD came to Jonah
a second time. (Jonah 3:1 HCSB)*

I remember well the day I was sitting by the window in our bedroom, so struck by a single verse from the book of Jonah, I found myself sliding to my knees on the floor. With my hands extended upward toward the heavens, I voiced a prayer more full of spontaneous thanks than maybe any prayer I've uttered in a long time. God was speaking, and it was powerful.

I was enthralled.

In the first place, studying the prophet's abrupt calling from God somehow mirrored the shock I had felt upon learning that our two-parent, two-kid household was about to expand by one. My third pregnancy had caught me completely off guard. Totally unexpected. My life had again become a "life interrupted," only in a more substantial way than ever before. And something about Jonah's familiar Old Testament story seemed to hold examples and answers God wanted me to apply here, in my situation.

But if I needed any more confirmation from His Spirit that this particular Bible book had something significant to say to me, it was this one special moment alone at home, set against a pivotal moment from Scripture when "the word of the LORD came to Jonah the second time" (Jonah 3:1).

Don't let the simplicity or brevity of this line disguise its depth and power.

God spoke . . . for a second time.

He specializes in second chances.

When we've messed up. When we've rebelled. When we've recoiled at the plans He's unfolded before us, we still get another chance.

And don't we all just need to know that sometimes?

I know I sure did. And still do.

- Because I am Paul—the chief of sinners.
- I am Peter—the one who's made multiple promises to God that I couldn't (or wouldn't) keep.
- I am Samuel—the person who has often required God to call out to me time and time again before I finally realized He was speaking.
- And I am Jonah—one who, even when hearing a word from God clearly, has been known to turn and run in the opposite direction.

I've been known to see Him lining up circumstances in my life, leading me in a different way than I wanted or expected, perhaps speeding up or slowing down the timetable I'd fixed in my mind, and I have sometimes rebelled against His intervention. I've seen it as nothing other than a rude, unwelcome interruption—I've often jumped to the wrong conclusions. And now, in my heart, I hadn't fully surrendered to the idea of our new baby and the changes required in this new phase of ministry God was calling us to. I wasn't doing a good job of yielding to His lordship and sovereignty. And I was ashamed of myself.

Yet God has given me a second chance. Again and again. He is truly a God of second chances.

Excerpt taken from *Life Interrupted* by Priscilla Shirer (© 2011).

Mercy Me

He has showed you, O man, what is good. And what does
the LORD require of you? To act justly and to love mercy
and to walk humbly with your God. (Micah 6:8 NIV)

I've been on a search my entire life. After accepting Christ at an early age, and then growing in my understanding through the years of what it meant to be a Christian, I began to wonder what His will for me was. I knew He had a purpose for my life but I often felt like it eluded me, as though it was always just out of reach and out of sight. As a younger woman, when I was navigating which subjects to study, which opportunities to accept, and which direction to pursue, I regularly wished that God would be more clear, more forthright, more plainly obvious about what He wanted me to do at that particular point in life.

Maybe you're wondering the same thing. In one area or another, you feel like you're just meandering, weaving aimlessly through your weeks and months, walking around with a continuous question mark floating above your head. You *want* to be in His will, but you just aren't clear what His will is. And so you wait. And keep waiting. Waiting for Him to make His will known so you can get busy doing it.

But what if the disclosure of His continued purposes for your life is at least partly dependent on your obedience to what He's *already* set before you? What if He wants to see your level of faithfulness in responding to what you *do* know before He fills you in on what you *don't*? It's like your child trying to get you to make plans for tomorrow when he hasn't yet taken care of his responsibilities for today.

Well, maybe the same idea applies in God's revelation of His will to *us*. For, yes, while some of what He retains in store for you and me is not yet known to us, some of it He has *clearly* and *explicitly* expressed. Case in point:

> He has showed you, O man, what is good. And what does
> the Lord require of you? To act justly and to love mercy
> and to walk humbly with your God. (Micah 6:8 NIV)

Doesn't get any clearer than that. "He has showed you." Never again can you say that you don't know what He "requires" of you, what His current will is for your life. Sure, there's much more to unfold, an array of details left to discover. But this much you *do* know:

1. Do justice.
2. Love mercy.
3. Walk humbly with your God.

So, sister, I ask you . . . are you doing *that?* Are you making the deliberate and conscious resolution to respond to what you absolutely know God has asked you to commit to? There's no better time to make this resolution than right this minute.

Excerpt taken from *The Resolution for Women* by Priscilla Shirer (© 2011).

Look Again

Why do You force me to look at injustice? Why do You tolerate wrongdoing? Oppression and violence are right in front of me. Strife is ongoing, and conflict escalates. (Habakkuk 1:3 HCSB)

I didn't want to see it. The images were too disturbing. The towering HD-quality screen perched overhead translated every single pixel of this devastating story into a larger-than-life reality for me, as well as for the fifteen thousand other women who were assembled there watching.

We were at a conference in Sydney, Australia, a gathering held once a year and attended by women from every corner of the globe. The convention, one of the largest of its kind, is intentional in its focus. It has become an ongoing, year-round sisterhood—a trans-global connecting of women seeking to serve Christ, pursue justice, and change humanity through specific outreach ministries.

Who can deny that this kind of active mercy is what Christ compels His church to do? And if so, why wasn't I doing it? Why wasn't I using the platform the Lord had given me to encourage women to look outside the tight orbits of their own lives and pressing concerns and see the grave suffering around them? Why wasn't American Christianity—from the best I could tell—as visibly broken by these gaping needs as believers from other countries seemed to be, some of whose nations and homelands are far less economically stable? These women, far from wanting to come for a conference for their personal edification alone, sensed a responsibility to impact culture as a result—as a goal—of their time together.

A steady chorus of gasps and sniffles resonated throughout the vast arena as the video presentation played. Tears streamed down our cheeks. We passed tissues down the rows. On more than one occasion, unable to bear any more, I had to lower my gaze momentarily to escape the visual assault.

This just couldn't be real! This kind of thing doesn't really happen. To real people. To mothers and daughters. In their own land. *Does it?*

I didn't want to see. I didn't want to look.

Seems like a God who loves us so fiercely wouldn't mind giving us a break from all this. Seems like with all we're required to shoulder in our own lives, with our own schedule and all our demanding circumstances, He'd give us a pass to look away, to ignore, to disregard. Right?

His answer to Habakkuk's question may surprise you. For after forcing the prophet to sit back and watch the suffering of his own beloved people, here's what God said to him.

> Look . . . ! Observe! Be astonished! Wonder! Because I am doing something in your days—you would not believe if you were told. (v. 5 NASB)

In other words, seeing is believing.

Diamonds are most brilliant against a blackcloth of velvet. Look. Again.

Until what takes your breath away is not the gravity of the problem but the power of God to heal it—one touch, one person at a time.

Excerpt taken from *The Resolution for Women* by Priscilla Shirer (© 2011).

A Delightful Lullaby

Yahweh your God is among you, a warrior who saves.
He will rejoice over you with gladness. He will bring
you quietness with His love. He will delight in you
with shouts of joy. (Zephaniah 3:17 HCSB)

In recent years as I have considered the aspects of God's fatherhood, Zephaniah 3:17 has become an absolute favorite verse for me. This verse says that God does three wonderful things for me. These three actions reveal His love for me in a way that touches the deep places of my soul.

He rejoices over me.

He quiets me with His love.

He joyously delights in me.

What a beautiful picture of the Father heart of God! When I read this verse, I imagine a father holding his young daughter in the middle of the night, rocking her and soothing her back to sleep with gentle, tender songs of love. The lessons reflected in this verse are profound and as tender as a lullaby.

- The Father is with you no matter how dark the night or how difficult the problem.
- He is mighty—your strong Father with whom you can feel safe and secure.
- He will save you, protecting and delivering you from the evil one.
- He delights in you; you are the pride and joy of his heart.
- He quiets you, soothing your fears and giving you confidence and peace.

- He rejoices over you with singing, with sweet songs of tender love.

Can you imagine the Father rejoicing over you with singing? He does, you know? Whenever your heart is inclined toward Him.

Delight was in God's heart when he created mankind (Prov. 8:30–31). He delighted in Abraham, Isaac, and Jacob (Deut. 10:15), and in David (2 Sam. 22:20). In contrast, He did not delight in Saul's outward appearance of religiosity (1 Sam. 15:22). Nor does He delight in those who do evil (Mal. 2:17). The Father delights in all those whose hearts are inclined toward Him to obey His Word.

The following list represents some of the attitudes that the Father delights in. As you read each one, consider whether you honestly try to have that particular attitude in your life. He delights in those who:

- Seek to obey his voice (1 Sam. 15:22)
- Have a teachable spirit (Prov. 3:12)
- Have a broken and contrite heart (Ps. 51:16–17)
- Try to walk blamelessly (Prov. 11:20)
- Deal truthfully (Prov. 12:22)
- Pray with an upright heart (Prov. 15:8)
- Demonstrate mercy (Micah 7:18)
- Demonstrate kindness, justice, and righteousness (Jer. 9:24)

The Father delights in all those children who are living as members of His family. Have you accepted the fact that the Father delights in you? He sings over you lullabies of love.

Beware of letting the legalistic lie that you can please God with your good works cloud the issue. The Father delights in his children. His delight has nothing to do with any virtue or greatness in the child but only because of His great love and faithfulness. He is, after all, the ultimate good Father.

Excerpt taken from *In My Father's House* by Mary Kassian (© 2005).

Timing Is Everything

These people say, "The time has not come for the house of the LORD to be rebuilt." The word of the LORD came through Haggai the prophet: "Is it a time for you yourselves to live in your paneled houses, while this house lies in ruins?" (Haggai 1:2–4 HCSB)

Sometimes we get so caught up giving our best that we don't stop to consider if we're giving our best toward what *God* wants us to be doing.

This balancing act took center stage during the latter part of the Old Testament, after a remnant of the Hebrews had returned to their native homeland from exile. The Lord spoke to them through the prophet Haggai, questioning the priorities they were demonstrating. The order in which they were choosing to rebuild both their nation and their lives was off-kilter. While the temple lay in ruins and disrepair, the people were spending considerable time and resources on the rebuilding of their own lavish dwellings.

They were likely feeling an incredible release of pent-up emotions, having been held for years against their will as a subjugated people group in a foreign land. This chance to start fresh—despite the many challenges of reclaiming a land gone to seed—must have come with an intoxicating sense of excitement as they sought to reestablish their own little corner of the world.

Their desire to give time and attention to the rebuilding of their own homes was understandable. It was even honorable. Why then did God express such concern?

He wasn't concerned with *what* they were doing as much as *when* they were choosing to get it done. See if you can detect the pattern:

- "This people say, 'The *time* has not come . . .'"
- ". . . even the *time* for the house of the Lord to be rebuilt."
- "Is it *time* for you yourselves to dwell in paneled houses while this house lies desolate?"

Rebuilding the destroyed temple (and thereby restoring the worship of God to a place of prominence in their lives) was obviously of greater priority to Him *at that particular moment* than construction of their elaborate dwellings. He wasn't saying their homes didn't matter. But the time for concentrating their efforts on their own houses was for later, not for now. Now was the season to focus on the house of God, to concentrate primarily on what God was telling them to do *today*.

As you're able to determine what you're current priorities should be, and as you're obedient in setting other things aside for the time being, don't fret that you'll never again have the opportunity to spend time pursuing them. Whatever moment you're living in will cue you toward the responsibilities that are inherent for you in this time and space.

Give yourself permission to say no to certain things that are not really yours to carry right now. And force yourself to delay certain things that aren't your primary mission for this moment. In doing so, you'll find that every *yes* comes with a lot more freedom and fulfillment.

Excerpt taken from *The Resolution for Women* by Priscilla Shirer (© 2011).

Covenant-Keeping God

Because, I, Yahweh, have not changed, you descendants
of Jacob have not been destroyed. (Malachi 3:6 HCSB)

I hear these phrases often coming from my children:

"But you *never* let me . . ."

"But she *always* gets to . . ."

"He *never* has to . . ."

"She *always* does that . . ."

The only truth to the "always and never" statements is that we, as humans, always and never "always and never." We will always be inconsistent. God, on the other hand, can truly say He "always" and He "nevers." He is always consistent. He is never inconsistent.

In His immutability and eternal existence, He has never needed anything or anyone. He did not create humans because He was lonely. He just wanted to. He didn't call a people for Himself through Abraham, Isaac, and Jacob because He needed them to worship Him. He just decided to show His unchanging nature to and through them. And against all appearances, He didn't change His mind toward His people, nor did He renege on His promise to them.

> God spoke to Moses and said to him, "I am the LORD. I appeared to Abraham, to Isaac and to Jacob, as God Almighty, but by my name the LORD I did not make myself known to them. I also established my covenant with them to give them the land of Canaan, the land in

which they lived as sojourners. Moreover, I have heard the groaning of the people of Israel whom the Egyptians hold as slaves, and I have remembered my covenant. Say therefore to the people of Israel, 'I am the LORD, and I will bring you out from under the burdens of the Egyptians, and I will deliver you from slavery to them, and I will redeem you with an outstretched arm and with great acts of judgment. I will take you to be my people, and I will be your God, and you shall know that I am the LORD your God, who has brought you out from under the burdens of the Egyptians. I will bring you into the land that I swore to give to Abraham, to Isaac, and to Jacob. I will give it to you for a possession. I am the LORD.'" (Exod. 6:2–8 ESV)

God introduced Himself to the patriarchs and established His covenant with them as God Almighty, El Shaddai. But it was when His beloved people were enslaved, broken down, crying in their despair, wondering if God had forgotten them, that He chose to make Himself known as Yahweh, "I AM WHO I AM."

He's assuring them, not only am I the covenant-making God, I am the covenant-keeping God.

This isn't just any god, this is the God who doesn't give up. This is the God who heard His people's groaning and remembered His covenant with them. He sent plagues, parted seas, and displayed His strength in redeeming His people. Nothing could stand in His way, not even the grumbling of His children.

Excerpt taken from *Steadfast Love* by Lauren Chandler (© 2016).

Remember the Lord

Then those who feared the LORD spoke with one another.
The LORD paid attention and heard them, and a book of
remembrance was written before him of those who feared
the LORD and esteemed his name. (Malachi 3:16 ESV)

Several years ago I had a really interesting conversation with my mother-in-law about the book of Malachi.

She told me she loved the idea that there was a record of the way they "remembered" the Lord, and the fact that it was important enough to God that He took the time to notate it. In the book of Revelation we are told that there are "books" opened as the dead are judged (20:12), and she wondered if this was one of the books referenced. We don't know what they are for certain because Scripture doesn't identify any of them by name (with the exception of the book of life), but I agreed with her that it was an amazing image. A giant scrapbook of sorts, including all the moments in our life that we remembered the Lord, or deliberately chose to recognize Him.

I love that visual because it encourages me to make the conscious decision to remember. I think there are a couple other interesting things about this particular verse, namely that these were people who feared the Lord. We need to remember that the book of Malachi was written in a time when the Israelites were living lives that did not honor God. Essentially, most of the people had stopped concerning themselves with the consequences of sin and were just doing whatever they wanted. There was obviously a group of people who chose not to go with the masses and encouraged one another in their desire to live holy lives in light of their fear of God. I love that they got together and made a point of talking with one another about their convictions. There is still a lot of wisdom in choosing to surround ourselves with people who also fear God and will hold us accountable and encourage us as we try to do the same.

The circumstances are different, but we, too, live in a society where we have become so self-sufficient that we don't always feel like we need God to sustain us.

It is so crucial that we have a group of people we can count on to remind us of our need for God. We get so caught up in what the world can do for us that we start to think we can do it on our own, and the greatest tragedies of life come when we turn from Him and rely on ourselves. If you have people around you who will allow you to walk in the opposite direction of God's commandments without confrontation, I suggest you find some that can love you better. That goes for us as observers too; if we are in the presence of sin and we don't act, then we need to consider our own hearts as well.

Let us nudge each other often to remember the Lord.

Excerpt taken from *What Women Fear* by Angie Smith (© 2011).

Your Biggest Fan

"They will be Mine," says the LORD *of Hosts, "a*
special possession on the day I am preparing. I will
have compassion on them as a man has compassion on
his son who serves him." (Malachi 3:17 HCSB*)*

One year my son was on an ice hockey team called the Green Gators. While some of the fathers were coaching the boys in hockey skills, one particularly enthusiastic mom was coaching the remaining parents in how to be good fans. She organized us into one of the most boisterous cheering squads minor hockey has ever seen.

We waved green and gold pompoms. We stamped our feet. We chanted, did the wave and our Gator Snap. More than once during a game, the eyes of the players from both teams, as well as all the coaches and referees, were directed with fascination toward the stands, where middle-aged women dressed in baggy sweatshirts were exuberantly doing the Macarena. (I hope there is no video footage to commemorate the event!)

Although I took part in cheering for the Gators team, the real reason I was there was my son. It was he whom my eyes followed as he skated around the ice. It was he who really thrilled my heart when he scored. And my heart froze, gripped with fear, when the body that went into the boards and lay motionless on the ice was his. (Don't worry, he was okay. Hip-hip-Hooray!).

If it weren't for my boy, I wouldn't have been at all those games. If it weren't for him, I would not have cared about the Gators. (And I certainly wouldn't have been doing the Macarena!)

I am my son's number one fan. He may not ever make the NHL, but he is the absolute best in my eyes. Of course he is! He is my child. And my heart belongs to him forever in a way that it does not belong to anyone else.

God the Father is your number one fan. His eyes are continually on you. He is thrilled when you play the best you can. And when you manage to score a goal, He and the throngs of angels in heaven cheer.

His heart is gripped when you fall. He is right with you, comforting you. He will encourage you and coach you and help you get back in the game.

The heart of the Father belongs to His children in a way that it does not belong to anyone else. Malachi 3:17 tells us that his children are His special and cherished treasure.

The Father is undeniably for you. He's your biggest fan. He delights in you. You are His treasure. He rejoices over you. He is totally committed to your happiness and well-being. And if God is for you, who can be against you? (Rom. 8:31).

Thank Him for His devotion to you and delight in you. Ask Him for increased confidence to spread your wings and fly higher, knowing that He's always nearby rooting for you.

Excerpt taken from *In My Father's House* by Mary Kassian (© 2005).

Cleaning House

Therefore produce fruit consistent with
repentance. (Matthew 3:8 HCSB)

One of my favorite television programs is *Clean House* on the Style Network. Ever seen it? They locate a family whose household clutter has pretty much overtaken their ability to function. Then the zany host and her team swoop in to help them tackle their heaping load of challenges.

While a handyman builds new shelves to store all the things that are currently strewn haphazardly across the floor and furniture, a decorator begins sorting through whatever he can find to incorporate into a new overall design scheme. A professional organizer sifts through mounds of papers and supplies to figure out the best way to systematize the chaos, while a yard sale expert hunts for stuff to sell on the front lawn. Each half-hour episode captures the enormity of the task and makes it highly entertaining to watch, even though it looks like a nightmare to actually do.

During the final minutes of each telecast, the owners return home, surprised to find their familiar rooms and corners completely organized, gorgeously decorated, and squeaky-clean, rid of all the debilitating junk and disorder that once weighed the place down. They are always stunned beyond belief to see the transformation that's occurred in the short time they've been gone. What had seemed so impossible to overcome has now been restored to manageability and freedom.

They feel like they've gotten their lives back.

The host never leaves these excited people behind, however, without addressing the amount of upkeep required to maintain all the work that's been done. She explains to the family that her team is now leaving, and the responsibility for keeping this house a livable home is up to the people who actually live there. If they want their house to stay clean, organized, and comfortable for friends and guests, they must make some changes to the way they operate.

They must choose to live differently.

And the same could be said for every one of us, as far as our personal lives are concerned. Just because we've *acknowledged our sin, accepted our discipline, and asked God's forgiveness,* the greatest blessings of repentance will continue to linger out there unrealized and beyond our grasp if—even after all of that, after doing all three of those things so well—we just end up going back to our old ways of living. Repentance requires walking down a different path, cooperating with God's Spirit to maintain what He has been working so hard to drain out of us.

We cannot stop at merely knowing and agreeing with God that we've taken a turn in the wrong direction. We must now *act in conjunction with God's direction.*

Instead of thinking of repentance like a single stop on the map, we see that repentance is four-wheel drive. Repentance means getting off at the first exit on the road out of town, turning the car around as quickly as possible, and steering ourselves onto the road coming back toward the life God has called us to.

Excerpt taken from *Life Interrupted* by Priscilla Shirer (© 2011).

When Loneliness Is Your Teacher

"This is my beloved Son, with whom I am
well pleased." (Matthew 3:17 ESV)

These are the words God the Father spoke just before Jesus was led into the wilderness. Jesus was baptized and the heavens literally opened up. The Spirit of God came down like a dove, and God's voice boomed approval from heaven. Talk about a spiritual high! But in a heartbeat, Jesus was led into the wilderness where He faced forty days of intense trial.

When reading about Jesus' forty days of testing in Matthew 4, I always imagined it as some sort of spiritual intensive. Jesus hung out by the campfire, sang worship songs, and occasionally got into a battle of wits with the Devil. Sounds like good ol' church camp stuff to me. But that's not what the wilderness was about.

The wilderness is the area that surrounded the Dead Sea. It was thirty-five miles long and fifteen miles wide with almost no drinkable water. Because of this, birds were known to drop out of the sky dead mid-flight if they attempted to cross. The ancient Jews called this spot "The Devastation." Not exactly worship songs by the campfire, if you ask me.

This nickname alone provides tremendous context for the forty days Jesus spent in the wilderness. This wasn't a serene camping trip. It wasn't a personal retreat. Jesus' time in "The Devastation" was a time of anguishing trials. My hunch is that it was also a season of intense loneliness.

Jesus did encounter Satan three times in those forty days. I think I can say with certainty that those interactions didn't ease the loneliness of this season for Jesus. Sometimes encounters with those who know us but aren't on our side are the loneliest encounters of all.

Matthew 4:11 tells us that Jesus was joined at one point by angels sent to minister to Him. All of heaven knew what was at stake. When the lonely season was over, it was the presence of the supernatural that Jesus needed most. Pay attention to that. There's a lesson to be learned.

Jesus' time in the wilderness is the first lonely season we read about from His life, but it was not the last. Chronic loneliness doesn't have to be a part of the human condition, but it seems that seasonal loneliness does. That's the cloud, but I believe there is a silver lining.

Hebrews 4:15 reminds us that Jesus is not a God who is unfamiliar with our experiences. This includes seasons of loneliness. He has been there. He has walked a mile in your lonely shoes and as we look at how He walked, loneliness takes on a new role. I've said that much of our loneliness is self-imposed. Jesus is different from us in this way, but if we will study how Jesus responded in seasons of loneliness, loneliness becomes our teacher, showing us how to connect with God and others in the way we were designed.

•

Excerpt taken from *Connected* by Erin Davis (© 2016).

When Temptation Comes

Then Jesus was led up by the Spirit into the wilderness to be tempted by the Devil. After He had fasted for 40 days and 40 nights, He was hungry. (Matthew 4:1–2 HCSB)

Christ was on the cusp of His earthly ministry when His loving Father took Him into the desert. The road ahead would be fraught with difficulty and trepidation, but it would yield immeasurable fruit.

Right on cue, Satan showed up.

"If You are the Son of God, tell these stones to become bread" (v. 3 HCSB).

The enemy called Jesus' identity into question and appealed to His instinctive desire for food. He wanted Jesus to doubt His true identity and cave to entitlement. Satan has no new tricks. He held out forbidden fruit to Jesus, but this time it was bread. And unlike Adam and Eve, Jesus remained firm in who He is and resisted presumption.

"It is written, 'Man must not live on bread alone'" (v. 4 HCSB).

And the devil took him up and showed him all the kingdoms of the world in a moment of time, and said to him, "I will give You their splendor and all this authority because it has been given to me, and I can give it to anyone I want. If You, then, will worship me, all will be Yours" (Luke 4:6–7 HCSB).

Of course, the blameless Son of God responded, "It is written, 'Worship the Lord your God and serve Him only'" (v. 8 HCSB).

Satan made one more attempt to trip up the Savior. He recited a twisted version of Scripture to hook Him. Taking Him up to the pinnacle of the temple in Jerusalem, he said, "If You are the Son of God, throw Yourself down from here. For it is written: 'He will give His angels orders concerning you, to protect you, and they will support you with their hands, so that you will not strike your foot against a stone'" (vv. 9–11 HCSB).

The Word made flesh was not thrown for a loop. He saw through the enemy's scheme. He used Scripture to interpret Scripture (v. 12 HCSB).

The record of Christ's temptation shows us a few things. It shows us how God might use temptation (although He is never the author of it) to further root our identity in Him, uproot entitlement, strengthen our desire to be about His glory, and burn Scripture into our hearts for the impending season. If you're in the midst of a desert, be looking for these evidences of God's work in your life. Be encouraged that He might be leading you through a time of suffering or wilderness so that you may bear much fruit in a time of ministry.

We can be encouraged that when we inevitably give in to the temptations that come our way, there was One who did not. We can claim His righteousness as our own because we know we have none apart from Him.

Excerpt taken from *Steadfast Love* by Lauren Chandler (© 2016).

The Other Perspective

*Then the Devil took Him to the holy city, had Him stand
on the pinnacle of the temple, and said to Him, "If You are
the Son of God, throw Yourself down. For it is written: He
will give His angels orders concerning you, and they will
support you with their hands so that you will not strike your
foot against a stone." Jesus told him, "It is also written: Do
not test the Lord your God." (Matthew 4:5–7 HCSB)*

Here we find Jesus at the second of three temptations by Satan.
The Devil has brought Jesus to the very center of religious life,
the temple in Jerusalem.

It should not surprise us that Satan knows Scripture. He often
knows it better than we do. For some reason, he thought he could
outwit the Word who became flesh with His own words. Even we
can see that the Scripture he quoted was out of context and being
improperly used. Of course, Jesus saw that, too. Instead of arguing
with the Devil, Jesus simply quoted Scripture that repelled the per-
version of Scripture.

When studying this second temptation, we often put ourselves
in the place of Jesus. We think, "I need to know God's Word well so
that I can know when Satan is twisting it." That is a great lesson to
learn from this event. It is important to know God's Word so we can
resist Satan's schemes to get us to sin and disrespect God. However,
do we ever put ourselves in Satan's place in this story and see what
lessons we can learn from that perspective?

Like the Devil, we too try to manipulate God. We do it with
prayer, with empty promises, with Scripture, and with challenges.
Most of us are guilty of praying a prayer similar to, "God, if You give

me a better job, I will tell all my new coworkers about You," or, "If You will just make my chronic pain go away, I will start a ministry to help other people with this problem. I couldn't possibly do it now." Or we might use His Word to try to get Him to do something. "God, Your Word says, 'Sons are indeed a heritage from the LORD, children, a reward'" (Ps. 127:3 HCSB). I have followed You and served You. Therefore, You should reward me with children." Or we try to challenge or test Him, like Satan did. "God, if you are all-powerful, then get me a better job. Heal my mom. Make my kids obey me. You can do anything, after all." In our finite minds, we are trying to bargain with the infinite Creator.

God sees through our schemes as we see through the infantile requests and manipulations from children. We cannot trick Him any more than Satan could trick Jesus. We need to be honest with God with our requests. He already knows what we need, and He responds and demonstrates His love for us.

Excerpt taken from *100 Days in the Gospels* (© 2016).

No Other Gods

Again, the Devil took Him to a very high mountain and showed Him all the kingdoms of the world and their splendor. And he said to Him, "I will give You all these things if You will fall down and worship me." Then Jesus told him, "Go away, Satan! For it is written: Worship the Lord your God, and serve only Him." Then the Devil left Him, and immediately angels came and began to serve Him. (Matthew 4:8–11 HCSB)

Idolatry is rampant. People seem to jump from one belief system to another on nothing but a whim or simply out of boredom. Worshipping just one god is nearly a thing of the past.

Missionaries who work with Hindu people talk about the difficulty of getting them to worship only the one true God. Many will easily accept Jesus as a "little-g" god, but they simply add Him to their collection of deities. They figure it won't hurt to add another god to the list of those they pray to and count on for various things.

But don't many Christians do the same thing? Jesus is just another god we put on our mantel of deities. We have introduced to our daily lives other idols, other objects of worship, and other false gods to serve. The One who created all now sits quietly among the gods of this world.

"Who and what are these other gods?" you may ask. Wealth. Sports. Status. Pleasure. Television. Social media. Kids. Grandkids. Church.

"I don't worship these!" you might exclaim. Perhaps not consciously, but many of us have given into a type of idolatry. There are some who treat sport teams and star players as objects of worship. There are those who idolize their children or grandchildren.

"But those things are important!" you say. "Especially kids!" Of course kids are important, but consider the parents who let all other relationships and ministry and attention to any semblance of a spiritual life go by the wayside because their sole focus is on their kids. Or think about the grandparents who expect their grandkids to fulfill them in a way only Jesus can.

Others idolize marriage. They think if only they were married, they'd be fulfilled. Or if only their husband or wife would do this or that, like their friend's spouse does, life would be perfect. Again, they're looking for a human to fill a spot only God should fill.

The idol that can be the hardest to spot is church, which might seem like an odd idol. But it's not uncommon for believers to look to church attendance or volunteerism as the most important thing in their lives. They seek human accolades and a feeling of accomplishment for diligently serving God instead of serving Him out of love.

Determine in your heart to make God the only god in your life. Reflect on what other things might be taking His place in your heart, and then remove them from His rightful spot.

Excerpt taken from *100 Days in the Gospels* (© 2016).

Immediately

While walking by the Sea of Galilee, he saw two brothers,
Simon (who is called Peter) and Andrew his brother, casting a
net into the sea, for they were fishermen. And he said to them,
"Follow me, and I will make you fishers of men." Immediately
they left their nets and followed him. (Matthew 4:18–20 ESV)

One of my favorite stories in the entire Bible is in Matthew 14, and it involves Peter. The short version is that Jesus told Peter to walk on water, so he stepped out of the boat in faith. He did okay for a little bit. Step by step he got closer to the Lord. But then he realized the waves were huge, and he doubted. He started to drown.

But then "Jesus immediately reached out his hand and took hold of him" (Matt. 14:31 ESV). *Immediately.* It's the same word used to describe how Peter responded when he first heard the voice of the Lord. Remember? He immediately dropped his net to follow. No dilly-dallying. Jesus called out to him, and he responded right away.

Does it surprise you that Jesus chose a man like Peter to be a "rock" of the faith? After all, let's not forget the epic failure Peter had yet to experience as his faith was challenged in the middle of the sea. Not long after he'd find himself at a dinner with Jesus washing his feet—the same dinner where Jesus told Peter he'd soon deny Him three times in one day. Peter passionately argues not just, "I won't do that, Lord," but "I WOULD RATHER DIE!"

I can't help but wince when I read those words, because as we know, he did deny Christ three times. And when he heard the rooster crow, he remembered the Lord's words, weeping bitterly at his betrayal. It was just hours after Jesus had washed his feet. And as the Lord was beaten, hung to die, and lay lifeless in a cave, was Peter weeping over his actions somewhere else that night?

Have you ever felt the kind of shame that says you're not worthy to be near God—maybe not even good enough to come near the cross? I'm afraid the enemy of our souls wouldn't have it any other way.

Regardless of where Peter was during Jesus' crucifixion and death, his denial of Christ wasn't the last we heard from him. In fact, Peter became a great evangelist, boldly proclaiming the name of Christ to people everywhere. When Mary Magdalene ran to tell the apostles news of the risen Christ, many didn't believe her. "But Peter rose and ran to the tomb; stooping and looking in, he saw the linen cloths by themselves; and he went home marveling at what had happened" (Luke 24:12 ESV).

I'd imagine he went immediately, wouldn't you?

Christ is real. And that means there's still a chance for us to dedicate the rest of our lives to Him—no matter how many times we've failed in the past. No matter many times we've denied Him in word or action.

Excerpt taken from *Mended* by Angie Smith (© 2012).

Leave a Mark

In the same way, let your light shine before men, so
that they may see your good works and give glory to
your Father in heaven. (Matthew 5:16 HCSB)

Sometimes you leave a legacy unintentionally, what seems small and ordinary to you is a lifeline for someone else. I only knew Kim from online, the way friendships these days blossom out of Facebook and forums. We both had February due dates and so our lives followed the same pattern of pregnancy cross-country with overlapping morning sickness and blurry sonogram pictures popping up in our news feeds on the same weeks. Our stories were in sync until week twenty-four, when Kim spontaneously went into labor and gave birth to her daughter whom she named Maelani Rose. I pulled up her pictures on Caring Bridge to show my husband, fingers on one hand trailing over the screen while my other hand curved protectively around my stomach. "It's like if I were to give birth right now," I said and we sat somber at the thought. Jeff and I followed her Caring Bridge updates every day, hoping that her daughter would survive and talking about how we did not even realize that someone could go into labor that early.

One week after Maelani Rose was born, I gave birth to Scarlette.

It was because of Maelani that I went to the doctor on that ordinary Wednesday. I did not have any signs of preterm labor. I had a weird feeling and the memory of Maelani lingering in my mind. Maelani's story saved my daughter's life. Shortly after Scarlette's birth, Maelani passed away. I cannot begin to tell you why one baby lives in body while another lives only in spirit. I do not know the

Author's purpose for this in the Story. I would not write it this way. I would give us all the happy ending in the here and now. I would be like that scene in *Bruce Almighty*, where Jim Carey answers "YES!" to everyone's prayers and millions of people win the lottery. (My love language is clearly gift-giving.) So no, I do not understand. I cannot make sense of it. But what I do know, emphatically and without question, is that it was because Kim shared her story that we were able to give our daughter a chance at survival. She will never know, though I've tried to articulate it, how deeply indebted to her I feel.

We leave our mark on this world no matter how small our stories seem. Maelani lived for one week and altered the course of my entire existence. My grandmother's funeral was held at one of the largest churches in our area at the time, and it could not hold the people who came to honor the life of a woman who worked at JCPenney. On Easter weekend, no less. Her story might have seemed small, but she blessed her community quietly and consistently and it became epic.

You did not know her.

But you do now.

Excerpt taken from *Anchored* by Kayla Aimee (© 2015).

Serve, Sacrifice, Love

"Be careful not to practice your righteousness in front of people, to be seen by them. Otherwise, you will have no reward from your Father in heaven." (Matthew 6:1 HCSB)

I don't know if you're like me, but every night as I climb into bed I have the same conversation with myself, and it starts with these four words: "Did I do enough?" Before I know it I am tangled up in the memories of the day, from the nods I gave to the kids in place of conversation, to the dishes piled high in the sink, to the phone calls I forgot to make and on and on. I torment myself with regret, apologizing to the Lord (and often others) about my shortcomings.

I want to walk away from today and every other day with the sense that I knew and fulfilled my purpose. As a writer, I can't help but see my life in a series of pages, all torn up and stapled together in a heap with the hope that there will be more days that were noteworthy than not. If I step back it's easy to see why the pages don't seem to matter; just scribbles on a page that had the potential to be beautiful.

More often than not I spend my time on what I *wish* I had done with the kids, what I *wanted* to do in my time with the Lord, the impact I *could* have had if I would have just gotten my act together. And the image of tattered pages, fresh with intention and promise, can haunt me long into the night.

It's so easy to believe the voice that tells us we could have been better. You know that voice, right? I, for one, can become so affected by these doubts about myself that I can't seem to tap into whatever it is that I'm supposed to be doing. I have moments that would certainly get a gold star; brief snippets in a day where I feel like I hit the nail on the head. I have many, many more moments that I want to cross off, rewrite, or erase. It's like a constant tipping of the scales—sometimes in my favor and other times not.

We long to be significant in this world and we feel desperately inadequate when we aren't. Yet, may I suggest to us that our primary problem isn't really the objective contribution we make to the world around us?

The bigger issue is whom I have placed in the front row of my audience.

We are significant in our insignificance, urged to have the faith of a child and the heart of a servant. And be assured, friend, that you are loved in a way that is infinitely different than any love you could know here on earth. It is the love of a Man who had the chance to exert His importance in the eyes of the world, and instead did exactly what He calls us to do.

Serve, sacrifice, love.

And be made great for His glory.

Excerpt taken from *What Women Fear* by Angie Smith (© 2011).

How to Give Well

"Be careful not to practice your righteousness in front of people, to be seen by them. Otherwise, you will have no reward from your Father in heaven. So whenever you give to the poor, don't sound a trumpet before you, as the hypocrites do in the synagogues and on the streets, to be applauded by people. I assure you: They've got their reward! But when you give to the poor, don't let your left hand know what your right hand is doing, so that your giving may be in secret. And your Father who sees in secret will reward you." (Matthew 6:1–4 HCSB)

One of the most difficult things in life is to be unnoticed. We want people to notice us, and this has never been more obvious than in this era of social media. How often do we post a picture of an amazing vacation spot, our kids doing something cute, or our trendy new living room design, hoping to get a bunch of "likes" and comments?

Barely a day goes by when we don't see an article in the news or a social media post about a celebrity who gave $20,000 to a charity or visited cancer patients in a children's hospital. We may roll our eyes, thinking that $20,000 to them is equal to $20 to us. Or we wonder if they're visiting those kids just for the photo op and publicity.

But don't we often do the same? Our small group serves a meal at a homeless shelter, and twenty pictures show up on Instagram. Or our child sets up a lemonade stand, giving the $5 earned to a charity, and we brag about it on our Facebook page. Or we see a stranger with a flat tire and stop to help, and we "live tweet" the entire experience.

We aren't always looking for a parade in our honor, but a digital "pat on the back" never hurts. Right? Wrong.

As Jesus taught on the life of faith, He reminded us that giving must be done simply for the sake of giving. When done for show, approval, or applause, it ruins the purpose. Rather than focusing on the one in need, we ask everyone to focus on us.

This passage in Matthew's Gospel is clear. We should be givers. In fact, our heavenly Father wants to reward us for doing so. Just as He looks after the poor and the outcast, so should His people. Jesus gives us the necessary guidance on how to live well.

The key Jesus points to is to give quietly or, perhaps, even anonymously. As we mature in our faith, this kind of giving allows us to not be the center of attention. By growing up, we will place others before the Lord for their needs to be met. As He makes use of us in the work, we find our full reward in our relationship with Him.

Excerpt taken from *100 Days in the Gospels* (© 2016).

Resisting Temptation

*"And lead us not into temptation, but deliver us
from the evil one." (Matthew 6:13 NIV)*

on't touch that! You don't know where it's been!"

I wonder how many little kids have heard their parents say something similar, usually while lunging across the playground or the sandbox, horrified at their son's or daughter's unsanitary sense of curiosity.

I know I'm not your mama. But I do think of you as a friend. And when it comes to the enemy's specific, strategic, most enticing temptations against you and against your purity, I hope you'll imagine me as a blur coming up fast in your peripheral vision, calling out to you with an urgent voice, both arms waving wildly, "DON'T! TOUCH! THAT!" . . . because both of us know *exactly* where's it's been.

That enticing temptation that tickles your curiosity, piques your interest, and placates your personal proclivities has been festering in the devil's sick, sinister mind all morning, all week, all year maybe. Just sitting there, soaking up vileness and filth. Cruelty and conspiracy. Waiting for the right time—the moment when you are most weakened and susceptible to attack. But once he's cleaned it up for presentation, sliding it meticulously into view, you'd think it was the shiniest, most desirable bit of unclaimed satisfaction you've ever seen. He sets it out there where your eyes can't help but be drawn toward it—at least, you know, to pick it up and look at it. Feel it. Play with it.

The moral compromise. The unhealthy habit. The enticing addiction. The allure toward sexual impurity. Do you think their uncanny ability to show up when you happen to be exhausted or hungry or lonely is just coincidence? Don't you detect some design at work in the timing, the placement, the package?

Look at what we know from Satan's temptation of Christ in Matthew 4. The devil came out into the wilderness where Jesus had been fasting for forty days, a time when (physically speaking) the Lord was hungry, alone, tired, depleted. What better setup and situation to make the suggestion of, well . . . bread? I mean, I don't know about you, but slide a warm roll in my direction, topped with a smear of soft butter, and I'm a goner. Even when I'm *not* hungry. But that's the enemy's way. Precision, personalization, and persistence. He's always scouting for what Luke's Gospel describes as the "opportune time" (4:13 NASB)—the moment when a well-placed temptation is most likely to be its most irresistible.

So again I ask—the devil's temptations, the ones he picks out and personalizes for you . . . coincidence? Uncalculated? Just happenstance?

Stop and see what's happening. Stop at the place where you first recognize the scent of temptation in the air. And before you touch it, remember . . . *remember where it's been.* Remember where it came from and who's behind it. And if it's one of those repeat temptations you've been battling against for years, remember the places it's taken you . . . the places it *always* ends up taking you. Because as soon as you say yes to it, you're headed there again.

And you know it.

Excerpt taken from *Fervent* by Priscilla Shirer (© 2015).

The Wrong Kind of Treasure

*For where your treasure is, there your heart
will be also. (Matthew 6:21 HCSB)*

The word *materialism* might bring to mind large houses filled with luxury furnishings and a jet-set lifestyle far beyond the reach of our income bracket. But while our checking account balance may not reach the sky, the god of materialism is more than willing to bend low and touch our more modest spending habits. When we allow our material comforts to crowd out our spiritual priorities, we are seeking the wrong treasure.

Some of us desire not to spend money but to save it, squirreling away for the financial winters that may pop up now and again. Being fiscally responsible certainly isn't sinful; rather it is prudent and wise. But hoarding cash far beyond that which you need in order to create a safety net against disaster, relying on your monetary discipline rather than God's provision, is neither prudent nor wise. While we may use the resources God has given in order to provide for ourselves and those in our care, we must always be mindful that our ultimate security lies with God, not our savings.

Not all materialism takes the form of spending money. Love of comfort doesn't have to be displayed with cold, hard cash. It can be finding time to make brownies and run to the store, but not to call a friend or write an encouraging e-mail. Our time is a great resource for good in this world, and it is something we have all been given. They say time is money and while my time is not billed by the hour, it is limited. How I "spend" it says a great deal about what I value most.

This may seem a bit harsh, but then God's commands often are. Consider Jesus' conversation with the man dubbed "The Rich Young Ruler." The guy came to Jesus and basically said, "Hey Jesus, what do I need to do in order to get into heaven?" Jesus gave him a list of dos and don'ts, at which point Mr. Rich Young Ruler must be feeling pretty good. He has done all those things. And then Jesus lowered the bomb. "If you want to be perfect, go, sell your possessions and give to the poor, and you will have treasure in heaven. Then come, follow me" (Matt. 19:21 NIV). Ouch. At this point I think I might be tempted to settle for less than perfection and I guess so was Mr. RYR. Matthew tells us that "When the young man heard this, he went away sad, because he had great wealth" (Matt. 19:22 NIV).

While we may not be called to literally sell everything we own, we are still seeking after that which the Rich Young Ruler sought—salvation. If this is truly our goal, then we must be willing to give up anything in order to obtain it. It isn't the object itself that hinders, but rather our unwillingness to lay it down.

Excerpt taken from *Letting Go of Perfect* by Amy Spiegel (© 2012).

The Remedy for Anxiety

"No one can be a slave of two masters, since either he will hate one and love the other, or be devoted to one and despise the other. You cannot be slaves of God and of money.

"This is why I tell you: Don't worry about your life, what you will eat or what you will drink; or about your body, what you will wear. Isn't life more than food and the body more than clothing? Look at the birds of the sky: They don't sow or reap or gather into barns, yet your heavenly Father feeds them. Aren't you worth more than they? Can any of you add a single cubit to his height by worrying? And why do you worry about clothes? Learn how the wildflowers of the field grow: they don't labor or spin thread. Yet I tell you that not even Solomon in all his splendor was adorned like one of these! If that's how God clothes the grass of the field, which is here today and thrown into the furnace tomorrow, won't He do much more for you—you of little faith? So don't worry, saying, "What will we eat?" or "What will we drink?" or "What will we wear?" For the idolaters eagerly seek all these things, and your heavenly Father knows that you need them. But seek first the kingdom of God and His righteousness, and all these things will be provided for you. Therefore don't worry about tomorrow, because tomorrow will worry about itself. Each day has enough trouble of its own." (Matthew 6:24–34 HCSB)

Living above worry is much easier said than done. Our most basic needs—what we eat, what we drink, and what we wear—are indeed recurring needs. There is never a day that we do not need them.

Many reading this do not often worry about whether we'll have enough money to put food on the table or clothe our families. But we still worry about being able to afford the things we don't really need: a bigger house, a college education for our children, the latest technological gadget, more clothes. These things all too often absorb much of our time, thought, and emotional energy.

In the Sermon on the Mount, Jesus challenges our natural inclinations: "Don't collect for yourselves treasures on earth" (Matt. 6:19 HCSB), "You cannot be slaves of God and of money" (v. 24 HCSB), do not obsess over your daily needs (see v. 31). These are many of the things that keep us earth-focused instead of God-centered.

In contrast, Jesus offers two challenging alternatives. "But collect for yourselves treasures in heaven . . ." (v. 20 HCSB). "But seek first the kingdom of God and His righteousness . . ." (v. 33 HCSB).

In effect, Jesus said, "Do this (seek Me first), and trust Me to provide (the things you are prone to worry about)." When we seek Him we find that all we truly need is found in Him alone, so we have no reason to be anxious.

Excerpt taken from *100 Days in the Gospels* (© 2016).

The Secret the Boxes Hold

*But seek first the kingdom of God and his righteousness, and
all these things will be added to you. (Matthew 6:33 ESV)*

I rapt softly on the door of her hotel room—a woman I'd long
admired from a distance; one I was thrilled for the chance to
spend time with. She'd been actively involved in ministry for more
than thirty years, and I—a young wife and new mom in the fledg-
ling stages of ministry—was feeling a bit strained in this season of
life. I was tired. Overwhelmed. Out of sorts and out of balance.

I needed a dose of her wisdom and perspective.

As I sat cross-legged on the floor of her hotel room, expecting
nothing in particular but everything at the same time, I knew if I'd
just listen, I'd glean a few nuggets of ageless truth to take away with
me.

Speaking in her delicate British accent, she whisked me on a
journey through her early years, revealing some of the lessons she'd
learned along the way, as well as the ones she wished she'd learned a
lot sooner. Each time I asked her another question, I'd lean in, chin
in my hands, elbows on my knees, listening for her thoughtful
answers. Not a single one failed to make an impression.

Especially the boxes.

No, she didn't pull them out from under the bed or fish them
from a hiding place in the closet. She simply painted them in my
imagination and then set them out before me, one beside another.
Clear, glass boxes, each with a lid on top that opened and closed
from a hinge fastened to the side. All were exactly the same size, and
each was filled to the same level with a clear, bluish, water-like

403

substance. "These boxes, Priscilla, are symbolic of the activities of one's life, the various undertakings into which we must invest our time, talent, and energy. Our tendency is to try keeping them just this way—equally filled with identical amounts of ourselves and our effort. This, we think, is what balance looks like.

"But in reality, this is the picture of a woman's life *out* of balance.

"The way we achieve balance, my dear, is to consider prayerfully God's priorities for us in this current season of life and then rearrange the boxes accordingly—pushing some of them into the background, bringing others to the front. Into these primary boxes we place the best of ourselves and our effort, while perhaps totally emptying some of the others—at least temporarily—not because they're of any less overall significance but because they're not where we need to be allocating the best of our abilities and attention for the time being.

"Balance is not when the boxes are equally filled but when we are free to fill only those that are important for now, without feeling guilt over the ones that we've left for another time and place. This is balance, little sister. Remember it."

I have.

Excerpt taken from *The Resolution for Women* by Priscilla Shirer (© 2011).

Acknowledge the Log

*Do not judge, so that you won't be judged. For with the judgment
you use, you will be judged, and with the measure you use, it
will be measured to you. Why do you look at the speck in your
brother's eye but don't notice the log in your own eye? Or how
can you say to your brother, "Let me take the speck out of your
eye," and look, there's a log in your eye? Hypocrite! First take
the log out of your eye, and then you will see clearly to take
the speck out of your brother's eye. (Matthew 7:1–5 HCSB)*

Jesus taught with authority. Beginning the Sermon on the Mount
(Matt. 5:1—7:29) with the Beatitudes, and ending with the parable of the wise man who built his house on a rock—from start to
finish, this sermon is packed with simple, yet hard-to-live-out
truths. Case in point: the command to not judge, and thereby,
become a hypocrite.

Have you ever been guilty of being a hypocrite? Once, while
driving, a father expounded eloquently to his young daughters
about how a very influential state politician had lied about his education. All agreeing that it was very wrong, they drove a short distance in silence. Then one of the daughters asked, "Dad, wouldn't it
also be lying to tell people we caught more fish than we really did?"
The father couldn't deny it. He had also been guilty of hypocrisy.

The previous verses paint a compelling visual of what hypocrisy
looks like. Can't you just imagine cartoon characters playing the
parts of the two men? There's one guy with a little speck of dust in
his eye. He's blinking hard and maybe even rubbing his eye. Then
there's the man with a tree trunk protruding out of his eye without
even noticing it. He just goes walking around, knocking people

down with that huge log but pointing out the speck of dust in the other guy's eye. One wonders how he could even get close enough to notice that speck without doing damage to the other man. The truth is, he can't. First, he has to acknowledge that he has a log, and then he has to remove it. Only then can he truly help the man with the speck.

Jesus made it plain enough, even for children, that while we may have different levels of accountability among family, friends, countrymen, and enemies, God has only one standard for us all: "Be perfect, therefore, as your heavenly Father is perfect" (Matt. 5:48 HCSB).

Let's strive to be self-aware enough to realize when we have a log in our eye. In fact, let's also be cognizant of our own specks, and ask Jesus to remove them. Then not only will we see others' specks properly, but we can also tell them from experience how they can be removed—only through the power of Jesus.

Excerpt taken from *100 Days in the Gospels* (© 2016).

Asking, Then Asking Some More

Keep asking, and it will be given to you. Keep searching,
and you will find. Keep knocking, and the door will
be opened to you. For everyone who asks receives, and
the one who searches finds, and to the one who knocks,
the door will be opened. (Matthew 7:7–8 HCSB)

'm watching. Waiting.

The view from my window seems to me the only thing beautiful in the whole situation, and it is the view that's kept me from quitting.

I've been asking God for a miracle.

I read a book recently that spoke of miracles, of the things God can do that we cannot do, and I realized that in the whole of my faith walk, I haven't often asked God to do the miraculous. I've asked Him to do a lot but not many things that are outside the normal—nothing crazy. Nothing like a blind person seeing or a deaf person hearing.

So I've decided to ask God for a miracle in my love life. That something would happen that would be so outside of the bounds of what humans could accomplish it would clearly be God.

The Bible says to ask, seek, and knock.

So I have been, and I'm going to keep doing it. Asking. Seeking. Knocking. And I'm expecting, fully expecting, to see God do something amazing.

I like looking for things—looking for deals on a new pair of boots, looking for my friends in the crowd at church, looking for the ball to hit the back of the net when a soccer player takes a penalty kick. But I'm not *looking* for a miracle. I'm *watching* for one. It's a subtle difference, but when you really think about it, the way you use the words, and the way I use the words, show you how they aren't exactly interchangeable.

When I am watching, like a sunset or a movie, I know it is going to happen. Things we watch for are bound to happen. We aren't hoping; we're expecting. When you show up at a theater to watch a movie, you aren't there with your fingers crossed, hoping the screen starts showing a film. You expect it. You may have to wait a few minutes for it to start, but it is coming. So you get your popcorn, your SnoCaps, your Coke ICEE, and you take your seat, facing the screen, and you wait, without worry or concern, without question, because you are here to watch a movie.

That's why I'm watching for a miracle. Because I'm believing it is coming. I'm not looking for a miracle like you look for a rainbow, fingers crossed, just hoping you'll maybe see one. I'm watching for a miracle like I watch a movie because I'm expecting one.

Excerpt taken from *Looking for Lovely* by Annie F. Downs (© 2016).

Polishing Up the Golden Rule

"So whatever you wish that others would do to you, do also to them, for this is the Law and the Prophets." (Matthew 7:12 ESV)

We've come to identify this teaching as the Golden Rule. Later in Matthew, Jesus presented this same concept in a slightly different wrapper by saying that loving others as yourself is the second greatest commandment (Matt. 22:39).

These verses urge us to love others in the same way we want to be loved, but they are not a guarantee that the favor will be returned. The Golden Rule is not an invitation to keep score.

When it comes to my relationships, I tend to think thoughts like these:

I was nice to you today, so you better always be nice to me.

I forgave you, but you better not ever hurt me again . . . or else.

I helped you, so you better help me.

But this is not the spirit of the Golden Rule. And let's face it; it doesn't make for great relationships. If we want to know and be known we need to stop keeping score. If we want to move toward worrying less about having the right friends and put effort toward loving like Jesus did, we've got to learn to love others well without constantly wondering, *What's in this for me?*

When Jesus gives us the second greatest commandment, what is He really commanding? John Piper puts it this way: "He is commanding that our self-love, which has now discovered its fulfillment in God-love, be the measure and the content of our neighbor-love. Or, to put it another way, he is commanding that our inborn self-seeking, which has now been transposed into God-seeking, overflow and extend itself to our neighbor."[1]

Jesus doesn't ask us to love others extravagantly simply so the neighborhood can hold hands and sing "Kumbaya." It's not about warm fuzzies. It's about giving teeth to our faith. It's about letting the abundant love God has demonstrated toward us overflow and impact others instead of keeping it bottled up and to ourselves.

When it comes to our relationships, this is a mark that so many of us miss.

In a culture completely obsessed with feeling good, we've been raised with the idea that our self-esteem should be fed into. We look to our relationships to satisfy our craving for constant ego strokes. This is not the formula that Jesus modeled or taught.

Paul is urging Christians in Philippi to be encouraged by Christ's example when he pens these words: "Do nothing from selfish ambition or conceit, but in humility count others more significant than yourselves" (Phil. 2:3 ESV).

Perhaps it's time we outgrow the notion that the purpose of our relationships is to provide a steady drip of feel-good fuel for our delicate self-esteem.

Excerpt taken from *Connected* by Erin Davis (© 2016).

---

1. John Piper, "Love Your Neighbor as Yourself, Part 2," *Desiring God*, May 7, 1995, http://www.desiringgod.org/resource-library/sermons/love-your-neighbor-as-yourself-part-2.

Mercy, Not Sacrifice

Just then some men brought to Him a paralytic lying on a mat. Seeing their faith, Jesus told the paralytic, "Have courage, son, your sins are forgiven."

At this, some of the scribes said among themselves, "He's blaspheming!"

But perceiving their thoughts, Jesus said, "Why are you thinking evil things in your hearts? For which is easier: to say, 'Your sins are forgiven,' or to say, 'Get up and walk'? But so you may know that the Son of Man has authority on earth to forgive sins"—then He told the paralytic, "Get up, pick up your mat, and go home." And he got up and went home. When the crowds saw this, they were awestruck and gave glory to God who had given such authority to men.

As Jesus went on from there, He saw a man named Matthew sitting at the tax office, and He said to him, "Follow Me!" So he got up and followed Him.

While He was reclining at the table in the house, many tax collectors and sinners came as guests to eat with Jesus and His disciples. When the Pharisees saw this, they asked His disciples, "Why does your Teacher eat with tax collectors and sinners?"

But when He heard this, He said, "Those who are well don't need a doctor, but the sick do. Go and learn what this means: I desire mercy and not sacrifice. For I didn't come to call the righteous, but sinners." (Matthew 9:2–13 HCSB)

Matthew's purpose in his Gospel was to show how Jesus fulfilled God's promises found in the Old Testament by offering a new way of life. Here we see where Jesus healed a man and engaged in an ongoing confrontation with the Pharisees, who refused to recognize His authority and power.

Blinded by their own sense of piety and arrogance, the Pharisees thought they were the only ones in right standing with God. Hence, they were openly critical of Jesus for eating and interacting with people who did not keep the ritual sacrifices as they did. Jesus responded by calling their attention to the words of the prophet Hosea (6:6). God is more interested in a person's loyal love than He is the ritual of sacrifice. Sacrifices are worthless when given to the Lord without mercy toward others.

Christians live in a world that does not always appreciate our sense of what is right, our faith convictions, and our commitment to a godly lifestyle. We must be strong in our faith and live the life we know God wants us to live. At the same time, we must guard against developing an attitude similar to that of the Pharisees where we act like we are better than those who do not believe, act, or think as we do.

Jesus came to save humble sinners, not the self-righteous who fail to see their need for Him. For this we can be eternally grateful. Like Jesus, we are to reach out to sinners so that they may know Jesus' grace, love, and mercy.

Excerpt taken from *100 Days in the Gospels* (© 2016).

Audacious Adventure

*"Let it be done for you according to your
faith!" (Matthew 9:29 HCSB)*

Enthusiasm, vivacity, energy, vitality. Those are four aerobic synonyms in anybody's dictionary. The fact is it's hard to audaciously love without a whit of animation. I'm not suggesting we have to bounce around on our tails like Tigger, but audacity does call for a little vivacity. The good news is, we don't have to rev ourselves up with a daily rant or shout "look alive!" every morning to the mirror. We could start beckoning Jesus to wake us up to a hike with Him that becomes a greater reality than anything we can see with human eyes or touch with human hands.

To grab hold of His unseen robe and hang on tight for the hike of our life, let's turn loose of every trace of the imaginary friend syndrome. You know what I mean: mostly playing like Jesus is there. Saying something to Him and hoping He heard it. Feeling a little silly like we're talking to ourselves but taking the chance in case the Bible is telling the truth. Walking to the car after a church service feeling almost high then pulling out of the parking lot wondering if we're all making this up. We've all done it. We've all treated Jesus like our imaginary friend and as though, if He turns out to be an illusion, at least we were better off safe than sorry. In fact, amid the first flickers of faith, nothing is more natural than taking the all-purpose approach:

God, if You're really out there then . . .

It's damage control in case it's a lie. It's half-hearted, so the other half won't risk proving foolish. And it's totally natural. But you and

I aren't pursuing something natural. The sentences of our stories are meant to be penned from the inkwell of the supernatural. We want God to be able to perform wonders in our clay and do the kinds of things with us that He did with His followers back in their day. If we stay wishy-washy, our little faith will see few results and our few results will breed littler faith. By God's sovereign design, faith is the fertilizer in the seedbed where wonders sprout. Jesus said it this way: "Go. As you have believed, let it be done for you" (Matt. 8:13 HCSB).

We are the very resting place of God's inconceivable favor. What if we awakened to it and took Him up on the animated relationship He's really offering? What if we quit suffocating our spiritual lives like pillows over our faces, being tentative and timid and unsure for the fifteen-thousandth time? What if, instead, we threw caution to the wind, took Him at His Word, and fully engaged in a wide-open, chain-breaking, story-making connection?

Then everything would come alive.

Because He is life and, what He invades, He infuses. What He permeates, He activates.

Excerpt taken from *Audacious* by Beth Moore (© 2015).

Don't Look Away

*When He saw the crowds, He felt compassion for
them, because they were weary and worn out, like
sheep without a shepherd. (Matthew 9:36 HCSB)*

What tugs at your heart?

What causes your stomach to feel uneasy?

It may be an issue effecting people on the other side of the globe.
Or it may be a situation involving some neighbors across the street.
It may require a long-term commitment or just a couple of hours on
one solitary afternoon. It could be an older woman or a newborn
baby. Opportunities to serve others come in all shapes and sizes—
none more valuable than another. But when you see the one that's
yours to do something about, He will cause your heart to be stirred,
drawn to an individual and her need, drawn to a family and their
pain, drawn to a group of people and their challenges, drawn to a
country and their crises.

Take that as your cue to respond, like a woman resolved to compassion. Don't let my words be the force that nudges you toward
compassion. There's a louder voice calling.

"The Lord of Hosts says this: Make fair decisions. Show faithful
love and compassion to one another" (Zech. 7:9 HCSB).

You may be a person who's not normally moved or emotionally
stirred, who just doesn't usually respond that way. And yet you can
have the same thing Jesus had—a divine compassion for that which
breaks the heart of God and tunes you into His purposes for you.

Perhaps you've been burned when trying to reach out too drastically. People have taken advantage of you or misunderstood your

motives. But when you go to minister Christ's love to another person, stop to consider: what is your real reason for going? Is there a better way to evaluate your success than with measurable, feel-good results alone?

This is why we must look often at Christ's example of compassion. He was never motivated by accolades or "Atta boys," but rather He saw people as image bearers and their needs as a sure sign of dependence on the Father. He knew He was their only hope.

When your heart melts to the touch of searing realities that others are facing, you're experiencing something your sanctification is designed to achieve. You are being changed into Christ's image. Breaking your heart. And in being broken, being called to respond.

Yes, you can have it—a godly sympathy that leads to action. You *must* have it. Because your world is waiting to experience Christ through you. *You* are the solution the problem is waiting for. This is why your heart is hurting. This is why it's so hard for you to look. This is the reason your tummy churns at the sight of it.

This is compassion.

So ask the Lord to break your heart, to reveal a need in all its horrible actuality until He gives you the courage to respond.

What is causing your heart to break? This is your cue.

Do something.

Excerpt taken from *The Resolution for Women* by Priscilla Shirer (© 2011).

He Loves You

*"Aren't two sparrows sold for a penny? Yet not one of
them falls to the ground without your Father's consent.
But even the hairs of your head have all been counted.
So don't be afraid therefore; you are worth more than
many sparrows." (Matthew 10:29–31 HCSB)*

I've always loved the verse that says God cares about us more than
sparrows. I'm not sure I've always believed it, though. For the
longest time I kept it to myself, always nodding at the right time
while in Christian circles, furrowing my brow in agreement when it
was brought up. As if I was considering the depths of this unfathomable love, and swallowing it like sweet tea in the hot sun.
Delicious.

But that wasn't what I was thinking. I was actually imagining
what it must be like to honestly believe God would love me that
way.

The image of a sparrow chased me everywhere I went. Years
passed. Decades, in fact. I continued to believe that a God who
would love someone like me wasn't worth loving back.

One day I decided I wanted to know what it was that made this
bird so important. I'd gone through a very dark time in my life, and
I was looking for Him, for answers, for a reason to believe He even
cared, let alone loved me. Why would He care about the number of
tears I cry, or the hairs on my head? I just wanted Him to know I
cried at all.

I came across an article on a particular type of bird. It wasn't a
Christian reference, but rather a zoological-type resource with

statistics and pictures for someone who knows much more about birds than I do. I skimmed it until I came across a sentence explaining how this type of bird learned how to sing. I didn't finish reading it before the tenderness overcame me.

This particular bird cannot learn to sing in the daylight because it's always concerned with the chatter around it. Instead, its cage must be covered, putting it in complete darkness. Then, it is able to hear its master and will learn to sing.[1]

More than a sparrow. More than the pitch-black darkness. He loves me.

And in that place of feeling left alone, unwanted, disregarded, abandoned, He whispered to my weary soul.

Sing, love.

In the black night, I listened to His voice and I heard Him in a way I never had before. Nobody watching, nobody to judge. Just me and the One who told me I was worth it.

Have you heard Him too? I pray so.

Sing, love.

Despicable as the shadows may be, they hold the promise of the Master's voice. Worry not about tomorrow, wondering if the sun will come again. It will, as it always does, in some sense or another. In the meantime, raise your voice to the One who loves you.

He loves you.

Sing, love.

The Master is listening.

Excerpt taken from *Mended* by Angie Smith (© 2012).

---

1. Source unknown.

If You Only Knew

*"Anyone finding his life will lose it, and anyone losing his
life because of Me will find it." (Matthew 10:39 HCSB)*

Those willing to give up their insatiable self-preoccupation to
identify with Jesus and follow Him furiously will find an ever-
unfolding life and love that they couldn't have scripted if they'd
tried.

We are dying to find someone worthy of our unabashed, wholly
unguarded trust. We're all looking for Jesus. We just keep looking
for Him in other faces, palms, and places. When we do find Him,
we find the Giver. That part of us dying to find someone to freely
give ourselves to was created in His image.

Nothing Jesus will ever woo us to lay down on His behalf is
worth what we'd miss if we didn't. If He wants your hands free, He
has something to put in them. If He wants your feet loose, He has
somewhere to plant them. If He wants your mouth shut, He has a
new set of words to put in it. He's not trying to cheat you or trick
you. He's not placing bets on you or playing games with you. He
does not dispense grace with an eyedropper. He drenches us with it.
He does not offer bare existence. He extends life abounding in blessing, power, passion, and purpose. If people told you God was stingy,
they didn't know their Bible.

There's this fabulous scene in the Gospel of John where Jesus
sends His disciples to town to grab some lunch and He stays behind
and meets a woman at a well. She'd been preoccupied for years,
repeating the same relational cycle, filling up the same empty jar the
same empty way, looking for the life she was longing for. We're not

told her name. It's easier that way to give her ours. She had no idea that audacious love was staring her right in the face. He said four words to her that I think He wants to say to each of us:

"If you only knew the gift God has for you and who you are speaking to, you would ask me . . ."

If you only knew.

That's what Jesus said. If you only knew what He has for you. Not only after you kiss this life good-bye but, here on this earth and now in this season. If only you knew, your heart would be so swept up in audacious love that nothing could keep you from the life you were born to live.

In Acts 16, a very successful businesswoman is just one verse removed from a girl enslaved and trafficked. Among the women who encountered Christ in the pages of Scripture, you find the devastated, bleeding, busy, grieving, sick, dying, doubting, thriving, adulterous, ambitious, wise, despised, demon-possessed, and severely oppressed. So, if you are drawing breath, you're Christ's type. If Mary Magdalene couldn't run Him off with seven demons, you're probably out of luck.

He has come looking for you. And somewhere deep inside of you is a girl looking for Him.

Excerpt taken from *Audacious* by Beth Moore (© 2015).

A Much-Needed God-Margin

*Are you tired? Worn out? Burned out on religion? Come to me.
Get away with me and you'll recover your life. I'll show you how
to take a real rest. Walk with me and work with me—watch how
I do it. Learn the unforced rhythms of grace. I won't lay anything
heavy or ill-fitting on you. Keep company with me and you'll
learn to live freely and lightly. (Matthew 11:28–30 The Message)*

Psalm 37:7 reminds us, "Be still before the LORD and wait patiently for him" (HCSB). The original Greek word for *still* is *dâmam* (daw-mam´), meaning "to be astonished, to stop; hold peace, quiet self, wait." Think back at the times in your life when you've been most astonished by God. Chances are, you were giving him your total, undivided, unburned-out attention. I mourn the God moments we miss when we rush through our days, too distracted with the things of the world to sit quietly at His feet. William Penn once said, "In the rush and noise of life, as you have intervals, step home within yourselves and be still. Wait upon God, and feel His good presence; this will carry you evenly through your day's business."

Are you running on fumes? Or are you completely out of gas?

How are you doing when it comes to "keeping company with him"? If you want to be the best possible wife and mother, you must build a God-margin into your day. Uninterrupted time. Quiet time. Time away from your computer, phone, household chores, noisy children, and the demands of life. Most of us fill up once a week at church, thinking an hour of worship and/or an hour of Bible study are enough to hold us over until the next week. We make the mistake of squeezing God into our busy schedules rather than building our schedules around our time spent with God. Our souls long to be nourished and will not be satisfied with trifle crumbs we grab on the run. Have you built a God-margin into your day? If you read that question and immediately entered into panic mode over the thought that you don't have time left in your day for God, then chances are you are a yes-aholic. Even Jesus took the time to be alone with God. If Jesus needed time alone with the Father, so do we.

Psalm 1:2–3 reminds us that those who delight in the law of the Lord and meditate on it day and night are "like a tree planted by streams of water, which yields its fruit in season and whose leaf does not wither. Whatever he does prospers" (NIV). Our souls are desperate for spiritual nourishment.

What nourishes your soul? Better yet, how can you get a bigger dose of it? Take a minute to think about what might work for you when it comes to building a God-margin into your day.

Excerpt taken from *Everafter* by Vicki Courtney (© 2013).

Storing Up Good Fruit

*Either make the tree good and its fruit good, or
make the tree bad and its fruit bad; for a tree is
known by its fruit. (Matthew 12:33 HCSB)*

I have an apple tree in my backyard that struggled for three years before it produced even one apple. The next summer, it produced five or six, and the next year, a few more. Even though it will occasionally produce a deformed or underdeveloped apple, the tendency to bear good fruit is there, and increasing yearly. As a result, I consider it to be a good tree.

When you enter into a relationship with Jesus, the tree of your heart is made good. That means that the inclination of your heart has changed away from producing bad fruit and toward producing good fruit. In spite of this, you may still struggle with bad speech and bad behavior. You may feel frustrated because you don't see the harvest coming quickly enough. Remember, just like my apple tree, it may take some time for you to mature. It is the tendency toward productive growth that indicates that your heart has changed and you are on the right track.

If the tree of your heart has been made good, why are you struggling with bad speech? What might be the problem?

May I suggest that we struggle with bad speech because we have not "stored up" enough good in our hearts?

In Matthew 12:35 Jesus said, "A good man produces good things from his storeroom of good, and an evil man produces evil things from his storeroom of evil."

A couple of years ago, I bought lots of new shelves and set up a pantry downstairs in our storage room. Every time I went shopping for groceries, I bought a few extra supplies for my new pantry. Over time, it became very well stocked. Now I am confident that I have the necessary reserves to manage the vociferous appetites of my teenage boys. No more running to the corner grocery store in a panic because I have run out of something. I have all the supplies I need. This is particularly helpful when something unexpected happens and I am unable to make supper as planned. It's wonderful to be able to go to the pantry and bring out something that's quick and easy to make.

When we speak, particularly in unplanned situations of being irritated, tired, sensitive, or stressed, we reach down into the pantry of our hearts and bring out what has been stored up over time. Words spring from the ground of our hearts. If we have stored up good in our hearts, our words will be good. If we haven't, or if our stores are meager, we may not have the resources available to respond gracefully (a.k.a. produce "good fruit"). Even the most well-stocked pantry will run out of supplies if it is not regularly restocked. Run to the Word of God today and fill your storehouse with His goodness.

Excerpt taken from *Conversation Peace* by Mary Kassian (© 2004).

Every Careless Word

*I tell you that on the day of judgment people will have
to account for every careless word they speak. For by
your words you will be acquitted, and by your words
you will be condemned. (Matthew 12:36–37 HCSB)*

"You make me so mad!"

"You're asking for it!"

"You're driving me crazy!"

Do any of these accusations sound familiar? Do you blame others for the words that come out of your mouth? One of the biggest barriers to peaceful communication is failure to claim responsibility for our own words and behavior. No one can force you to speak improperly. What you say is your own choice. Whether you like it or not, you—and you alone—are responsible for what comes out of your mouth. Remember the words of Jesus?

"I tell you that on the day of judgment people will have to account for every careless word they speak" (v. 36).

We can begin practicing for that day right now and learn to curb careless words before they slip past our lips. An important step to becoming an effective communicator is to accept responsibility for the part of the communication loop that belongs to me. This involves relinquishing my attempt to control the part that does *not* belong to me. When I expect and demand that the other person thinks or behaves the way I want him to, I claim ownership for a part of the loop that is not mine and thereby enter into a power struggle. The net result is conflict and miscommunication. Healthy communication can only take place when each person accepts responsibility for his or her own part of the loop.

Taking responsibility for my part of the loop means that I try to be aware of how my personality, feelings, attitudes, assumptions, habits, past experiences, and current environment affect the way I encode and decode messages. It means that I carefully observe all parts of the other person's message—verbal, vocal, and visual—and that I observe my own behavior and seek to be clear and consistent in the messages I send. Being responsible for my part of the loop means that I bear sole responsibility for what I think and what I say. No matter what the other person says or does, I choose how I respond. *I am responsible for me.*

An effective communicator is acutely aware of the complexity of the communication loop, her own limitations, and the potentials for miscommunication. She enters an exchange with the attitude. Being responsible for her part of the loop means she is susceptible to misinterpreting the other person's behavior. She is open to the possibility that she might be wrong or that her behavior might be sending an inconsistent message. So she relies on feedback to confirm or correct the way she is decoding and encoding.

Humans are not mind readers, and we are not all-knowing. Adjusting our attitudes to be open to learn from others—even those with whom we disagree—is an important step toward effective communication.

Excerpt taken from *Conversation Peace* by Mary Kassian (© 2004).

Embracing the Paradox

Immediately Jesus made the disciples get into the boat and go on ahead of him to the other side, while he dismissed the crowd. After he had dismissed them, he went up on a mountainside by himself to pray. (Matthew 14:22–23 NIV)

We cannot know and be known in the leftover slots on our calendar. We cannot have deep intimacy in the midst of constant chaos. We cannot nurture a relationship with God when there is no time for Him. So, how do we fix what we've broken?

Take a look at how Jesus did it: *Jesus spent time alone.*

One of the pivotal moments of Jesus' ministry was the feeding of the five thousand, but the story has an odd ending. Jesus had thousands of people waiting for Him and yet, He walked away. It wasn't as if His schedule suddenly cleared up and He had time to feed His spirit. He left when everyone was clamoring for more of Him. He took control of His schedule and figured out a way to be alone.

This wasn't a rare occurrence. In Matthew 13:1, we find Jesus sitting alone by a lake. In Matthew 15:29, He is sitting alone on the side of a mountain. In Luke 22:41, He pulled away from the pack of disciples to pray by Himself. Luke 5:16 tells us that spending time alone was part of Jesus' usual rhythm: "But Jesus *often* withdrew to lonely places and prayed" (NIV, author emphasis).

Jesus didn't ask permission from others for quietness and solitude. Nor did He apologize for it. He took it because it was best for Him. It filled His tank with the fuel He needed to continue to pour into the lives of others. We should pay attention and follow His lead.

It's paradoxical that spending time alone can ease our loneliness, but God's way rarely jibes with our natural instincts. If we want to be less lonely, we must make time to be alone. It's extra critical that we make time to be alone with God. We've got to find a way to turn away from all that's on our plates and walk toward peace.

Psalm 46:10 is a well-worn verse, but perhaps it's become so familiar we've started to ignore it. "Be still, and know that I am God. I will be exalted among the nations, I will be exalted in the earth!" (NIV).

Be. Still.

Slow down.

Tell the "to-do's" to take a chill pill. Because God is God and you are not.

If you don't get it all done, or make it to every church function, or have the planet's most well-rounded children, the world will keep spinning. Making it a priority to spend time alone and alone with the Father will fill you up. When you are full, you are able to pour out. And when you pour out you are very likely to find yourself connected. Go figure.

Excerpt taken from *Connected* by Erin Davis (© 2016).

Confidence in Christ

When evening came, He was there alone. But the boat was already over a mile from land, battered by the waves, because the wind was against them. Around three in the morning, He came toward them walking on the sea. When the disciples saw Him walking on the sea, they were terrified. "It's a ghost!" they said, and cried out in fear.

Immediately Jesus spoke to them. "Have courage! It is I. Don't be afraid."

"Lord, if it's You," Peter answered Him, "command me to come to You on the water."

"Come!" He said.

And climbing out of the boat, Peter started walking on the water and came toward Jesus. But when he saw the strength of the wind, he was afraid. And beginning to sink he cried out, "Lord, save me!"

Immediately Jesus reached out His hand, caught hold of him, and said to him, "You of little faith, why did you doubt?" When they got into the boat, the wind ceased. Then those in the boat worshiped Him and said, "Truly You are the Son of God!" (Matthew 14:23–33 HCSB)

Jesus came to bring us peace. In fact, He is called the Prince of Peace. The wrath and judgment of God against sin may promote fear in the heart to draw us to Him. But the end result is that we can have peace with God and confidence of spending eternity with Him.

Many people go through life living in fear. Some people are deathly afraid of spiders. Others fear commitment. Many fear falling or flying, and some fear the future. But with Jesus, we do not have to live with the fear of death and judgment.

The disciples saw what they thought was an apparition coming toward them in the night, walking on top of the water. Who can blame them for their fear? Yet it was Jesus, and He spoke to them to calm their fear.

Moments later, Peter stepped out of the boat in faith, but he quickly became scared when he realized how strong the wind was. But he called out to Jesus, who immediately came to his rescue. What's important to note, though, is that Jesus didn't accuse Peter of having no faith at all. He said he had "little faith." But even when we have little faith, Jesus reaches out to us when we call to Him.

However, the overall message is clear: When Jesus is with us, we can be confident in any situation; we have no reason to be afraid. He will see us through any predicament or malady because we have His promise that He will never leave us. Our future is secure in Christ, and even death has no power over us. He is the Prince of Peace.

Excerpt taken from *100 Days in the Gospels* (© 2016).

Getting to the Root

*Don't you realize that whatever goes into the mouth passes
into the stomach and is eliminated? But what comes out of
the mouth comes from the heart, and this defiles a man. For
from the heart come evil thoughts, murders, adulteries, sexual
immoralities, thefts, false testimonies, blasphemies. These
are the things that defile a man, but eating with unwashed
hands does not defile a man. (Matthew 15:17–20 HCSB)*

I didn't know what the problem was. My African violet looked sick.
Many leaves had curled and darkened; a few appeared translucent
and jellylike. The flowers, which had once bloomed vibrant purple,
had all but died. Not having inherited my mother's green thumb, I
assumed that tiny insects were to blame. Finding a can of Raid in
the shed, I generously sprayed the leaves.

A few days later the violet looked worse than ever. It was time to
call in the expert. Hearing the symptoms, my mom quickly diag-
nosed the ailment: Root rot. I had an inverted perspective on what
was causing the problem. I thought the problem originated in the
leaves when the problem was actually with the root.

In Jesus' day some people had an inverted perspective on the
connection between the mouth and the heart. They believed that
the mouth could contaminate the heart. Jesus showed that the heart
and the mouth are indeed connected, but the flow of contamination
goes from the heart to the mouth and not the other way around.

The Pharisees were a Jewish sect noted for their strict interpretation and observance of religious law. The religious leaders had all
sorts of rules about what was and what wasn't acceptable behavior.
One of their rules was that people needed to ritualistically wash

their hands before they ate a meal; otherwise they would be spiritually defiled. The religious leaders had precisely defined the process: you had to use a volume of 11/2 eggs worth of water, hold your hands in the right posture, and let the water flow in the right direction. Your cleanliness and your spirituality depended upon perfectionist attention to details. The religious leaders' excessive concern about external appearances had resulted in an inauthentic spirituality.

Jesus exposed the contradiction. He pointed out that what comes out of a person's mouth is a better indicator of their spiritual condition than what goes into their mouths. If the heart is bad, the words or actions are also bad, regardless of how good they look to observers.

When Jesus died to pay the penalty for our sins, the need for these external symbols of holiness changed (see Heb. 9:13–14). If the heart is bad, the words or actions are also bad, regardless of how good they look to the observers. External symbols of holiness— doing the right things and saying the right words—are of no worth if the thoughts and attitudes of our hearts are not right. He dug past the superficial soil, straight to the root.

Excerpt taken from *Conversation Peace* by Mary Kassian (© 2004).

All In

Then Jesus told his disciples, "If anyone would come after me,
let him deny himself and take up his cross and follow me. For
whoever would save his life will lose it, but whoever loses his
life for my sake will find it. (Matthew 16:24–25 ESV)

"C hildren, do you have any fish?" (John 21:5 ESV).

They told the stranger they didn't have any fish, and He suggested that they cast their nets on the right side of the boat instead. After they obeyed, they could not even pull the nets onto the boat because of how heavy with fish they were. As soon as this happened, everything clicked for John and he shouted, "It is the Lord!" (v. 7 ESV).

When Peter heard this, he put on an outer garment and "threw himself into the sea" (v. 7 ESV). Isn't it the same for us? Once we have seen the power of Jesus, we're much more likely to jump. Forget the fish and the nets. Who needs a boat? He's here, and I'm going to get to Him now. Immediately, although Jesus was all the way on the shore, Peter gave himself over to the One who saved him. Not only from the sea, but also from his sin. Wow.

It makes me want to throw myself into the sea over and over again. Whatever it takes to get to the shore. Not because it's safe. *But because He's there.*

Do you ever feel like you crossed an invisible line in the sea and can't get to the shore? That you have finally pushed so hard that He has just given up on you?

Scripture tells us Peter didn't hesitate—he leapt into the water after Jesus. But I wonder if he was worried about what Christ would say to him?

The Bible says that when they got to the shore, there was a fire burning. The Lord asked Peter to go get the fish from the boat so they could cook them. After they'd finished eating breakfast, Jesus turned His attention to Peter.

"Simon, son of John, do you love me?" One. "Yes, Lord; you know that I love you."

"Simon, son of John, do you love me?" Two. "Yes, Lord; you know that I love you."

"Do you love me?" Three. "Lord, you know everything; you know that I love you" (see vv. 15–17 ESV).

Do you think you've sinned one time too many? He says it isn't so. He still calls to you from the shore. He still invites you to Him. And when you come, He welcomes you at His table. But that's not all.

His desire is for you to throw yourself into the water, leave your nets, and run where He calls you. There you'll be healed, and when you have, I daresay, you'll have a story that's begging to be told.

Be bold, sisters.

Jump.

Immediately.

One.

Two.

Three.

Excerpt taken from *Mended* by Angie Smith (© 2012).

The Lord's Desire

At that time the disciples came to Jesus and said, "Who is greatest in the kingdom of heaven?"

Then He called a child to Him and had him stand among them. "I assure you," He said, "unless you are converted and become like children, you will never enter the kingdom of heaven. Therefore, whoever humbles himself like this child—this one is the greatest in the kingdom of heaven. And whoever welcomes one child like this in My name welcomes Me. . . .

"See that you don't look down on one of these little ones, because I tell you that in heaven their angels continually view the face of My Father in heaven. [For the Son of Man has come to save the lost.] What do you think? If a man has 100 sheep, and one of them goes astray, won't he leave the 99 on the hillside and go and search for the stray? And if he finds it, I assure you: He rejoices over that sheep more than over the 99 that did not go astray. In the same way, it is not the will of your Father in heaven that one of these little ones perish." (Matthew 18:1–5, 10–14 HCSB)

Jesus always welcomed women, children, lepers, and those who were hurting. He showed great love and acceptance toward the vulnerable. In today's Christian culture, that might not sound so surprising, but in Jesus' day, it was a radical way of thinking and living. Children, women, and the sick were to be pitied, not helped, and definitely not seen as being "greater" than the religious men of the day.

It's important to note that Jesus isn't talking to the Pharisees here in Matthew 18, but to His disciples. It's also interesting that in the following chapter, those same disciples tried to keep children from coming to Jesus, who responded, "Leave the children alone, and don't try to keep them from coming to Me, because the kingdom of heaven is made up of people like this" (Matt. 19:14 HCSB).

Going back to chapter 18, Jesus tells His followers about His Father. As a Shepherd, God goes after a lost sheep, because it is not His will that even one should perish.

What a challenge and a warning to all of us. Are we that welcoming to those who are vulnerable and hurting? Or are we easily irritated and annoyed by those who are wounded and needy? Being surrounded by children is a chaotic, fussy, clamoring business. But that is exactly where Jesus willingly placed Himself: in the mess, noise, and chaos.

He was driven by an awareness of His Father's will, so He loved the loud children and the "unclean" lepers, because He was focused on their souls. He loves people, even the most demanding, because He sees past the immediate moment into eternity. And we can follow Him and love the needy people in our lives by keeping our Father's desire in mind.

Excerpt taken from *100 Days in the Gospels* (© 2016).

Forgive, as You Have Been Forgiven

Then Peter came to Him and said, "Lord, how many times could my brother sin against me and I forgive him? As many as seven times?"

"I tell you, not as many as seven," Jesus said to him, "but 70 times seven. For this reason, the kingdom of heaven can be compared to a king who wanted to settle accounts with his slaves. When he began to settle accounts, one who owed 10,000 talents was brought before him. Since he had no way to pay it back, his master commanded that he, his wife, his children, and everything he had be sold to pay the debt.

"At this, the slave fell facedown before him and said, 'Be patient with me, and I will pay you everything!' Then the master of that slave had compassion, released him, and forgave him the loan.

"But that slave went out and found one of his fellow slaves who owed him 100 denarii. He grabbed him, started choking him, and said, 'Pay what you owe!'

"At this, his fellow slave fell down and began begging him, 'Be patient with me, and I will pay you back.' But he wasn't willing. On the contrary, he went and threw him into prison until he could pay what was owed. When the other slaves saw what had taken place, they were deeply distressed and went and reported to their master everything that had happened.

"Then, after he had summoned him, his master said to him, 'You wicked slave! I forgave you all that debt because you begged me. Shouldn't you also have had mercy on your fellow slave, as I had mercy on you?' And his master got angry and handed him over

to the jailers to be tortured until he could pay everything that was owed. So My heavenly Father will also do to you if each of you does not forgive his brother from his heart." (Matthew 18:21–35 HCSB)

The religious leaders of Jesus' day taught that while we should at first forgive people, there should be a limit on it. They set the bar at three times, so Peter likely thought he was being generous with seven. But Jesus dispensed with that notion very quickly, saying we should forgive seventy-times-seven times. Before you do the math, just know that Jesus wasn't really giving a limit. He was essentially saying: forgive as many times as you have the opportunity to do so.

This parable illustrates why we should forgive. Just as the slave was expected to forgive a debt because his owner had forgiven him one, we should forgive others because God has forgiven us.

It's that simple—but it's not always that easy, is it? When you find it hard to forgive, take some time to remember all the things God has forgiven you for. You may find it a little bit easier to show mercy to the other person and forgive just as God has forgiven you.

Excerpt taken from *100 Days in the Gospels* (© 2016).

House of Mercy

". . . with God all things are possible." (Matthew 19:26 HCSB)

I have long been fascinated by the questions the Lord asks in the Bible. It started when I was reading through Genesis and came to the part where Adam and Eve had sinned, then decided it would be a brilliant idea to run from Him. Because, as you know, God isn't so great at finding people.

God asks, "Where are you?"

When I first read this passage years ago, I thought maybe He was serious. I mean, why would He ask the question if He already knew the answer?

Because God is constantly asking us where we are, even while His eyes are fixed upon us. He wants our accountability, our recognition, our understanding of who we are compared to Him.

In John 5:2–9, we see that Jesus was traveling through Jerusalem when He passed a pool of water called "Bethesda." In Hebrew, the word *Bedazzle* means "house of mercy" or "the flowing water." Many sick, crippled, blind, and diseased people sat beside the pool because it was believed angels periodically came and stirred the water, causing it to cure the first person who entered it.

There was one man there who'd been an invalid for thirty-eight years. The Lord saw Him and asked, "Do you want to be healed?" (v. 6 ESV).

I imagine he did, and I'd venture to guess the Lord knew the answer. I think Jesus wanted the man to hear his own answer.

The man replied, "Sir, I have no one to put me into the pool when the water is stirred up, and while I am going another steps down before me" (v. 7 ESV).

But that's not what Jesus asked; He asked if the man wanted to be healed. And then it hits me: it has nothing to do with the stirring, and everything to do with the stirrer.

Which is exactly why He asks.

When Jesus hears the man's doubtful answer, He tells him to be obedient and to disregard the pool. He doesn't need water—just to obey the One who controls far more than the water.

"Get up, take up your bed, and walk" (John 5:8 ESV). And so he did.

He may not heal you the way you want Him to. But He's in our midst, and if you love Him the way I hope you do, listen for Him in the stillness of night:

Do you want to get well?

Do you believe I can make you well?

Do you trust Me to determine what that will look like?

That's when I kneel deep and nod yes, believing He can handle the rest.

After all, it's *His* house of mercy. *His* unending grace and love.

Whether it's been thirty-eight minutes or thirty-eight years you've been waiting, one thing is for sure. He's the same God now as He was in Jerusalem years ago.

So get up, friend.

It's time to walk.

Excerpt taken from *Mended* by Angie Smith (© 2012).

Love God and Love Others

When the Pharisees heard that He had silenced the Sadducees, they came together. And one of them, an expert in the law, asked a question to test Him: "Teacher, which command in the law is the greatest?"

He said to him, "Love the Lord your God with all your heart, with all your soul, and with all your mind. This is the greatest and most important command. The second is like it: Love your neighbor as yourself. All the Law and the Prophets depend on these two commands."

While the Pharisees were together, Jesus questioned them, "What do you think about the Messiah? Whose Son is He?"

"David's," they told Him.

He asked them, "How is it then that David, inspired by the Spirit, calls Him 'Lord':

"The Lord declared to my Lord, 'Sit at My right hand until I put Your enemies under Your feet'?"

"If David calls Him 'Lord,' how then can the Messiah be his Son?" No one was able to answer Him at all, and from that day no one dared to question Him anymore. (Matthew 22:34–46 HCSB)

Rules are all around us. Most of us grew up with a list of rules in the classroom. We got our driver's licenses and learned to follow rules of the road. As adults, we have workplace rules and just common-sense unwritten rules that we must follow. And, of course, there are all the laws of our land—we cannot escape them.

The Old Testament lays out more than 600 laws/rules, and the Pharisees added many more. So in Jesus' day, there was a major focus on rules in Jewish life.

Jesus was confronted by a Pharisee who would've been considered a very religious man. In an attempt to discredit Jesus, the Pharisee asked which commandment was the greatest. Jesus boiled them all down to two—to love God and to love people. He said that all other laws and prophetic teachings hinged upon this. The Pharisees had to be shocked and angered by this answer. This man had taken all of the rules and laws that they had so carefully crafted and followed and thrown them out the window. In their place, He said we just needed to do two things.

Jesus then followed up with a question of His own about who they thought the Messiah was and, to put it bluntly, His answer shut them down. Scripture tells us they stopped questioning Him after that. They must have known they couldn't win.

And neither can we. Jesus' answer to the question about the greatest commandment poses a problem for all of us, because we don't have it in us to obey it perfectly. But that is what makes the gospel the good news. Jesus loved the Father and loved people so much that He perfectly kept all of the laws, thus making Him a perfect sacrifice. Believers can now stand before God based on Christ's perfect righteousness. We, too, should strive to love God and people like Jesus.

Excerpt taken from *100 Days in the Gospels* (© 2016).

The Truth Is Love

*"Heaven and earth will pass away, but My words
will never pass away." (Matthew 24:35 HCSB)*

It is God Himself, the Perfect One—the whole of His Truth and His covenant to us as His people—who covers us when we're hanging on the side of life's mountains, just trying to weather the storm without losing our grip.

This world is still passing away, just like autumn leaves do and like you and I will. But God and His Word will never pass away. He is the one permanent thing we find when we frantically grasp in the dark of our doubt and fear. He is the perfection we long for in the midst of our suffering and brokenness. He is the one sure thing we seek in our uncertainty.

God is our only immovable mountain, and we can find Him in His Word.

What we want is Him.

We want faith, hope, and love.

We want help and healing.

We want to hear and be heard, to see and be seen.

We want things set right.

We want to know what is true—not partly true, or sometimes true, or almost true. We want to see Truth itself, face-to-face.

But here, now, these things are all cloudy. Hope is tinged with hurt. Faith is shaded by doubt. Lesser, broken things masquerade as love.

Real love is the God who became flesh—a living, feeling human being. He is God with us, rescuing the dying, calling the sinners, and embracing those who are wasting away. Real hope is the God who came to set things right. He came to set the cloudy mirror aside for good so we can see Him, face-to-face. Real Truth is the Word that created the world, the Truth that never ceases to be true.

Counterfeits of these no longer interest us; we are looking for the realest thing. This is why we read. We read Truth to find Jesus.

And He is there, on every page, greater than our triumphs and shame, vaster than our needs and our pain. Those are real, to be certain. But they are the partial, the passing away. Jesus—and Jesus alone—is the Perfect, the Permanent.

The Truth does not magically erase our suffering or cure our disappointment. It does not negate our struggle or invalidate our sorrow. It does something even better—it leads us into relationship with the One who made us and makes us new, the One who is greater than all of these. The Truth brings us face-to-face with the God who has never stopped loving His children, who has never failed to do what He says He will do. The Truth is love in black and white—a love that does not change, even when our Bibles are closed.

One day the cloudy mirror will be gone. One day face-to-face is the only way we will see.

Until then, we read Truth—not just for answers or equations, help or how-tos. We read Truth to find the perfect and permanent One. We read Truth because we need Jesus.

Excerpt taken from *She Reads Truth* by Raechel Myers and Amanda Bible Williams (© 2016).

Be Prepared

"Then the kingdom of heaven will be like 10 virgins who took their lamps and went out to meet the groom. Five of them were foolish and five were sensible. When the foolish took their lamps, they didn't take olive oil with them. But the sensible ones took oil in their flasks with their lamps. Since the groom was delayed, they all became drowsy and fell asleep.

"In the middle of the night there was a shout: 'Here's the groom! Come out to meet him.'

"Then all those virgins got up and trimmed their lamps. But the foolish ones said to the sensible ones, 'Give us some of your oil, because our lamps are going out.'

"The sensible ones answered, 'No, there won't be enough for us and for you. Go instead to those who sell, and buy oil for yourselves.'

"When they had gone to buy some, the groom arrived. Then those who were ready went in with him to the wedding banquet, and the door was shut.

"Later the rest of the virgins also came and said, 'Master, master, open up for us!'

"But he replied, 'I assure you: I do not know you!' "Therefore be alert, because you don't know either the day or the hour."
(Matthew 25:1–13 HCSB)

I t is possible to understand the main point of the parable of the virgins without understanding wedding rituals in the first century, but let's have a quick lesson anyway. The virgins were what we'd call bridesmaids. The wedding would start at the bride's house with the bride and her maids in attendance. The groom would arrive and escort her to his home, where the ceremony would be completed. The bridesmaids would go along, and if the wedding were an evening or nighttime event, they would light the procession with lamps (or torches).

Now that you can picture the scene better, the story might make a little more sense. The bridesmaids were waiting at the bride's house, but the groom was late. Apparently, they all had oil in their lamps, but only half of them were prepared for a delay by bringing along extra oil.

You'd think the bridesmaids with oil would just share theirs with the ones who hadn't brought extra. That would be the charitable and compassionate thing to do, right? But remember, this isn't a true story—it's a parable—and compassion isn't the point. Being prepared for the delayed coming of the Lord is the point.

The bridesmaids couldn't share their oil with their friends any more than we can share our salvation with our friends. Each one must prepare on his or her own. Those who have only a little oil—an interest in or knowledge of the gospel—will not be allowed to go with Jesus when He returns. Only those who are fully prepared will be ready when the groom comes.

Are you fully prepared? Remember we "don't know either the day or the hour" when Christ will return. Make the decision to follow Him today.

Excerpt taken from *100 Days in the Gospels* (© 2016).

A Faithful Servant

"For it is just like a man going on a journey. He called his own slaves and turned over his possessions to them. To one he gave five talents; to another, two; and to another, one—to each according to his own ability. Then he went on a journey. Immediately the man who had received five talents went, put them to work, and earned five more. In the same way the man with two earned two more. But the man who had received one talent went off, dug a hole in the ground, and hid his master's money.

After a long time the master of those slaves came and settled accounts with them. The man who had received five talents approached, presented five more talents, and said, 'Master, you gave me five talents. Look, I've earned five more talents.'

His master said to him, 'Well done, good and faithful slave! You were faithful over a few things; I will put you in charge of many things. Share your master's joy!'

Then the man with two talents also approached. He said, 'Master, you gave me two talents. Look, I've earned two more talents.'

His master said to him, 'Well done, good and faithful slave! You were faithful over a few things; I will put you in charge of many things. Share your master's joy!'" (Matthew 25:14–23 HCSB)

What does it mean to be a faithful servant? Jesus praised those who took what had been given to them and used it wisely. In the case of this parable, the servants each received some amounts of money. The servants who used his resources in appropriate ways were given more resources to use.

You probably know some five-talent and two-talent people. They exercise their God-given resources, skills, and abilities effectively and productively in kingdom service. We admire their accomplishments, most often by pointing to some measure of increase. We may conclude the greater the increase, the greater the person must be.

The emphasis in this parable is not on the different amounts given to the servants or the amounts of total increase. Rather, Jesus tells the story to urge those who would follow Him to do well, model goodness in character, and exercise faithfulness in their service. The Lord has entrusted to each of us that which we can use in His service. He gives us opportunities to honor Him.

What resources do you have at your disposal that could be used for God's kingdom? Do you have a talent for working with children? Do you play an instrument or sing, or even compose music? Are you good with your hands and able to make repairs? Do you have good organizational skills? Any of those resources could easily be put to use in a local church.

Maybe you don't feel like you have any special talents. Take time to pray and ask the Lord to show you ways in which He has gifted you, and then become a faithful servant as the Lord leads you.

Excerpt taken from *100 Days in the Gospels* (© 2016).

The Vulnerability of Faith

Then he said to them, "My soul is very sorrowful, even to death;
remain here, and watch with me." (Matthew 26:38 ESV)

I'm afraid that with pride there are no happy endings.

Jesus made a similar confession when He found Himself at a painful crossroads. He and His disciples had just finished the Last Supper. Knowing that His arrest, trial, and crucifixion were right around the corner, Jesus chose to press into His community. For some reason, I've always sort of imagined that the Last Supper was some sort of favor to the disciples, that maybe Jesus would have preferred to spend His last night alone. But if we fast-forward just a few verses, we see that this isn't true.

After Jesus ate and sang with His disciples, they moved out to the Garden of Gethsemane. Jesus wasn't stoic. He didn't slap on a brave face. He said, "I am sad to the point it feels like dying." He demonstrated what vulnerability really looks like.

Jesus was fully God and fully man. He didn't experience weakness at the level that the rest of us do, but in this moment He chose not to take care of everything Himself. He chose to defer to the sovereignty of His Father. He chose to get real and to press into the friends that surrounded Him. He chose not to face His darkest moments alone. We'd do well to follow His lead.

Jesus is not the only example of vulnerability in the Bible. The prophet Isaiah's prayer found in Isaiah 6 is one of the most vulnerable prayers in the entire Bible. After seeing God on His throne, Isaiah uttered these words: "Woe is me! For I am lost; for I am a man of unclean lips, and I dwell in the midst of a people of unclean lips; for my eyes have seen the King, the LORD of hosts!" (Isa. 6:5 ESV).

Seeing how perfect God is only exposes how messed up and weak we really are. Isaiah didn't try to gloss over his imperfections. He didn't spin his culture or justify his failures. There was no pride in Isaiah's heart in that moment. He was painfully aware of his shortcomings. Preserving the image of perfection was not an option.

And what was the result? He got to see God. He was with the Lord in the throne room. He had an intimate conversation with Him about the things that were to come.

A prideful man would not have been granted such a privilege. Someone bent on appearing perfect would almost certainly miss the wonder of the flawlessness of God.

Excerpt taken from *Connected* by Erin Davis (© 2016).

The Power of Jesus

While He was still speaking, Judas, one of the Twelve, suddenly arrived. A large mob, with swords and clubs, was with him from the chief priests and elders of the people. His betrayer had given them a sign: "The One I kiss, He's the One; arrest Him!" So he went right up to Jesus and said, "Greetings, Rabbi!" and kissed Him.

"Friend," Jesus asked him, "why have you come?"

Then they came up, took hold of Jesus, and arrested Him. At that moment one of those with Jesus reached out his hand and drew his sword. He struck the high priest's slave and cut off his ear.

Then Jesus told him, "Put your sword back in its place because all who take up a sword will perish by a sword. Or do you think that I cannot call on My Father, and He will provide Me at once with more than 12 legions of angels? How, then, would the Scriptures be fulfilled that say it must happen this way?"

At that time Jesus said to the crowds, "Have you come out with swords and clubs, as if I were a criminal, to capture Me? Every day I used to sit, teaching in the temple complex, and you didn't arrest Me. But all this has happened so that the prophetic Scriptures would be fulfilled." Then all the disciples deserted Him and ran away. (Matthew 26:47–56 HCSB)

It's a spectacularly dramatic scene. There's betrayal, bloody confrontation, and imminent death. There's a kiss, a sword, and a human ear on the ground. It could've come straight out of the latest blockbuster movie—or an episode of a popular reality television show.

The crucifixion story had begun. Disciples Peter, James, and John were there when a crowd of armed men—along with one of their former comrades—arrived to arrest Jesus. Peter impulsively grabbed a sword and sliced off a soldier's ear!

Jesus responded by reminding Peter that His power is limitless. He could've easily asked God for legions of angels to protect Him. He didn't need Peter's brave ear-slicing for defense.

When life gets dramatic, do you start wielding your own defense weapons like Peter, wildly trying to take things into your own hands? Peter was often brave in the face of adversity, but he also often didn't understand that he could wholly trust in the power of the One he followed. Jesus had tried to explain to the disciples who He was and what He was there to accomplish, but until they had experienced Jesus' death, burial, and resurrection, they didn't begin to understand what He was all about.

But we know. We've read God's Word. So why do we sometimes forget the extent of Jesus' power? We've read the stories, and we've experienced His power in our own lives, yet somehow we still think we can do something to help Him out.

Let's stop underestimating God's power and remember what He did for us on the cross—and after the cross. That's power we cannot deny.

Excerpt taken from *100 Days in the Gospels* (© 2016).

Pick Up Your Cross

As they were going out, they met a man from
Cyrene, named Simon, and they forced him to
carry the cross. (Matthew 27:32 NIV)

There are only two times we are told that someone is "behind" Jesus. The first is the woman with the issue of blood (Luke 8:43–48), and the second is Simon of Cyrene, carrying the cross behind the King of all kings. Carrying the cross that would eventually bring His death and our life.

Simon was a righteous Jew, but he wasn't a disciple of Christ's. It's not likely he even knew who He was. He was just one man, in a crowd, who thought he might escape notice. And as his hands lifted the beam, I wonder if he saw himself as a victim: wrong place at the wrong time, and nothing more.

It's unclear whether Simon was carrying the entire cross, or whether the crosspiece was still on Christ. It was customary for a victim to carry His own cross, so it's possible this kept the weight of the cross on Christ, but a portion was granted to another person for some distance until they had reached Golgotha.

What a horrific responsibility. To walk in the bloody footsteps of a man about to be executed, all the while painstakingly trying to keep balance and not succumb to the intense physical agony. Step after step, seeing enough of the man ahead of you to know there is life in Him now that will soon be snuffed out.

Simon carried the cross to the place where Jesus was crucified, and while we don't know the specifics of what he saw, we know he saw enough to believe Christ was the Messiah. He returned to his tiny hometown, where he informed his family of what he'd seen and they too believed. From there, a church began in Cyrene, and one of the members from that church would eventually gather with others in sending Paul and Barnabas on their missionary journey years later. We learn that Simon's wife was like a mother to Paul, and he sent his greetings to her and their family in the book of Hebrews.

So let me ask you this:

Was Simon of Cyrene randomly chosen from the crowd? Forced into submission by an angry officer?

Or could it be that before there was time, God saw this town, this crowd, and this moment? I daresay we safely assume the latter. Not just with the bleeding woman or the man visiting for a time, but for every one of us.

Will you chase Him out of your own doubt, or bear His cross from the faith you have to offer? Jesus said that in order to follow Him, we must be willing to carry our own crosses (Matt. 16:24). They're crosses chosen for each of us, tailored to our lives, and always designed to bring us closer to our Savior.

Excerpt taken from *Chasing God* by Angie Smith (© 2014.

Unfathomable Love

From noon until three in the afternoon darkness came over the whole land. About three in the afternoon Jesus cried out with a loud voice, "Elí, Elí, lemá sabachtháni?" that is, "My God, My God, why have You forsaken Me?"

When some of those standing there heard this, they said, "He's calling for Elijah!"

Immediately one of them ran and got a sponge, filled it with sour wine, fixed it on a reed, and offered Him a drink. But the rest said, "Let's see if Elijah comes to save Him!"

Jesus shouted again with a loud voice and gave up His spirit. Suddenly, the curtain of the sanctuary was split in two from top to bottom; the earth quaked and the rocks were split. The tombs were also opened and many bodies of the saints who had fallen asleep were raised. And they came out of the tombs after His resurrection, entered the holy city, and appeared to many.

When the centurion and those with him, who were guarding Jesus, saw the earthquake and the things that had happened, they were terrified and said, "This man really was God's Son!"
(Matthew 27:45–54 HCSB)

Think about the most unbearable physical or emotional pain you've ever personally experienced. Imagine the most horrific scene you've ever seen on the news or in a movie. Now breathe. Those events don't come close to this one. It's doubtful that even an actual crucifixion scene from a movie about Jesus can come close to depicting the horror of that experience. After all, we just watch it for several minutes. Jesus lived it for hours.

When we get to this passage, the crucifixion had begun six hours before, and the agony worsened each minute. He'd been tortured and beaten almost to death, then nailed to the cross to die a slow, painful death. Strangers gawked at His naked form. People taunted Him and challenged His seeming lack of power to get down off the cross. Soldiers mocked Him relentlessly and gambled for His clothes. Mark tells us, "Even those who were crucified with Him were taunting Him" (Mark 15:32 HCSB).

Every breath was difficult. Death was imminent. But Jesus was not only dying—He was dying for our sin. As part of God's salvation plan, Jesus was voluntarily substituting His life for our sins. Your sin. My sin.

Imagine the raw pain in Jesus' voice as He loudly cried from the crucifixion cross, "My God, My God, why have You forsaken Me?" Jesus was quoting from Psalm 22. The entire psalm depicts elements of physical suffering, similar to what Jesus experienced. But He was also expressing the enormous weight of desperation and loneliness as He hung dying, carrying the weight of the world's sin.

We can't fathom the depth of Jesus' pain as He cried out those words. But we can get a small glimpse of His love for us. Let's take time to reflect on all the ways He has shown His love to us.

Excerpt taken from *100 Days in the Gospels* (© 2016).

Christ Is Risen from the Dead

The next day, which followed the preparation day, the chief priests and the Pharisees gathered before Pilate and said, "Sir, we remember that while this deceiver was still alive He said, 'After three days I will rise again.' Therefore give orders that the tomb be made secure until the third day. Otherwise, His disciples may come, steal Him, and tell the people, 'He has been raised from the dead.' Then the last deception will be worse than the first."

"You have a guard of soldiers," Pilate told them. "Go and make it as secure as you know how." Then they went and made the tomb secure by sealing the stone and setting the guard.

After the Sabbath, as the first day of the week was dawning, Mary Magdalene and the other Mary went to view the tomb. Suddenly there was a violent earthquake, because an angel of the Lord descended from heaven and approached the tomb. He rolled back the stone and was sitting on it. His appearance was like lightning, and his robe was as white as snow. The guards were so shaken from fear of him that they became like dead men.

But the angel told the women, "Don't be afraid, because I know you are looking for Jesus who was crucified. He is not here! For He has been resurrected, just as He said. Come and see the place where He lay." (Matthew 27:62–66; 28:1–6 HCSB)

Sometimes those intent on stamping out Christianity end up assisting it. As any high school physics student can attest, fire burns brighter under pressure.

Interestingly, the Lord's opponents remembered that He predicted He would rise from the dead—even if His disciples did not remember.

It appears the wrong guys were taking Jesus' words literally! The disciples, forgetting the Lord's promises, were mired down in their sadness and their grief. Matthew records multiple instances in which Jesus said He would rise again on the third day. But somehow the disciples didn't get it. It doesn't seem to have occurred to them that Jesus actually might defeat death like He said He would.

When the opponents of the Lord went to such lengths to protect the tomb, they inadvertently provided extra evidence for His resurrection by ruling out all other explanations. Many historians assure us that the only explanation that makes sense and satisfies all the evidence is Jesus Christ rose bodily from the grave.

There are silly theories concocted by people who refuse to believe. Some say He wasn't completely dead to begin with. Others say He faked His death. Anticipating this, Scripture goes to lengths to establish His death and burial, too. It even goes so far as to record the elders' and chief priests' plan to cover up the resurrection with a story about the disciples stealing the body. However, the history is solid; our faith is well-grounded.

Christ was dead. He is risen. He is alive and well today, and He is the Savior of the world!

Excerpt taken from *100 Days in the Gospels* (© 2016).

Go and Make Disciples

*The 11 disciples traveled to Galilee, to the mountain where
Jesus had directed them. When they saw Him, they worshiped,
but some doubted. Then Jesus came near and said to them,
"All authority has been given to Me in heaven and on earth.
Go, therefore, and make disciples of all nations, baptizing
them in the name of the Father and of the Son and of the
Holy Spirit, teaching them to observe everything I have
commanded you. And remember, I am with you always,
to the end of the age." (Matthew 28:16–20 HCSB)*

We often call this passage the Great Commission. And it might be surprising to some that the term is not found in Scripture. In fact, scholars think it was coined by Dutch missionary Justinian von Welz in the 1600s, and it was popularized in the 1800s by Hudson Taylor, British missionary to China. So Christendom existed for more than sixteen hundred years before this term came about.

Traditionally, the focus has been on the word "Go." Basically, the point is that we are to go into all the world and tell others about Jesus. Mission-sending agencies really like this focus.

However, in the last few decades there has been a lot of press about the idea that verse 19 is not so much about going and more about making disciples. The reasoning behind this is based on the verb tenses of the words. Technically, the only imperative verb (command, for those of you who are many years removed from third grade grammar) is the one translated as "make disciples." The Greek word for "Go" is not an imperative, and therefore many have recently translated it as "As you are going." As a result, the application has been something like, "As you are going about your life, be on the lookout for ways you can make disciples." Sounds pretty good, especially if you're not sold on the idea of going to other nations to be a missionary.

So we have two camps on what it's all about. Is it about going, or is it about making disciples? New Testament scholar Dr. Bob Mounce has some input on that. He argues that the "go" verb, while not an imperative, takes on the mood of the main verb, which makes it act as an imperative. So, he says, "Jesus' instructions are proactive; we are to move out into the world, not simply [sic] make disciples when we happen to be there."

Now that you've gotten your Greek lesson for the day, let's talk about what this means for us. Are we to go? Yes. Are we to make disciples? Yes. Do we have to go to China or Sudan or Peru to do so? No. But we should be willing to do so. And what can give us the strength to do that? Jesus' often-overlooked promise: "I am with you always, to the end of the age."

Excerpt taken from *100 Days in the Gospels* (© 2016).

All Will Be Tempted

Immediately the Spirit drove Him into the wilderness.
He was in the wilderness 40 days, being tempted by
Satan. He was with the wild animals, and the angels
began to serve Him. (Mark 1:12–13 HCSB)

We often hear people say, "Stay away from the things that tempt you, and you'll be okay," or "Avoid your temptation triggers." That's not bad advice, but it is not the whole story. No matter what we do to avoid temptation, there is one who desires to draw us into sin, and he will work his wiles on even the holiest of believers. No one is above the reach of temptation. After all, Satan himself tested Jesus.

Consider these words of nineteenth-century pastor Charles Spurgeon:

> A holy character does not avert temptation—Jesus was tempted. When Satan tempts us, his sparks fall upon tinder; but in Christ's case, it was like striking sparks on water; yet the enemy continued his evil work. Now, if the devil goes on striking when there is no result, how much more will he do it when he knows what inflammable stuff our hearts are made of. . . . In the haunts of men we expect to be tempted, but even seclusion will not guard us from the same trial. Jesus Christ was led away from human society into the wilderness, and was tempted of the devil. Solitude has its charms and its benefits, and may be useful in checking the lust of the eye and the pride of life; but the devil will follow us into

the most lovely retreats. Do not suppose that it is only the worldly-minded who have dreadful thoughts and blasphemous temptations, for even spiritual-minded persons endure the same; and in the holiest position we may suffer the darkest temptation. The utmost consecration of spirit will not insure you against Satanic temptation. Christ was consecrated through and through. It was his meat and drink to do the will of him that sent him: and yet he was tempted! Your hearts may glow with a seraphic flame of love to Jesus, and yet the devil will try to bring you down. . . . If you will tell me when God permits a Christian to lay aside his armour, I will tell you when Satan has left off temptation.

We will be tempted. There is no escape from it. But there is hope in the midst of temptation. When we know Scripture, we can fight the Devil's schemes with God's Word, as Jesus did. And we must put on the full Armor of Christ. Paul tells us, "In every situation take the shield of faith, and with it you will be able to extinguish all the flaming arrows of the evil one" (Eph. 6:16 HCSB).

Excerpt taken from *100 Days in the Gospels* (© 2016).

Obey Me the First Time

As He was passing along by the Sea of Galilee, He saw Simon and Andrew, Simon's brother. They were casting a net into the sea, since they were fishermen.

"Follow Me," Jesus told them, "and I will make you fish for people!" Immediately they left their nets and followed Him. Going on a little farther, He saw James the son of Zebedee and his brother John. They were in their boat mending their nets. Immediately He called them, and they left their father Zebedee in the boat with the hired men and followed Him. (Mark 1:16–20 HCSB)

In an early learning center, the teachers help parents say to their children, "Obey me the first time." For example, when a parent asks a child to do a task, such as putting his shoes away, the parent says, "Go put away your shoes. Obey me the first time." Hearing this statement helps young children learn to respond respectfully to their parent's directive the first time the request is made. (The jury's still out on how well this method works, but it seems like it would be worth a try!)

Imagine for a moment what might have happened if Simon and Andrew had not obeyed Jesus the first time He extended to them the invitation to follow Him. Not only would they have missed blessings in their own lives, they would have forfeited being a blessing to an infinite number of others—past, present, and future.

Contrast the disciples' story with that of the "rich man" we read about in Mark 10. He asked Jesus how one receives eternal life. The man said he had followed all the commandments in Scripture (which could be debatable), but he obviously knew something else was involved, or he wouldn't have asked Jesus the question. Jesus said to him, "You lack one thing: Go, sell all you have and give to the poor, and you will have treasure in heaven. Then come, follow Me." (Mark 10:21 HCSB). Jesus told the man what he needed to do to follow Him. Did the man do it? No. Mark says the man "went away grieving, because he had many possessions" (v. 22 HCSB). Just imagine! This man could have spent time with Jesus, but he didn't obey. Did he obey later? Perhaps. We would hope so. But even if he did, we know how short Jesus' time on earth was, and the rich man missed out because he didn't obey the first time.

As we seek direction from the Lord, are we ready, any time He calls, to obey Him the first time? Are we willing to do whatever He says, whenever He asks, for as long as He asks? He may not call us to give up our jobs and leave everything we know. He may not ask us to sell everything and give to the poor. But He might. Are we willing to deny ourselves and follow Him?

Excerpt taken from *100 Days in the Gospels* (© 2016).

The One and Only

*Very early in the morning, while it was still dark, He
got up, went out, and made His way to a deserted place.
And He was praying there. (Mark 1:35 HCSB)*

Two times of day.

Two fascinating looks at our Jesus—the One and Only.

Luke 4:40 tells us that the sick and suffering came out to see Jesus "when the sun was setting." To those of us who are Gentiles, the reason for this is not so obvious. Christ had previously left the synagogue when He went to the home of Simon, meaning it was the Sabbath day. Remember, at this point Christ primarily had been ministering in various synagogues to Jews. It was unlawful for them to carry the sick on the Sabbath. But God-fearing people counted the moments until the sun set over the Sea of Galilee, marking the close of day. So as the darkness fell, they bundled their sick and brought them to the Light. The thought almost makes me cry. It was as if they watched the clock of the law tick until it finally struck grace . . . and they raced to Him with their need. How blessed we are to live in the liberty of a completed Calvary! The pharmacy dispensing God's grace is open 24/7.

But a second snapshot of time also appears in our passage. Early the next morning, Jesus rose and went out to pray (Mark 1:35). I wish I had words to express the feelings such scriptural moments stir in me. The thought of Christ ducking out the door while it was still dark to find a place to be by Himself with God floods my soul with emotion. I love every glimpse of the unique relationship Father and Son shared while Christ was on earth and His Father was in heaven.

Never before had such a bridge connected the celestial and the terrestrial. I always wonder what Christ said to His Father and what He heard in those intimate moments. Did God the Father speak audibly to Him? Or did He speak in His heart like He does to you and me through His Word? I can't wait to find out someday in glory.

We have no idea how often Jesus got to steal away with His Father, but Scripture says He was soon interrupted by his disciples, excitedly shouting, "Everyone is looking for you!" (Mark 1:37 NIV). I'm convinced we don't give enough thought to how challenging Jesus' prison of flesh must have felt to Him. Prior to His advent, He was completely unencumbered by the natural laws governing the human body. Suddenly He experienced for Himself the pull to be in many places at once and the challenge to prioritize not just the good but the goal: proclaiming the good news of the kingdom of God. "That is why I have come" (v. 38 NIV).

Excerpt taken from *Portraits of Devotion* by Beth Moore (© 2014).

The 14 Challenge

*Then He told them, "The Sabbath was made for man
and not man for the Sabbath." (Mark 2:27 HCSB)*

If a regular rhythm of rest (a.k.a. Sabbath) is tough for you (psst. . .
it's tough for most of us) start with what I call the "14 Challenge."
Historically the Sabbath was one day out of every seven. This
amounts to 14 percent of a week. So let's just keep it simple by starting with the number *fourteen*. Look at your schedule and decide
when you can block out a Sabbath space of fourteen minutes each
day. Doesn't sound like much, but you might be shocked at how difficult this may be for you to achieve and maintain. You may also be
amazed at how much this block of time could rejuvenate you.

On the weekends, encourage your children to spend at least
fourteen minutes each day having some down time where they just
go to their rooms to read or play quietly. This teaches both toddlers
and teenagers that it's okay not to be constantly barraged by television, video games, and other forms of entertainment that someone
else provides for them with very little of their input.

If you're married, I also want to encourage you to determine
what weekend or full week you can devote as a couple to Sabbath
space, to rejuvenate and recalibrate from the other fifty-one weeks
of the year. You need this and so does your husband. So does your
relationship.

This doesn't necessarily mean taking a costly vacation *to* a particular destination. Sometimes it only means taking a vacation *from*
certain activities. A simple week "off" from inundating technology
and the normal schedule can give you a refreshing boost, as well as

the opportunity to do some things you don't usually have time for. Prioritizing a Sabbath will cause you to be fresher, lighter, and more prepared to take care of your home without becoming so easily frustrated and stressed out.

Beyond just planning breaks in your time, consider creating Sabbath spaces in the tangible areas of your home. As easy as it is for our calendars to become overrun with responsibilities, our own homes can also turn into pits of clutter and chaos, causing them to feel less like a haven and more like a cave or dungeon we want to get out of. So why not create some "margins" in your home as well? Just as you cleared fourteen minutes from your daily schedule, clear fourteen inches of space somewhere in your living area once a week.

As an act of obedience to God—even an act of praise-filled worship—start giving your home some breathing room. Deliberately own that small section of your world until you've transformed it from piles of junk into peace and joy. Do it consistently enough, and you'll wake up one day a few months from now with a living space that's orderly, balanced, and more available for God's use, all in fourteen-inch increments at a time.

Excerpt taken from *The Resolution for Women* by Priscilla Shirer (© 2011).

In the Eye of the Storm

And they were terrified and asked one another, "Who then is this? Even the wind and the sea obey Him!" (Mark 4:41 HCSB)

It was Jesus' idea to set foot on the boat that would take them to the other side. The phrase "let us" is repeated countless times in the Old and New Testament. Most often it precedes an act of the will—man's will or God's will—depending on who is saying it.

When Jesus says, "Let us go across to the other side," we can count on two things: it's the will of God and it will be accomplished. That's why He was able to fall asleep in the stern. He knew what was coming and He knew how He would handle it.

We don't have that luxury—neither did the disciples. Some had experience on the Sea of Galilee: Andrew, Peter, James, and John had been called from their lives as fishermen to become "fishers of men." A trip across the sea wasn't a new thing for them. They were familiar with the sea but not comfortably so. Stepping onto the boat, they knew there was an element of risk.

It was in the storm that they began to grapple with who Jesus really was. It was in the storm that He became more than a good teacher, more than a movement leader, but what He was—what He is—was still not fully known to them. But they got a glimpse.

When the storm hit they struggled to stay afloat and found Jesus was *napping.*

How can He sleep at a time like this? Doesn't He even care that we are going to die?

God can come off that way in the midst of the storm, can't He? When we're reeling from the wind and the waves, it sure can feel like

God is taking a nap. I can find myself asking Him, *Do You even care about me, about what I'm going through?* In the vast sea, it can seem reasonable that He doesn't—why should He? We are but a speck in the endless ocean!

We see that He does, in fact, care. Although the disciples could have used the rebuking, Jesus instead reprimanded the wind and waves. He spoke as a superior to an inferior, like a parent to a child: "Stop it and be quiet." And they did. It says the wind ceased. It didn't die down, it stopped completely. The waves went from liquid mountains to glassy calm in an instant. The same power that "raises the stormy wind" and "lifts up the waves of the sea" is the same power that "makes the storm be still" and "hushes the waves of the sea."

The pain inflicted by the storm is God's grace to help us quit trusting in our circumstances—whether the good or the bad. We come to the end of ourselves and discover there's only one anchor for our soul—only One who is able to manage the unmanageable storm.

Excerpt taken from *Steadfast Love* by Lauren Chandler (© 2016).

Go In Peace

"Daughter," He said to her, "your faith has made you well. Go in peace and be free from your affliction." (Mark 5:34 HCSB)

She had just touched His robe, and the crowd was breathless with anticipation. The sheer nerve of this woman, thinking she deserved something from Jesus. Who was she, anyway? Who touched Him?

He hardly let another moment pass before He blessed her.

He wasn't identifying her so that He could ridicule her or expose her shame. He was affirming her faith. Because in that moment, she believed Him to be more powerful than the condition that had crippled her for over a decade of her life. She was a woman with nothing left to lose and He recognized her faith in Him.

I imagine her weeping with relief, not just at her healing, but because she had felt something true rise up in her bones as He spoke.

He knows who I am.

We come with our infirmities and our feebleness and we beg for Him to heal us. But we fear His methods; we can't help but see ourselves as the exception to His mercy. Maybe He won't forgive me. Maybe my sin was too great. Maybe He doesn't even care. He'll just go on His way to more important things. I'm one in a crowd of millions. Who in the world do I think I am, calling out to the King?

On a dusty road leading to Nazareth, Jesus' actions answer that question.

You are the one I stop for.

You are the one I long to heal.

I know your name. I know your heart. I know everything about you, including that we would meet here today.

You are the one who sought me and I delighted in knowing your hand would reach for My hem in faith. What you saw as an act of desperation, I saw as an act of love. How many never reach out to Me at all because they don't think it would make a difference?

Now go in peace and newness of life.

Jesus makes it clear in this moment that she is not to be known as the woman with the issue of blood, but rather the woman *who had faith in Him.* She will not be known for what she was, but by what she had in spite of it.

Faith.

Don't trade your legacy for your reputation. He is here, and He is able.

I don't want to miss that blessing either, despite how hard it is to acknowledge my sins and my weaknesses while the crowds look on. What matters in this moment is not their eyes, but His. Never mind them; just remember that they are here to witness your faithfulness to Him. They have no power over you. Go to the Lord and tell Him your name. Tell Him the depth of your brokenness and regret.

You will walk for the rest of your days telling the story of redemption, not in words or deeds, but in your very existence.

Excerpt taken from *What Women Fear* by Angie Smith (© 2011).

I Knew You When

He went away from there and came to His hometown, and His disciples followed Him. When the Sabbath came, He began to teach in the synagogue, and many who heard Him were astonished. "Where did this man get these things?" they said. "What is this wisdom given to Him, and how are these miracles performed by His hands? Isn't this the carpenter, the son of Mary, and the brother of James, Joses, Judas, and Simon? And aren't His sisters here with us?" So they were offended by Him.

Then Jesus said to them, "A prophet is not without honor except in his hometown, among his relatives, and in his household." So He was not able to do any miracles there, except that He laid His hands on a few sick people and healed them. And He was amazed at their unbelief. (Mark 6:1–6 HCSB)

A pastor's son attended seminary, and his dad's church asked the son to preach one weekend when his father was out of town. Those who were new to the church thought he preached well and were moved by His sermon and what God stirred in their hearts through the teaching of the Word. But those who had seen the little boy grow up in the church had trouble seeing this young man as a preacher. To them, he was still the little kid who purposefully picked his nose during the preschool Christmas program, mooned the ladies' prayer group when he was ten, and later got caught throwing a party with alcohol when his parents were away. They had a hard time seeing him as something other than a rambunctious child who liked to stretch (or break) the rules.

A similar thing happened to Jesus in the passage on the previous page. The people of Nazareth knew Him well, they thought. Sure, they had heard that His birth was unique, but they assumed the stories were just that—stories. They had watched Him run in the streets as a boy. They watched Him grow into a young man, gaining the skills of a carpenter and working hard at His craft.

But now, they had heard He was teaching spiritual truth like none before Him. They had even heard He was healing the sick and casting out demons. Rather than come to Him, they took offense at Him. How could one of their own be telling them how to follow God? They missed His truth and His miracles because they believed He was no different than they were.

Maybe you know somebody who believes that Jesus was not the Son of God. Perhaps you have friends who don't accept that Jesus actually worked miracles. "He was just a man like us," some think. But we know He wasn't, and we know they need Him. Take time now to pray that those who do not believe Jesus is the Son of God will learn the truth and decide to follow Him.

Excerpt taken from *100 Days in the Gospels* (© 2016).

The Pace of Life

*"Come with me by yourselves to a quiet place
and get some rest." (Mark 6:31 NIV)*

The first roadblock for many of us is simply a pace of life that keeps us running so fast, we never purposefully think about the big picture—much less take proactive steps to course-correct. We are too stressed, too overloaded, and just plain tired too much of the time. But Jesus doesn't want us to be overloaded or stressed. And He *does* have an answer for us in Matthew:

> "Come to me, all you who are weary and burdened, and I will give you rest. Take my yoke upon you and learn from me, for I am gentle and humble in heart, and you will find rest for your souls. For my yoke is easy and my burden is light." (Matt. 11:28–30 NIV)

God does not want us to be weary or burdened. Jesus illustrates this by speaking of a yoke, an apparatus and a system designed to protect and help an animal as it tries to pull a heavy load. In our lives this would be the heavy load of life that we are trying to pull around by ourselves.

What Jesus is doing here is holding out His design, His boundaries, and His calling on our lives and saying, "Come hitch yourself to Me, take this life and this *way* of living I have designed for you, let Me lead you, and you will find rest even if you pull a heavy load."

Too often the reason we are overwhelmed or unclear is that we are trying to live in a way that is completely contrary to what God has planned for our lives. We are carrying a yoke, but it is not the one God has designed for our direction and protection as we walk through life with Him. Essentially we are living life in a way God does not intend us to.

It may sound as if we are talking about making sinful choices, and it is true that willful choices that go against God's principles will eventually catch up with us and will usually make us more stressed. But many of us are honestly trying to follow God's principles, and we are still stressed.

Most of us are living contrary to God's design specifications for us and His callings on our lives. We don't even realize it. The Bible says God knew us all before we were born, and He has created us each in a specific way, for a specific purpose, with specific callings. If we don't live according to those callings, we will feel off track. And if we get really far off track, we might find ourselves, at the end of our lives, looking back not with satisfaction and peace but with regret. But if we live according to those callings, life will just seem right.

Excerpt taken from *The Life Ready Woman* by Shaunti Feldhahn and Robert Lewis (© 2011).

The Space Between

"I believe; help my unbelief!" (Mark 9:24 ESV)

In the dark of night, 2,000 years ago, Jesus left a linen shroud and an empty grave, along with the imprints of His feet in the words of Scripture. Whether or not you feel like it's true is irrelevant.

I can't help but hear the echo of a man, begging for healing as he came across Jesus one day. It isn't a contradiction—his believing, yet asking for help for our unbelief—it is a confirmation of our humanity due to our sin nature, despite the desire to believe perfectly. With our mouths we say "I believe," and with our hearts we confess our inability to eliminate doubt. Our actions should always come from what we know is true, not what we are struggling to fully embrace in that truth.

Jesus knows the deepest measure of our own motivation. He fully recognizes the difference in a person who doubts while earnestly seeking God and a person who rejects God entirely. Instead of rebuking the man, He honors the plea for faith and heals his son.

It's interesting to note that the man had gone to the disciples (presumably believing they could heal his son) before he went to Christ, but they weren't able to cast out the demon. It stands to reason that his belief in Christ's ability may have wavered because of the disciples' failure, and by the time he spoke to Jesus, the word "if" had worked its way into his vocabulary. We're reminded that even today, the perceived inability of others has no relevance to the ability of God, nor can it change the sovereign will of God.

I love this story and the heart of the man who came to Jesus out of desperation, hungry to fill the gaps in his faith with belief. And what's the first thing he does in order to make progress in that direction?

He says he believes.

Do you think he *felt* differently after he stated it? Probably not. He has no reason to believe that's going to change based on physical evidence. He doesn't know that his son is about to be healed.

But he says he believes.

Many times in our lives as Christians, we'll be standing in the midst of what looks to us to be chaos, not knowing what the next scene will bring. That's the place of true faith. It's the space between, where we declare it without having seen the miracle yet.

I imagine that after the man watched his son be completely healed and restored to life, his feelings about belief changed. And many people today live out their faith the same way, telling the Lord they will believe when they see proof of Him.

Don't wait for the miracle you think will make it clear. Confess your belief and then act out of that determination. When unbelief comes to cloud our paths, may we step forward anyway, with these words on our lips: Lord . . . *I believe.*

Excerpt taken from *Chasing God* by Angie Smith (© 2014).

Compelled to Action

"This is the most important . . . Love the Lord your God
with all your heart, with all your soul, with all your mind,
and with all your strength." (Mark 12:29–30 HCSB)

Surely I love Jesus. *Right?*

Only love actually qualifies as love. And love carries a feeling. Not every second of every minute, of course, but it has frequent enough feeling involved in it to characterize the whole attachment. Is that fair enough? We know this instinctively with every other relationship in the human experience. Set aside all the times we toss around the word *love* to convey how we feel about a movie or a meal and let's limit it to the real thing.

We don't give a second thought to characterizing love primarily by feelings in our human relationships but, somehow, when it comes to Jesus, the definition shifts. The difference is understandable, of course. He is not visible. It's easy to subconsciously conclude that, since Jesus is unseeable, love for Jesus is probably unfeelable. With this view, love for Jesus is most about doing and least about feeling. Not only is this view misleading, it's woefully dissatisfying. In fact, Christ's point with Simon Peter in their dialogue in John 21 was that *the doing* He was assigning him ("feed My sheep") could only be sustained and satisfied for the long haul through *the loving*.

The love Jesus longs for is not just devotion. It's also emotion.

It's not just volition. It is also affection.

It is not just discipline. It is also passion.

It's not just routine. It is also romance.

And not just for Christ's sake but also for ours. Love is the cata-lyst. The holy cause and effect. The person you are when you love Jesus with everything in you—with your whole heart, soul, mind, and strength—is the real you. The brilliant you. The *bring-it* you. The breathtaking, *born-for-this* you. The person you were born to be crawls out of the shell of a heart cracked wide-open to the audacious love of Christ. When your heart, soul, mind, and might are engaged in a wholly invasive holy affection, march yourself into the nearest bathroom and look in the mirror over the sink.

That's you.

When the blood in your veins runs hot with holy affection for the living Christ, what do you want to do most? Paul put it this way: *Christ's love compels us.* When Christ's love invades every cell in your body, what are you compelled to do? The follow-up question is criti-cal. The answer to it is where the rubber meets the road, where dreams become realities and destinies that defy gravity finally get fulfilled. This is it: What would it take to do it? You answer those two questions: *What are you most compelled by the love of Christ to do?* and *What would it take to do it?*—then identify one first step toward that direction, and, child, you will find the next place to plant your foot on your divinely planned path.

Excerpt taken from *Audacious* by Beth Moore (© 2015).

The Things That Will Last

But in those days, after that tribulation: The sun will be dark-
ened, and the moon will not shed its light; the stars will be falling
from the sky, and the celestial powers will be shaken.

Then they will see the Son of Man coming in clouds with great
power and glory. He will send out the angels and gather His elect
from the four winds, from the end of the earth to the end of the sky.

Learn this parable from the fig tree: As soon as its branch
becomes tender and sprouts leaves, you know that summer is near.
In the same way, when you see these things happening, know that
He is near—at the door! I assure you: This generation will cer-
tainly not pass away until all these things take place. Heaven and
earth will pass away, but My words will never pass away. (Mark
13:24–31 HCSB)

Logic says that when the leaves on the trees begin fading from
green into yellow, red, or orange, the days are getting shorter
and winter is coming. The world is ordered so that we have constant
signs of things to come.

We also know everything is moving toward decay. We try to
prevent it. We spend money trying to impede physical decay. We
repair things when they wear down or break. If time has taught us
anything, it's that nothing lasts forever. The very earth we are standing on is winding down.

Scientists even say that half of the earth's heat is caused by radio-
active decay. The fact that our world will someday fade away is actually proof that Jesus' statement about His words is true. What He
says will come to pass, and what He says is reliable. Our hearts can

turn to doubt easily, but no matter how long we think it is taking for Jesus to keep His Word, He always does.

Today's devotional passage contains powerful statements about Christ's return. Jesus said these reassuring words in response to His disciple's inquiry about the end of the age. He spoke about some of the signs of the times. However, He cautioned them against trying to predict when the end would come, reminding them that no one knew the time—not the angels or even the Son—except the Father.

Sometimes we are so engrossed in the daily grind of life that we fail to give appropriate attention to the things that really matter, to things with Kingdom value, to the things of Christ. Our belief that this world is not our home and will pass away should encourage us to look for that which is truly eternal. Only that which is of Christ will last.

We can be certain that the words of the Lord are true and enduring; they will not pass away. Therefore, we should live in anticipation of their being fulfilled. Rather than trying to figure out a time line for Christ's return, we are to live each day as if He were coming at any moment. That is what really matters.

Excerpt taken from *100 Days in the Gospels* (© 2016).

Loneliness When There's a Cross to Carry

"And at the ninth hour Jesus cried with a loud voice, 'Eloi,
Eloi, lema sabachthani?' which means, 'My God, my
God, why have you forsaken me?'" (Mark 15:34 ESV)

I think Simon of Cyrene may be one of the most blessed men in all
of history.

Simon was an average guy—a father of two who was likely visiting Jerusalem for the Passover when a cross was placed on his back
(Mark 15:21). But this was not just any cross. This was the cross of
Christ. This was the greatest instrument of grace the world would
ever know. This was the scene of the most important rescue mission
there would ever be. This was the place where Jesus would die for
Simon's sins. For all our sins.

Jesus carried that cross for us, and for the briefest of moments
Simon carried it for Him. But Simon could only go so far. Ultimately,
the cross was a burden that only Jesus could bear. That walk up the
hill to Golgotha was surely a lonely one, and as Jesus later hung on
the cross that Simon carried, He did so alone.

None of us will ever bear a literal cross the way that Jesus did.
That fact alone is enough to cause us to rejoice even in lonely valleys, but we do have crosses to bear. There are things that we must
carry alone. Whether it's an illness, or a fear, or an experience, or a
wound, we all have things that we cannot successfully pass off to
someone else to carry. When that happens, we can take courage that
we are in good company.

Once on the cross, Jesus repeated a pattern we saw throughout
His entire life. He cried out to God the Father (Mark 15:34). In that

lonely season Jesus craved the presence of God. It was what He needed most in His most desperate moment.

The antidote to our loneliness is the presence of God.

This is the loneliest moment in all of history. God, who had always been steadfast before and has always been steadfast since, allowed His Son to bear our sins on that cross alone.

Jesus bore a season of unthinkable loneliness so that you could be reconciled to the Father. He bore the cross alone so that you could know and be known. He was lonely so that we never have to be. God's presence is the eternal answer to our lonely state.

But this was the story of Christ's agonizing death. It was the story of God's great sacrifice. The gospel can become so familiar to us that we forget the gravity of it. Life has a strange way of rocking us to sleep so that we miss the big stuff. But we need a wake-up call now and then, to remember the truth about who God is and how much we need Him.

Excerpt taken from *Connected* by Erin Davis (© 2016).

Embracing Mission Impossible

For nothing will be impossible with God. (Luke 1:37 HCSB)

I was seventeen when I visited Haiti on a mission trip, where I met a tiny young girl by the name of Manette. She was nine years old, living in what were undeniably the most deplorable conditions I had ever witnessed. It was one of those moments when you feel so full of compassion and desire to help yet so small and helpless.

I couldn't get her out of my mind. Even back at home in my comfortable air-conditioned existence, I thought back to the heat and filth and want of that impoverished island nation and the look on Manette's face. She had captured my heart. And though insecure about how to communicate with her, doubting that such a small effort from one person like me could do any good, and tempted just to put the whole thing out of my mind, I decided to try. By God's grace and through the partnership of those who minister there in Haiti on a daily basis, I began sending letters and dollars and tightly compressed care packages to Manette, hoping she'd sense the love of Christ through me.

In January 2010, news broke that a devastating earthquake had rocked the island of Haiti. Thousands were dead. Whole villages and buildings demolished. Even the president had been forced to flee his palace and relocate to other quarters. And Manette, who had e-mailed me only a few days earlier, was likely in the hard-hit capital city of Port au Prince, having just entered her first year of nursing school.

It would be three long, anxious days before my phone calls and messages to the missions organization finally triggered a response.

To my great relief I learned that Manette had made it through with only a few scratches—not only surviving but now busy helping in nearby Pignon where many had fled for safety. She was serving and sharing the love of Christ, a young woman transformed by our Savior's seeking heart.

I thought back to the day when I first met her, when the challenge of making a connection with a little girl so far away and so desperately in need seemed so terribly impossible. These many years later I've enjoyed a deep personal friendship for two decades with someone only God could've placed in my path. His intervention became an opportunity to love and be loved and be a small part of His plans for a young girl He had been drawing to Himself before the foundation of the world.

Sometimes His interventions feel like they're asking more than we can do. Costs too much. Hurts too much. Involves too much work, too many other people. Honestly there's probably a lot of truth to such concerns. But because God is calling, our job is not to obsess over the challenges but merely to trust what He's saying—not to focus on how little one person can do but embrace the opportunity of watching God do something incredible.

Excerpt taken from *Life Interrupted* by Priscilla Shirer (© 2011).

Lost and Found

Every year His parents traveled to Jerusalem for the Passover Festival. When He was 12 years old, they went up according to the custom of the festival. After those days were over, as they were returning, the boy Jesus stayed behind in Jerusalem, but His parents did not know it. Assuming He was in the traveling party, they went a day's journey. Then they began looking for Him among their relatives and friends. When they did not find Him, they returned to Jerusalem to search for Him. After three days, they found Him in the temple complex sitting among the teachers, listening to them and asking them questions. And all those who heard Him were astounded at His understanding and His answers. When His parents saw Him, they were astonished, and His mother said to Him, "Son, why have You treated us like this? Your father and I have been anxiously searching for You."

"Why were you searching for Me?" He asked them. "Didn't you know that I had to be in My Father's house?" But they did not understand what He said to them.

Then He went down with them and came to Nazareth and was obedient to them. His mother kept all these things in her heart. And Jesus increased in wisdom and stature, and in favor with God and with people. (Luke 2:41–52 HCSB)

How could Mary and Joseph not know their child was missing for an entire day? Likely, everyone thought He was with someone else. We know they were in a "traveling party," which could have been made up of hundreds of people. Additionally, it's possible that the women and children traveled in one party, followed by the men. As a twelve-year-old boy, Jesus could have been part of either group.

Regardless of how He was left behind without anyone noticing, Jesus was still in Jerusalem. But how were they to find Him? At the time, up to a hundred thousand people lived in Jerusalem, and another several hundred thousand would've been there for the Feast of the Passover. Frankly, it's amazing they found Him as quickly as they did.

We read that Mary and Joseph were astonished when they saw Him, but Jesus was astonished they hadn't known where to find Him. His parents didn't understand why He was there or how He knew the things He was discussing with the teachers—let alone His explanation of why He was there. This gives us a pretty good indication that Jesus' childhood was a fairly normal one. He obviously hadn't been performing miracles or doing other supernatural things, as some early Christian writings claimed, or His parents wouldn't have been surprised by His actions.

Instead, we're told He grew "in wisdom and stature, and in favor with God and with people" (Luke 2:52 HCSB). This is a good reminder that while Jesus was fully God, He was also fully human. He grew as children naturally grow up—mentally, physically, and spiritually.

The Perfect Substitute

Then Jesus returned from the Jordan, full of the Holy Spirit,
and was led by the Spirit in the wilderness for 40 days
to be tempted by the Devil. He ate nothing during those
days, and when they were over, He was hungry. The Devil
said to Him, "If You are the Son of God, tell this stone to
become bread." But Jesus answered him, "It is written:
Man must not live on bread alone." (Luke 4:1–4 HCSB)

When we think of a substitute, our minds likely take us back to school. The substitute teacher was never as good as the "real thing." It seems to be a fact of life that school kids tend to treat the substitute teacher with disrespect. (Spitballs, anyone?) Even young students are able to figure out that substitutes have little to no authority. They don't create the lesson plan or determine student grades, after all. Our experience of a classroom substitute is quite different than the Bible's presentation of Jesus as a substitute for sinful humanity. We think of a substitute as a temporary and poor replacement for the "real thing," but the Bible presents those who came before Jesus as the copies who pointed to Jesus.

Jesus is the real thing.

Let's go back to the beginning of humanity and look at Adam as an example. Adam, the first man, represented us before God. God spoke His Word to Adam, letting him know how to live as God's obedient son (Gen. 2:15–17).

Adam failed to live the righteous life God designed for him. He and Eve listened as the serpent distorted God's Word, leading them to disobedience (3:1–8). That very first sin changed our nature so that we've been sinning against God ever since the Garden. We are all guilty of sin that is unacceptable to the holy God who formed us (Rom. 5:12, 18–19). In this way, Adam was a true representative for mankind.

This unpleasant reality is hard to stomach. We want a different representative. In our individualist society, it is difficult to understand how one person's sin can affect other people in ways that are so unilaterally devastating.

Yet Satan is still up to his old tricks of distorting God's Word. It's still his goal to deceive God's children into thinking God meant something other than what He said. We're all capable of falling for the same old lies and living in ways contrary to God's best for us.

But remember, Jesus is the perfect substitute. He's not a lame excuse for the "real thing," but the only one with the authority to set things right.

Adam came face-to-face with the Serpent and forgot all that God said. Not Jesus! He came face-to-face with the Serpent and stood His ground. When Satan twisted God's Word, Jesus countered with rock-solid Truth. He lobbed more than spitballs in the direction of the Enemy. He took aim with the unapologetic Word of God. May He teach us to do the same.

Excerpt taken from *90 Days with the God Who Sees* (© 2017).

A Beautiful Reversal

*When the sun was setting, all those who had anyone sick with
various diseases brought them to Him. As He laid His hands
on each one of them, He would heal them. Also, demons were
coming out of many, shouting and saying, 'You are the Son of
God!' But He rebuked them and would not allow them to speak,
because they knew He was the Messiah. (Luke 4:40–41 HCSB)*

Because of sin, God's good creation has been infiltrated by all
kinds of evil. You are likely all too familiar with the things on
that list. Things like:

Disease

Chaos

Poverty

Conflict

Death

Sin has tarnished God's good creation. We see its awful effects
all around us. Even our own bodies have become living dioramas for
the devastating sin causes as they waste away due to age and disease.
The Bible goes so far as to say that we are enslaved to sin and its
effects (Rom. 6:17–22). Sin works like a ball and chain, tethering
each of us to this broken, groaning world.

That's the cloud. Here is the silver lining.

Jesus fulfilled all righteousness by taking on our human nature
and obeying where we've failed. He also announced the good news
of God's kingdom (Luke 4:42–44), prying our eyes off the sin and
destruction all around us and toward a future where holiness has

infiltrated all things instead of sin. Jesus' arrival marked the beginning of the kingdom of God, it was the start of the reversal of sin's devastating effects. He ushered in the rule of God where the effects of sin on creation were to be halted and reversed and God's people were to be liberated from sin's hold on them. Jesus healed many physical bodies to tell a bigger story. The decay and disease that has impacted people's bodies could be reversed because of Jesus. That's the lower story Jesus used to highlight that the death and decay that has infiltrated our hearts can be reversed too.

Since Jesus was the Messiah, anointed by God's Spirit to accomplish God's mission, Jesus had authority over all creation (5:1–10; 8:22–25). Jesus displayed this authority when He liberated people from physical bondage by healing their diseases (4:38–40) and from spiritual bondage by casting out their demons (vv. 41–44).

B. B. Warfield, the famous Princeton theologian, described Christ's work this way: "When our Lord came down to earth He drew heaven with Him. The signs which accompanied His ministry were but the trailing clouds of glory which He brought from heaven, which is His home. The number of the miracles which He wrought may easily be underrated. It has been said that in effect He banished disease and death from Palestine for the three years of His ministry."

All manor of diseases lost their grip in Jesus' presence. Most significantly, the disease of sin is reversed forever because the Messiah has come. One day we will exchange these broken bodies for heavenly ones and this sin nature for righteousness.

Excerpt taken from *90 Days with the God Who Sees* (© 2017).

His Gifts Runneth Over

*Give, and you will receive. Your gift will return to you in
full—pressed down, shaken together to make room for more,
running over, and poured into your lap. The amount you give
will determine the amount you get back. (Luke 6:38 NLT)*

It appears there's nothing exact about God's recipe of return to us.
His gifts are overflowing. When you choose to give, He promises
you'll have enough—more than you think—filling you back up
with even more than you had to begin with. Not just a good measure, not just one that's been pressed down and shaken together—
not even one that's fair, equal to what you deserve—but one that is
brimming over, unable to be contained.

Now, by no means am I suggesting that you should always and
without question give of yourself at the expense of the relationships
and purposes that should be prioritized in your life. Sometimes the
best, most empowering word you can learn to utter is *no.* But on
those occasions when you feel genuinely led by God to give, you
needn't be worried about what appears to be a dwindling amount of
personal resources to suit the task. If He has endorsed your involve-
ment, you can proceed with complete contentment and willingness,
knowing He will always give back far more than you every expended.
The contented woman, required to give of her time, her love, her
resources . . . herself . . . is secure in the knowledge that she possessed enough to do it. And she looks forward to experiencing the
promise of an outlandish return on her investment.

I can imagine what you may be thinking because I've thought it
too . . .

- My energy level is so low.
- My "love tank" is running so close to empty. I'm sure I'm about to stall.
- It's only Tuesday, but my patience quota has already been used up for the week.
- My wallet is even emptier than I remember, and my financial needs aren't going away.

Yet just when you feel as though you're completely void of anything worthwhile to offer, or when your situation makes you feel justified in not being the one to participate, you'll often hear Him whispering . . .

"Give, and it will be given to you."

And when He scoops up the dividends that He'll be sending back your way, He won't be short and scanty about it. He won't skim off the excess or be bound by an "exact" measurement. He will supply you a portion that is abundantly good and beyond what is warranted. He'll shake and press, shake and press, to make sure no pockets of air are taking up space reserved for His blessing. And then He'll pile up His favor and grace into such a rounded heap that it will spill off the sides, more than you can hold.

So, "give, and it will be given to you; a good measure—pressed down, shaken together, and running over—will be poured into your lap."

Excerpt taken from *The Resolution for Women* by Priscilla Shirer (© 2011).

Underneath it All

A good man produces good out of the good storeroom of his heart.
And evil man produces evil out of the evil storeroom, for his
mouth speaks from the overflow of his heart. (Luke 6:45 HCSB)

Controlling my own tongue is a quest I'm sure will require all the maturity every year of my life will bring. That's because so far along this journey, I've already discovered that the "cracks" I make with my mouth are actually symptoms of a much deeper, much more intimate issue, something much more difficult to address. It's down below the surface. Closer to the ground than my mouth is.

"For [my] mouth speaks from the overflow of [my] heart" (Luke 6:45).

Turns out, my mouth is only a barometer that divulges whether I'm immersed in humility and surrendered in obedience to the Lord, or I'm housing a malnourished spirit that stubbornly refuses to yield to the wisdom of God's own Word.

It's a foundational issue.

So taking inventory of your tongue's track record is an instructive way to uncover what's hidden within it. Let's try it.

- *Symptom:* Are you always quick to offer an opinion, inserting your assessments into conversations at every conceivable opportunity? *Diagnosis:* This could reveal a haughty tinge in your heart, which causes you to feel the need to impress and be at the center of attention.
- *Symptom:* Do you frequently find yourself quarreling with your spouse or being divisive among others? *Diagnosis:* You're lacking a spirit of peace and unity deep inside, a true

desire for your relationships to be strengthened and reflect the grace of Christ.

- *Symptom:* Does gossip continue to come easily for you, so that even the steeliest self-restraint is unable to stop you? *Diagnosis:* You find others' problems and difficulties entertaining and don't think of them as people needing your support, prayer, and companionship.
- *Symptom:* Do your words often reveal a doubtful, skeptical outlook? *Diagnosis:* You're low in the faith and belief department, not operating from a deep trust in God's ability and His wise handling of the details and timing of your life.

The words of our lips are like cracks in the wall, revealing what's going on at the foundation, in our "heart."

Jesus' use of the word *heart* in this verse signifies the inner being of an individual, the place where our thoughts, attitudes, and beliefs are cemented. The heart is a reservoir, a holding tank for every attitude and belief we've either placed there or allowed to hang out there. It is a storehouse containing the essence of who we are and—because of its direct link to our ongoing habits and actions—the picture of who we're becoming.

So I ask you . . .

What are you putting inside?

What treasures are you storing?

If you don't know, just listen to yourself, because your words and tone and topics of conversation will tell you.

Any lasting change you make in controlling your speech will have to start at the base, the foundation, down where the cracks are really formed.

Excerpt taken from *The Resolution for Women* by Priscilla Shirer (© 2011).

More Than Enough

In the presence of all the people, she declared the reason she had
touched Him and how she was instantly cured. (Luke 8:47 HCSB)

In Luke 8:42, we read that the crowd pressed so closely to Jesus
they were almost crushing Him. Yet a woman behind Him
touched only the edge of His cloak—she never even touched His
skin—and He discerned the difference. Amazing! Notice, too, that
when Christ asked, "Who touched me?" they all denied it. Odd,
isn't it? The people were so close they were nearly crushing Him, but
no one admitted to touching Him. Their response reminds me of
children too afraid of getting into trouble to admit to something.
Did they not realize He wanted few things more than for them to
reach out to Him?

When the woman realized she could not go unnoticed, she
"came trembling and fell at his feet" (v. 47 NIV). Beloved, no one
goes unnoticed by Christ—least of all a person acting on faith. I
love the fact that the woman came trembling, even though she had
exercised enough faith to draw forth the healing power of Jesus. It's
good to know that the faithful still come trembling. In fact, their
reverence is a critical part of their faith. The truly believing will most
certainly also be the bowing.

Why do you think Christ asked her to identify herself? I think
one reason might have been so that she could enjoy the healing she
had received. Most modern Bible translations don't record one
phrase found in the King James Version of verse 48: "Daughter, *be*
of good comfort: thy faith hath made thee whole; go in peace" (author
emphasis). In this way I believe Christ was saying, "Do not go forth

as someone who feels like they have stolen a gift! Be of good cheer! I freely give it to you!"

Verse 42 also tells us Jesus was on His way to heal the dying child of Jairus when the woman in the crowd touched the edge of His cloak. Christ Himself described what happened: "Someone touched me; I know that power has gone out from me" (v. 46 NIV).

Hear this: Jesus has more than enough power! Does He seem to be on His way to another need, one that you perceive may be more important than yours? More a matter of life and death? No problem! Reach out and grab that hem! You are not going unnoticed—not even if He's on His way to raise the dead!

Would you dare to believe that He is completely able? If He doesn't grant you what you ask in faith, it is never because He lacks the power. I believe it's because He wants to release an all-surpassing power and reveal an even greater glory through another answer. Will we laugh at the thought like the foolish mourners outside Jairus's home? Or will we be invited into the house to behold a miracle?

Excerpt taken from *Portraits of Devotion* by Beth Moore (© 2014).

Storms of Grace

*Then He got up and rebuked the wind and the raging waves.
So they ceased, and there was a calm. He said to them, "Where
is your faith?" They were fearful and amazed, asking one
another, "Who can this be? He commands even the winds
and the waves, and they obey Him!" (Luke 8:24–25 HCSB)*

In Luke 8 we find the disciples sailing into the eye of the storm. All the while, Jesus was sawing logs in the back of the boat (He was a carpenter, after all)? Their boat was already taking on water when they finally woke Jesus.

Jesus spoke and it was all over.

"Then He got up and rebuked the wind and the raging waves. So they ceased, and there was a calm" (v. 24 HCSB).

After Jesus calmed the storm, He asked the disciples this question: "Where is your faith?" (v. 25 HCSB).

Location, not existence, becomes the issue. They're putting their faith somewhere; it's just not where it should be. Their faith is in the power of the storm—the wind that knocks them off their feet and the waves that threaten to drown them. I don't fault them for putting their faith there—for believing the storm will overcome them. When we're in the storm, the wind and the waves feel real.

The diagnosis

The prognosis

The anxiety

The unknowns

The bills piling high

The job loss

The empty crib

The death of a loved one—those things feel real. Those things we can taste, touch, hear, smell, and see.

Yet, the pain inflicted by the storm is God's grace to help us quit trusting in our circumstances—whether the good or the bad. It peels back the veil from our eyes. Before the storm, we are easily fooled into thinking that we have something to do with our well-being, or that having certain things in our lives ensures stability. But when we're eyeball to eyeball with the wind and the waves, we quickly see through the veneer. We come to our "wit's end" just like the men in the ships in Psalm 107.

"Then they cried out to the LORD in their trouble, and He brought them out of their distress. He stilled the storm to a murmur, and the waves of the sea were hushed. They rejoiced when the waves grew quiet. Then He guided them to the harbor they longed for" (vv. 28–30 HCSB).

When we face life's storms, we reel, we stagger, our courage melts. We come to the end of ourselves and discover there's only one anchor for our soul—only One who is able to manage the unmanageable storm.

If all our hope is tied to what cannot sustain, wouldn't it be God's wrath to let us stay tethered to the false anchors? So when we ask Him in the midst of the storm, "Do You even care?" We can be confident that He replies with a resounding "YES." If He didn't care, we wouldn't be where we are. We would be floating along merrily, oblivious to our peril.

Excerpt taken from *Steadfast Love* by Lauren Chandler (© 2016).

Take Up Your Cross

But He strictly warned and instructed them to tell this to no one, saying, "The Son of Man must suffer many things and be rejected by the elders, chief priests, and scribes, be killed, and be raised the third day."

Then He said to them all, "If anyone wants to come with Me, he must deny himself, take up his cross daily, and follow Me. For whoever wants to save his life will lose it, but whoever loses his life because of Me will save it. What is a man benefited if he gains the whole world, yet loses or forfeits himself? For whoever is ashamed of Me and My words, the Son of Man will be ashamed of him when He comes in His glory and that of the Father and the holy angels. I tell you the truth: There are some standing here who will not taste death until they see the kingdom of God." (Luke 9:21–27 HCSB)

Knowing some details of what Jesus went through at His crucifixion, we may shudder to think He might ever call us to do the same. The cross reminds us of suffering, pain, rejection, scorn, self-sacrifice, hardship, and even loving and forgiving those who have harmed us. Yet in Luke 9:23, Jesus is calling us, as His followers, to do just that: to lay aside our own gain for the sake of others and for His glory. And we have His power and grace to carry us through.

Nineteenth-century pastor Charles Spurgeon said,

> Mark then, Christian, Jesus does not suffer so as to exclude your suffering. He bears a cross, not that you may escape it, but that you may endure it. Christ exempts you from sin, but not from sorrow. Remember

that, and expect to suffer. But let us comfort ourselves with this thought, that in our case . . . it is not our cross, but Christ's cross which we carry. When you are molested for your piety; when your religion brings the trial of cruel mockings upon you, then remember it is not your cross, it is Christ's cross; and how delightful is it to carry the cross of our Lord Jesus! You carry the cross after him. You have blessed company; your path is marked with the footprints of your Lord. The mark of his blood-red shoulder is upon that heavy burden. 'Tis his cross, and he goes before you as a shepherd goes before his sheep. Take up your cross daily, and follow him.

Our inclination is to use our skills, talents, and resources to further our cause and gratify our own pleasures. Yet, Jesus is calling us to do something we consider radical: to identify with Him, obeying His commands, regardless of the cost.

The world teaches us to do just the opposite. Today's media push us to give our preferences priority. But to follow Jesus, we must do what He did—to serve and not seek to be served. Then we will truly be His disciples.

Excerpt taken from *100 Days in the Gospels* (© 2016).

The Greatest

Then an argument started among them about who would be the greatest of them. (Luke 9:46 HCSB)

Jesus gathered His disciples around Him and urged them to remember Him when He was gone. It must have been a sober time as the disciples considered what life would be like without the Man they had come to love so much. Jesus broke bread with the people He had shared life with for the last three years. Surely the taste of death was bitter in His cup.

At the close of the Lord's last supper with His disciples, an argument broke out among the disciples. It takes my breath away to consider the subject of the argument. For a moment, envision yourself reclining at the table with the Lord as He shares some of His last words, anticipating a time very soon when He will be betrayed, forsaken, and killed. I would probably ask Him to tell me over and over again, all the while trying to figure out a way to protect Him and to make sure I did everything in my power to show Him how much I loved Him.

I would scarcely be able to eat from that table, knowing that His betrayer was nearby. Wouldn't I have done anything to show my devotion to Him? Surely I would have offered to lay down my life for His if it would be permissible.

Wouldn't I?

I would like to say I would.

I bet the disciples would have said the same, but the sad truth is that all the love they could humanly feel for Christ was not enough for them to escape their own fear and selfishness on their own. In a matter of hours, Jesus would be taken, beaten, and hung with arms outstretched to the point of death to bear the penalty for their sin and for ours.

I would love to believe that I would have comprehended the magnitude of this moment; that I would break bread with only thoughts of Him, myself made small in my own eyes.

Instead, they argued.

They weren't expressing rage over His death, or fighting to know how they could serve Him. What they wanted to know in this critical moment was this:

Who is the greatest among us?

Who is Your favorite, Jesus? Who am I in Your eyes?

The cup is passed and the wine is drunk.

And instead of tasting His goodness, they fight over their own fear of insignificance.

Like the disciples, my fear gets the best of me sometimes. As troubled as I may be for Him, truth be told I am no different from the disciples. In the recesses of my heart, in more moments than I want to admit, I have asked Jesus the same.

Do I matter, Lord? Am I important to You?

And Jesus whispers to me in those moments just as He did to them so long ago, asking the question that speaks right to the heart of the fear.

Who is greater?

Excerpt taken from *What Women Fear* by Angie Smith (© 2011).

The Way to Fight

*"Behold, I have given you authority to tread on serpents
and scorpions, and over all the power of the enemy,
and nothing shall hurt you." (Luke 10:19 ESV)*

Prayer is how we isolate the real problems. It's how we get up behind those problems and attack them at the roots. It's how we isolate the real enemy and keep him on his heels and off our man.

And prayer is also how God gets through to *us*, leading us to pray for our husband. For our children.

So even if things are going pretty well for you right now, even if you don't have a lot to complain about or feel upset over, the enemy is still there, whether in full-on attack mode or lurking, waiting for the next possible opportunity to infiltrate. So pray. And pray fervently.

And what about your children? How are you praying for them? The Bible says our children are "like arrows in the hand of a warrior" (Ps. 127:4 NASB). We raise them up to shoot them out into the culture, bearing the image of Christ to the world. Sounds again, then, like a place that would qualify as a major area of concern for an enemy who doesn't want any vestige of Christian valor and virtue running loose out there where they might take bold stands of faith. Might pastor a church or serve in all kinds of missions and ministry opportunities, honoring Christ and serving hundreds of people. Worst of all, they might marry and raise up a whole *other* generation of little Christ followers, keeping your family burning red hot on enemy radar long beyond your lifetime, spinning up a legacy of faith that spirals forward undaunted into the future.

Your enemy can't be having any of that, now, can he?

So don't be surprised when he starts coming after your kids. And don't think it's all because they're being headstrong or peer dependent or careless or lazy. Satan knows the parts of their character—both their strengths and their weaknesses—where he can worm in and try stunting their growth, their potential, and their confidence.

Let the enemy run roughshod over my kids? No way. And I have a strong feeling you won't allow him to do it to yours either.

An enemy is after your children, I'm telling you. Believe it. Know it. But most important, *deal with it*—by tunneling deep into your prayer closet and fighting back with every parental and spiritual weapon at your disposal.

As much as the devil loves stirring up trouble in churches, he loves stirring up trouble in families. He's a relationship destroyer, causing immeasurable amounts of senseless hurt and distraction within your family.

But if we're wise, we can stand against him, putting prayer into effect. Then as God's Spirit does His work in us and in these situations, the rest of our family will be standing close enough to watch it all happen, to see the kinds of change and impact our prayers are able to accomplish.

Excerpt taken from *Fervent* by Priscilla Shirer (© 2015).

Letting Go of Perfect

*But one thing is necessary. Mary has made the right choice
and it will not be taken away from her. (Luke 10:42 HCSB)*

I love the characters found in God's Word. Like watching an infant taking his first steps, you really want to see them succeed but are holding your breath for the disastrous tumble you know is coming.

Of course, these stories haven't been given to us for their entertainment value but rather for our edification. We can learn much from the characters' examples, good and bad. I tend to gravitate toward the "bad" examples rather than the good. They shore up my ego a bit and serve to remind me that "God chose the foolish things of the world to shame the wise" (1 Cor. 1:27 NIV).

There aren't many "foolish" women like this in the Bible. Most of those mentioned are of the never doubting, always believing sort. Ruth is loyal, Rahab shows great faith, and the Virgin Mary is humble in the face of great honor. Certainly these are women I strive to emulate; but despite my great respect for their faithful ways, I just don't see us hanging out together. There are a few, though, that I definitely could see myself chatting on the phone with while my children run amuck and dinner burns on the stove: Sarah, a control freak who can't help but take things into her own hands and laughs at God's "alternative" plan; Rachel, who's frankly a big fat liar and a thief and a little whiny about the whole naming her kid "son of my trouble" thing (Gen. 35:18). These are women I can identify with— the ones that mess everything up and then complain about how messed up everything is.

In the New Testament there's Martha (Luke 10:38–42). Martha, Martha, Martha. How can you not love Martha, or at least feel really sorry for her? She is like the first-century version of Martha Stewart, wanting everything to be nice for her guests. And her guest is the Son of God, after all. Certainly if there is anyone for whom you want to make napkin animals, it would be Jesus, right? Isn't that what service is all about? Getting it right? I guess not, because despite the fact that she is working her tail off, probably whipping up a creative centerpiece and tasty hors d'oeuvres, Jesus doesn't seem too impressed. I can relate. While I wish to be Mary, listening at the feet of Jesus, doing the thing that is better, I know I would be the one running around like a chicken with its head cut off.

We *are* told to show our faith by our works (Phil. 2:12) and are given gifts and abilities in order that we might accomplish them. Too often, though, we are so busy exercising those gifts that we forget why we are running the race in the first place. The end game is not perfection, but to sit at the feet of Jesus and learn how to better glorify Him.

Excerpt taken from *Letting Go of Perfect* by Amy Spiegel (© 2012).

Our Father

"Lord, teach us to pray." (Luke 11:1 ESV)

We don't know the name of the disciple who asked, but we hear his voice as he bravely inquires of Jesus. The Lord has just finished a time of prayer, and all eyes were on the one who took a chance and spoke up.

It should be noted that nobody (in any of the Gospels) ever asks Jesus to teach them how to disciple others. Nor do they ask Him to teach them how to perform miracles or how to be effective preachers. And yet they ask Him how to pray.

If our role is to constantly become more like Him, we want to model His behavior and His decisions, but in this case He was often gone for hours (even nights) on end where they didn't have the benefit of observing Him pray. It seems they're essentially asking Him to reveal what it is that makes those hours so necessary to Him, and to help them see a glimpse of the power of prayer.

A mere seventy words long, it provides us with a beautiful structure for our own prayer lives. Jesus didn't teach them this prayer in order for it to simply be repeated, but rather to give them (and us) a model of prayer.

Don't beat yourself up if prayer doesn't come naturally to you, and don't get caught up in what everyone else is doing. This isn't something that should frustrate you or make you feel bad about yourself. It's an opportunity to have real intimacy with the Lord, and that's no small privilege.

It begins with a heart that is humbly seeking God, asking Him to teach us what we don't already know. We're acknowledging that it's going to be a process, and we're going to move forward a little and likely back again before we make real progress. That's the nature of being a disciple.

Jesus doesn't waste a single word, beginning with the phrase, "*When* you pray . . ." (Luke 11:2 ESV). He's clearly saying this isn't an "if" situation we're talking about. It's not a suggestion; we're commanded to pray. So when? How?

Immediately after this statement, Jesus begins the actual prayer portion with a short sentence we often breeze past: "Our Father in heaven" (Matt. 6:9 ESV).

Even as we read "Our Father," we're urged to remember we exist in a community of believers. There is an inherent humility in recognizing we are a part of the whole and not simply an individual whose life can be untangled from everyone else's. He isn't just my Father, but the Father of many, and my prayer and life should reflect that I am aware of that.

He uses the word *Father* intentionally. The biblical perspective of God is that of a Father who desires to give good things to those who love Him. He is our Abba Father. It's an intimate term, reserved for those who have identified Him as our Savior. And because of Christ's blood, we can approach Him as such.

Excerpt taken from *Chasing God* by Angie Smith (© 2014).

Oxygen

He replied, "Blessed rather are those who hear the
word of God and obey it." (Luke 11:28 NIV)

God knows His children and what they need. And—in His sovereign care and His sovereign timing—He gives it to them. He writes faith into our stories, not by any merit or action of our own, but simply because it pleases Him to do so.

In his letters to young churches, the apostle Paul often prayed that these believers who were new to the faith would be carried along by the work of the Holy Spirit within them—a gift given by God's grace to them—not by their own merit (1 Cor. 1:4–9).

We don't have to fret if our feelings of faith seem weaker today than yesterday, or worry about our circumstances today or tomorrow. God has written the whole of our stories, start to finish, and what He has written into them—including the faith He gives us through Christ—no one can erase.

When you're in Christ, faith is woven into the fabric of your story. Not even death can unravel it. That heavy quilt of circumstance can feel stifling, but the gospel is always true. The gospel is for the moment Christ calls us to repent and follow Him, and for every moment before and after.

It is for our times of joy and fervor, and of doubt and despair.

We need it every minute. The gospel is our oxygen.

But, here in our temporary home, the gospel can seem intangible. So where do we turn when the heavy blanket is closing in, when we're in the dark, gasping for air?

We turn to God's Word.

We find Truth in its pages, the very breath of God fills our lungs, our heart, our mind, our soul. Whether we come to Him doubting, praising, weeping, laughing, His Word is for us and it is true. It never fades. We can approach it in any condition, under any circumstance, and IT IS STILL TRUE. When our will is weak, our faith fragile, our hearts are heavy, and even in our doubt—God's Word is true.

The gospel is the reason we can take Paul seriously when he writes, "Rejoice always! Pray constantly. Give thanks in everything" (1 Thess. 5:16–18 HCSB). It is the reason we can put away our faith formulas and walk side by side with the One who wrote faith into our stories and has promised to finish what He started.

Jesus promised His disciples they'd have trouble, and we're guaranteed to have it too (John 16:33; 1 Pet. 4:12). Darkness and death are weighty, and our emotions, our actions, even our beliefs may bend at their pressure. But our God does not. There is no one like Him (1 Sam. 2:2).

Let your chest rise and fall today with the knowledge that the gospel is true. It is oxygen, available every moment of every day, and you can breathe it in.

Excerpt taken from *She Reads Truth* by Raechel Myers and Amanda Bible Williams (© 2016).

Burst Into Praise

"Son," he said to him, "you are always with me, and
everything I have is yours. But we had to celebrate and
rejoice, because this brother of yours was dead and is alive
again; he was lost and is found." (Luke 15:31–32 HCSB)

He's an easy to miss character in the story of the prodigal son—
the older brother. His response to his rebellious sibling is
indignant. The father had already given the younger son his inheritance, so what remained was by right the older son's. So the robe,
ring, and shoes the father put on the prodigal? Technically, those
belonged to the older brother. The food for the feast and wares for
the party? The older brother's. The only way the younger brother
could be accepted back as a son was at the expense of the older
brother.

In the parable of the prodigal son, the older brother acted badly.
He resented his father's generosity on his behalf. Rather than joining
the celebration for his brother's return, he threw himself a pity party.
I probably would have done the same. Praise the Lord, though, we
have a better Older Brother.

"For those whom he foreknew he also predestined to be con-
formed to the image of his Son, in order that he might be the first-
born among many brothers" (Rom. 8:29 ESV).

Jesus is the better Older Brother. We are accepted, clothed, and
celebrated at His expense. He paid the price for the grace we freely
receive. His righteousness covers our unrighteousness. His blood
atones for our sin. We walk in the newness of life because we no
longer live, but Christ lives in us. And the life we now live in the

flesh we live by faith in the Son of God, who loved us and gave Himself for us (Gal. 2:20).

Such grace! Such thanks in response! It overflows into praise. It's the "let them extol him in the congregation of the people" and the "praise him in the assembly of the elders." The gratitude we feel cannot be contained, it bursts into praise.

For those of us who have been in distress and were delivered by the Lord, we have a responsibility to tell it. For the health of our own hearts, the praise must flow forth. As our physical hearts pump oxygenated blood to the rest of the body, so our spiritual hearts pump praise to the Body, the Church—encouraging growth and endurance.

Don't picture "cheerleader" praise, a rah-rah chant and spirit sprinkles. This kind of praise I'm talking about is deep-seated and genuine. It's not for God so that He can "win the game." It's for us and those who hear us. Praise lets us tell on God—to recount all the ways He has been faithful. It's an invitation to join the chorus that has been singing the same song from the beginning:

> Whoever is wise, let him attend to these things; let them consider the steadfast love of the Lord.

Excerpt taken from *Steadfast Love* by Lauren Chandler (© 2016).

Give to Caesar

Then the scribes and the chief priests looked for a way to get their hands on Him that very hour, because they knew He had told this parable against them, but they feared the people.

They watched closely and sent spies who pretended to be righteous, so they could catch Him in what He said, to hand Him over to the governor's rule and authority. They questioned Him, "Teacher, we know that You speak and teach correctly, and You don't show partiality, but teach truthfully the way of God. Is it lawful for us to pay taxes to Caesar or not?"

But detecting their craftiness, He said to them, "Show Me a denarius. Whose image and inscription does it have?"

"Caesar's," they said.

"Well then," He told them, "give back to Caesar the things that are Caesar's and to God the things that are God's."

They were not able to catch Him in what He said in public, and being amazed at His answer, they became silent. (Luke 20:19–26 HCSB)

The religious leaders took every chance they could to try to trap Jesus into saying or doing something that would break their laws. But Jesus was very clever in answering their questions. In this passage, the religious leaders sent a group to try to trip Jesus up by asking if they should pay taxes to Caesar. But this time, before questioning Him, they tried to butter Him up with flattery.

Then the leaders asked whether or not they should pay tribute to Caesar by recognizing as lawful the personal (head count) tax with a coin bearing Caesar's inscription. This was an additional tax above the other taxes each Roman citizen was required to pay. If Jesus approved payment of the tax, it would contradict the Law of Moses, which said allegiance was to be given only to God. If He said the tax should not be paid, Jesus could be found guilty of treason.

The answer Jesus gave began with a concrete object. He had them pull out a Roman coin and He asked them whose picture and title are stamped on it. Of course, everyone knew that Caesar's image was on the coin. Then Jesus replied, "Give to Caesar what is Caesar's and to God what is God's." It was more than a thoughtful response. Our willingness to submit to authority magnifies God's greatness because we obey for God's sake, not the government's. When paying taxes, we fulfill what the government requires of us, which honors God.

We read about taxes again in Romans 13: "For government is God's servant. . . . And for this reason you pay taxes, since the authorities are God's public servants, continually attending to these tasks. Pay your obligations to everyone: taxes to those you owe taxes, tolls to those you owe tolls, respect to those you owe respect, and honor to those you owe honor" (vv. 4, 6–7 HCSB). We honor God when we honor those He puts in authority over us, including our government officials.

Excerpt taken from *100 Days in the Gospels* (© 2016).

Empty Inheritances

*Jesus sent Peter and John, saying, "Go and prepare the
Passover meal for us, so we can eat it." (Luke 22:8 HCSB)*

Christ's appointments are never haphazard. He can accomplish anything He desires by merely thinking it into existence. Yet He sovereignly chooses to employ mortals to flesh out an invisible work in the visible realm . . . even Jesus the perfect Word made flesh.

I believe Peter and John were not only chosen for the job of preparing the Passover but that the job was chosen for them. In their letters, Peter and John repeatedly refer to Christ as the Lamb. Perhaps a large part of their understanding came in retrospect after their preparation for the last Passover with Christ. Both men were also influenced early on by John the Baptist, having been directly influenced by him. John 1:29 tells us that these disciples first encountered Jesus through the words of the Baptizer: "Look, the Lamb of God, who takes away the sin of the world!" (NIV).

Jesus would not rest until Peter and John knew exactly what that title meant. The pair didn't run by the Old City market and grab a plastic-wrapped package of trimmed lamb for a buck fifty a pound. No, they picked out a live lamb and then had the sweet thing slaughtered, very likely holding it still for the knife. Most of us can hardly imagine all that was involved in preparing for a Passover, but you can be sure that none of it was wasted.

Christ isn't into waste management. If He assigns us to a difficult task or season, every ounce of our experience is meant for our instruction—if only we'll let Him finish the work.

Psalm 25:14 says, "The LORD confides in those who fear him; he makes his covenant known to them" (NIV). I believe these treasures are hidden in secret, not because He shares them with a chosen few, but because not many seek to know Him and tarry with Him long enough to find out.

As Peter and John prepared the Passover meal that day, they were privy to many secrets that became clearer and clearer to them as time passed. Ecclesiastes 3:11 says God makes everything beautiful in its time. Too often we settle for the bearable when beauty was just around the corner, waiting.

Surely many years and Passover celebrations passed before Peter and John fully assimilated the profound significance of the one in which Jesus became the Lamb. John wrote over twenty references to the Lamb in the Book of Revelation. And it was Peter who wrote of the old, "empty way of life inherited from the fathers" (1 Pet. 1:18 HCSB).

Once Peter knew the true Passover Lamb, an Old Testament Passover meant nothing without its fulfillment in Jesus. He knew that the ritual "inheritances" were empty without Jesus. Christ became everything, and all former things were empty without Him.

Excerpt taken from *Portraits of Devotion* by Beth Moore (© 2014).

Moment By Moment

*"Father, if You are willing, take this cup away
from Me—nevertheless, not My will, but
Yours, be done." (Luke 22:42 HCSB)*

The Bible is littered with stories of people who believed they had a better solution than the one God was offering to them. What we notice upon reading these stories is that the Lord doesn't respond the same way to each one; it seems that individuals who plead their case to Him while expressing a genuine desire to remain in His will have influenced His response.

For example, when Abraham pleaded to God on behalf of a sinful, disobedient city, we see them "negotiating" about the number of righteous men that must be found in order to save that city. Throughout the conversation we see Abraham humbling himself to the Lord, saying things like, "though I am nothing but dust and ashes . . ." (Gen. 18:27 NIV) and "may the Lord not be angry" (Gen. 18:32 NIV). Abraham wanted God to change what He had already told him, but it is also abundantly clear that Abraham knew who is God and who was not. Abraham recognized in this moment what I fail to so many times in my life.

I have every right in the world to ask God to intervene if it is still in accordance with the purpose of His will. But I must kneel low before Him in humble submission, recognizing that at the end of the day, it just might not look the way I want it to. What a beautiful image we allow Him to paint when we trust Him in seasons of life that feel ugly.

After all, our Lord did the same.

As His blood mingled with sweat and the hours passed in the garden, He knew He would soon be crucified. Three times He asked His Father to let the cup pass if He was willing. Even in the face of death, Jesus recognized the sovereignty of God and submitted to it.

You don't just have to be at the end of your rope to cry out to Him. In fact you may not recognize His leading in that moment if you haven't relied on Him before.

What if we deliberately made the Lord a part of our hours and not just our hour of need?

As Christians we can look ridiculous to the outside world when we say we "prayed for a parking spot," or "asked the Lord to get us there in time." It does sound silly when compared to the heavy issues being faced if not by us, then by those around us. I am certainly not making the case for a "gumball machine God" who gives us whatever we ask. Rather, I want to encourage you to invite Him into your days. Speak to Him while you do the laundry, play with your children, or sit in a stadium full of people.

Be in constant communion with Him so that when times get hard, you will have relationship instead of requests.

Excerpt taken from *What Women Fear* by Angie Smith (© 2011).

Sweet Indeed

He said to them, "How unwise and slow you are to believe in your hearts all that the prophets have spoken! Didn't the Messiah have to suffer these things and enter into His glory?" Then beginning with Moses and all the Prophets, He interpreted for them the things concerning Himself in all the Scriptures. (Luke 24:25–27 HCSB)

Many of us are not used to thinking of God's commandments—and Scripture in general—as "sweeter than honey," something that is delicious and desirable and yet, that is how the psalmist describes God's Word.

How sweet Your word is to my taste—sweeter than honey in my mouth. (Ps. 119:103 HCSB)

Even if we can reckon with the idea of loving God's law, we may have trouble figuring out how not to think of it in the context of a religious duty or a "chore chart" (something sometimes followed but not particularly enjoyed in my home!). But the psalms speak of God's children delighting in God's law. How in the world do we get to that perspective?

Here's one way we find God's commands delightful and His instruction tasty like honey: by moving beyond what God requires of us and seeing what He has accomplished Himself. God Himself is the Hero of God's story, and as it pertains to His desire to be known, He Himself bridges the communication gap we are unable to span ourselves. His commands become a delight to us when He becomes a delight to us. He does this first by speaking into the shadows of general revelation revealed through creation in the special revelation of Scripture. He does this by speaking in the special revelation of Scripture the great announcement of the gospel of Jesus.

The point of special revelation, then, is to reveal the gospel. God's written Word points to Jesus, the Living Word. Don't take my word for it, however. Listen to Jesus Himself:

> "He said to them, 'How unwise and slow you are to believe in your hearts all that the prophets have spoken! Didn't the Messiah have to suffer these things and enter into His glory?' Then beginning with Moses and all the Prophets, He interpreted for them the things concerning Himself in all the Scriptures."

After Jesus was raised from the dead, He caught up with a couple of disciples making a trek to Emmaus. He sidled up alongside them and preached the greatest Christ-centered, expository sermon from the Old Testament ever preached in the history of the world. In the shadow of the cross, soon after the resurrection, at the dawn of the New Covenant when the world's understanding of God had been thoroughly flipped in it's head, "The point of all that," Jesus essentially said, pointing to the varied wonders of what we call the Old Testament, "is Me."

Jesus is the true Messiah long awaited by the people of God. He was asserting Himself as the culmination of human history, worthy of our allegiance and obedience. That truth is sweet indeed.

Excerpt taken from *90 Days with the God Who Speaks* (© 2017).

The Word

In the beginning was the Word, and the Word was with God, and the Word was God. He was with God in the beginning. All things were created through Him, and apart from Him not one thing was created that has been created. Life was in Him, and that life was the light of men. That light shines in the darkness, yet the darkness did not overcome it.

There was a man named John who was sent from God. He came as a witness to testify about the light, so that all might believe through him. He was not the light, but he came to testify about the light. The true light, who gives light to everyone, was coming into the world.

He was in the world, and the world was created through Him, yet the world did not recognize Him. He came to His own, and His own people did not receive Him. But to all who did receive Him, He gave them the right to be children of God, to those who believe in His name, who were born, not of blood, or of the will of the flesh, or of the will of man, but of God.

The Word became flesh and took up residence among us. We observed His glory, the glory as the One and Only Son from the Father, full of grace and truth. (John 1:1–14 HCSB)

John began his Gospel with a concise and powerful statement. "The Word" is a wonderful, descriptive title for Jesus, the Son of God. Jesus is the eternal, pre-existing Word-become-flesh. He is the direct message from the Father who reveals His purpose through the very life of Christ.

The Word (Jesus) is the Author and Creator of all things. Not one thing was made apart from Him. He was there when the Father spoke the heavens and the earth into being.

Have you ever noticed the first-person plural pronouns in Genesis 1:26? Scripture reads: "Let Us make man in Our image, according to Our likeness" (HCSB). It's likely that many of us imagine just God the Father present during creation. But it was the Trinity—they were all there, including Jesus, as John tells us in his Gospel. Jesus "was with God in the beginning." This gives us a bigger picture of Jesus' role. He didn't just begin to exist and work when He was born in Bethlehem. He's existed since the beginning.

He was there in the garden when God called out to Adam. He was there when God gave the law to Moses and dwelled among His people in the tabernacle. He was with God and He was God.

Jesus is the culmination of the Father's plan for salvation. The One who made everything, from the highest angel to the lowliest insect, came to be our salvation—the Author and Finisher of our faith. Who else is more qualified to offer new life than the One who created life? God gave us His Word, and this is good news indeed!

Excerpt taken from *100 Days in the Gospels* (© 2016).

Called

"Behold, the Lamb of God!" (John 1:36 ESV)

I n the first chapter of John, we see John standing with two other men, Andrew and Simon Peter. Jesus walked by, and John immediately declared, "Behold, the Lamb of God!"

It's possible John had been telling them all about His experience with Jesus the previous day, revealing that he'd seen the Spirit descend like a dove on the Lord. His heart had no doubt been stirred. The other men were all too anxious to follow Him themselves. Scripture doesn't mention them asking Him anything, nor even greeting Him. It's as if they were so moved by His presence that they simply started *walking*.

That's the first important thing we can do as disciples of Christ. No big questions, no interrogations, no agenda. Just our steps, one after another, as we seek to walk the road His feet are carving.

Don't worry. He won't leave things silent for long.

"What are you seeking?" Jesus asks them when He sees them following (John 1:38 ESV).

In other words, "What are you hoping to gain here? What do you want from Me?" It isn't a rebuke, but rather a question posed in love and interest.

Imagine the scene; they've started walking behind Him when He turns to ask them what it is they desire. What a beautiful image of our Lord, ever loving and wanting us to know we're valuable to Him. We walk and He turns to us. What a gift it is to serve a God so interested in the personal details.

They answer Him with a question of their own.

"Rabbi, where are you staying?"

Well, that didn't really tell Jesus what they were seeking, did it? Actually, if we dig a little deeper we will see that it just might. The term *rabbi* means several things, most notably, "teacher." So right away they are acknowledging that He has some authority, even though they have yet to even be introduced to Him. The fact that they asked where He was staying isn't to dodge His question. It was likely to tell Him they were interested in going with Him, but they weren't being presumptuous that He would allow them to do so. In one brief sentence, the first we hear the disciples speak, they give two references to the fact that they look up to Him and, in a sense, defer to Him.

"Come and you will see."

So few words, yet so profoundly important to incorporate into our own understanding of God. It sets up the journey so succinctly and identifies our roles as we go. We aren't to be passive about it, but instead, we're to take action, making His example our highest calling, constantly aware of our need for His grace in the process. We're not the ones in charge of finding Him, but rather, our goal is to walk in a way that makes us more like Him every day.

He is leading and you are following. It's His map, His road, and His time line.

Excerpt taken from *Chasing God* by Angie Smith (© 2014).

Jesus' First Miracle

On the third day a wedding took place in Cana of Galilee.
Jesus' mother was there, and Jesus and His disciples were invited to
the wedding as well. When the wine ran out, Jesus' mother told
Him, "They don't have any wine."

"What has this concern of yours to do with Me, woman?" Jesus
asked. "My hour has not yet come."

"Do whatever He tells you," His mother told the servants.

Now six stone water jars had been set there for Jewish purifi-
cation. Each contained 20 or 30 gallons.

"Fill the jars with water," Jesus told them. So they filled them
to the brim. Then He said to them, "Now draw some out and take
it to the chief servant." And they did.

When the chief servant tasted the water (after it had become
wine), he did not know where it came from—though the servants
who had drawn the water knew. He called the groom and told
him, "Everyone sets out the fine wine first, then, after people have
drunk freely, the inferior. But you have kept the fine wine until
now."

Jesus performed this first sign in Cana of Galilee. He displayed
His glory, and His disciples believed in Him.

After this, He went down to Capernaum, together with His
mother, His brothers, and His disciples, and they stayed there only
a few days. (John 2:1–12 HCSB)

We might think that a wedding at noon, followed by an infor-
mal reception, then followed later by an evening dinner is a
long wedding. But in Jesus' day, wedding celebrations could last a

week. The groom was financially responsible for this extended party, and we know the guests weren't limited to family, since Jesus, His mother, and His disciples were all present for the celebration in John 2. A wedding was quite a financial undertaking.

Added to the financial stress was the knowledge that running out of food or drink would bring great embarrassment to the family. This was just the situation Jesus found Himself in.

Mary saw the problem, and she informed Jesus. He responded in what might seem to be a rude fashion, but by using the word "woman," He was simply distancing Himself from her, for reasons that we can only speculate upon. Jesus wasn't ready to start revealing His power to the world, but His mother insisted, and He acquiesced.

We don't know exactly what Mary expected Jesus to do, but those there to witness it were likely surprised to see Him turn six large containers of water into wine—quality wine.

Not everyone knew where this wine had come from, but we can rest assured that those who knew were astonished by His power. We read that because of this display of His glory, His disciples believed in Him.

We, too, can believe in the power of Christ. He can and does work miracles, the most amazing of which is the miracle He does in our hearts when we choose to trust in Him.

Excerpt taken from *100 Days in the Gospels* (© 2016).

You Must Be Born Again

> *There was a man from the Pharisees named Nicodemus, a ruler of the Jews. This man came to Him at night and said, "Rabbi, we know that You have come from God as a teacher, for no one could perform these signs You do unless God were with him."*
>
> *Jesus replied, "I assure you: Unless someone is born again, he cannot see the kingdom of God."*
>
> *"But how can anyone be born when he is old?" Nicodemus asked Him. "Can he enter his mother's womb a second time and be born?"*
>
> *Jesus answered, "I assure you: Unless someone is born of water and the Spirit, he cannot enter the kingdom of God. Whatever is born of the flesh is flesh, and whatever is born of the Spirit is spirit. Do not be amazed that I told you that you must be born again. The wind blows where it pleases, and you hear its sound, but you don't know where it comes from or where it is going. So it is with everyone born of the Spirit." (John 3:1–8 HCSB)*

Have you ever wondered what the phrase "born again" means? Nicodemus approached Jesus at night, curious about both Jesus and the Kingdom of God. Jesus told him he must be born again, but Nicodemus was confused by this answer.

A highly moral and respected leader of the Jewish community, Nicodemus was no doubt a fine man. Yet something was lacking. Like Nicodemus, many people today confuse religion with new birth in Christ. Phrases like "I pray regularly" or "I believe there is a God" are often confused with a real new-birth experience.

New birth begins with the Holy Spirit convicting us of our sin and need for a Savior. Because of sin, we are spiritually dead. For this reason, spiritual birth, as Jesus described it, is necessary. God loves us and gives us spiritual birth when we ask Him for it.

The Bible says all persons are sinners (Rom. 3:23). Jesus died on a cross and was raised from the dead to save sinners. To be born again means that a person admits to God that he or she is a sinner, repents of sin, believes in or trusts Christ, and confesses faith in Christ as Savior and Lord. Jesus told Nicodemus that everyone who believes in (places faith in) Christ would not perish (John 3:16). Jesus is the only One who can save us (John 14:6).

To believe in Jesus is to be born again. Confess your sins and ask Jesus right now to save you. "Then everyone who calls on the name of the Lord will be saved" (Acts 2:21 HCSB). After you have received Jesus Christ into your life, share your decision with another person. Then follow Christ's example by asking to be baptized by immersion in a local, Bible-believing church, as a public expression of your faith (Rom. 6:4; Col. 2:6).

Excerpt taken from *100 Days in the Gospels* (© 2016).

All for You

For God so loved the world that he gave his one and only Son, that whoever believes in him shall not perish but have eternal life. For God did not send his Son into the world to condemn the world, but to save the world through him. (John 3:16–17 NIV)

The Son of God, conceived by the Holy Spirit, born of a virgin: He crawled and toddled and skinned His knees. The one called *the Word* learned to talk. He laughed and cried. He, who'd never slumbered, slept and He, who'd never hungered, ate. Jesus grew into manhood and walked on callous feet of flesh to the banks of the Jordan River. There in the waters He'd once parted for the children of Israel, John the Baptizer dunked His head.

He went to a wedding and turned water into wine. He cleansed the lepers, healed the sick, loosed the tongues of the mute, gave sight to the blind and hearing to the deaf. He walked on water as if it were dry ground. He confounded the wise, called the simple, dined with the sinners, dipped bread with a betrayer, and took up for the looked-down upon. He fed thousands from a few fish and loaves, and preached the Scriptures to multitudes and droves.

And He raised the dead.

Then, He did what He'd come most to do. Sweating blood, He submitted Himself to the will of His Father to give over His life and hang on a cross, letting the full weight of humanity's sin rest bloody and mean on His body. He cried out "It is finished!" then He bowed His head and gave up His Spirit.

Stone cold dead.

Three days later, He sat straight up and walked out of that tomb. He appeared to His disciples and some five hundred others and, after a period of forty days, entrusted the gospel to His followers, promised to send the Holy Spirit for comfort and power, and ascended right before their eyes straight up into the heavens. Don't you know they were glad to get Him home?

Dear God.

If that's not adventure, I don't know what is. Here's the part that connects the point straight to you. John 3:16–17 tells us exactly why the Father sent His only beloved Son: "For God so loved the world . . ." (NKJV).

For God so loved *you*.

He knew your name before creation, what all your life would entail. He knew both strands of your DNA by heart. He chose the generation in which you'd live and planted you in an exact spot on the planet to initiate divine purpose. His Son took on flesh, gave His life, and rose from the dead for all humankind—including you. He sits at the right hand of God to intercede for you. He sent His promised Holy Spirit to seal, sanctify, thrill, and fill you.

Every single day Jesus pursues and fights valiantly for you. Every single day He gazes on your face, bringing you one step closer to seeing His.

Excerpt taken from *Audacious* by Beth Moore (© 2015).

Jesus' Spokesperson

So they came to John and told him, "Rabbi, the One you testi-
fied about, and who was with you across the Jordan, is baptiz-
ing—and everyone is flocking to Him."

John responded, "No one can receive a single thing unless it's
given to him from heaven. You yourselves can testify that I said, 'I
am not the Messiah, but I've been sent ahead of Him.' He who has
the bride is the groom. But the groom's friend, who stands by and
listens for him, rejoices greatly at the groom's voice. So this joy of
mine is complete. He must increase, but I must decrease."

The One who comes from above is above all. The one who is
from the earth is earthly and speaks in earthly terms. The One who
comes from heaven is above all. He testifies to what He has seen
and heard, yet no one accepts His testimony. The one who has
accepted His testimony has affirmed that God is true. For God sent
Him, and He speaks God's words, since He gives the Spirit without
measure. The Father loves the Son and has given all things into
His hands. The one who believes in the Son has eternal life, but
the one who refuses to believe in the Son will not see life; instead,
the wrath of God remains on him. (John 3:26–36 HCSB)

In today's world, it's not unusual for a celebrity, an athlete, or a
person of power to have an authorized spokesperson speak on his or
her behalf. The job of this person is to be the voice of someone else,
to speak with authority and integrity. Perhaps the most visible of
these spokespeople today is the White House Press Secretary. This
person is tasked with telling the media—and through them, the
American people—what is happening around the world and in the

country, as well the reactions of the president and other senior government officials. The press secretary doesn't speak for herself; she speaks for something bigger: the White House. Her job is to lift up the president, not herself.

John the Baptist had the unique and daunting assignment of speaking for the Savior of the World. As the one who prepared the way for Jesus, John's role was to point people to the Messiah, the Son of God. In order to do his job effectively, John had to lift up someone other than himself—not an easy task for most humans.

In today's passage, John executed his job well. He declared that Jesus was sent from God the Father. Jesus spoke the very words of God. Everything God had and was and possessed, Jesus had and was and possessed. Jesus and the Father were and are one.

What a declaration! What a promise! What a Savior! And for those of us who call Him Lord, what an example for us to emulate. John was bold and unswerving in his proclamation of Jesus. Can we do any less?

Excerpt taken from *100 Days in the Gospels* (© 2016).

His Word Brings Life

The words that I have spoken to you are
spirit and are life. (John 6:63 HCSB)

God's Word always brings life. It was with a word that He brought forth all creation. The commandments that He spoke to Moses were for the good of His people—that they would live long in the land He promised them. It's not just the Law through which God speaks life, but all of Scripture.

The Scriptures are the food that Jesus talked about when He answered Satan's temptation to turn stones into bread. We don't live by physical food alone, but on the "manna and quail" generously provided in God's Word.

The psalmist croons delight in meditating on Scripture, "Oh how I love your law! It is my meditation all the day" (Ps. 119:97 ESV).

The psalmist's desire was God's Word. He'd gotten a taste of it and dreamed about every bite from then on. It had proven sweet and sustainable.

In our folly, we stuff ourselves with what may taste sweet at first, but it leaves a bitter aftertaste. And we are always emptier than we were before we indulged. We feed on our own wisdom and it makes us sick. However, when we turn to God, when we cry out to Him, He gives us back our appetite and fills us with good things—namely, His Word.

For over a year now, I have been meeting almost weekly with a group of women. We open the Bible and talk about what it says and how that bears on our lives. Some weeks are easier than others; the pages lay before us and truth is easy to discern and apply. Other times, we either wrestle to understand or struggle to humbly submit to what it says. In addition to mining the Scriptures for gems, we memorize and recite it. It's like 2nd grade Sunday school all over again—but without the stickers. Our reward is having God's Word written on our hearts and minds. It's work but it's worth it.

There's a warning we should heed, though. In John 5, Jesus had just healed a man who had been lame for thirty-eight years. To the Pharisees (the most religious Jews) though, this healing act was an abomination. Jesus had healed the man on the Sabbath. In their eyes, He had broken the Sabbath. The act of healing was not on their list of acceptable practices on what was meant to be a day of rest. They had taken what God had said and twisted it to suit their preferences. The Pharisees missed the whole point. Jesus calls them on it saying, "You search the Scriptures because you think that in them you have eternal life; and it is they that bear witness about me, yet you refuse to come to me that you may have life" (John 5:39–40 ESV).

Our healing is only found in Jesus—the Word made flesh. We devour Scripture so that we may know God, that we may see Him and love Him.

Promised Land Living

"I came that they may have life and have
it abundantly." (John 10:10 ESV)

M ilk. And honey.

Milk may be what I need, but honey is what I love.

That's why I'm glad God didn't promise the Israelites a land flowing with nothing but milk. Life is good, just like milk is good. But the life Jesus came to give is a whole lot more than good. It's not just the good life; it's the great life, the kind of life He intends for us to experience "abundantly."

Our God is indeed a God of abundance. Wherever you happen to travel in the Bible, you're never far away from some mention of His fondness for going above and beyond.

- He supplies everything we need out of His "glorious riches" (Phil. 4:19 NIV).
- He's able to brighten our hearts with "joy inexpressible and full of glory" (1 Pet. 1:8 NASB).
- The woman in Song of Solomon envisioned Him as being "altogether lovely" (Song of Songs 5:16 NIV).
- He promised to make His people "abound in prosperity" as they obeyed Him (Deut. 28:11 NASB).
- He presented even the prodigal with the "best robe" and a "fattened calf" (Luke 15:22–23 NASB).
- He has blessed us with "every spiritual blessing in the heavenly places" (Eph. 1:3 NASB).
- He has "lavished on us" the "riches of His grace" (Eph. 1:7–8 NASB).

- David could hardly come up with the words to describe His "unfailing love" (Ps. 36:7 NIV).
- His new Jerusalem is said to have gates of "pearl" and streets of "pure gold" (Rev. 21:21 NASB).

So we're not talking about a God who's thrifty in His tastes or stingy in His gifts. On the contrary, He is sitting on the edge of His seat to give us more than we can "ask or think" (Eph. 3:20 NASB). Bread and wine. Milk and honey. Abundant life. He brings us:

Confidence—the sweet assurance that you've been anchored in right standing with God. No longer hounded by guilt and condemnation but fully alive in the afterglow of forgiven sin.

Joy—not because your trials and difficulties have necessarily let up but because you've been graciously relieved of wallowing in worry.

Discernment—being so saturated in the truth of His Word and attuned to recognize His voice, you can be clear on His direction, no matter how hard the path.

Anticipation—an excitement that no circumstance can dull, no setback can silence, no doubt can quench. You just know that God is actively working.

Power—a life overflowing with supernatural evidence of God's Spirit alive and at work in you, around you, and through you.

Oh, sure, there's lots of milk in what God has to offer—lots of depth, substance, and faith-based fiber. But it's not just a life of Bible knowledge and Sunday school coffee. It's a life filled with colors and textures and unexpected opportunities. It's honey—a life enhanced with all the juicy flavors of the Promised Land—deeply satisfying but, oh, so sweet.

Excerpt taken from *One in a Million* by Priscilla Shirer (© 2010).

In the Dark of Night

So Jesus then told them plainly, "Lazarus has died.
I'm glad for you that I wasn't there so that you may
believe. But let's go to him." (John 11:14–15 HCSB)

We know from commentaries on the story of Lazarus that after He received Mary and Martha's letter, the Lord waited another two full days before beginning His journey to Judea.

As I've tried to imagine what it must have felt like to be Mary and Martha, I so easily associate with their limited viewpoint. They have sent word they trust will be received by the Lord who loves them. They know that He will recognize the urgency in their voices and surely will come and heal their beloved brother. Each morning they wake to another seemingly hopeless day, watching the hours tick by until eventually they begin to lose hope. They weren't given an explanation. They sat in silence and hurt because they felt like the only One who could make it right had abandoned them.

I am sure that somewhere along the way they wondered if they had angered or offended Jesus.

Maybe He was punishing them for something they had done in the past.

Maybe He was too busy.

Maybe He didn't care.

Maybe they just didn't matter to Him as much as they thought they did.

Maybe He wasn't powerful enough for this situation.

Maybe He wasn't who He said He was after all.

However theologically flawed they were, all of those thoughts entered my mind during my high risk pregnancy. On dark nights when the rest of the neighborhood was asleep, I was awake, battling with my brokenness and asking Him why He wouldn't come. I have no doubt that Satan was thriving on my angst and doing everything he could to convince me that I had been forsaken.

Have you been there?

In the dark of night, it is easy to surrender to the lies.

What Mary and Martha could not see is what the Lord was doing and how He was responding to the situation. Jesus tells His disciples that Lazarus is dead but that He is glad He wasn't there so that they will be able to witness the miracle and believe.

Think about this for a minute.

The letter that Jesus has received from the sisters says that Lazarus is *sick*, not that he has died.

The Lord knew exactly what was happening to Lazarus just like He knew exactly what was happening to my baby. Yet we, just like Mary and Martha, are not privy to His thoughts.

Sometimes He just feels so faraway and so indifferent from where we are. Of course we see glimpses of Him and reasons to believe. Yet we are human. We want to *know* He is coming.

Yet, even in the dark of night, we can hold on to the promise of His coming. Take comfort! He knows exactly what is happening in our lives as we wait for Him to say "But let us go to her."

Excerpt taken from *I Will Carry You* by Angie Smith (© 2010).

Do You Believe?

Everyone who lives and believes in Me will never die—
ever. Do you believe this? (John 11:26 HCSB)

After Lazarus has been in the tomb for four days, Martha received word that Jesus was coming. Jesus halted by the city gates, and she ran to meet Him there. The first thing we are told about their conversation is that Martha tells the Lord her brother would still be alive if He had been there (John 11:21).

Was she blaming Him? Was she angry with Him?

Based on reading several commentaries on this passage, it seems likely that she wasn't angry but was declaring her faith in Him. This faith is evidenced by her next statement, "But I know that *even now* God will give you whatever you ask" (John 11:22 NIV).

If You are who You say You are, it is not too late.

Jesus responded by saying that Lazarus would rise, which Martha misinterpreted as a referral to His resurrection into heaven on the last day. It is easy to jump to the assumption that He is going to intervene but not in the way we want Him to. I love what happens next. He has a way of doing things like this in our lives, doesn't He?

He began by reminding her who He is, "I am the resurrection and the life. He who believes in me will live, even if he dies; and whoever believes in me will never die" (John 11:25 NIV, author paraphrase). Then He asked the hard question.

"Do you believe this?"

Ouch.

Not much room for negotiation, is there?

He knew she believed in Him because He knew her heart and her mind. I believe He asks us this question in our lives because sometimes we need to hear our own voices responding to His call. I see more of Martha in myself than I want to admit. I have expectations of Him, and although at my core I know that *He* is God, I am hurt when I feel like He hasn't met me where I wanted Him to be. In these moments we are faced with the question that must be answered as we look deep into the eyes of the Father.

Either He is or He isn't.

There is no middle ground.

He didn't ask her if she was sad or if she was disappointed. He didn't tell her anything more about her brother. He paused, mid-conversation, and asked her where her faith was.

"'Yes, Lord,' she told him, 'I believe that you are the Christ, the Son of God, who was to come into the world'" (John 11:27 NIV).

Beautiful, isn't it?

Jesus simply and comfortably showed patience with her questioning and misunderstanding, using it as an opportunity for her to hear her own words of faith. This is Who He is to me, as so many times He has taught me in this same way. My doubt is diffused by the simplicity of His request.

Yes, Lord. I believe.

Excerpt taken from *I Will Carry You* by Angie Smith (© 2010).

Jesus Wept

When Mary came to where Jesus was and saw Him, she fell at His feet and told Him, "Lord, if You had been here, my brother would not have died!"

When Jesus saw her crying, and the Jews who had come with her crying, He was angry in His spirit and deeply moved. "Where have you put him?" He asked.

"Lord," they told Him, "come and see."

Jesus wept.

So the Jews said, "See how He loved him!" But some of them said, "Couldn't He who opened the blind man's eyes also have kept this man from dying?"

Then Jesus, angry in Himself again, came to the tomb. It was a cave, and a stone was lying against it. "Remove the stone," Jesus said.

Martha, the dead man's sister, told Him, "Lord, he's already decaying. It's been four days."

Jesus said to her, "Didn't I tell you that if you believed you would see the glory of God?"

So they removed the stone. Then Jesus raised His eyes and said, "Father, I thank You that You heard Me. I know that You always hear Me, but because of the crowd standing here I said this, so they may believe You sent Me." After He said this, He shouted with a loud voice, "Lazarus, come out!" The dead man came out bound hand and foot with linen strips and with his face wrapped in a cloth. Jesus said to them, "Loose him and let him go." (John 11:32–44 HCSB)

It has long been a staple in Bible quizzes: "What's the shortest verse in the Bible?" Hands shoot up, and at least one kid shouts it out before being called on: "Jesus wept!"

This miniscule verse comes right in the middle of the story of Lazarus being raised from the dead. At this point, he's still dead. Jesus had just spoken to Lazarus' sister Martha. Lazarus' other sister Mary is weeping at Jesus' feet, and she's telling Jesus that if He had been there, Lazarus wouldn't be dead. She was heartbroken.

So why did Jesus weep? Scripture doesn't tell us, exactly, but we can take a few guesses. His friends were suffering, and He would have had compassion for them. Even though He knew what was about to happen, they didn't, and they were hurting. He also may have been angry over the reality of death in this world, as a result of our sin. And He knew that He was about to have to die Himself in order to rectify that situation.

Jesus wept with His friends, and He had compassion on them, and He did what only He could have done—He raised Lazarus from the dead. Jesus also weeps with us when we weep, He has compassion on us, and He died and rose from the grave Himself so that we can also be raised from spiritual death. Take a moment to praise Him for that today!

Excerpt taken from *100 Days in the Gospels* (© 2016).

Remove the Stone

"Remove the stone," Jesus said. Martha, the dead man's
sister, told Him, "Lord, he's already decaying. It's been four
days." Jesus said to her, "Didn't I tell you that if you believed
you would see the glory of God?" (John 11:39–40 HCSB)

Jesus could have healed Lazarus without even coming to Bethany. He chose to resurrect him the way He did for the benefit of those who saw it. It's the same today. Have you ever felt like you have been invited to be a part of His miracle? As Jesus, Mary, and Martha arrive at the tomb, He asks those present to move the stone that is blocking the entrance. Instead of running to it in obedience, Martha questions him, telling Him that the stench of decomposition would be too strong.

It sounds ridiculous to be worried about something as silly as a smell when there might be a chance to see your brother again, but this is much more powerful than Martha's words.

It is not about the stench. It is about trust.

He asked them, and He asks us, to be a part of the miracle. How do we respond to this? Are we so distraught over our perceived fears and disappointments that we are paralyzed, or do we trust Him enough to put our hands on the rock? There is no middle ground. Those are our two options: fear or trust.

We all have some Martha in us, so it is easy to focus on the potential problems with what we feel the Lord leading us to do, but that is exactly why He does it. I would love to say I always followed His requests, but I haven't. Many times I stood, hands behind my back, explaining all the reasons I was not moving. After all, what could be worse than walking in front of everyone, mustering up all of my strength, and being let down? Sometimes staying put just feels easier, where there's no more room for disappointment.

Of course, we also may never see what's on the other side of the stone.

Jesus addressed this in His reply to Martha's objection over His request to remove the stone, "Did I not tell you that if you believed, you would see the glory of God?" (John 11:40 NIV).

Jesus isn't saying that her faith enables Him to perform the miracle but rather that it allows her to *see* the glory of God. I want to love Him this way.

I love this part of the story because as we walk through trials, He invites us to trust Him. We aren't guaranteed anything as Christians as far as the outcome, but we are loved enough to be a part of the greatest story ever written. To imagine the same God whose hands marked out the world is allowing us to enter into His plan is profound and humbling. What we are called to do (and I say this with full *belief* but less *earthly comprehension*) is to agree to move the stone, no matter what happens next.

Excerpt taken from *I Will Carry You* by Angie Smith (© 2010).

Wash One Another's Feet

Before the Passover Festival, Jesus knew that His hour had come to depart from this world to the Father. Having loved His own who were in the world, He loved them to the end.

Now by the time of supper, the Devil had already put it into the heart of Judas, Simon Iscariot's son, to betray Him. Jesus knew that the Father had given everything into His hands, that He had come from God, and that He was going back to God. So He got up from supper, laid aside His robe, took a towel, and tied it around Himself. Next, He poured water into a basin and began to wash His disciples' feet and to dry them with the towel tied around Him.

He came to Simon Peter, who asked Him, "Lord, are You going to wash my feet?"

Jesus answered him, "What I'm doing you don't understand now, but afterward you will know."

"You will never wash my feet—ever!" Peter said.

Jesus replied, "If I don't wash you, you have no part with Me."

Simon Peter said to Him, "Lord, not only my feet, but also my hands and my head."

"One who has bathed," Jesus told him, "doesn't need to wash anything except his feet, but he is completely clean. You are clean, but not all of you." For He knew who would betray Him. This is why He said, "You are not all clean."

When Jesus had washed their feet and put on His robe, He reclined again and said to them, "Do you know what I have done for you? You call Me Teacher and Lord. This is well said, for I am. So if I, your Lord and Teacher, have washed your feet, you also ought to wash one another's feet. For I have given you an example that you also should do just as I have done for you.

"I assure you: A slave is not greater than his master, and a messenger is not greater than the one who sent him." (John 13:1–16 HCSB)

In ancient times, foot washing was something that was done by a slave for his master, or by a child for his parent, or even a disciple for his teacher. It was not something that a master ever did for anyone else. This is why Peter was so adamant that Jesus would not wash his feet; it was well beneath Jesus' standing. But Jesus insisted.

The situation was odd enough that when Jesus finished, He had to explain what He'd done. He leveled the playing field. In His Kingdom, masters are no more important than slaves. Disciples are no less important than their teachers. All ought to serve each other in humility.

Are you willing to "wash others' feet," or do you feel that is beneath you? According to Jesus, serving others—no matter who they are—should be beneath no one. If the Son of God could clean the smelly, dirty feet of His disciples, surely we can serve anyone!

Excerpt taken from *100 Days in the Gospels* (© 2016).

My Father's House

*In My Father's house are many dwelling places, if
not, I would have told you. I am going away to
prepare a place for you. (John 14:2 HCSB)*

The first few verses of John 14 contain some of the most often
quoted words of Jesus. The occasion was the night before the
crucifixion. For months Jesus had been telling His thick-headed disciples that He was going to Jerusalem to die. Finally the message
began to soak in. On the eve of His own suffering, Jesus comforted
His friends:

> "Your heart must not be troubled. Believe in God;
> believe also in Me. In My Father's house are many dwell-
> ing places; if not, I would have told you. I am going
> away to prepare a place for you. If I go away and prepare
> a place for you, I will come back and receive you to
> Myself, so that where I am you may be also." (John
> 14:1–3 HCSB)

The Father sent His Son to bring us into the Father's house. In
the future we will go there and see Him face-to-face. But we do not
have to wait to begin to enjoy this privilege. We can begin to enjoy
the Father's house the moment we meet Jesus.

Knowing Jesus is not the ultimate goal of Christianity. God's
purpose has always been that we know the Father through Jesus.
Coming into the Father's house through His Son is what the
Christian journey is all about. We come to Jesus so that we can get
to know our heavenly Father.

In the following verses note who initiates the invitation for you to come to the Father's house:

> "Everyone the Father gives Me will come to Me, and the one who comes to Me I will never cast out. (John 6:37 HCSB)

> "No one can come to Me unless the Father who sent Me draws him, and I will raise him up on the last day. It is written in the Prophets: And they will all be taught by God. Everyone who has listened to and learned from the Father comes to Me." (John 6:44–45 HCSB)

> "Praise the God and Father of our Lord Jesus Christ, who has blessed us in Christ with every spiritual blessing in the heavens. For He chose us in Him, before the foundation of the world, to be holy and blameless in His sight." (Eph. 1:3–4 HCSB)

The Father gave the invitation for you to come to his house! He sent His Son to make it possible for you to come. You have entered the door of His house through Jesus. But are you content to stay just inside the door? Or do you long to travel further in to get to know its owner, your Father?

If you are drawn to Jesus, you will really love the Father! That's because Jesus reveals the Father to us. The fatherhood of God is the reality that Jesus came to reveal and the relationship He came to restore.

Excerpt taken from *In My Father's House* by Mary Kassian (© 2005).

Friendly Friction

*"No one has greater love than this, that someone would
lay down his life for his friends." (John 15:13 HCSB)*

Nineteen times in the proverbs, we're told how something apparently undesirable is actually "better" than something we think we all want. These verses teach us, for example, that sharing a big, fancy house with people who can't tolerate each other, or who are hardly ever in it . . . well, we'd probably be better off in a much *smaller* place that didn't require two jobs to pay the mortgage, insurance, taxes, and utility bills, and where we could actually be there to enjoy it, as well as spend time with the precious family who lives there.

You know, *that* kind of thing.

One of these "better" verses is Proverbs 27:5—"Better an open reprimand than concealed love" (HCSB). In other words, the best kind of friends are the ones who'll tell you when your zipper's down, rather than just sit there while everybody in the room is privy to an unspoken embarrassment that you're not aware of . . . not yet.

Love is honest. Love is daring. Love is sacrificial (John 15:13). Love is not willing to be "concealed." Love is dedicated solely to someone else's welfare, even if the path to help them get there is occasionally lined with the barbed wire of their temporary anger with you. As the Kenny Rogers/Dolly Parton duet says, "You Can't Make Old Friends." And you can't *find* a better friend than someone whose relationship with you is brave enough to say what you need to hear, even if it makes you mad.

"Iron sharpens iron" is another way to put it (Prov. 27:17 HCSB*f*). "One man [or woman] sharpens another." The heat and friction and pressure and digging that go into sharpening a knife or construction tool involves sparks of discomfort. Apply this same picture image to the realities of a dear friendship, and it's not hard to see how we run the risk of rubbing each other the wrong way. But if I care about you the way I've always claimed—and if you care about me the way *you've* always claimed—we'll know that nothing we say or do is ever meant to do *anything* but help the other.

Sometimes this sharpening action means helping a friend see a talent that's buried inside them, which they don't seem capable of appreciating. Sometimes it means alerting them to a warning sign we've picked up on, one that's caused us to wonder—knowing it's better to ask and thankfully be told no, rather than hold it all in while danger is playing out underneath, undetected.

The literal meaning of this verse's original language speaks of a man who "sharpens his friend's face," which—given the rasping, filing, whetstone analogy—is a little gross to contemplate. But people who are blessed with authentic, redemptive, honest relationships . . . they simply have a *look* about them. The joy of steady growth. The freedom of consistent purity and integrity. The celebration of shared community. The reward that comes from giving and sacrifice.

Iron sharpens iron. Who's sharpening you?

Excerpt taken from *100 Days in the Proverbs* (© 2016).

An Ever-Present Help

*Nevertheless, I tell you the truth: it is to your advantage that
I go away, for if I do not go away, the Helper will not come
to you. But if I go, I will send him to you. (John 16:7 ESV)*

We are God's children by grace through faith. We stand on this side of Christ's atoning cross and empty tomb and walk around each day with the blessed Holy Spirit guiding, directing, pointing things out, turning our focus, setting up encounters, putting thoughts in our heads and words in our mouths.

How easily we forget what a blessing and privilege this is.

Think of Jesus' disciples in John 16, tense amid the electric atmosphere leading up to what appeared to be an imminent death threat to their beloved Master. Alone with His closest followers on that scary, emotional night, Jesus confirmed to them that, yes, He would be leaving them, but He would send a Helper.

This Helper surely seemed to them like a poor substitute for having Jesus right there in the flesh. They *loved* hanging out with Him. And the last thing they wanted was to see this interrupted.

But with Jesus preparing to leave them in the near future, they would need an internal compass to help them find their way. They had not been able to take enough notes over the course of their three years with Him to navigate every obstacle and interruption that lingered on the horizon. Couldn't have. But they *needn't* have because God's wise and wonderful Spirit would be there to guide them the rest of the way with step-by-step instructions, like a tour guide shepherding them from place to place, giving them the ideal amount of information they needed, precisely when they needed it. If they'd listen, He'd speak and direct them. If they'd follow, He'd lead. And when it was all said and done, they'd be assured a life well lived and a journey well taken.

This presence of God that was promised to Jesus' disciples is the same Holy Spirit available to each of us as we walk in obedience to Him. When we're unclear on what to do, not knowing what to say, a bit fuzzy on how all of this fits together into some semblance of meaning and purpose, or tempted to take the shortcut route because we aren't sure we can handle what's being asked of us, we can trust with full assurance that He is here, doing His job, supplying just what we need exactly when we need it.

Friend, we've just got to learn to lay back in that. His arms are big and strong enough to hold us through anything! By offering us His eternal presence on an intimate, personal level, God is not making our lives more difficult. On the contrary He is giving us exactly what we need to keep from being mired down in guilt, agitation, and distance from Him. He is providing us full supply for every circumstance, even the hardest, most unexpected ones.

Excerpt taken from *Life Interrupted* by Priscilla Shirer (© 2011).

Before the World Existed

*"Father, glorify Me in Your presence with that glory I had
with You before the world existed." (John 17:5 HCSB)*

One of the most astonishing statistical comparisons between the
Gospel of John and the three synoptics is how much more God
inspired him to tell us about the world. Based on a word count comparison, Matthew mentions the world ten times, Mark five times,
and Luke seven times. The Gospel of John? A whopping seventy-
three times! In fact, the totality of John's New Testament contribu-
tions informing us about the world constitutes almost half the
mentions in the entire New Testament. Obviously we will miss a
very important concept in John's Gospel if we overlook what he tells
us about the world.

Perhaps the most overwhelming is a concept to which we've
grown inordinately casual: Jesus was sent by God to the world.

John 17 tells us that the Father and Son had fellowship and
shared glory before the world even existed. Jesus said, "Father, glorify Me in Your presence with that glory I had with You before the
world existed" (John 17:5 HCSB). In fact, I am absolutely convinced
that mankind exists out of the holy passion of the Trinity to draw
others into their fellowship. Thus, the plan of salvation was already
completely intact before the creation of the world. Then when the
Holy Trinity was ready, each member participated in the creation.

Genesis 1:1: "In the beginning God created the heavens and the
earth" (NIV). Stay with me here. The Word of God delineates
between one little planet He called the earth and the entire rest of
the universe. We have no idea what is out there. What little science

documents and hypothesizes makes Genesis 1:1 inconceivably impressive.

Our solar system is in a galaxy called the Milky Way. Scientists estimate that more than 100 billion galaxies are scattered throughout the visible universe. Astronomers have photographed millions of them through telescopes. The most distant galaxies ever photographed are as far as 10 billion to 13 billion light-years away. The Milky Way's diameter is about 100,000 light-years. The solar system lies about 25,000 light-years from the center of the galaxy. There are about 100 billion stars in the Milky Way.[1] Imagine, 100 billion stars estimated in our galaxy alone, and Psalm 147:4 tells us God "counts the number of the stars; He gives names to all of them" (HCSB).

Impressive, isn't it? In the beginning God created the sun, the moon, every star, all their surrounding planets, and the earth. You and I have no idea what God's activities may have been elsewhere in the universe, but according to the Bible and as far as He wanted us to know, He picked out one tiny speck upon which to build a world. Our world. And He picked it out so that when the time had fully come, He could send His Son (Gal. 4:4).

Excerpt taken from *Portraits of Devotion* by Beth Moore (© 2014).

---

1. *The Worldbook Encyclopedia 2001*, vol. 8 (Chicago: World Book Inc., 2001), 8–8a.

8 Days

"Unless I see the nail marks in his hands and put my
finger where the nails were, and put my hand into
his side, I will not believe." (John 20:25 NIV)

It's unfortunate that Thomas has become known as "the doubter," because if his life with Christ before the resurrection is any indication, he was actually a man of pretty strong faith.

Have you ever stopped to consider the fact that Jesus chose to come at a time when Thomas wasn't there? It wasn't an accident. He is the God of the universe. I'm pretty sure He knows when people step out for a bit. He knew that Thomas was not there.

And He knew that Thomas would doubt.

Thomas would not take their word for it. Plain and simple.

Eight days went by with no sign of Him and then suddenly, in the same room, the Lord came and stood before them. But this time, Thomas was present.

Upon entering, Christ used the same greeting He had before, "Peace be with you" (v. 26 ESV).

"Then he said to Thomas . . ."

Our Lord—our tender, loving, ever-gracious Lord—turned to the one disciple who was the least convinced and *He spoke directly to him*. He wasn't angry. He wasn't calling him out on his sinful lack of trust; He came to Thomas to speak face-to-face with him out of love.

He came back.

"Put your finger here, and see my hands; and put out your hand, and place it in my side. Do not disbelieve, but believe" (v. 27 ESV).

Thomas had made it clear that nothing less than touching the risen Christ would make him believe. *Nothing.* And here was Jesus, steps away from him, inviting him to do exactly that.

But it was not the sound of Thomas's feet that broke the silence—it was his voice.

"My Lord and my God!"

It is the first time anyone in the New Testament calls Jesus God.

Thomas is lost in truth, swallowed entirely by the grace given to him. He is so unaware of himself that it seems he forgets his required task. Or maybe he realizes he doesn't need to chase God anymore. I've seen it depicted in art dozens of times, and I've resisted standing up and embarrassing myself in sermons, but the truth of the matter is this: Scripture gives us no reason to believe Thomas ever actually touched Jesus.

Do you hear your own voice in the conversations?

"This is what I need to do in order to believe."

He hears our doubts and He knows our requirements. And yet He knows more than what we really need and that is what He offers.

You don't have to chase God in order to believe God.

Look up, take Him in, and acknowledge His majesty with the mouth you used to question Him. He is here where He has always been, but you've been so busy with the chase that you didn't recognize Him.

No more chasing. It isn't the way.

He is.

Excerpt taken from *Chasing God* by Angie Smith (© 2014).

Faith and Doubt

Put your finger here; see my hands. Reach out your hand and put it into my side. Stop doubting and believe. (John 20:27 NIV)

For years I have considered this passage, envious of those who got to touch His humanity and walk in total belief. But it wasn't until recently that I noticed something interesting about the story. We assume that Thomas touched Jesus and as a result he believed, but we aren't told that explicitly in the text. Nowhere in the account is there a moment where Thomas actually lays a hand on Him. Instead, we hear him exclaim, "My Lord and my God!"

I ask Him to reveal Himself to me in ways that would make Him impossible to doubt too.

In a sense, it's irrelevant if Thomas actually touched Him. More importantly, God provided the evidence to swallow the doubt. Thomas wanted to touch Him, and he said he wouldn't believe until he did. Maybe he did put his hands in the wound, but then again, maybe he didn't.

It's possible that he saw enough of the risen Lord to know that his way didn't matter anymore, and cried out in awe to the One Who stood before him.

Beauty and blessing don't come from our hands being in the evidence, but from the faith that comes from trusting Him *in spite of* the evidence.

We must have faith, yes. But to remove every single bit of doubt? Friend, not even those closest to Jesus Himself were able to accomplish this.

I can think of several times in my life when Satan wanted me to believe I wasn't really a believer, taunting me with images of people who never seemed to question. The more I pressed into Christ, the more clearly I saw Him. Was it perfect? No. But that's what made it so precious to me.

I used to watch as He did incredible things for people around me, and I envied their relationship with Him. I would love to tell you that I saw an infomercial that walked me through the three-step program to get to know Him, or that I simply woke up one day and I believed.

Here's the hard part of what I want you to hear.

We are not called to be passive in our relationship with the Lord.

Is it possible that you doubt much because you are waiting instead of moving?

I'm not talking about enrolling in a class or volunteering at a homeless shelter because you know you are supposed to learn and live a sacrificial life.

No one who truly wants to know Christ and opens up their heart (and Bible) to Him will walk away empty-handed. That's a pretty bold claim to make, isn't it? Well, it isn't my claim to make . . . it is God's. He promises that His Word will not return to Him empty (Isa. 55:11), so I challenge you to read through the Scriptures with a heart that is seeking truth, inviting Him to reveal Himself as you go.

Excerpt taken from *What Women Fear* by Angie Smith (© 2011).

Follow Me!

When they had eaten breakfast, Jesus asked Simon Peter, "Simon, son of John, do you love Me more than these?"

"Yes, Lord," he said to Him, "You know that I love You."

"Feed My lambs," He told him.

A second time He asked him, "Simon, son of John, do you love Me?"

"Yes, Lord," he said to Him, "You know that I love You."

"Shepherd My sheep," He told him.

He asked him the third time, "Simon, son of John, do you love Me?"

Peter was grieved that He asked him the third time, "Do you love Me?" He said, "Lord, You know everything! You know that I love You."

"Feed My sheep," Jesus said. "I assure you: When you were young, you would tie your belt and walk wherever you wanted. But when you grow old, you will stretch out your hands and someone else will tie you and carry you where you don't want to go." He said this to signify by what kind of death he would glorify God. After saying this, He told him, "Follow Me!" (John 21:15–19 HCSB)

When you consider the condition of your relationship with Jesus Christ, you have to ask yourself a very simple question: Do I love Jesus Christ more than anything else? That's the simple substance that is foundational to the relationship. That's the question Jesus was asking Peter.

Jesus led Peter through an experience that would remove the cloud of his denial. Peter had denied Jesus three times after Jesus was arrested and subsequently sentenced to die. A short time later, three times Jesus asked Peter if he loved Him. When Peter answered yes, each time Jesus gave him an instruction. Why? It is one thing to say you love Jesus, but the real test is willingness to serve Him.

Love is the kind of affection that has to be demonstrated, and in our relationship with the Lord it will show up in obedience. When we truly love Him, we will want to please Him and do as He asks.

We know that the two greatest commandments are to love God and to love others. Jesus showed in this passage that when we love God, we must serve others, which is one way we demonstrate our love for both them and for Him.

Three times Peter said that he did not even know the Lord, now three times he said he loved the Lord. No matter how great a person is, he may fall. But God's grace and forgiveness will restore the repentant. At the end of this passage, Jesus said, "Follow Me!" Peter had to have been filled with joy that the One he had betrayed still wanted him to not only serve His followers but also follow Him.

He calls us to follow Him as well, even knowing all the ways we have betrayed Him. Let that knowledge fill you with joy today!

Excerpt taken from *100 Days in the Gospels* (© 2016).

An Inconvenienced God

And they devoted themselves to the apostles'
teaching and the fellowship, to the breaking of
bread and the prayers. (Acts 2:42 ESV)

As I read the Gospels, one fact is undeniable to me—Jesus valued people. Over and over He allowed Himself to be stopped, inconvenienced, and used by the people around Him.

There was the time He retreated to a mountain hideout for some much-needed rest only to be chased down by a crowd of needy seekers. What did Jesus do? He healed them. Then there was the time He was literally on His way to heal a sick girl when another woman grabbed His robe and got His attention. He stopped and tended to her need. There was the time He went way out of His way to heal a demon-possessed man that others saw as a lost cause. Oh, and there were the children Jesus urged to come to Him even though they seemed to pull Him away from His many ministry responsibilities.

As I study the book of Matthew, I am dumbfounded by Jesus' patience for inconveniences. The entire book reads like a string of interruptions to His life. Everywhere He went people stopped Him, asked Him for His attention, and sought to redirect His path.

Valuing people means adopting an overt willingness to be inconvenienced. It means doing things that cannot be measured. It means developing relationships based on who people really are and not who we want them to be.

But let me be clear, it is not convenient.

Meeting together regularly interrupts our schedules. It interferes with extracurricular activities and bed times. It takes effort to care for each other. Needs rarely pop up on weekends and evenings. But that's what valuing people looks like. It means accepting a dirty house because people have been loved, cared for, and entertained within the walls of your home. It means accepting a schedule in flux because you are determined to make time for others whenever necessary. It means considering the tasks on your to-do list as less important than the people you're doing them for. It means measuring success through relationships—not how neat and tidy your life looks.

Being known won't fit onto a checklist and it won't be convenient. Christian community has become a buzzword for something we do, something we can put into our day planner, but that's not true community.

Jesus knew all about this. His community was no cakewalk. Judas betrayed Him. Peter denied Him. Paul persecuted His flock and yet . . . Jesus pursued a relationship with them.

If you want to be known, you must be willing to get messy; and you've got to ditch the idol of convenience our culture worships so freely. I'm shooting straight with you because I want you to know it's not an easy road. But it is one that God has always walked, and it leads to a life more meaningful and connected than anything we could ever dream of.

Excerpt taken from *Connected* by Erin Davis (© 2016).

The Family of God

*Now all the believers were together and held all things
in common. They sold their possessions and property and
distributed the proceeds to all, as anyone had a need. Every
day they devoted themselves to meeting together in the temple
complex, and broke bread from house to house. They ate their
food with a joyful and humble attitude, praising God and
having favor with all the people. And every day the Lord added
to them those who were being saved. (Acts 2:44–47 HCSB)*

Even in the midst of our busy lives most families come together on Thanksgiving and Christmas. For many of us, these twice a year gatherings define what it means to be a "family." The New Testament believers described in the book of Acts seemed to define family differently. They certainly gave the family of God more real estate on their calendar than we often do. They were not satisfied with coming together just for special occasions. They met together *daily.*

Not long after Jesus ascended into the clouds, what appeared like tongues of fire descended and settled on the believers who met together, and they began to speak in other languages (Acts 2:3–4). After Peter stood up to explain what was happening, about three thousand people were baptized and added to the church in a single day (v. 41). As a result of this supernatural gathering a "family" was formed. They worshipped together, shared in the Lord's Supper, and met together daily. They shared meals in various houses. If someone had a need, others filled it. They were more than a Thanksgiving and Christmas family. They became a day-in-day out family, a lives woven tightly together family.

The Church is still a family. As the adopted children of God we are brothers and sisters and co-heirs to the kingdom. Yet, the Thanksgiving/Christmas model that's so common in our families of origin seems to have infiltrated the Church. We meet as a huge group once or twice a week for an hour or two in a building that may or may not be in our neighborhood. Some of us may also meet in smaller groups occasionally in someone's home or at a coffee shop. We might "serve the city" together two Saturdays a year. We're still a family, we're just . . . disconnected.

Why did the early church spend so much time together? We don't know for sure. Perhaps they saw it as the way God would want His children to interact with each other. Maybe there was such persecution from non-believers that they needed to stick together for support. It could have been a cultural thing. Whatever the reason, the Lord impressed Luke to record their family-like actions in his book, so we know it's important.

How? Like all families, God's family isn't best served by a list of rules. The point is that those early followers of Jesus lived like the family they were—as sons and daughters of the one true God. We can too.

Excerpt taken from *100 Days in the New Testament* (© 2016).

Laid at Their Feet

And the apostles were giving testimony with great power to the resurrection of the Lord Jesus, and great grace was on all of them. For there was not a needy person among them, because all those who owned lands or houses sold them, brought the proceeds of the things that were sold, and laid them at the apostles' feet. This was then distributed for each person's basic needs.

Joseph, a Levite and a Cypriot by birth, the one the apostles called Barnabas, which is translated Son of Encouragement, sold a field he owned, brought the money, and laid it at the apostles' feet. (Acts 4:33–37 HCSB)

Aren't you struck by the description in this passage?

"And laid it at the apostles' feet" (v. 37).

The church had barely even begun when this happened. Despite the church's infancy at the moment this passage describes, these Jerusalem Christians were experiencing the Old Testament ideal of Deuteronomy 15:4, "There shall be no poor among you" (HCSB). The tenses in the original text show that this was not a move to become the first Christian commune. Nor was this a rash divesting of all property in immediate expectation of Christ's return. Rather, members voluntarily gave presumably out of either their excess or their sacrificial willingness to downsize so that all might have enough. All these years later, though the church has moved beyond the infant stage, Acts 4:34 remains a model of voluntary godly giving for the church.

Does this describe today's global church?

Does it describe your local church?

Does it describe *you*?

There's a good chance it doesn't. The kind of giving described in Acts 4 is not very common today. It wasn't very common then either. Their radical giving is part of what made the early church stand out like a sore thumb. We might think we're generous, but let's use the early believers as our litmus test. Are we willing to sell our belongings and lay them at the feet of our fellow believers? This isn't meant to be a guilt trip. We've been conditioned by our society—and yes, possibly even our churches—to put our own needs first. There are two problems with that mind-set.

First, we tend to confuse needs and wants. Perhaps we can start there. Can we give up some "wants" in order to provide for a fellow believer's "needs"?

The second hurdle we have to jump in order to continue to put our own needs first is this: it's not biblical. We're told to "consider others as more important than yourselves" (Phil. 2:3 HCSB) and "Love your neighbor as yourself" (Mark 12:31 HCSB). To put it bluntly, we should not be the most important people in our own lives.

These passages about the early church are descriptive, not prescriptive. But when others have needs, and we have the ability to help them, let's consider how we can use our resources to provide aid for those who don't have enough.

Excerpt taken from *100 Days in the New Testament* (© 2016).

The Problem with Chains

On the night before Herod was to bring him out for execution,
Peter, bound with two chains, was sleeping between two soldiers,
while the sentries in front of the door guarded the prison.
Suddenly an angel of the Lord appeared, and a light shone in
the cell. Striking Peter on the side, he woke up and said, "Quick,
get up!" Then the chains fell off his wrists. (Acts 12:6–7 HCSB)

The problem with chains is that we get used to them. They become so entangled with our identity that we resign to the idea that being hurt, hooked, or hung up is a part of who we are. An encounter with a woman named Donna put flesh on this problem for me.

Donna's appearance hinted at the life she'd lived: her weathered skin, stained and soiled clothes, and hair that hadn't seen a brush in days. Her approach toward us as we exited the pizza parlor was anxious and desperate. Much to my shame, I spoke to my heart, "Not now, I don't have time for this."

"Ma'am? I am so hungry. Could you buy me just a slice of pizza?"

My dad walked up as I listened to Donna's story and struggled to decide how to help her. She began stepping backward, waving her hands in front of her, taking a defensive posture as he neared us.

Dad's hands came up in reassurance. He meant her no harm. She wasn't easily convinced. She brought out her identification card and flashed it in my face. It indicated that she had recently been released from prison. Her desire was not to harm us but to put all her cards on the table.

It was as if she was saying, I am a felon. This is who I am.

My daughter had witnessed the whole encounter. A thought dawned on her and she rushed to the car. She raced back and handed Donna a jar full of coins.

The loose change had previously occupied a plastic jar with "New Saddle Fund" scribbled on the front in a 5th grader's handwriting.

"Take this," she said.

"I can't take money!"

I assured her that this is how grace comes. It humbles. There's nothing we can do but receive it with gratitude. A dam broke. Tears, cries, and heavy sighs rushed out of Donna. We laid our hands on her and offered up a prayer to the God who knows Donna, the God who sees her.

I can't shake the snapshot of her waving the ID in front of me. Before her time in prison maybe she was known as a wife, a mother, a daughter, a sister, a coworker, or a neighbor. Now, she's a felon. She didn't just accept it, she absorbed it.

Our chains are connected to who we are, but they don't have to stay that way. The Lord of steadfast love is able to break any chain— if we are willing. He invites us to trace them back to the source and watch Him work.

Excerpt taken from *Steadfast Love* by Lauren Chandler (© 2016).

Our Damascus Road

"Brothers and fathers, listen now to my defense before you."
When they heard that he was addressing them in the Hebrew
language, they became even quieter. (Acts 22:1–2 HCSB)

Acts 22 contains Paul's account of his own Damascus-road conversion. His approach contains several elements that build a powerful testimony. We can learn from the following four elements in sharing our own testimonies.

1. Paul communicated simply and clearly. Paul spoke in Greek to the commander and in Aramaic to the Jews. Few of us are fluent in several languages, as Paul was, but we can apply his example, learning to communicate more effectively by speaking the language of our hearers.

2. Paul honestly described his former conduct. We lose our listeners the moment they sense an attitude of superiority in us. Paul spoke with honesty and humility. As he explained his background and his persecutions of the church, he related with them as one who had been exactly where they were. Not all of us have a background as dramatically different from our present lifestyles as Paul did, yet we have all been lost. Lost is lost.

3. Paul related his experience of conversion. Few of us have experienced the dramatic conversion Paul described in Acts 22:6–16, but we can tell how we accepted Christ. Don't think your testimony is meaningless if you didn't have a dramatic conversion. Every conversion cost the same amount of Christ's blood shed on the cross. Yours is just as meaningful as the most dramatic conversion ever told.

In the parable of the prodigal son, the elder brother felt insulted because the father accepted his brother after a season of wild living (Luke 15:29–30). He didn't understand the biggest difference between the two brothers was that the prodigal son had to live with the personal loss and suffering. If your conversion was less sensational than others, praise God for less drama! With it probably came less pain. The determining factor is not how exciting your conversion was but how excited you are now about your conversion.

4. Paul shared how he received his commission. He was very clear that God had a purpose for his life. The people we talk to need to know that there is life after salvation! Salvation is not only about eternity. Salvation is also the open door to a rich earthly life in which we enjoy the love and direction of an active God.

Many unbelievers are repelled by Christianity because they are afraid they'll have to give up so much in order to live for Christ. As we share our testimonies, we can help them see all we've gained since Jesus came into our hearts, all the ways our lives have been blessed and enhanced by His presence within us. Make your sense of ongoing purpose a part of your testimony. We often have no idea how much people are struggling to find a reason to live and to persevere through difficulty.

Excerpt taken from *Portraits of Devotion* by Beth Moore (© 2014).

Without Excuse

For His invisible attributes, that is, His eternal power and
divine nature, have been clearly seen since the creation of
the world, being understood through what He has made. As
a result, people are without excuse. (Romans 1:20 HCSB)

Suppose you came home one day to find a package with this note attached: "These are the personal effects of your twin brother Joe, recently deceased." Once you got over the initial shock of discovering you had a twin brother you never knew about, you'd open the package and look at the contents, hoping they might tell you something about this long lost brother.

If the package contained a leather jacket, a set of brass knuckles, and some cigarettes, that wouldn't tell you everything about your brother, but it would certainly give you a general impression, wouldn't it? Likewise if you opened the box to find an expensive suit, a portfolio of healthy investments, and the keys to a condo in Cabo, you'd get a different impression. The package's existence would tell you that you had a brother, but the package's contents would tell you a bit about him.

In the same way, the created world tells us we have a God, and what we see in the created world tells us some general things about Him. By seeing the general revelation of "the heavens" and the rest of the world, we can get a sense of God's glory, the sum of His attributes.

Nobody can rightfully say, "I never heard the gospel message contained in the Bible, so I am not responsible for my own sin," because there is enough evidence of God's sovereign rule (over both people and their sin) in general revelation that nobody can say they weren't directed to seek Him out in special revelation.

Just like a box containing a few belongings can't tell us everything there is to know about another person, general revelation does not tell us all there is to know about God, nor can we hear the specific gospel message of salvation in the declarations of the heavens. Still, enough is communicated that "people are without excuse." Paul says the visible world reveals God's invisible attributes, namely, His "eternal power and divine nature." We can look around us and see that God's power is without end or limit. This is an affirmation of His omnipotence.

We see God's eternal power revealed through the vastness of the cosmos and through the mighty forces at work in nature. The expanse of space or the unfathomable depths of the ocean are meant to humble mankind. The same is true of an eruption of a volcano or the strength of a tsunami. These shows of power give us an otherworldly and overwhelming sense of being in the presence of the divine Being.

These clear declarations of God's power aren't just meant to remove our excuses, but to usher us toward wonder-filled worship. Stop. Look up. The evidence of God's power is all around you.

Excerpt taken from *90 Days with the God Who Speaks* (© 2017).

Idol Factories

*They exchanged the truth of God for a lie, and worshiped
and served something created instead of the Creator,
who is praised forever. Amen. (Romans 1:25 HCSB)*

If you filled a basket with the temporary, good things in your life, what would be in it? It would probably have your people in it—family and friends; it may have your work—how you feel called to spend your days; laughter over good food with the people you love; beautiful landscapes and sounds and smells. I imagine your basket is lovely, and that it contains things that are special just to you, that may not have any meaning for others. These are the things you love.

We know many of these things are good because God calls them good in His Word. And so, these things exist for God's glory and our enjoyment, but none of them is deserving of our worship. But because we live in a fallen world, we are often tempted to worship "something created instead of the Creator" (Rom. 1:25 HCSB).

Are you ever tempted to worship your good things?

Is there anything in your basket that you just "can't live without"?

The good stuff is what the Tempter uses to draw our affections away from the Creator and onto the creation. We are tempted to care for, consider, and rely on the good thing more deeply than we care for, consider, and rely on God. That's all it takes for something to become an idol—our eternal souls placing their greatest affection on something that will turn to dust.

In his book *Counterfeit Gods*, Tim Keller calls the human heart an "idol factory that takes good things like a successful career, love, material possessions, even family, and turns them into ultimate things. Our hearts deify them as the center of our lives, because, we think, they can give us significance and security, safety and fulfillment, if we attain them."[1]

There is nothing innately wrong with sports, or climbs to the top of Everest, or master's degrees, or big beautiful homes, or even a really lovely pair of earrings. They only become idols when we turn a good thing into an ultimate thing.

It makes sense, but it sure does sting. My family is one of the most important things in my life. My kids are my own flesh and blood, and if we had adopted children, they would be just as fiercely ours. A lot of times, I am compelled to say "no" to good things because I've chosen to make my family a priority.

I wonder how many times I've chosen my family over God.

I wonder how often I've elevated the good work of pointing women to God's Word over actually opening and studying Scripture myself.

Sometimes, something important but temporary becomes more valuable to me than that which is permanent. Sometimes, we find ourselves holding tight to outdoor adventures or career milestones or teeth whitening, relying on them for our joy and fulfillment, and we stop holding tight to God.

Excerpt taken from *She Reads Truth* by Raechel Myers and Amanda Bible Williams (© 2016).

1. Tim Keller, *Counterfeit Gods: The Empty Promises of Money, Sex, and Power, and the Only Hope that Matters* (New York, NY: Penguin, 2011), xiv.

Only One

As it is written: There is no one righteous, not even one. There is no one who understands; there is no one who seeks God. All have turned away; all alike have become useless. There is no one who does what is good, not even one. (Romans 3:10–12 HCSB)

When I was fourteen, I had a moment of panic. I later learned that's not the same as having a moment of repentance. While sitting in church on a Sunday morning, I started to realize that the way I was living did not line up with the stories that I heard in Sunday school. So I did what I had watched others do, I waited until the end of the worship service and went to the front. When our pastor stepped down to greet me, he asked what had brought me to the altar.

"I want to straighten my life up," I told him.

My pastor replied by saying, "Okay. You're going to get baptized." I didn't fully understand the implications of baptism, but I'd seen other folks from my church go into the water before. Maybe baptism could help me turn away from my sin and set my feet on the straight and narrow path. I left church that morning on cloud nine. I was ready to change! By evening, I had fallen from cloud nine without a parachute!

I went ahead and got baptized anyway, hoping that it would do me some good. No change. Despite my best efforts, I wasn't able to straighten my life up. Good intentions couldn't save me.

In Romans 3, Paul quotes a number of Old Testament texts to drive home the point that "there is no one righteous, not even one.

There is no one who does what is good, not even one" (Pss. 14:1–3; 53:1–3; Eccles. 7:20; Pss. 5:9; 10:7; 140:3; Isa. 59:7–8; Ps. 36:1).

Why do so many verses point out that we aren't good? The shocking truth is that we need such overwhelming evidence to snap us out of the idea that we can save ourselves, that we can bridge the gap between us and God and ford the river of sin, with good intentions and hard work. We cannot.

None of us really pursues God on our own. The bottom line is this: If a person is seeking God, it is because the Spirit is at work.

Baptism is a beautiful thing, instituted and modeled by God, but it's only an outward picture of the inner workings of the Holy Spirit. There isn't a baptismal tub big enough to wash away our sin. That's what Jesus' blood is for. The Scripture reminds us that there is no one righteous, no one who understands, no one who seeks God, no one who does what is good.

Except for one.

> But it is from Him that you are in Christ Jesus, who became God-given wisdom for us—our righteousness, sanctification, and redemption. (1 Cor. 1:30 HCSB)

Excerpt taken from *90 Days with the God Who Speaks* (© 2017).

Bad News, Good News

For all have sinned and fall short of the
glory of God. (Romans 3:23 HCSB)

Ask people what the greatest problem in the world is, and you will get a myriad of answers:

- the economy
- poverty
- hunger
- greed
- misused power . . .

But Christians know the main problem in the world is the problem that has plagued humanity since the garden of Eden: sin. It is good to know that in heaven there will be no sin, and, therefore, there will be no problems!

Satan is skilled at distracting people from the problem of sin. He keeps people focused on the cares of the world and on their own selfish gain. In fact, sin is an unpopular word in our modern culture. No one wants to be judged by anyone else for their attitudes, actions, or beliefs. Though sin causes many problems in life, many people prefer to blame others. But, deep in our hearts, God has written a moral law.

In Romans 3, Paul describes that deeply ingrained moral code this way:

> Now we know that whatever the law says speaks to those who are subject to the law, so that every mouth may be shut and the whole world may become subject to God's judgment. (v. 19 HCSB)

They may not recognize it as God's law, but even those without the Bible understand that there are certain things that are wrong. And according to God's Word, it's a law we've all broken. All. Every. The entire lot of humanity has rebelled against God's law.

Many people have sat in a doctor's office and heard frightening news that they have cancer. Such bad news shocks us to our core. But the good news is that medical science has advanced so much that many cancers that were previously a death sentence can be treated today. Many cancer survivors live happy and satisfying lives for decades after being treated for this terrible sickness. Hearing bad news does not always mean that there will be a bad ending.

Though sin is always bad news, there is also the good news about Jesus: He loves us and stands ready to forgive us, if we will turn to Him. Yes, Paul reminds us that we've all missed the mark of God's law, but don't stop there! We're just getting to the good part.

> They are justified freely by His grace through the redemption that is in Christ Jesus. (vv. 24 HCSB)

In other words,

> For the wages of sin is death, but the gift of God is eternal life in Christ Jesus our Lord. (Rom. 6:23 HCSB)

Jesus came to free people from the power of sin and death, and to rid the world of its pressing problem. His atonement on the cross solved the problem—if only people would repent and believe in Him. We cannot solve the problem with human power. The only solution is to put our faith in Christ, and He'll make all things right again.

Excerpt taken from *100 Days in the New Testament* (© 2016).

Slaves of Sin

*For if by the transgression of the one, death reigned through
the one, much more those who receive the abundance
of grace and of the gift of righteousness will reign in life
through the One, Jesus Christ. (Romans 5:17 NASB)*

The connection between the Israelites in Egypt and our own experience today is not hard to link together. Biblical typology gives us permission to view many Old Testament events as patterns that take on ultimate meaning in the New. For instance:

- *Pharaoh* correlates to the role of Satan.
- *Egypt* is equivalent to a life in bondage to sin.
- *Moses* is a forerunner of Christ and His deliverance.
- *Canaan* represents the abundance of life in Him.

So as we look back at Israel's enslavement, we see that they were held captive by a person (Pharaoh) and a place (Egypt). Like them we were each born with a double-bolted chain that held us back from any opportunity to experience freedom and abundant living. The bolts are a *person* and a *place*. This was all we'd ever known. Life on the chain was our normal. We started out thinking this was all it could ever be, that this was what it was supposed to be like, the way it was for everyone else around us. Like the Egyptians handcuffed hopelessly to Egypt, like a baby elephant held by a shackle too strong for him to tear through, we came into this world hindered by a chain that was locked by two strong bolts, locked too tightly to be sprung by human willpower. The chain went by lots of different names and excuses, but we eventually learned to know it by one that, for such a little word, really packs a wallop.

Sin.

Some may think of the chain as simply a problem to overcome, an identity issue to resolve. The Bible, however, calls it sin and declares it an unavoidable curse. The first bolt that must be loosened on the chain is the *curse* of sin so we can be free from our captor, our true enemy, Satan. Though Adam and Eve were born into ideal conditions, enjoying perfect relationship with God and total freedom to be everything He'd created them to be, their choice to sin resulted in a chain being handed down to every single one of their descendants—to us. "Death spread to all men, because all sinned" (Rom. 5:12 NASB).

But we know that's not the end of the story.

The power of sin was broken at the foot of the cross. We couldn't break it ourselves any more than the children of Israel could negotiate their own liberation pact. The only way they were getting loose from Egypt was for their deliverer to come. And the same goes for us. As Romans 5:17 says, we don't go out trying to find deliverance; we "receive" Christ's abundance of grace, His gift of righteousness, His ability to walk free from sin's enslavement.

Excerpt taken from *One in a Million* by Priscilla Shirer (© 2010).

Numb

*So you also must consider yourselves dead to sin and
alive in God in Christ Jesus. (Romans 6:11 ESV)*

"Unclean! Unclean!" The shout resounded through the narrow
streets of Palestine.

Perhaps you've read the stories littered throughout God's Word
about people suffering from leprosy. Jewish ceremonial law rendered
anyone with leprosy to be unclean. Any physical contact with lepers
(even their shadow) would make you ceremonially unclean and
exclude you from worship activities.

Why were lepers treated with such disdain? One reason concerned the disfigurement caused by the skin disease. Let's face it, a
face without a nose is a scary sight. Fingers, toes, and other extremities were often missing. Since this disease was highly contagious and
the evidence of its power were as obvious as the nose missing from a
sufferer's face, anyone who had this infectious disease was considered an outcast by the rest of society. Colonies of lepers formed in
order to provide social interaction for this ragged bunch of cast
aways.

Leprosy is a disease that adversely affects the nervous system. It
gradually numbs a person's extremities to the point that pain is no
longer felt.

You might think that never feeling pain would be a good thing,
right? After all, if you're going to get a filling in a tooth, you're
thankful for that shot of Novocain! And if you're going to have surgery, you schedule an anesthesiologist. Pain is bad, right? In the case
of a cavity or a cut, we want to avoid needless pain. But what if the

numbing from the Novocain was permanent? What if the sensation of pain never returned to your mouth? Over time, you'd chew your tongue right off! Ew.

Pain serves a purpose. In fact, it is a gift from God and part of His creation order. Pain tells a child not to touch a hot stove. Pain tells a carpenter to aim skillfully with a hammer. Pain warns and guides. Lepers are numb to pain, which means they don't know when their hand is burning or when they've just hit their thumb with a hammer. They don't sense that anything is wrong until it's too late.

What about feeling good things? A leper doesn't feel pain, but neither can lepers feel the gentle touch of someone who cares for them. Numbness eliminates all feelings—the painful feelings given to protect you and the good feelings given to bless and encourage you.

But there is a worse condition.

More horrible than physical leprosy is spiritual numbness—the inability to recognize our sin and how it harms us and the inability to recognize God's grace and how it benefits us. Sin sears our consciences, leading us away from life—in all its beauty and complexity.

God's Word brings us a refreshing truth that starts our hearts beating again. Because of Jesus the nerve endings of sin are dead in us. We are alive in Christ! He has reoriented us from outcasts to the family of God.

Excerpt taken from *90 Days with the God Who Speaks* (© 2017).

Your Finalized Adoption

For you did not receive a spirit of slavery to fall back into
fear, but you received the Spirit of adoption, by whom
we cry out, "Abba, Father!" (Romans 8:15 HCSB)

As Christians, we have received the Spirit of adoption. The word *adoption*, also translated "sonship," refers to the process and status of being a son or child of God. For some of us, the concept of adoption carries the idea of being "second best," but this is not the concept communicated in the Bible.

In the Roman culture of Paul's day, an adopted child, particularly a son, could have greater prestige and privilege than a natural child. This was because a father's rule over his children was, by law, absolute. If a natural son did not have the skill, character, or other attribute that the father desired, the father could diligently search for a boy available for adoption who demonstrated the desirable qualities. If this boy proved himself worthy, the father could initiate the legal process of adoption. At the father's death a favored adopted son would then inherit the father's title, the majority of the estate, and be the primary progenitor of the family name.

Because of the privileges of adoption, the Roman process involved several carefully prescribed legal procedures. To begin, the boy's legal and social relationship to his natural family was totally severed. All previous debts and other obligations were paid in full. Next, the boy was placed permanently into his new family, receiving all the rights and privileges that are bestowed upon one naturally born.

You have been chosen by God the Father. He has adopted you.

This means that:

- Your legal and social relationship to your natural "family" root of sin has been severed.
- All of your sin debts and obligations have been paid and eradicated.
- You have been permanently placed into the family of God and now live in the house of the Father.
- You have received all the rights and privileges associated with being a child of God.

Roman law required multiple witnesses for an adoption to be legal. We know that we have been adopted when God's Spirit joins with our spirit in bearing witness that we are children of God. We cry out to God as Father (Rom. 8:15), and the Holy Spirit in us also cries out to the Father (Gal. 4:6; Rom. 8:26).

Your adoption is legal and binding because it has been witnessed by the Holy Spirit. The Bible reinforces the teaching with the names used to refer to this witness to your adoption. Scripture calls the Holy Spirit:

- The Spirit of his Son (Gal. 4:6)
- The Spirit of sonship/adoption (Rom. 8:15)
- The Spirit of your Father (Matt. 10:20)
- The Holy Spirit (Luke 11:13)

Our spirits long for the Father. There is a void, an empty gap within us that cannot be filled by anything else. An intimate relationship with the Father is the "something more" for which we yearn. Through Jesus we already have entered into relationship with the Father of our dreams.

Excerpt taken from *In My Father's House* by Mary Kassian (© 2005).

A Needle for the Thread of Sin

We know that all things work together for the
good of those who love God; those who are called
according to His purpose. (Romans 8:28 HCSB)

We all feel like there is something from our past that could pop up and ruin us. We believe that if people really knew who we had been, they wouldn't love us anymore. They would judge us and look at us like the one who "barely made it into the club."

Maybe it's a relationship you know you handled wrong, or choices you made with regard to your virginity, your sobriety, or your integrity. You can't possibly think of everything (and praise God for that!), but ask the Lord to bring those things to mind that stand in the way of your relationship with Him. The first time I did this I immediately thought of two seasons of life where I got really off course. One was before I was a believer and the other was after. I know there are many, many more, but I trust that these were the ones that God wanted me to deal with at that time.

I allowed myself to grieve the missed opportunities, but I didn't give Satan the right to convince me that the Lord couldn't use these times for His glory.

It's hard to believe, isn't it?

He can be glorified in spite of our mistakes.

It used to scare me that I was accountable for my sins, but I have come to trust Him in even these matters, knowing that He makes all things work together for the good of those who love Him. It might not feel good at the time, but the fruit is a life more closely aligned with Jesus, and that is where restoration lies.

Sometimes the hard part isn't setting it down and surrendering it, but rather resisting the urge to go back to it over and over again. I assure you that the Lord is not glorified when we replay sin in our minds, and I don't think any good can come of it once we have already repented and sought restoration. Instead of becoming consumed with the desire to change that, or to spend my time beating myself up, I do something I think has a lot more power. I write down the sin pattern I am seeing in my life, I look for a Scripture that has to do with this topic, and I ask the Lord to give me a needle for the thread of sin I am seeing run through my choices.

When I am face-to-face with the kind of choice that usually makes me stumble, after I have gone through this process of conforming my thoughts to those of Truth, I let this go through my mind and I meditate on what God has for me.

When I have His Word in my quiver, I am ready to defend myself against my own weaknesses, calling on the Lord to battle for me.

Excerpt taken from *What Women Fear* by Angie Smith (© 2011).

A Common Enemy

*So then we pursue the things which make for peace and
the building up of one another. (Romans 14:19 NASB)*

Friendly fire is the term used in military circles to describe soldiers killed in the line of duty by their own fellow fighters.
Sadly, this type of tragedy isn't only a reality on battlefields. It's also
happening far too frequently amongst the hearts of fellow believers,
people who are supposed to be fighting with us against a common
enemy.

But when it happens in these circles, it's no accident. Friendly
fire in the church or in our most vital relationships is almost always
code for enemy activity. He knows his odds of success jump mark-
edly whenever he can cause heart-wrenching division between us,
isolate one or two of us, and separate us into warring or stonewalled
camps. We cannot leave these kinds of openings for the enemy to
infiltrate.

So one of our most important strategies—a call for our most
fervent praying—must be to stand against all forms of disharmony
in our relationships and to battle for oneness among ourselves and all
of God's people. We owe it to the Lord and we owe it to one another.
The gospel we share in common is meant to continue to be shared
together, both the giving and receiving of grace, inspiring each of us
to pure living and spiritual fervency so the gospel can shine outward
to others through our loving, enriching relationships.

Together, we are a mighty force. Satan knows that.

And by remaining united, we let him *feel* that.

He hates—*hates!*—when God's people get their act together, when we're unified as a couple, a family, a local church, as well as the global, "capital-C" Church. He hates when we're all praying for one another's needs and potential and mission and unity, going to the throne for (and even with) those around us and closest to us.

Our job now is to make sure we're clinging to that gospel and not letting personal, friendly-fire skirmishes hammer away at our unity from the inside.

If we're not praying for oneness—seriously, specifically, strategically—we're leaving our hopes for togetherness to the fickle weather patterns of emotion, misunderstanding, and imposed pressure from outside sources and circumstances. We're giving the enemy room to create cracks in our relationships.

Prayer helps us stay focused on bigger things, on much more eternal things than the petty stuff that threatens to puff itself up beyond actual size and become some huge deal it doesn't deserve to be. In prayer we experience the kind of hard-fought *peace* that unites us into an army of soldiers for Christ.

So if we can pull back for a moment from whatever's creating distance and disrespect among the people we know and among the church where we worship, you can bet your bottom dollar there's a demonic tint to most of it. Our job as people who've caught on to his schemes is to remember the truth, and pray against his schemes. To move forward in peace and unity. Together.

Excerpt taken from *Fervent* by Priscilla Shirer (© 2015).

Why Weren't You Moses?

For consider your calling, brothers: not many of you were wise according to worldly standards, not many were powerful, not many were of noble birth. But God chose what is foolish in the world to shame the wise; God chose what is weak in the world to shame the strong; God chose what is low and despised in the world, even things that are not, to bring to nothing things that are, so that no human being might boast in the presence of God. And because of him you are in Christ Jesus, who became to us wisdom from God, righteousness and sanctification and redemption, so that, as it is written, "Let the one who boasts, boast in the Lord." (1 Corinthians 1:26–31 ESV)

They need you. Not Moses.

I don't know who your "Moses" is, but I can think of several people in my life whom I have seen myself as such a pale shadow of—people I look up to and want to emulate in some sense. At the heart of it, it isn't even what I see as greatness in them, but rather the way it casts light on the weaknesses I perceive in myself. How much time do I spend comparing, evaluating, doubting, and allowing myself to feel like a disappointment when the Lord tells me over and over that He loves me?

There will be no measuring stick when we see our Savior face-to-face. I have images of apologizing to Him, fumbling for words as I've tried to convince Him that I want to be as good or brave as "so and so."

I'm realizing more and more that it's not my job to compare myself and my failing to others' successes, imagining I've failed the Lord, somehow disappointed Him. What a waste it is to watch each other, longing for what they have and how they do it so well. How wildly ridiculous, right? Then why is it that we spend our days doing exactly this?

May we all hear the words so truly spoken in this amazing story, and may the message soak you with truth that permeates your insecurities, your doubts, and your misgivings about what you have to offer. Thank God for you, just as you are. God doesn't want you to be Moses, friend. He wants you to be you loving Him.

You aren't Moses (or whomever you put in his place), and you won't be. God wouldn't have it any other way. May the peace of that gentle reminder fall on you, and may it secure something in you that may have been rattling around, determined to find a satisfactory answer.

Face what's before you with confidence and with a heart aligned with the One who knew your name before time began. He sings songs over you and quiets you with His love (Zeph. 3:17). If you're brave enough to listen, you might hear the sound of your own name echoing back from the great I AM.

Excerpt taken from *Mended* by Angie Smith (© 2012).

I Will Not Be Mastered

"I have the right to do anything," you say—but not everything is beneficial. "I have the right to do anything"—but I will not be mastered by anything. (1 Corinthians 6:12 NIV)

In 1 Corinthians 6:12 Paul writes one of my favorite declarations in the entire Bible: "I will not be mastered by anything."

Part of living the Christian life is to be mastered, governed, by the Holy Spirit alone. Paul's declaration should be our declaration too. "I will not be mastered by anything." I will not be mastered by my selfishness, by my lust, by my hunger, by my alcoholism, by my substance abuse, by my anger, by my own impulses. I will not be mastered by pride or bitterness or unforgiveness. I will not be mastered by my hormones, my circumstances, or my thought-life. And I will not be mastered by my emotions.

My emotions do not control me; Christ controls me.

It is a crucial life skill for the believer to be able to say:

I will not retaliate just because I feel hurt. I will show grace because Christ controls me.

I will not have sex just because I feel love. I will remain pure because Christ controls me.

I will not scream at my family just because I feel misunderstood. I will show love because Christ controls me.

I will not quit my job just because I feel tired. I will work hard because Christ controls me.

The ability to feel something and respond, instead of react, is the essence of maturity. My forever-favorite definition of maturity is this:

> Maturity is not a vague philosophical concept, but a trained ability to meet the demands of reality.[1]

The degree of maturity in a person is the degree to which that person can meet the demands of reality, whether or not those demands seem fair. Meeting the demands of reality means doing things we don't feel like doing.

The inability to get emotions under control is what gives women everywhere a bad name. A woman who lets her emotions run amok is a fiery train wreck waiting to happen.

A woman mastered by her emotions is in just as much bondage as a woman mastered by other destructive vices. It's more socially acceptable, but if she doesn't learn how to get out, how to get control, the habits she forms will be detrimental, negatively impacting her relationships, her career, and ultimately her own fulfillment and satisfaction.

The Word of God centers us, focuses us, and tells us the truth. When your emotions are threatening to leech the sense and logic right out of you, when they feel oppressive and suffocating and like the only real thing in the world, the Word of God is a lifeline back to reality. May we be women mastered only by His Word!

Excerpt taken from *Enough* by Kate Connor (© 2014).

---

1. Dr. Ted Roberts and Diane Roberts, *Sexy Christians: The Purpose, Power, and Passion of Biblical Intimacy* (Grand Rapids: Baker Books, 2010), 94.

Free to Serve

Although I am a free man and not anyone's slave, I have made myself a slave to everyone, in order to win more people. To the Jews I became like a Jew, to win Jews; to those under the law, like one under the law—though I myself am not under the law—to win those under the law. To those who are without that law, like one without the law—not being without God's law but within Christ's law—to win those without the law. To the weak I became weak, in order to win the weak. I have become all things to all people, so that I may by every possible means save some. Now I do all this because of the gospel, so I may become a partner in its benefits. (1 Corinthians 9:19–23 HCSB)

If you were in prison, would you purposefully do something that would send you into solitary confinement? That seems crazy, but apparently there are those who have done so. Why? To share the gospel.

I've heard stories of men who come to know Christ while behind bars and then take on the task of spreading the gospel within their small part of the world. In order to reach all of their fellow prisoners, they must go to all parts of the prison—even solitary confinement. While nobody in solitary can see anyone else, they can often hear each other. So these prison missionaries volunteer for solitary confinement in order that they can read Scripture to and pray with the others in hearing distance. They are willing to do what many would not, in order that they can tell people about Jesus. Can you imagine?

While not all of us are called to send ourselves to solitary confinement in a prison, we are all commanded to be servants to others that we might win them to Christ. If that doesn't look like preaching from a cell for us, what *does* it look like?

Perhaps it means we move to a part of our city that might not be as safe or pretty, but where we can live among people who desperately need to hear about the love of Christ. Maybe we ask our immigrant neighbors about their culture and join them in some cultural practices that do not go against what the Bible teaches. Perhaps we defer to the preferences of others on non-gospel issues, so that dialogue about salvation can flow more freely. There are many ways we can "become like a Jew," as Paul did.

Those of us who are not in prison have a wide world to reach out to. And our neighbors who do not know Christ are as imprisoned by sin as a prisoner confined behind physical bars. We cannot expect the lost to simply show up on our doorstep ready to listen to the gospel. Let's be as bold and courageous as those prisoners who are willing to put themselves into even more dire circumstances in order to reach others for Jesus.

Excerpt taken from *100 Days in the New Testament* (© 2016).

Anything, Everything, and Whatever

Therefore, whether you eat or drink, whatever you do, do everything for God's glory. (1 Corinthians 10:31 HCSB)

One of the richest blessings that comes from deciding to shift some things into the background for a season of life so you can focus on what currently matters more—is that it unlocks your ability to finally do things well, to do them in a way that magnifies and honors God. Perhaps like many women, you constantly feel like you're failing. You end most days with the sense that you're inadequate, that you don't have what it takes, that you just don't have it together like everybody seems to.

This is the burden the perfectionist carries. She's often paralyzed because her standards are at such an impossible height. She can't do *anything* well because she's exhausted from doing *everything* halfway. She looks at all the half done and undone tasks around her and melts into despair. Perfection is a surefire way to live in shame and guilt your entire life, never satisfied with yourself or your surroundings.

In passages like Matthew 5:48, where Jesus instructs us to "be perfect . . . as your heavenly Father is perfect," He's not saying He expects you to live without a single flaw or bobble. You are being invited to a life of *wholeness* and *completeness*. That's what the biblical word *perfect* means. It's not a standard of faultless accuracy and precision but rather an invitation to devote the *whole* of yourself—your time and your talents—toward the *completion* of the tasks He's appointed.

God's Word is pointing you in the *opposite* direction of perfectionism. It's encouraging you to cut back, to engage in only those activities in which God's glory will be seen in this season of your life, and then apply yourself more fully to those. As a wise friend once said to me, "You cannot do a thousand things to the glory of God, but you can do one or two." When you choose to do *everything,* you can't do *anything* well. But when honoring God is your focus, it pares down your purpose and narrows your focus.

And for the record, doing things well is something *you can do!*

The Bible promises it.

Why else would Paul admonish his "whatever you do" encouragement as a living reality—not just once, but again in Colossians 3:17.

He said it (twice) because it's true. If you and I will take the time to zero in on our unique, divinely given set of "whatever you do" and then commit to bring them wholeheartedly to the tasks the Lord has given us, He will help us not only accomplish those tasks sufficiently but also in a way that brings Him glory.

Set your sights on displaying God's glory through today's calling, and then watch Him inspire and empower you to bring your A game every step of the way.

In anything, everything, and whatever you do.

Excerpt taken from *The Resolution for Women* by Priscilla Shirer (© 2011).

Internal Injuries

Let a person examine himself, then, and so eat of the bread
and drink of the cup. (1 Corinthians 11:28 ESV)

No sooner had I curled up on the sofa to watch one of my favorite hospital/medical TV dramas than the action immediately captured my attention. A devastating crash brought dozens of wounded into the emergency room, overwhelming the staff with the sheer number of those needing attention. Among the flurry of new patients were two women—best friends—who had both been involved in the accident and whose story line was setting up to be featured in the show.

One of the women appeared to be fine. But the other, strapped to a gurney, was obviously in grave danger. The attendants rushed to her aid, whisking her into triage, while several nurses offered the less injured woman a quick check of her vitals, just to be sure she was okay. Far more concerned about the health of her closest friend, she declined.

As the program continued, chronicling the various stories and traumas surrounding this event, the camera kept circling back to this frantically worried woman. She prayed by her friend's bedside. She hailed the doctors' and nurses' attention, requesting assistance for her ailing companion. She made cell phone calls to family members. Finally, when the stricken woman's condition appeared to be stabilizing, her relieved friend relaxed a bit and began to entertain the medical staff with her effervescent, engaging personality and wit. Everything seemed to be turning out all right. Not only was her friend going to be fine; so was she.

Then all of a sudden, with absolutely no warning, she collapsed. Just like that.

I sat forward in my seat, stunned, just like the fictional hospital staff. Highly trained individuals, who seconds before had been laughing at her jokes while caring for her injured friend, now gathered around the woman, quickly administering the help she so desperately needed.

But nothing they could do was of any value. Within sixty seconds she was dead.

Gone.

A mandatory X-ray report revealed that she had apparently suffered internal wounds and bleeding in the accident. And throughout the day—though neither she nor any of the hospital staff had been aware of it—her life had been slowly ebbing away. For hours on end, she had been within an arm's length of treatment and healing procedures, while secretly dying on the inside.

This graphically illustrates the internal trauma of unforgiveness. How easily it goes undetected, buried beneath the disguises of external smiles and laughter. We pour ourselves into activity and busyness to avoid having to think about it, medicating ourselves on others' needs instead of tending to the surgery we need ourselves. We continually operate at surface level, masters at managing the externals, even though the church of sickness and unrest is always at work underneath, wreaking havoc and decay to our very souls.

Let us pause to examine ourselves. Asking the Lord to test our vitals to ensure that the poison of unforgiveness is not leaching poison into our system.

Excerpt taken from *The Resolution for Women* by Priscilla Shirer (© 2011).

Shared Suffering, Shared Joy

*So the eye cannot say to the hand, "I don't need you!" Or again,
the head can't say to the feet, "I don't need you!" But even more,
those parts of the body that seem to be weaker are necessary.
And those parts of the body that we think to be less honorable,
we clothe these with greater honor, and our unpresentable
parts have a better presentation. But our presentable parts have
no need of clothing. Instead, God has put the body together,
giving greater honor to the less honorable, so that there would
be no division in the body, but that the members would have
the same concern for each other. So if one member suffers, all
the members suffer with it; if one member is honored, all the
members rejoice with it. (1 Corinthians 12:21–26 HCSB)*

After playing piano for many years, a pianist suffered from carpal
tunnel syndrome. When numbness turned to pain and even
simple tasks were hindered, she resorted to surgery. Amazed that
something so insignificant as a nerve in her wrist could wreak such
havoc and impede activity, she was thrilled to be restored to normal
function.

Compared to a human body, Paul taught that the church is
composed of many members, each indispensable with an important
role to fill. When we see ourselves through the lens of this description,
perhaps you are the tendon that makes the wrist function perfection,
and I am one of the muscles that makes the mouth smile.
Even those whom the world might say are weaker or not honorable
are necessary parts of the body and are given greater honor by God.
There's an important bottom line we shouldn't rush past: None of
us are more important than others in the body of Christ.

When you stub your toe, the source of the pain may be isolated, but your whole body reacts. So it is with God's people. Just like when one part of a physical body struggles, and the rest of the body suffers with it, when one member of Christ's body suffers, the other members are to share the pain. They are to help restore that one to spiritual health. Just as the pianist never considered amputation to cure her wrist, fellow believers should be so important to us that we strive to keep them vitally connected in our congregations.

It's not just our shared suffering that connects us to each other. Equally significant as shared suffering, however, is shared joy, unimpeded by grudges, envy, or rivalry. How it must bless our Lord when His children take such delight in each other!

Do you consider other believers to be part of the same body as you and realize that the actions and circumstances of each part affects all the others? Do you weep with others' suffering and rejoice with their victories? Remember we are members of one body. Our identity in Christ and joy in His promises are the tendons that connect us.

Excerpt taken from *100 Days in the New Testament* (© 2016).

A Rotten Cherry

Love . . . does not keep a record of wrongs.
(1 Corinthians 13:4–5 HCSB)

If a wife expects to find joy in marriage, she must be able to quickly forgive her husband when he upsets her. If a mother expects to enjoy her children, she must rapidly release any hurt they inflict on her, not letting it settle inside and fester into resentment. If a daughter expects to fulfill the biblical requirement to honor her parents, she must write off any debt she feels owed as a result of her parents' failings. If a friend expects to relate with any depth and vulnerability toward another, she must not feel entitled to her well-dusted collection of cataloged offenses. If we want to keep our relationships healthy, we must unshackle them from the built-up resentment over issues from the past.

Truly a wounded heart cannot open up either to fully love or receive love. And one who harbors her wounds as some kind of protection against further wounds only tightens the hard places in her heart that keep her locked in circles, never escaping what's happened, stuck in her predictable ruts and reactions.

So I'm urging you to make this first decision. To clear the decks and stop keeping count.

And here's how you'll know you're doing it. If someone does something today that causes you to be angry and you immediately begin rehearsing everything they did yesterday and the day before, you'll know you're still living in unforgiveness. If what this person has just done becomes the cherry on top of a cake you've been baking for days, weeks, and years, you'll know that you still have a tendency to store up offenses.

But as you start releasing them from your debt—and releasing yourself from the burden of carrying it around and keeping up with it—your treatment of them will no longer have the past continually reflected in it. You'll be free.

Second, you must leave room for God to act on your behalf. It's quite natural to feel as though forgiveness lets the other person just get away with it. You're still the victim, and they're still the oblivious, unpenalized offender. You're especially likely to feel this if you never hear this other person express any regret for their actions, or if their lame attempt at an apology is more like self-justification, trying to shroud *you* in as much or more blame as themselves. Their pitiful way of saying "sorry" only reveals how they obviously still don't get it.

Yes, repentance is an important, necessary step on their part if they are ever to experience freedom from what they've done. But if they don't, or can't, or won't admit to the harm they've caused you, it is not your job to ensure they get what's coming to them. By giving them your forgiveness, you leave it up to God to deal with them. And deal with them, He will—in His own way, in His own timing, much better and more thoroughly than *you* ever could.

Excerpt taken from *The Resolution for Women* by Priscilla Shirer (© 2011).

Rock of Ages

Love never ends. As for prophecies, they will pass away; as for tongues, they will cease; as for knowledge, it will pass away. For we know in part and we prophesy in part, but when the perfect comes, the partial will pass away. (1 Corinthians 13:8–10 ESV)

Sometimes the path we're on grows steep. Before you know it you are precariously perched on a mountain with no way down and nothing to do but keep climbing.

When you're in that place—clinging to the side of a wall made of rock, a storm of uncontrollable circumstances swirling around you—what you're holding on to becomes clear. Place your foot on shale, and it will crumble beneath you. Grab hold of a loose ledge, and your hand will slip. But hold tight to the mountain itself, and it will hold you up.

God's Word gives us firm handholds along the journey. He knew how much we'd need them, and He knew they would bring us peace (John 16:33).

We hold tight to the promises of God in Scripture. But their immutability is inseparable from the Promiser. These rocks of promise are part of the steadfast mountain of God's covenant. His Word is true because He Himself is true (Heb. 13:8). When everything around us is withering and fading away, God and His Word stand firm (Isa. 40:8).

The apostle Paul warned us about this in his letter to the new believers at Corinth. Love—the love that is the essence of our God and His Son, our Savior—will last. But nothing else on earth will.

It's easier to focus my efforts on crafting something solid than it is to acknowledge that this temporary world is passing away just like the leaves of that fading tree signaling the end of another season. Still, when I try to force permanence where there is none, I am always disappointed. We cannot know the eternal weight of this temporary life we've been given unless we understand that it is, indeed, temporary. Paul knew this about us too.

"For now we see in a mirror dimly, but then face to face. Now I know in part; then I shall know fully, even as I have been fully known" (1 Cor. 13:12 ESV). The things we cling to can be good and true, but only because they are part of something much greater and truer than the world can offer: the immovable mountain of God's eternal Truth.

God's Word is more than a foothold, more than a verse to chant when life's foundations are crumbling and you're trying like mad to caulk the cracks. God's Word itself is our stronghold—a place to hide, a place to dwell, a place to be safe.

The gospel of Jesus Christ is not a rock we stand on to climb a mountain; it is the Rock, the Mountain. It is His faithfulness that holds me, not mine that holds Him. The footholds only hold because they are part of the Rock of Ages.

Excerpt taken from *She Reads Truth* by Raechel Myers and Amanda Bible Williams (© 2016).

A Hint of What's to Come

*"For now we see in a mirror dimly, but then face to face.
Now I know in part; then I shall know fully, even as I
have been fully known." (1 Corinthians 13:12 ESV)*

If you've been to many Christian weddings, you know the love chapter of the Bible. It's the chapter that tells us what love should look like. After a vivid description of what love is, Paul seems to take a hard left turn here into the subject of being known. For now, our concept of love is a little hazy, our concept of knowing perhaps even hazier. Knowing God has to be squeezed through the filter of sin and sometimes things get lost in translation. But a day is coming when we will know Him fully. Love is like the appetizer to the best feast we will ever enjoy.

God's love is a precious gift, but the reason He loves me is even more beautiful. He loves me because He knows me. He knows every hair on my head, every thought in my brain, every worry in my heart. He sees all of me, from beginning to end, and He loves me. He invites me to knit my heart into His in a bond so tight that we can never be pulled apart. Being so intimately known is the vaccination we all need to cure our deep feelings of loneliness.

I hope you realize that dealing with the pandemic of loneliness isn't going to be easy. We can't simply make a new friend or cram more people into church pews and see the tide start to turn. Our relationships with God and others are as intertwined as a big ol' plate of spaghetti. We've got to reexamine some of our most basic understandings of who He is and how He made us in order to connect. I'm afraid we've been singing a song all wrong since preschool.

Yes, Jesus loves me, this I know. But when loneliness comes, I need to be reminded that Jesus *knows* me. This I love.

Yes, God loves you and that is a beautiful truth, but maybe we find ourselves unsatisfied because we've missed the wonder of His knowing. Is it possible that has trickled down into our other relationships—causing us to crave love while missing opportunities to knit our souls with others?

Many of us have experienced deep heartache, starting in childhood. If we started to compare relationship scars, I'd have some big ones to show. I get that being known can be very, very scary. Relationships are complicated. Knowing and being known doesn't always work out like a Lifetime Original movie. Sometimes we step on landmines, and the whole thing gets blown to bits. But loneliness doesn't effectively insulate us from pain, does it? It just transfers the hurt to another corner of our hearts. Though, when it comes to dealing with loneliness, God's Word is a deep well with the answers to our ache to connect.

Excerpt taken from *Connected* by Erin Davis (© 2016).

Where Is Your Sting?

*Then comes the end, when He hands over the kingdom to
God the Father, when He abolishes all rule and all authority
and power. For He must reign until He puts all His enemies
under His feet. The last enemy to be abolished is death. For
God has put everything under His feet. But when it says
"everything" is put under Him, it is obvious that He who
puts everything under Him is the exception. And when
everything is subject to Christ, then the Son Himself will also
be subject to the One who subjected everything to Him, so
that God may be all in all. (1 Corinthians 15:24–28 HCSB)*

Death is a stark, and sometimes dark, reminder that we live in a
fallen world. Most of us have faced the reality of death through
the loss of a loved one or dear friend. Eventually, we will face it ourselves. Death is inevitable. We were born to die.

We have made attempts to forestall death. And in some ways,
we've succeeded. Medical science advancements have resulted in
cures for many diseases that in earlier human history led to the death
of thousands. We are grateful for these advances, but in the long
run, all attempts to avert death will fail. All the research, and medicine, and cures can only delay the inevitable.

That is, except one.

Through Christ's resurrection, all enemies of the Lord have been
vanquished, including the greatest enemy of all—death. So why is
death still so scary?

Think of it this way. A father and son were driving down the
highway one day with the windows down when the child began
screaming. The dad spotted a honeybee flying inside the car and

began slowing down. His child was allergic to bee stings and doctors had warned that the next one could be fatal. As the father pulled the car onto the side of the road, he reached out and grabbed the bee out of the air.

Turning off the motor, he turned to his son, held out his hand, and opened his palm. As soon as he saw the bee, the little boy began crying again. Why would his dad put him in harm's way again? But the father said, "Look in my hand, son. There is his stinger. That bee cannot ever hurt anyone again."

In 1 Corinthians 15:55, the apostle Paul taunts death. "Death, where is your victory? Death, where is your sting?" (HCSB). Like the honeybee without his stinger, death is still flying around frightening people, but for all who are in Christ, death has lost its sting.

By His own death, Jesus paid the price to redeem us from death and the grave. By His resurrection, He conquered death and gave us the victory. Yes, physical death still will come to us all (unless the Lord returns first). However, death is not the end for believers in Christ, but rather a transition into the presence of the Lord. The sting of death has been replaced with victory!

Excerpt taken from *100 Days in the New Testament* (© 2016).

The Same Amount of Faithful

We are pressured in every way but not crushed; we are perplexed
but not in despair; we are persecuted but not abandoned; we
are struck down but not destroyed. (2 Corinthians 4:8–9 ESV)

Maybe you're familiar with the chaos of nothing being certain.
Maybe you've gone to bed not knowing what the next morning will bring, checking for signs of life the moment you wake up. A pregnancy or a child, a spouse or a friend; perhaps a relationship on life support.

You've been given a particularly bitter cup and you've asked the Lord to take it from you, asking yourself if you're willing to drink it to the dregs if that is what He asks of you.

You've wanted to run, but known drinking from the cup in the Lord's presence is better than escape. You lean in, knowing it will be the most difficult season of your life, like a tidal wave growing to slam you into the Rock. You know this suffering may save you.

Maybe you, like me, have learned over time to name this bitter cup Mercy.

It is God's exquisite mercy that asks us to drink the cup of suffering. As we drink, with only our present circumstances in view, God is right there, faithful and at work, with all of eternity in view.

Allowing us to be pressed, but protecting us from being crushed.

Permitting persecution, but never abandoning.

Striking us down, but not destroying us (2 Cor. 4:8–9).

Every day seems more fragile than the next. Every new wave slams into us, threatening to shake us loose, but because the Rock doesn't move, neither do we. The Truth of God's Word echoes in our ears and we go to sleep at night knowing whatever tomorrow holds—life or death or things present or things to come—nothing "will have the power to separate us from the love of God that is in Christ Jesus our Lord!" (Rom. 8:39 HCSB).

God is faithful in both our joy and our sorrow.

Our cup may be filled with something completely different tomorrow than it is today. Much to our chagrin, God is not bound by our planners. And so tonight, before we close our eyes, we pray and scribble across the pages of our agendas: Not my will, but Yours.

When we rise, we give thanks for whatever we find in our cup. We call it mercy—exquisite mercy. And because we read Truth, we know:

Nothing can separate us from Christ (Rom. 8:38–39).

Even if we pass through the fire, we will not be burned (Isa. 43:2).

The waves will not overcome us (Isa. 43:2).

And we know His power is made perfect in our weakness (2 Cor. 12:9).

We have learned to trust the One who fills our cups with sweet and bitter things. We know He may take the cup away, and He may ask us to drink it to the dregs, but He will never not be faithful.

Excerpt taken from *She Reads Truth* by Raechel Myers and Amanda Bible Williams (© 2016).

Glorified Saint

*For we must all appear before the judgment seat of
Christ, so that each one of us may be recompensed for
his deeds in the body, according to what he has done,
whether good or bad. (2 Corinthians 5:10 NASB)*

On the earth you made only the barest beginning to your life.
You knew it. Your heart told you so. Your Bible said it, too. You
believed your greatest adventures and your best joys were being
reserved for this last season of your life.

And now you're here!

You are in eternity; your beautiful personality, gifts, interests,
relationships—all living in a heavenly, "glorified" body! And what a
place to live! Heaven is better than you could have ever imagined.
There are surprises everywhere. But before you plunge into them,
there is a powerful meeting you must have with God—one on
One—to sum up the life you lived on earth. This should not come
as a surprise. You were told throughout your life this moment would
arrive. God spoke of it in His Word (2 Cor. 5:10).

Everything will be clear in this moment of infallible evaluation.
Everything you did in your earthly life—as God's feminine image
bearer—will be taken into account by the God who never forgets. For
your acts of courageous faith and obedience, you will receive a reward
that will awe and humble you (1 Cor. 3:10–14). For faithlessness and
worldly compromise, your loss of reward will hurt (v. 15).

God will also give you new responsibilities and new treasures in
heaven. Exactly what those are will be based on how well you followed Christ and God's Word while on earth (Matt. 19:27–30;

25:14–29). This is the clear teaching of Scripture (Matt. 6:20; Luke 12:33; 1 Tim. 6:18–19). For sure you are in heaven by the grace of God alone (Eph. 2:8–9). But it is equally true that your experience, standing, and life in heaven will be shaped by the kind of life you lived while on earth.

So choose wisely before you reach this final season of life. Live a reward-winning lifestyle so that you can walk away from your coming appointment with God with His praise and commendation ringing in your ears (Matt. 25:21) as you step into a heavenly life of unimaginable rewards. No, you won't live a perfect life on earth. No one does that. You will know failure, compromise, and shame at times. But cling to faith. Repent from periodic bouts with unbelief and worldliness. And when you finish this life, finish as one who trusted God and was blessed by Him. Live this kind of life, and you'll find that one of God's greatest delights is in giving you and others eternal rewards in heaven.

Every godly woman will find the same reality as she enters this final, glorious season of life. Faith pays off. This promise is what every godly woman should hold onto and treasure in her heart.

Excerpt taken from *The Life Ready Woman* by Shaunti Feldhahn and Robert Lewis (© 2011).

Brand New

Therefore, if anyone is in Christ, he is a new creation;
old things have passed away, and look, new things
have come. (2 Corinthians 5:17 HCSB)

If I'm supposed to be like this, if this is who I really am, why did I still hate me sometimes? If God made me on purpose, what's with all the broken crazy?

I thought I needed to be repaired. But my need was significantly deeper than that. I actually needed to be rebuilt. And rebuilding anything that is more than thirty years old takes a lot of time and strength and perseverance. All the nuts and bolts of my old ways of thinking were rusted in place, and what the broken crazy had done was reveal that the rust was eroding away at my soul, and it was time to tear down the old and build up the new.

I think that's what Paul must have been talking about in his second letter to the Corinthians (2 Cor. 5:17). A fresh start. A new creation. Yes and amen. I needed both of those things. But I also needed the strength of heart to hold on until God could complete the work He had begun.

It was going to take a lot of looking for lovely. I needed to find a reason to show up and not give up on this critical step in my journey. As I thought back over my own life, the beautiful things, though few and far between, were the knots on the rope that helped me keep climbing. When I looked out the window, I had just enough hope that something more beautiful was just outside my view.

There is a correlation, I'm finding, between beauty and perseverance. It feels like beauty might be knots in the rope you are climbing, gas stations along the cross-country journey, the water stations strategically set up on a racecourse. Beauty is what makes it possible to keep going. And beauty is in the eye of the beholder, isn't it? It's not just in the things everyone sees, but it is what YOU see, what sticks out to you, the unique moments God gives you to collect up and hold and draw strength from. Had I seen any beauty in me, maybe I wouldn't have walked such an unhealthy path for so long.

I needed to find beautiful if I was going to hang in there. I need it in my life. I need it in my heart. I need it in the bank of my soul to withdraw to when things feel hard. So I decided to start looking. And as I watch for my miracle and wait for it, I'm looking around for lovely. I'm filling my mind and eyes and memories with good things, good gifts from God, so that my tank is refueled, so that my parched throat is soothed, before the journey continues.

Excerpt taken from *Looking for Lovely* by Annie F. Downs (© 2016).

Shame on Repeat

The weapons we fight with are not the weapons of the world. On the contrary, they have divine power to demolish strongholds. We demolish arguments and every pretension that sets itself up against the knowledge of God, and we take captive every thought to make it obedient to Christ. (2 Corinthians 10:4–5 NIV)

If I were your enemy, I'd constantly remind you of your past mistakes and poor choices. I'd want to keep you burdened by shame and guilt, in hopes that you'll feel incapacitated by your many failings and see no point in even trying again. I'd work to convince you that you've had your chance and blown it—that your God may be able to forgive some people for some things, but not you . . . not for this.

It's awful. And it's personal.

A personal, unwelcome, unwarranted attack.

Using your forgiven past to poke holes in your future.

But that's exactly what the enemy does. He absolutely loves living in the past.

In *your* past. In *my* past.

And why not? Some of his best opportunities to sabotage our potential come from there.

He carefully archives footage from our history so he can pull from those files and remind us what our days of defeat, sin, and failure looked like. You've seen them, same as I have, a million times. If your life is anything like mine, I'd imagine he's turned every room in the house into a screening room at one time or another—for his amusement, for our shame and humiliation.

It's a painful thing to watch. *Especially* in reruns . . . because every time he cues it up again, it's with the fresh intent of mocking and maligning us, making us feel as unforgiven and unforgivable as possible. If he can't make us feel judged, he'll try turning us into judges. So it's quite a depressing show he puts on.

Under more constructive circumstances we might actually be able to *learn from it*—see another option we could've taken to avoid what ultimately happened. We might be able to *teach from it*—help steer others who might one day face the same set of choices (our children, for example). But in the hands of the enemy, it's always a horror film—*run from it, hide from it*—keep living and reliving it, over and over again. With no resolution—just when we thought we and God had finally settled it for good.

And that's how, instead of living with assurance, we become bombarded with *shame*. Instead of celebrating God's grace, we feel undercut by continual *guilt* over the same old things. Instead of experiencing the ongoing, residual blessings of being regenerated by His Spirit—all things new—we're caught in the spin cycle of ceaseless *regrets*.

But prayer—fervent, strategic prayer—can change things. Even unchangeable things. Even things as unchangeable as real-life scenes from your past—what you did, what you didn't do, why you did it, why you didn't. No, prayer doesn't wipe them all away, doesn't pretend they never happened. And, no, it doesn't remove every natural, logical consequence from playing itself out. But just as God says to the ocean waves, "Thus far you shall come, but no farther" (Job 38:11 NASB), He has given us prayer to raise us up above the sea level of Satan's assaults from our past.

Excerpt taken from *Fervent* by Priscilla Shirer (© 2015).

Sufficient Grace

*But he said to me, "My grace is sufficient for you, for my power
is made perfect in weakness." (2 Corinthians 12:9 NIV)*

After my baby was born at twenty-four weeks, she spent months in the NICU. People tell me all of the time that I am so brave to have shouldered this burden with grace, but I am not brave and it was not my grace. They say it with kind eyes that I am strong, but I know that I was not strong. I was a broken, fragile weak—the sort of weak that is left bereft in the raw chafing of exposing such tender vulnerabilities. Where they saw strong, I saw survival, and I was acutely aware that they were all wrong about me and that I had been all wrong about God.

I didn't feel brave at all. I often hear people say that God will meet us wherever we are or that in times of difficulty God will "show up." But what I found was that when I reached the place of desolation, God was already there. He was there as I fumbled my way toward it through the forsaken feelings, and He was there when I landed knees hard in the dust left by what burnt down, and He was there as I watched Him create something beautifully new from the rubble. He was. He is. He will be.

I did not need all of those fancy answers. I did not need to be strong. Everything I needed to live fully in both happiness and in hardship was nothing I could do myself; instead, I found myself completely reliant on the receipt of grace. It was always there, stored away with the rest of the Scripture verses I had memorized as a child. It was accessible and quotable and looked great on the framed print hanging in our hallway, but it was never my heart song until now.

"But he said to me, 'My grace is sufficient for you, for my power is made perfect in weakness.' Therefore I will boast all the more gladly about my weaknesses, so that Christ's power may rest on me. . . . For when I am weak, then I am strong" (2 Cor. 12:9–10 NIV).

The strong was not in the stoic or the stiff shoulders or the sweet singing of hymns in praise. The strong was in giving in to the weakest and finding a grace so sufficient it redeemed the worst.

As I stood there at the glass, I knew that if I walked back into that room only to find myself holding her lifeless form against my still beating heart, everything else would change and God would not. That in the middle of this crushing chaos, spinning senseless with heartache, this would be constant and I would cling to it and it would not fail me.

That if all else were lost, I would have this hope as an anchor.

It felt like coming home.

Excerpt taken from *Anchored* by Kayla Aimee (© 2015).

The Perks of Gratitude

So I take pleasure in weaknesses, insults, catastrophes,
persecutions, and in pressures, because of Christ. For when I
am weak, then I am strong. (2 Corinthians 12:10 HCSB)

Many by-products come from a grateful spirit. Gratitude pro-duces freedom, courage, peace, and satisfaction. Worry, cow-ardice, strife, or unhappiness absolutely cannot coexist with a genuine spirit of thanksgiving.

A thankful spirit is also a sure comfort and defense in the midst of distress and tragedy. There is always *some* cause for thanks, and *everything* offers a reason for thanksgiving. The apostle Paul—the shackled man who with his co-laborer sang hymns of praise to God from a dark and desolate dungeon—certainly has a right to recom-mend to everyone the same attitude of grateful faith that he himself exhibited. After all, your thanksgiving does not spring from circum-stances or people but from an immutable source—your own per-sonal relationship to Jesus Christ.

"And whatever you do, in word or in deed, do everything in the name of the Lord Jesus, giving thanks, to God the Father through Him" (Col. 3:17 HCSB).

Music sung without gratitude of spirit is hollow and heartless.

Some years ago I faced an unexpected serious surgery. Having already had several surgeries of the same type, I resented the fact that I had to go through the same ordeal again. My consternation was heightened by the fact that the late August timing meant that my children were preparing to enter school. My husband was in the midst of his busiest days with a faculty retreat and the student orientation for the fall semester. The surgery was a surprise. There was not even time to prepare and plan for the lengthy period of down time. However, the Lord used that very painful, agonizing experience to give me and my family many unexpected spiritual benefits.

Personally, in my frustration and confusion, I was driven closer to God. I was compelled to search the Word more earnestly for comfort and peace in those difficult days; I was forced to receive the loving ministries of family and friends. Countless blessings reached our family. For example, during those lengthy days of recovery our son, on his own initiative, began a personal quiet time. I, of course, had far more time for thoughtful introspection over the providence of God and His gracious hand, which is moving all the time in everything to care for you and me and to edify us. The Lord is the blessed controller of all things (1 Tim. 6:15). God's sovereign dispensation is a matter for gratitude and not for murmuring. It should provide a joyful forum and not a woeful dirge. It should prompt a happy attitude and not a bitter spirit.

Let me challenge you to face today with your own expression of genuine gratitude of heart to the Creator-Redeemer—whatever your circumstances may be. After all, your trial of difficulty, or even your tragedy, may well be a benediction in disguise!

Excerpt taken from *A Woman Seeking God* by Dorothy Kelley Patterson (© 2013).

Crucified by Love

I have been crucified with Christ. It is no longer I who live, but Christ who lives in me. And the life I now live in the flesh I live by faith in the Son of God, who loved me and gave himself for me. (Galatians 2:20–21 ESV)

Why do you choose to be crucified with Christ? You know, it's never been the nails that held you there with Him. It's always been love. The nails themselves aren't strong enough to hold you.

You can only live the life He's calling you to through the love He's given you. The love that has taken up residence in your very being is what makes the wounds bearable. But we do have a choice—two of them. We can be crucified with Him, or climb down.

We who are followers of the King must daily wake up and look in the mirror, seeing our reflection with a crown of thorns balanced on our heads. We must feel the burden of the cross at different points in our life. In the power of Christ, we will look back solemnly at ourselves and say, "I am choosing to bear the crown because I cannot live without the love."

That's easy to say, isn't it? Will you trust me enough to try it? Tell Him, the One who knows your deepest fears and most secret desperation, that you are choosing the thorns.

Every day.

And one day, not so far from now, I believe we will be made complete, and pain will cease completely.

Oh, Lord, come quickly.

But until then, make your life an offering, and allow the hands of the Father to carry you through what you think is impossible. He will show you His boundless, freeing love, which allows us the strength to make it another day. And another day. And then, one glorious day, He will call for us. I can't prove it to you, but I know it deep, deep within myself.

The stone has been moved.

He is risen.

And I love Him, even in the excruciating pain I feel. If you are trying to pursue relationship out of forced conviction, you will miss out on the glory of falling in love with the Maker of your soul.

There's such a difference between religion and relationship. Because, you see, the thing about the nails in this life is that they are temporary. We choose to bear them because we know that we will lay our crowns at His feet in the blink of an eye. We will join Him for eternity, and will worship the One who was scarred on our behalf.

We praise Your name, Lord. For You are who You say You are.

And that is enough.

Excerpt taken from *Mended* by Angie Smith (© 2012).

Spiritual Daughters

*For it is written: Rejoice, childless woman, who does not give
birth. Burst into song and shout, you who are not in labor, for
the children of the desolate are many, more numerous than those
of the woman who has a husband. (Galatians 4:27 HCSB)*

S ingleness and childlessness.
My Aunt Ruth's journey had been filled with the longings
and losses of both. She'd never been married. Over time she'd made
peace with it, with what appeared to be God's calling on her life to
remain purely satisfied in Him.

And yet . . . childlessness. Perhaps something even deeper in a
woman's psyche than the desire to find her heart's true love. That's
why when she went to the doctor complaining of certain pains and
discomforts in her body, his recommendation that she undergo a
hysterectomy struck her at a depth of sorrow she didn't realize she
was capable of feeling. To permanently close off from her the opportunity to reproduce life erupted in the form of deep, raw, lonely
emotions. It was the ripping away of a desire that dwells at the core
of womanhood.

Coming to grips with singleness had been hard, she told me.
Coming to grips with childlessness had unexpectedly been harder.

By the time of her surgery, however, she had let God deal with
much of her pain and loss. In fact, one day while recovering in the
hospital, she heard a baby crying in the near distance. And amazingly, instead of the sweet sound rushing over her with another wave
of heartache and grief, it compelled her to seize the moment as an
opportunity to receive her season of barrenness and to walk within

it wholeheartedly—to surrender instead of fight against what the Lord was allowing. As she did this, God placed a blanket of His peace and contentment around her in a remarkable way. She felt like He was saying to her, "You have given up the physical womb, but I have given you a spiritual womb."

Nearly six months later, while attending a meeting at church, she and a small gathering of brothers and sisters were praying passionately and earnestly for God's work and God's people. During the course of their praying, a wise, godly mentor—who actually knew nothing about her experience of release and surrender those many months earlier—slipped over to where she was, placed a loving hand across her shoulder blades, and said to her in words that supernaturally confirmed God's leading, "You are not barren. Out of your womb will come new life. There is life to be produced and a legacy to be left through you. You have daughters, many of them."

Many of them.

Perhaps you know my Aunt Ruth's heartache. Perhaps you feel cheated from experiencing a biological legacy. But maybe, if you look carefully, you'll see the same thing God opened my sweet aunt's eyes to see—spiritual offspring, a plethora of daughters, just waiting to be imprinted with wisdom and counsel and encouragement and favor . . . with the embrace of someone's motherly love.

Excerpt taken from *The Resolution for Women* by Priscilla Shirer (© 2011).

Under Pressure

*"It was for freedom that Christ set us free; therefore
keep standing firm and do not be subject again
to a yoke of slavery." (Galatians 5:1 NASB)*

Pressure.

Pressure to keep up. Pressure to keep going. Pressure to stay ahead, stay afloat, stay relevant. Pressure to perform a certain way, look a certain way, dress a certain way. To be the perfect parent, wife, daughter, friend, and employee—the perfect image of everything that everybody else expects you to be.

Oh, the *pressure.*

Ever notice how many of the pressures in your life resemble *slavery*? The enemy's intention is always to enslave you. First, by keeping you bound up by all the sins Christ has already died to set you free from. But when that doesn't work, he can enslave you to *good* things, too—your job, ministry, family—nothing is so life-giving that he can't turn it into a cruel taskmaster to ruin your life.

When God delivered the ancient Israelites from four hundred years of bondage in Egypt, slavery was all they'd ever known (Exod. 1:8–14). I'm sure they didn't like it, but what could they do about it?—till the Lord sent Moses and ten mighty plagues and delivered them from the iron clutches of Pharaoh.

Israel was free. They were no longer a slave people.

But being officially declared free doesn't automatically take the slave mentality out of a person's heart and mind, now, does it? God knew He'd need to radically adjust their perspectives in order to get them thinking like people who weren't slaves anymore.

Enter . . . the Sabbath.

"Six days you shall labor and do all your work, but the seventh day is a sabbath of the LORD your God; in it *you shall not do any work*" (Exod. 20:9–10 NASB, author emphasis).

Don't. Work?

You'd think the prospect of being allowed (no, *told*) to take regular breaks from their weekly work would sound incredible, right? Think again. They balked against their seventh-day vacation allotment and went to work anyway (Exod. 16:27–30).

Why does this concept of stopping, resting, shutting off, stepping away, pulling back, taking a deep breath—the biblical *command* of Sabbath—why was it so hard for them?

Same reason it's so hard for us.

Because to some degree, we're slaves just as they were.

The thought of deliberately choosing a rhythm of rest and margin around our full slate of activities feels almost unthinkable—because it lands on people who still think the way a slave thinks. People who've been trained through the years not to say no, who are the unwitting servants to their master calendars, going ninety-miles-an-hour through life.

That's a slave talking. And you're free.

We can sit back in the freedom that helps us start again tomorrow with our spirits rested, alert, and renewed. We can rest in Jesus, the One who made us free. "For My yoke is easy," He said, "and My burden is light" (Matt. 11:30 NASB).

Excerpt taken from *Fervent* by Priscilla Shirer (© 2015).

Baros

Bear one another's burdens, and so fulfill the
law of Christ. (Galatians 6:2 ESV)

Have you ever noticed that sometimes the Bible can seem con-
tradictory? When I read Galatians 6:2, it seemed pretty clear
that this "sharing of burdens" is important: "Bear one another's burdens, and so fulfill the law of Christ."

Okay. Got it.

But then, just a few verses later in Galatians 6:5, it says this:
"For each will have to bear his own load."

Interesting. So what gives?

The Bible isn't supposed to be intimidating. It shouldn't make
you afraid to dig further, or to seem like an academic, far away,
untouchable instruction manual. It's one amazing story, and you are
a part of it.

So, ladies, let's dig and learn about the story that defines us.

Why did the apostle Paul write that we are to carry one another's
burdens and then just a few sentences later say that we are all supposed to carry our own loads?

Here's what I discovered.

In verse 2, the Greek word being translated into English as "burdens" is *baros*, which means "heaviness, weight, burden, trouble."

Now onto verse 5. The Greek word translated in this passage as
"load" is different. This word is *phortion*. The word *burden* is in its
definition, so at first glance it can seem as though it really could be
a contradiction. However, when I dug down to the full meaning of
the word, I discovered something interesting. The word *phortion* is

also the same Greek word used in the passage that says, "For my yoke is easy, and my burden is light" (Matt. 11:30 ESV). So how does this all come together? Well, one of the most well-respected biblical scholars, W. E. Vine, put it this way,

> The difference between phortion and baros is that phortion refers simply to something to be borne without reference to its weight, but baros always suggests what is heavy or burdensome. Thus, Christ speaks of His "burden" (phortion) as "light," where baros would be inappropriate; but the "burden" of the transgressor is baros, "heavy."[1]

Phortion is what we are called to carry as disciples of Christ. Baros is the type of weight that is only of this world—the difficulties that come from living in a fallen world as a fallen person and with fallen people. It includes a sense of weight that is burdensome. I know that weight, as do you. We feel it every day.

While we can't shoulder the burden of someone's walk with Christ, we can shoulder the earthly burdens put on our friends. And, not only could we do this, I really believe it's more than a suggestion.

Isn't that incredible? I hope that this accomplishes two things in you—to prompt you to dig into your Bible and also to encourage you to bear one another's burdens and so fulfill the law of Christ.

I am honored to share the load.

Excerpt taken from *Mended* by Angie Smith (© 2012).

---

1. W. E. Vine, *Reflections on Words of the New Testament* (Nashville: Thomas Nelson, 2011), 21–22.

Truth Suppressed

*And you were dead in your trespasses and sins in which you
previously walked according to the ways of this world, according
to the ruler who exercises authority over the lower heavens, the
spirit now working in the disobedient. (Ephesians 2:1–2 HCSB)*

In Ephesians 2:1–2, we learn that apart from Christ we are spiritually dead. Since you can't put a dead soul in a casket or attend a funeral to commemorate spiritual death, we are left to wonder: What does it look like for us to be dead in our trespasses and sins? How exactly do we walk (or not walk) according to the ways of this world? The apostle Paul shines further light on this spiritual deadness in Romans 1–2 by pointing out that we suppress the truth made available to us in general revelation through creation and also the truth made available to us in special revelation that is God's direct Word to us.

"Since what can be known about God is evident among them, because God has shown it to them. For His invisible attributes, that is, His eternal power and divine nature, have been clearly seen since the creation of the world, being understood through what He has made. As a result, people are without excuse" (Romans 1:19–20 HCSB).

How does spiritual deadness lead us to suppress the truth of general revelation? This suppression comes out in several ways.

- The pantheist declares that all of nature is God.
- The deist declares that God has nothing to do with the day-to-day workings of nature.

- There are some who worship an object in nature, such as birds or trees, rather than the Creator of the natural elements.

One evidence of spiritual deadness is an obsession with creation that fails to honor the Creator. Each of these positions misses the truth about who God is. They lead us to a warped view of the world around us and the God who spoke it all into existence.

In His goodness, God has shown Himself to us in creation. But rather than glorify God or show gratitude, mankind has suppressed and disobeyed this God-speech and turned to idolatry. Our acts of suppression, disobedience, and idolatry always lead to death because they cut us off from the One through whom all life exists.

When we are walking according to the ways of the world, we also suppress the truth of special revelation, meaning we disregard God's direct Word to us. Paul often spoke of his own people as resting in their identity as God's chosen, in their possession of the Law, in God's ownership of them, and in the ability to know His will. The tragedy was that God's people had abused these gifts and disobeyed God's law. If the Gentiles were guilty for suppressing their general knowledge of God, how much more the Jews for their outright disobedience of their special knowledge of God! What's worse, Jewish hypocrisy had resulted in God Himself being blasphemed.

Only when we are alive in Christ, and walking according to His Word, can we embrace His Truth.

Excerpt taken from *90 Days with the God Who Sees* (© 2017).

But God

But God, who is rich in mercy, because of His great love that He had for us, made us alive with the Messiah even though we were dead in trespasses. You are saved by grace! (Ephesians 2:4–5 HCSB)

Death comes from following the prince of the power of the air (Satan). The way he walks and those who follow him. Disobedience. To what does he appeal? The passions of our flesh. And then two words interject. Two words that change everything.

But God.

Even in the garden of Eden, when the enemy thought he had God right where he wanted Him, when he bet everything on his seemingly indomitable hand, God pulled up a chair and laid down a royal flush. He called for Adam and Eve. He sought them out fully knowing what had transpired. He found them scrambling to cover themselves. He gave them the chance to fess up without blame-shifting. And like children caught in the act, they pointed fingers and wagged tongues, "But she . . . but he . . ."

But God.

Although it must have pained Him to dispense justice, it's what was right. He pronounced their punishment—Adam's, Eve's, and the enemy's. In the serpent's sentence He whispered hope of the coming rescue, "I will put enmity between you and the woman, and between your offspring and her offspring; he shall bruise your head, and you shall bruise his heel" (Gen. 3:15 ESV). There would be One coming whom the enemy would harm but not enough to keep Him from fatally wounding him in return.

But God.

Before Adam and Eve were driven from Eden with heads low and hearts heavy, God exhibited His unmerited kindness and love, He shadowed future redemption. In desperation, to cover their guilt and shame, Adam and Eve had sewn fig leaves together. They had the right idea but it was insufficient in so many ways. Adam and Eve knew they needed to be covered but all they could come up with just wasn't enough. God compassionately made a covering for them. In order to do so though, something had to die. There had to be a sacrifice of one life for another. An animal was killed, its blood drained, its hide flayed. Adam and Eve? Covered.

One day, on this side of Eden, Jesus would be the ultimate sacrifice, the covering for those who would be called children of God. His perfection would swallow up their imperfection, the source of their guilt and shame. For those who would trust Him, He would step in and turn over the table, ending the game with the enemy.

He has done that for me. When I think all is lost, that I've blown it again and wonder how can He put up with me, and I hear the enemy snickering in triumph, Jesus taps me on the shoulder and stands in my place. He reminds me that only He can end it. And He will, by crushing the enemy's head.

Belief and Unbelief

*For you are saved by grace through faith, and this is
not from yourselves; it is God's gift—not from works,
so that no one can boast. (Ephesians 2:8–9 HCSB)*

One of my favorite Bible stories takes place in Mark chapter 9.
Jesus had just come down from the Mount of Transfiguration
with Peter, James, and John, when they found the rest of the disciples in a heated debate with some religious leaders over a young,
demon-possessed boy. Here was Jesus, having just been physically
glorified while standing atop a mountain—with none other than
Elijah and Moses at His side as the audible voice of God the Father
said from a cloud, "This is My beloved Son; listen to Him!" (Mark
9:7 HCSB)—all in plain view of three of His disciples. Then He
comes down from that very mountain to see the rest of His disciples
calling into question His power and authority.

"You unbelieving generation!" Jesus said to the crowd, His disciples included (v. 19 HCSB).

That's how I feel sometimes. I know full well that Jesus is who
He says He is; I know He's the Son of God, yet I still question His
power. His authority. His goodness. *You unbelieving generation,* I say
to the mirror, shaking my head in shame.

But Jesus doesn't shake His head in disgust and walk away. Jesus
continues the conversation.

"Bring him to Me," Jesus said to them. He asked the boy's father,
"How long has this been happening to him?"

"From childhood," the father said. ". . . But if You can do anything, have compassion on us and help us."

This, of course, was an absurd thing to say to the Son of God. "'If You can'?" Jesus said to the man. "Everything is possible to the one who believes."

Immediately, Scripture says, the boy's father cried out, "I do believe! Help my unbelief." Then Jesus rebuked the spirit and it came out of the boy, and, taking the hand of the very Son of God, the boy stood up, healed (vv. 19–24 HCSB).

Immediately. As soon as the father's hopes in Jesus' divinity were reaffirmed, he spoke up—immediately. "I do believe! Help my unbelief."

I'm not one for big, bold statements, but this is one I'll dare to make: Were each and every believer to be transparent with ourselves, with each other, and with our God, we'd admit this man's cry is ours too: We believe! And, oh, how we need His help for our unbelief.

Like that boy's daddy—riddled with doubt and panic, his son convulsing on the ground between him and the Son of God—we've no reason to hesitate. Our desperation for Jesus isn't a confession we have to hide; the faith was never our doing to begin with.

Those early disciples believed the gospel of Jesus—and I, too, believe—but our human hearts are fickle and the strength of our conviction wanes. Our muddied-up view will not become crystal clear until we're face-to-face with Jesus in Glory (1 Cor. 13:12).

We believe! Help our unbelief.

Excerpt taken from *She Reads Truth* by Raechel Myers and Amanda Bible Williams (© 2016).

Made This Way

*For we are his workmanship, created in Christ
Jesus for good works, which God prepared ahead
of time for us to do. (Ephesians 2:10 CSB)*

I feel like God's given me a couple of songs to sing with my life. I have to live them first, mind you, but then the choruses seem to just keep repeating. No matter how many stages I stand on or how many conversations I have or how many books I write, a few common themes come out.

First, God made us on purpose. I think this is literally a baseline truth you have to believe. It's a pillar of our faith. If you don't believe the way you are is God-made and God-loved, the good and the bad, the tight and the flabby, the old and the new, the strengths and the weaknesses, you are missing out on connecting with God on a level that only comes to those who embrace and love His creations. (And that includes you.)

You're different. Whether you call yourself that or you tend to believe you can just fade into the background, you are different. You are unique. You are the only you there is. God did that on purpose. Because God made you that way. On purpose.

Your looks. Your loves. Your losses. They're you.

Second, God made you to be brave. We were never meant for a wimpy life. Now don't hear me saying we weren't meant for a simple life or a stay-at-home life or a famous life. There isn't a right answer for what a brave life looks like. Just as God made you uniquely, your call to courage is unique as well. But believe me, it's a call. You're called to be brave. You're called to face whatever dragons come into your life and scale the mountains that show up in your view. It may be a literal mountain, a mountain of work, or a mountain of laundry, but it's your journey to walk. And you must walk it bravely.

But I think we were made for it. Every act of obedience is an act of courage. Every hard yes, every difficult no, every moment of moving and shaking takes bravery. I've felt it in my life, way down deep in my bones, and I've seen it in a hundred lives around me.

To me these two things go hand in hand. One needs the other. You have to be brave to believe you are made on purpose—to go after your passions and walk in who you were made to be. When you believe God made you on purpose, you are willing to be brave because the root questions are already answered.

Am I enough?

Yes, God made you on purpose.

Am I alone?

No, God never leaves you. God loves everything He makes, and He loves you unconditionally, so you're never alone.

If I mess up, if I fail, if things don't go well, am I done?

No, you are always loved, you are never alone, you are enough.

Excerpt taken from *Looking for Lovely* by Annie F. Downs (© 2016).

I Love You This Much

[You] may be able to comprehend with all the saints what is the length and width, height and depth of God's love. (Ephesians 3:18 HCSB)

In the 1970s and 1980s, shoppers could buy cute porcelain statues that had their arms spread out as wide as possible. On the chests of the statues were red, plastic, heart-shaped plaques that declared, "I love you this much!" These kitschy gifts were designed to communicate that the giver loved the person receiving the statue as much as they possibly could. Given the arm span of the average person, the maximum amount of human love possible measured in at a distance of about six feet.

Let's compare that human measure of love capacity to the capacity of the love of the Father. How much does Father God love you? Paul prayed that we would be able to grasp the dimensions of God's love. David gives us some practical suggestions for measuring it. He said that the earth is filled with the love of God and that God's love is as high as the heavens are above the earth (Pss. 119:64; 36:5; 103:11).

If we go by the first suggestion of God's love "filling the earth," it would cover an area of approximately 196,951,000 square miles. If we take into consideration the mass of the earth, his love would weigh approximately 6.6 sextillion tons.

And what of the second suggestion? Just how high are the heavens above the earth? If David meant the moon, the distance from the earth to the moon is approximately 250,000 miles. That is about the same distance as ten trips around the equator, or 220 million adult men standing with arms outstretched, fingertip to fingertip. The distance to the sun is roughly four hundred times further.

The nearest star in our galaxy, Alpha Centauri, is 4.3 light years away. A light year is 5.88 trillion miles. So if you could travel the distance from the earth to the moon every day, it would take almost three hundred years to reach the nearest star. That would be nearly a quadrillion adult men standing fingertip to fingertip.

The nearest galaxy, the Great Andromeda Galaxy, is two million light years away from the edge of our galaxy. That is more adult men standing fingertip to fingertip than I have the numeric vocabulary to express.

The height of the heavens above the earth is so staggering as to be incomprehensible.

Of course, the Father's love, like human love, cannot really be measured. David's suggestions are figurative, not literal. But quantifying the love of the Father in comparison with our human capacity to love does point to an important truth. God's love for you is untold times bigger than the best, most devoted love of any human. The magnitude of His love is so large as to be incomprehensible.

In describing how much He loves you, your Father, the Creator, stretches out His arms to the right and the left, past all the galaxies of the universe, and says to you, "I love you this much."

Excerpt taken from *In My Father's House* by Mary Kassian (© 2005).

The Secret to Spiritual Maturity

But speaking the truth in love, let us grow in every way into
Him who is the head—Christ. (Ephesians 4:15 HCSB)

We often go to my in-laws' lake cabin. It is beautiful there, peaceful and relaxing. I particularly enjoy watching the birds. There are hummingbirds, sparrows, wrens, pelicans, ducks, geese, and loons. A loon is a diving waterfowl with a sharp, pointed bill and a yodeling, laughter-like call. It hovers about fifteen feet above the water and then rapidly dives down below the surface to snatch fish.

When my children were young, they used to run on the pier. Tired of warning them not to run and not to go out so far, my husband called out, "Hey you kids, don't run out on the pier. And watch out for the loons; they hunt in pairs. They'll carry off small children that go too close to the edge."

At that exact moment a loon cackled and dive-bombed down into the water just a few feet away from where the children were standing. Their eyes grew wide in terror, and they ran back to shore, screaming. Over the years it has become somewhat of a family joke. A child's dad, an uncle, or a grandpa will put on a worried look, shake his head gravely, and say, "Watch out for those loons. They hunt in pairs, you know, and carry off small children!"

It has been fascinating to watch how the children react. The young ones can be playing happily in the sand, but if they hear or see loons, they will jump up in fear and run to the safety of mom's arms. The children who are somewhat older suspect that the stories are a hoax. Grandma has repeatedly told them so. They have studied the loons enough to notice they never seem to be hunting humans.

The idea that loons attack and carry off children is a family myth. It is a myth the children learned from their fathers. Though untrue, belief in the myth causes the young ones to run away from loons. It is not until they mature and choose to believe the truth they hear from Grandma that they gain confidence in the character of loons and do not run away.

We often operate in a strikingly similar manner. We avoid God the Father because of our faulty beliefs about His character. However, as we discover and believe the truth and become more mature, our confidence in Him always increases.

Ephesians 4 holds out a wonderful prospect. After we have grown up in Christ, "we will no longer be little children." Instead "let us grow in every way into Him who is the head—Christ" (vv. 14–15 HCSB).

When we do not pursue truth we put ourselves in danger of exchanging the truth about God for lies (Rom. 1:25), and remaining spiritual toddlers forever. By contrast, the truth sheds light on falsehood. It exposes it (Eph. 5:8–13), helping us to mature in our understanding of God.

Truth helps us grow up.

Excerpt taken from *In My Father's House* by Mary Kassian (© 2005).

Anger Defined

"In your anger do not sin": Do not let the sun go down while you are still angry. (Ephesians 4:26 NIV)

Anger is the emotion we'd rather not talk about. It's much harder to feel compassion for an angry child. We get angry back. We take it personally and get hurt. We come up against it too much and get overwhelmed. Or all of the above.

If you have a child who battles with anger, or more likely, battles with you because he's angry, you are exhausted. You're exhausted from her anger and exhausted with yourself for the way you feel in response.

Define anger? Not sure we need to—you know what it looks like. It looks like a six-year-old boy who kicks and throws punches every time he hears the word *no*. It looks like a ten-year-old girl whose teachers describe her as a "delight" but who rages at you every night at bedtime. It looks like a fourteen-year-old girl who stomps rather than walks, screams, and slams her door with every opportunity. It looks like a seventeen-year-old boy who thinks everyone and everything is "stupid" and lives life in a constant state of disdain. Anger can be subtle or explosive. It can emerge in calculated cruelty or exaggerated outbursts.

The problem with anger does not lie so much in the feeling as it does the expression of that feeling. One of the most important things we can do for any child, not just an angry one, is to teach him healthy, appropriate ways to handle anger. He will feel anger. She will feel angry as part of those oceans of emotions. But the problem comes in what she does with it.

It's important to remember that anger isn't an isolated emotion—it feeds off the emotions of others. When your child is angry, he wants to express it. He wants an emotional if not physical release from the tension that anger creates. But that release often comes at the expense of others. It may be you or her siblings. It may be his teacher or best friend. But often with kids, because they have not yet learned how to express their anger constructively, it becomes destructive.

Almost all psychologists and counselors agree that anger is a secondary emotion. In other words it's coming from somewhere else. Underneath the anger lies sadness, fear, shame, or some other emotion. But anger makes us feel in control. It's less vulnerable. We know. We've been there ourselves a time or two.

It's often hard to get to what's underneath, to hear past the screaming to the hurt. But, even with all of the yelling and screaming, the likelihood is that something else is going on. Angry children feel shame, helplessness—an inability to control their outbursts. As their parents, we've got to somehow learn how to handle their anger and also help them dig down to the underlying emotion. Listen to them. Engage their hearts and give them a safe place to talk about what's going on inside.

Excerpt taken from *Modern Parents, Vintage Values* by Melissa Trevathan and Missy Goff (© 2010).

Give and Get

And be kind and compassionate to one another,
forgiving one another, just as God also forgave
you in Christ. (Ephesians 4:32 HCSB)

My sister Susan and I are guilty of choosing books for each other that we want to read just so we can borrow them. Forgiveness is like that. You give it to others because you want to have it as well.

One of Jesus' parables I find most uncomfortable to listen to is the story of the unmerciful servant (Matt. 18:21–35). Just when I am ready to shake my head in disgust at the first servant's obvious lack of gratitude after being forgiven much and then failing to forgive another servant little, I realize I am that servant. I complain to my children about their complaining; I feel slighted when a friend forgets to ask about an event important to me, all the while neglecting to inquire about what is going on in her life. I fail to forgive as I have been forgiven. Though it humbles me greatly, it sends me running to the cross. Where else can I go? Seeing my shame, nailing my Brother to the cross, I know how much I have been forgiven. At the foot of the cross, I am transformed from the unmerciful servant into the thief by Jesus' side who turned to Him in repentance and faith at the very last moment possible. Undeserving of mercy but destined to be with Him in Paradise.

The cross serves not only as a reminder of God's love and mercy, that He would send His Son to die in our place, but also as a reminder of the fate of God's children here on earth. As Paul says, "If God is for us, who can be against us? He who did not spare his own Son, but gave him up for us all—how will he not also, along with him, graciously give us all things?" (Rom. 8:31–32 NIV). This might seem like one of those feel-good verses in which we get to wallow in the excess of God's love. Wallow away, but just remember that if God didn't spare His own Son, His perfect and blameless Son, then why would He spare his adopted children the pains and sufferings of this world? If we want to be joint heirs with Jesus, picking up the cross is part of the deal. This same passage in Romans 8 goes on to list some of the things that can't separate us from the love of God, including some of the really unpleasant things that Paul assumes we will face—distress, persecution, and danger among them. I say this not to scare you but rather to encourage you in the face of the inevitable, which you have already faced and will face again. Suffering isn't a sign you aren't loved but rather a sign that you are a child of God. You have love, acceptance, and forgiveness. Now go, give it away.

Excerpt taken from *Letting Go of Perfect* by Amy Spiegel (© 2012).

The Three Percent Difference

But among you there must not be even a hint of sexual immorality, or of any kind of impurity, or of greed, because these are improper for God's holy people. (Ephesians 5:3 NIV)

Rat poison.

I've never really paid much attention to it . . . until today, when I found out from a friend that most varieties are made up of 97 percent food and only three percent poison. These products lure those nasty rodents by the smell and taste of something they actually like, a delectable treat that feels good going down. But along with a tasty meal, they also ingest trace amounts of fatal toxins that are enough to end their reign of terror. Rats die (and aren't we glad they do) because of a small thread of poison laced within an enticing serving of food.

Three percent.

Couldn't this also describe the way our virtue is stolen? Our integrity compromised? Our hearts hardened? Our spirits desensitized to the things of the Lord? Lured in by something seemingly harmless—an enjoyable form of entertainment, the camaraderie of an initially innocent relationship—but then . . .

Poison.

Strategically hidden, craftily disguised. Underneath the surface, just below radar. We lick our lips and go about our business, thinking that everything's going fine. It may take days, maybe weeks, before we begin to notice. But eventually our spiritual organs start to fail. Our passion quells. Our sensitivity and discernment wane. We lose our gag reflex.

We're dying a slow death.

Three percent at a time.

Yet the fact that something like this can so easily happen is one reason I think Paul went to such links to tell us to avoid "even a hint" of sexual immorality or "any kind of impurity." Even a trace or suggestion is too much for God's people—we who have been made holy through His deliberate act of grace, and who bear the responsibility to protect the tender hearts and minds of those who we dearly love.

Three percent is where it starts.

Who knows where it might lead?

And while the first part of Paul's admonishment speaks of "sexual immorality"—a spiritual poison that permeated the culture in which Paul lived—his use of the catchall phrase "any kind of impurity" broadens the scope to all the other polluting activities that need to be completely foreign to the believer's lifestyle. These, he says, have no place in our lives. None.

Try as we might to wage our own integrity battles, this kind of living requires accountability. It just does. Our willingness to support one another helps us remain strong in our promises.

We can't make it without this.

Because it doesn't take a lot of poison to take us down. Three percent is all it takes. Three percent can kill.

But by spreading it out among a whole group of us who are constantly helping each other whittle that 3 percent down to 2, to 1, till it's not "even a hint," we're able to stand strong to our feet again.

Excerpt taken from *The Resolution for Women* by Priscilla Shirer (© 2011).

Fighting for Your Family

Wives, submit to your own husbands as to the Lord, for the husband is the head of the wife as Christ is the head of the church. He is the Savior of the body. (Ephesians 5:22–23 HCSB)

According to Scripture, the number-one purpose of marriage—more than the unique partnership between a man and woman or conceiving and raising of children—is how it represents the mystery of the gospel in active, living form. At its deepest level, this primary human relationship between husband and wife is meant to be a living witness to others of the love of Christ for His Church (Eph. 5:22–33).

Marriage stands for the creation of unity among two people who were once separated in every way before love reached out and found the other—the way God reached out, found us, and covenanted to love us. This is exactly what the enemy wants to denigrate.

When Scripture counsels husbands to love and lead their wives, even when it counsels us wives to submit to our husbands—[gulp!]—the ultimate motivation for these lofty directives is not just so we'll get along better on the weekends but that our homes will reflect on earth the order of God's relationship with us. Husbands are to love their wives "just as Christ also loved the church and gave Himself up for her" (v. 25 NASB). "Wives are to submit to their husbands "as the church submits to Christ" (v. 24 NLT).

Again, big deal, all around. Much bigger deal than we thought.

So when you and I begin to feel the pressure, tension, and conflict building at home—is it just because of the husband? The kids?

Are we just being overly sensitive? Is it just all of you going to your own rooms—disconnected, disjointed, fragmented?

No, it bears all the marks of an outside enemy—the one who wants your marriage to suffer and your home to become a battleground. The one invested in sending each of you out the door every day vulnerable to temptation, desperate for the unconditional love you've committed to giving and receiving from each other.

But is *he* the one on the receiving end of your frustration? Is *he* the one you're splattering with juicy comebacks? Because the fact is, *he's* most likely the one who's pulled the wool over your eyes, fooling you and leading you to focus all your indignation on your man and kid instead.

He wants you miserable, exhausted, joyless, and undone. He wants that picture of the gospel—your marriage and family—tarnished. Ripped apart in failure. He wants you to turn on each other. As much as the Father loves and embodies unity, our enemy loves and embodies division.

But maybe he wasn't counting on you—a woman who's had enough, who's ready to start taking some prayer action for her family. It's time to bring your family issues out in the open, to put a bulls-eye on the real source of your family strife. Let's show him the kind of resistance that a steady dose of prayer is able to exact against his demolition plans.

Excerpt taken from *Fervent* by Priscilla Shirer (© 2015).

Weapons That Work

*Put on all of God's armor so that you will be able to stand
firm against all strategies of the devil. (Ephesians 6:11 NLT)*

Through intentional, deliberate, strategic prayer, you grab hold
of Jesus and of everything He's already done on your behalf. It's
how you tap into the power of heaven and watch it reverberate in
your experiences. It's a key part of your offensive weaponry against a
cunning foe who prowls around and watches for your weaknesses,
your vulnerable places, for any opportunity to destroy you. In prayer
you gain your strength—the power to gird yourself with armor that
extinguishes every weapon your enemy wields.

Strategies. Schemes and deceptive plots being concocted for
your demise by a very real enemy who is always primed to make his
next move. He works overtime to destroy the relationships and circumstances you want to preserve. He laughs at your attempts to fix
your own issues with timely words and hard work—tactics that
might affect matters for a moment but can't begin to touch his
underhanded, cunning efforts down where the root issues lie, or up
in those spiritual "heavenly places" where such physical weapons
were never meant to work.

> For we are not fighting against flesh-and-blood enemies,
> but against evil rulers and authorities of the unseen
> world, against mighty powers in this dark world, and
> against evil spirits in the heavenly places. (v. 12 NLT)

So we strap on the weapons that work—weapons divinely
authorized for our success in spiritual warfare: the belt of truth, the

breastplate of righteousness, the shoes of peace. Then we take up the shield of faith, the helmet of salvation, as well as the sword—the very Word of God. But we don't stop there. Because neither does Paul in his description of our spiritual armor in Ephesians 6:

> Pray in the Spirit at all times and on every occasion. Stay alert and be persistent in your prayers for all believers everywhere. And pray. . . . (vv. 18–19 NLT)

There it is. The fuel that drives everything. *Prayer.* We pray till our hands are worn and wrinkled. We pray until our granddaughters are old enough to understand and learn and copy our example. We pray until they can one day place their hands across ours, gently rubbing our aging skin, and we smile because now they'll never forget the things we had the good sense to record in writing for their generation. They will look back on our legacies and know we stood strong, fought the good fight, and finished a race in which we would *not even think* about letting the enemy have his way in our lives or in the lives of those we love.

We pray because our own solutions don't work and because prayer deploys, activates, and fortifies us against the attacks of the enemy. We pray because we're serious about taking back the ground he has sought to take from us.

That's what we do. But make no mistake: this enemy will seek to discourage you from doing it.

Excerpt taken from *Fervent* by Priscilla Shirer (© 2015).

The Belt of Truth

Stand your ground, putting on the belt of truth and the
body armor of God's righteousness. (Ephesians 6:14 NLT)

As adopted daughters of the living God, if we're not strategically praying in accordance with who our Maker and Redeemer says we are, if we aren't calling ourselves by name according to that list from Ephesians, serving the devil notice that we know (like *he* knows) who we really are, we'll always be subject to his attempts at devaluing us. We'll downplay our real strength. He'll diffuse our power simply by downplaying our true position.

If he can get you to believe his lies, you won't feel equipped or entitled to stand up against him. You'll be weak and helpless, and then he can run roughshod over you and over the things and people you love. The farther he can separate your practical reality from your true, living reality, he can wedge himself into the space between the two and short-circuit the free-flowing effectiveness of your influence as a wife, a mom, a friend, a daughter, a sister—all the relationships where God has placed you to be a light of His grace, His power, His love, His well-placed confidence.

That's why you and I need to be praying—to keep the truth about our real identity in constant, unbroken focus before us.

The *truth*.

One of the pieces of spiritual armor supplied to us as believers centers in on this issue precisely. It is what's commonly known as the "belt of truth." More accurately, based on the history of what a first-century soldier's gear was like, think of it as sort of a *girdle*, worn close around the body, with all his other pieces of armor tucked into it and held together by it. Underwear, kind of. A foundation garment. The first thing a soldier would put on before going into battle.

Truth—God's standard and viewpoint about us—must come first in our hearts and minds if we want to be effective in battle against the enemy. We need to put it on as our foundational garment and then reorient everything else around it. Before we accessorize with trendy add-ons, we should start with the underpinnings of truth, secured through prayer by the declarations of God's Word. Because unless our whole ensemble is framed around this undergarment, we're not really suited for spiritual battle. We're not dressed for the occasion. Not ready for what's coming.

That's why the apostle Paul prayed so fervently that the true identity of those first-century believers would be unveiled in their hearts. He wasn't asking God to make sure the early believers *received* these things. They already *had* them. He was praying they'd *realize* they already had them.

Because sometimes, even with a closet full of clothes, we can look in and think there's nothing to wear. But look again. Through the eyes of truth. And you might finally see that not only have you been given what you need but a whole, *whole* lot more.

Excerpt taken from *Fervent* by Priscilla Shirer (© 2015).

Playing Dress Up

I am sure of this, that He who started a good work
in you will carry it on to completion until the
day of Christ Jesus. (Philippians 1:6 HCSB)

There is a delicate balance between embracing our natures and making excuses for our failures. If I make jokes about snapping at the kids while trying to do my devotions, then no one can accuse me of being inauthentic. But they can't accuse me of being morally serious either. This is one of the reasons I generally avoid the blogging world. Too often blogs by Christian women fall into two basic categories: Category One is the "authentic" blogger who braggingly blogs about the disarray in her life, the unfolded laundry, the extra pounds she has decided to accept. While I appreciate her honesty and certainly identify with her struggles, maybe we should spend less time being authentic and more time creating order out of chaos. Category Two is the "excellent" blogger who spends every minute of the day enriching the lives of all those around her, alphabetizing her food pantry and developing a cure for leprosy. Again, I appreciate her zest for life, but maybe Miss Category Two needs to go over to Category One's house for a while and then take a nap.

If we put these women in a blender, metaphorically that is, the end product seems to be the perfect balance of honesty and determination. Honesty in that we are fearfully and wonderfully made, loved and accepted by our Maker. Christ died that we might approach the throne of God, as well as our next PTA meeting, without fear of judgment. Category One women encourage us to be honest about our shortcomings and embrace who God has created us to be. But we are also sinful and corrupt and are called to make war with our fleshly nature (Pss. 58:3; 139:14). Without a clear picture of our sinful nature, there is no good news to be found in the gospel. Coming out and admitting our faults and weaknesses can be a great comfort to those with similar struggles. We don't want, however, to give others or ourselves an excuse. We are diseased, but there is a cure, however long the recovery process.

Time and time again I realize the futility of playing spiritual dress-up. I can't write out spiritual goals in the same way that I write out a list for groceries, as if closeness to God or increased patience were merely items in a store that we can acquire for the right price. Blood is what is required to obtain what I desire but not my own. If I want to see myself transformed spiritually I must first take off—through confession and repentance—all the stolen parts in which I have covered myself. I must confess the ways in which I have counterfeited spiritual growth and repent of my envious ways. Only then can I humbly request that God work through me as He wills. Through prayer and the study of His Word, my creation will be brought to life.

Excerpt taken from *Letting Go of Perfect* by Amy Spiegel (© 2012).

Your Need for Trust

And I pray this: that your love will keep on growing in knowledge and every kind of discernment, so that you can approve the things that are superior and can be pure and blameless in the day of Christ, filled with the fruit of righteousness that comes through Jesus Christ to the glory and praise of God. (Philippians 1:9–11 HCSB)

How do you teach your children safety without freaking them out? How do you feel safe when your child is out exploring in this world of warning?

It is easy to answer that question with a blanket statement like, "Trust God with your children." But that blanket statement often doesn't do much to quell our anxiety. It leaves us a little flat. Anxiety makes it hard to trust.

We'll say it anyway. *Trust God with your children.* We serve a God who allows pain but redeems it. Maybe He knows the secret, too. Strength comes from struggle. Strength comes in struggle . . . His strength, not ours. His strength comes for us, and His strength comes for them. The blanket statement is true. God loves your children more than you could ever imagine—more than you could ever love them. He wants good for them, the best for them, and He will bring it to completion.

Fear paralyzes us and keeps us from being free to enjoy and have relationships, with our children or with God. But the Bible uses that blanket statement and uses it often. Sixty-seven times Scripture tells us to "fear not."

We would venture to say that the opposite of fear is not a lack of fear but trust. Somewhere deep down all of us know we're powerless to change things or truly protect our children the way we long to. But we don't want to parent out of fear. When we do, the emphasis is more on preventing than on encouraging. It becomes more about control than it does relationship. It centers on what is wrong in the world rather than who you and your child can be in the midst of it.

Trust God. Fear not. Studying God's Word can help hide these words inside your heart. They are words to learn on—words to bring His peace, confidence, and our trust to fruition. "For God did not give us a spirit of timidity, but a spirit of power, of love and of self-discipline" (2 Tim. 1:7 NIV).

This truth gives us confidence. He is our reason not to fear. He gives us the ability and grace to teach our children safety without freaking them out—without freaking us out. Instead of parenting out of fear, we can echo for our children the prayer Paul prayed for those who were like his children: that our love, knowledge, and discernment may abound (Phil. 1:9–11).

Excerpt taken from *Modern Parents, Vintage Values* by Melissa Trevathan and Missy Goff (© 2010).

The True Fairy Tale

Make your own attitude that of Christ Jesus, who, existing
in the form of God, did not consider equality with God as
something to be used for His own advantage. Instead He emptied
Himself by assuming the form of a slave, taking on the likeness
of men. And when He had come as a man in His external
form, He humbled Himself by becoming obedient to the point
of death—even to death on a cross. (Philippians 2:5–8 HCSB)

Imagine a righteous king who creates a special place, a sanctuary, where he and his people can share together in joy, peace, and love. There is no shame in this sanctuary because there is no evil present; there is only fellowship and joy and life. However, the people are not satisfied with serving the righteous king. They want to be their own kings, so they rebel and seek to establish their own kingdoms.

As punishment for rejecting his rule, the king casts the rebels out of the sanctuary and into a dark kingdom ruled by an evil prince who wields the power of death. Without realizing it, the rebels have become slaves of their own rebellion and of the evil prince who uses the fear of death as a weapon against them.

Because the king loves his people, he chooses to rescue them. But since he is a righteous king, he cannot simply overlook their rebellion. Therefore, in order to rescue the rebels, the king must send his righteous son, the heir to the throne, to this dark realm. In submitting to his father, the righteous son must step away from all his royal privileges. But he is still the prince; the royal blood still flows through his veins. In obedience to his father, he enters a different and dark realm where no one acknowledges his authority.

The righteous prince becomes like the captive rebels in order to take their place and rescue them. He obeys all the laws the rebels broke, but he also receives the punishment the rebels deserve. Ultimately the righteous prince must suffer the shame and ridicule of a public trial where the charges against the rebels are read. Then he must face the humiliating, public execution that their crimes require.

Only through the son's obedience can the righteous king and the rebels be reconciled. The Gospel accounts reveal that Jesus is the righteous Prince sent by the righteous King to rescue a rebellious people held captive by the Evil One.

The apostle Paul reminds us that Jesus submitted to the Father's will in humbling Himself in order to rescue us, even though it brought Him great shame. Thankfully our story does not end with Christ's shameful death, for His humiliation lead to exaltation.

God raised Jesus from the dead, defeating the evil prince of darkness, conquering sin and death, Jesus was crowned Lord and King over all, and the entire universe will bow down to Him and confess His lordship.

What a happy ending!

Excerpt taken from *90 Days with the God Who Speaks* (© 2017).

The Law of Love

A Hebrew of Hebrews; in regard to the law, a Pharisee;
as for zeal, persecuting the church; as for righteousness
based on the law, faultless. (Philippians 3:5–6 NIV)

S aul himself was a Pharisee and probably returned from Jerusalem to Tarsus to serve as a teacher of the law. Imagine how his thinking was influenced by his contemporaries. I believe Saul had set sail to Jerusalem as a young adolescent with a pure heart; but somewhere along the way the negative influences outweighed the positive, and his purity began to erode. The law became his god.

That's what happens when you take the love out of obedience. Without love for God and His Word, we're just trying to be good. Trying to obey God and serve Him before we've come to love Him can be exhausting. The first-century Jews became so obsessed with the law that they forgot their purpose. They argued endlessly about washing hands or observing the Sabbath, but they forgot about loving God.

Saul epitomized such pharisaic obsession. He packed his diploma and headed for a place to serve. Whether he divided his time between teaching and his father's business is unknown. But one thing you can count on: he was absolutely miserable. Why? In Philippians 3:6, he said his zeal was so great that he persecuted the church, and that his legalistic righteousness was "blameless."

We cannot begin to comprehend what Saul's life was like as he sought to live by the letter of the law because most of us do not have a Jewish background. Daily rituals determined the first words out of Saul's mouth in the morning, the way he took off his nightclothes and put on his day clothes, and how he sprinkled his hands before breakfast. He carefully avoided eating or drinking quickly and never ate while standing. Saul pronounced numerous benedictions throughout the day. His entire day and night was filled with rituals—rituals that paled in comparison to all the laws regarding the Sabbath.

The Sabbath observance could not have been further from God's intent by the time Christ "became flesh and took up residence among us" (John 1:14 HCSB). The day of rest was hardly recognizable to the One who ordained it.

Saul was strangled by the letter of the law. He tried desperately to keep all the outward acts of obedience while his heart slowly eroded. Saul gradually became the model for Isaiah 29:13: "These people approach Me with their mouths to honor Me with lip-service, yet their hearts are far from Me, and their worship consists of man-made rules learned by rote" (HCSB). Inevitably, Saul's faraway heart would turn to faraway actions.

Oh, God, forgive us when we act like modern-day Pharisees. Convict us at the very moment of our departure from the law of love You have written on our hearts. Give us hearts of devotion, not heads full of religion.

Excerpt taken from *Portraits of Devotion* by Beth Moore (© 2014).

The Greatest Treasure

But everything that was a gain to me, I have considered to
be a loss because of Christ. More than that, I also consider
everything to be a loss in view of the surpassing value of
knowing Christ Jesus my Lord. (Philippians 3:7–8 HCSB)

Just after the Civil War ended, a husband and wife in Chicago, Illinois, came to understand what it would mean to find rest in God's permanence, even as their treasures were destroyed.

The family was wealthy; he was a successful lawyer with influential friends. They had four beautiful children—three girls and a boy—until scarlet fever stole the life of their only son. The boy was just four years old.

A year later, the man invested a sizeable portion of their money in Chicago's growing real estate market. Several months later, it was gone—the property and the family fortune destroyed by the Great Chicago Fire of 1871.

But what came next revealed what he treasured most.

The year was 1873, two years after the fire. They added another child to their family in that time, a total of four daughters. He sent his wife, Anna, and their children ahead to England for a family holiday. The man stayed back on business with the plan of following shortly after. Only, something went terribly wrong. The ship collided with another in the Atlantic, and the daughters perished at sea. A grieved Anna reached shore and sent her husband a telegram: "Survived alone."

When Horatio Spafford sailed past the very spot on the Atlantic where his four baby girls sank into the depths, he grieved their passing away. Then he offered up these words of worship to the God who never moved, who presides over all the sorrows and all the seas:

> *When peace, like a river, attendeth my way,*
> *When sorrows like sea billows roll;*
> *Whatever my lot, Thou has taught me to say,*
> *It is well, it is well, with my soul.*

Spafford penned the hymn "It Is Well with My Soul" at sea that day, weeping for what was lost, holding tight to what could never be lost.[1]

Maybe you've never felt the depth of that Job-like sorrow, but like me, you've probably stood stunned, in the wreckage of what was or what might have been. It's hard to imagine those circumstances could ever be truly "well" with our souls in the face of a tragedy like Spafford experienced.

But when we hold tight to Permanent, and trust Him to carry the rest, we really can count all else as loss, long before it is ever lost.

Like Paul said in his letter to the Philippians, we say this with much joy, even knowing the chains of trial we're sure to one day endure. Because those chains, though real and grievous, cannot bind the love and grace and mercies that are ours in Christ. When we hold tight to Permanent, knowing we are also held by Him, our greatest treasure is always safe.

Excerpt taken from *She Reads Truth* by Raechel Myers and Amanda Bible Williams (© 2016).

---

1. Derek W. H. Thomas, *Tabletalk* magazine, March 1, 2008.

Don't Look Back

Not that I have already obtained this or am already perfect, but I press on to make it my own, because Christ Jesus has made me his own. Brothers, I do not consider that I have made it my own. But one thing I do: forgetting what lies behind and straining forward to what lies ahead, I press on toward the goal for the prize of the upward call of God in Christ Jesus. (Philippians 3:12–14 ESV)

God told Abraham that if there were ten righteous men in Sodom, He wouldn't destroy the city. Unfortunately, there weren't ten righteous men to be found, so God sent two angels to warn Abraham and his nephew Lot to get out of town. Lot tried to warn his sons-in-law, but they thought he was joking and apparently didn't listen. It says in Genesis 19:16 that Lot hesitated, so the angels grabbed he and his wife by the hand, along with their daughters, and led them out of the city.

As soon as they were safe, the angels said, "Flee for your lives! Don't look back, and don't stop anywhere in the plain! Flee to the mountains or you will be swept away!" (Gen. 19:17 NIV). But Lot wanted to go to a different town—one that wasn't in the mountains, but in the plains. God told Lot where to go, but Lot thought he had a better idea.

Sounds silly, right?

Well, as silly as it can sound to someone who does the same thing nearly every day.

God granted Lot permission to go to the nearby town instead of the mountains, telling them to hurry. So Lot, his wife, and their daughters headed toward the nearby town. As they did, Lot's wife made a critical mistake: She looked back. She looked back at the city filled with sin and wickedness, and as she paused, God turned her into a pillar of salt.

We don't even know her name, but that's her legacy: looking back. She'd been rescued from death and depravity, yet something still haunted her, causing her to stop moving toward whatever lay ahead. Why? Did she want to see her home one more time? Did she wonder if it would really be ruined? Was she looking for someone, or reflecting on a life she wanted to keep living?

I don't know, but I do know this: God has been gracious to me for many years as I've looked back at what could've been—a temptation that makes me question my faith. I've wandered to a closer city, while knowing He desires for me to climb.

Whatever you're walking away from right now, ask the Lord to remind you that there's a reason you've left that life behind. It's been swallowed by grace. Leave it be. The Lord has told you where to go, and it's time to walk, eyes straight ahead, tangled up in the spectacular love of a Savior who wants nothing less for you than the summit.

Excerpt taken from *Mended* by Angie Smith (© 2012).

Eyes on the Prize

Brothers, I do not consider myself to have taken hold of it. But one thing I do: Forgetting what is behind and reaching forward to what is ahead, I pursue as my goal the prize promised by God's heavenly call in Christ Jesus. In any case, we should live up to whatever truth we have attained. Join in imitating me, brothers, and observe those who live according to the example you have in us. (Philippians 3:13–14, 16–17 HCSB)

Have you ever watched a triathlon? The athletes that choose to participate in the swimming, biking, and running competition are clearly very serious about their task. (Just look at their triceps and hamstrings!) Most of the participants know they're not likely to win the grueling race, but they compete anyway. Why? There's sweet satisfaction in setting a very lofty goal and attaining it. No runner decides to compete in a triathlon on the day of competition. That would be lunacy! It would be impossible to just jump in with no preparation and expect to succeed; they would fall far short of their goal, perhaps not even making it past the first event. Every triathlete will tell you that there is much training involved with their sport. The athletes prepare for the race both physically and mentally. They acquire the proper clothing and gear that will best help them reach their goal of the finish line. So much of the race happens before they ever step up to the starting line.

Once the starting gun is fired and the race begins, the athletes are hyper-focused. They don't turn to wave at the fans, stop to gaze at the pretty clouds, or lie under a tree and take a break. They fix their sights on where they're going next, not where they've already been. There's no point in going back or even looking back; it would only detract from their goal of the finish line. They continue on to their goal with focused determination, and when they reach the end, there is a medal-wearing, Gatorade-dumping, finish line-crossing celebration!

In writing to the Philippians, Paul borrowed the language of athletes and compared the life of a Christian to that of an athlete who trains to compete. As believers we may never run an actual triathlon, but we are certainly in a race. We can model the athlete's complete focus and energy, fixed on that goal of knowing Christ and being more like Him.

Maybe our days of serious athletic competition are past (or maybe we never were the athletic type). But we can all be like runners in setting aside any distractions and pursuing Christ as our first priority. With our eyes fixed on Jesus, we can be champions in running the race of the Christian life. And when we reach the end of our earthly lives, there will be a celebration unlike any we've ever experienced.

Excerpt taken from *100 Days in the New Testament* (© 2016).

Re-telling the Secret

I don't say this out of need, for I have learned to be content in whatever circumstance I am. . . . I am able to do all things through Him who strengthens me. (Philippians 4:11, 13 HCSB)

My boys like secrets. In fact, we have a whole game we play that is centered around them. Sometimes when their friends come over, we'll all stand in a single-file line. The person in the front whispers a secret to the one behind him, and then the mysterious dialogue is sent from one to another until it reaches the end. Almost always by that time, whatever was shared between the first two participants has become misunderstood. Somehow the message just never gets translated clearly all the way back.

And judging from our current position in line as women today, in this culture, the same thing has happened to us. What we hear described as the secret of our satisfaction sounds a lot different than it did when it was first spoken and handed down many centuries ago.

Today we hear a philosophy of happiness that's actually been training us for a long time *not* to be happy. It says there's always something else, something more, some additional requirement we need before we can really enjoy life the way it was meant to be enjoyed. So the advertisements bombard us with suggestions, dripping with recommendations intended to whet our appetites and tantalize our taste buds, encouraging us to get rid of the old and acquire the new, to be dissatisfied with what we already have.

If you're single, you should have the security of marriage.
If you're married, you should have the freedom of singleness.
If you live in an apartment, you should own a home by now.
If you own a home, it should be bigger than the one you've got.

Getting the message?

Your appearance should look like *that trend*.

Your kids should be more like *those* kids.

Your standard of success should be measured by *these* standards.

The fallout from this is inevitable. Fed by such a steady diet of unclaimed desires, we can hardly help but develop a level of distain for our current circumstances. Caught in this vicious cycle, we consequently feel incomplete and substandard. Unhappy. Uncontrolled. Unfulfilled.

Dissatisfied.

This is precisely why a satisfied woman is such a surprising woman. She is shockingly noticeable to a world that lives on a watered-down version of the secret—a secret that she obviously got the truth about. You can tell it by her peace and serenity, by her solace and restfulness, by the mysterious sense of ease that accompanies her.

A satisfied woman knows that God has already given her enough. He always does.

And when you and I chose to recognize this and trust in His continued supply, we'll be able to engage in life in a way that we never have before. We'll finally be living life to the fullest.

You've found the secret.

Now you can pass it on.

Excerpt taken from *The Resolution for Woman* by Priscilla Shirer (© 2011).

No More Circles

*Just as the Lord has forgiven you, so you must
also forgive. (Colossians 3:13 HCSB)*

A young woman e-mailed me yesterday. In the throes of her letter, she told me an odd fact that had led her to a profound observation. Her sister, it seemed, owned a retired circus pony. But even though his days of working the circuit were now over, this little pony did nothing but wander in circles all day. Here he was, in a newfound place of freedom, fully able to range and explore and experience all that his new life had to offer. Yet his old life still haunted him. Defined him. Restrained him. Controlled him. He kept to the same pattern to which he'd been relegated for so long. He apparently didn't know how to operate any other way.

This is the burden of unforgiveness. It fits you with blinders, keeping you from seeing anything other than the offense done against you, making it hard to view anything else in your life except through its lens. Unforgiveness forces you to stay one-dimensional, unable to experience the joys that only exist on the periphery. Instead it keeps you narrowly relegated to the artificial boundaries created by yesterday's disappointments—a circle of mundane living that's far less than the abundant life you were created for.

I'm not judging you for this, okay? I understand. What's happened is bad. Terrible. In many ways—in every natural sense—unforgiveable. Perhaps it's still going on, in fact. You've *tried* to forgive. You've *thought* you were there. But then here it comes again—another betrayal, another broken promise, another blow to your fragile trust—and as a result, deeper hurt. Closed loops. Tighter circles.

So, while not pretending to be a counselor, and not able in this small space to discuss everything the Bible says about forgiveness—and certainly not implying that this equates to flipping a switch at 6:30 and enjoying a nice coffee at 6:45—I'm just here to tell you the truth.

I want your abundant life back. No more circles.

Please, God, no more circles.

Forgiveness is reached through a combination of several actions. *First, refuse to store up and harbor a grudge.* Make an active decision not to hold a debt over someone else's head or to keep an ongoing record of their wrongdoing. Choose instead to release them of that liability, and then to trust God—who knows every detail of everything that's happened—to work on your behalf and bring healing to your heart, even if not a clean resolution to the problem or a restoration of relationship. Forgiveness means releasing into His hands the person, the circumstance, and the outcome. All of it.

That's the way He did it with us, right?

"He forgave all our sins. He canceled the record of the charges against us and took it away by nailing it to the cross" (Col. 2:13–14 NLT).

This is our offering. Extending forgiveness. Just as He has so wonderfully, abundantly, and outlandishly poured it out on us.

Excerpt taken from *The Resolution for Woman* by Priscilla Shirer (© 2011).

Becoming Grace-Givers

Your speech should always be gracious, seasoned
with salt, so that you may know how you should
answer each person. (Colossians 4:6 HCSB)

G*race produces grace.* Grace motivates us to do gracious works
(Eph. 2:8–10) and to be gracious to others (1 Cor. 15:10). This
is not because we "owe" God or could ever hope to pay him back.
No. Grace is free. We owe nothing. But our conduct changes as a
result of being filled. We become like the one who pours His grace
into us.

In Bible times, salt was used as a seasoning and preservative to
add flavor to food and to keep it from spoiling. In rabbinical literature, salt is used metaphorically, as a symbol of wisdom. Salt was
included in Old Testament grain offerings as a symbol of friendship
and communion with God (Lev. 2:13). The idea communicated by
Paul is that just as salt seasons and preserves food, gracious, wise
words season and preserve our relationships.

Here are some of the ways in which God's grace enables our
speech to be gracious:

- It enables us to be humble, consider the perspective of oth-
  ers, and respect their strengths (Rom. 12:3–6).
- It enables us to be authentic, showing others who we really
  are (1 Cor. 15:9–10).
- It enables us to have an attitude of service (2 Cor. 4:1).
- It enables us to have an attitude of gratitude (2 Cor. 4:15).
- It enables us to be wise in how we speak (Col. 4:6).
- It enables us to conduct ourselves with holiness and sincer-
  ity (2 Cor. 1:12).

If God's grace changes our speech so dramatically, why do Christians still struggle with their mouths? The Bible explains that it is possible to "receive God's grace in vain" (2 Cor. 6:1) or to "miss" it (Heb. 12:15).

It's like the bee in my empty glass soda bottle at the lake last summer. The bottle was lying on its side on the picnic table. The bee exhausted itself trying to get out of the bottle by flying up against the top, toward the sky. The opening of the bottle was in the other direction. It was there the whole time and was, in fact, the way the bee got in. But that bee was not wise enough to fly toward the opening.

The grace of God has opened up a way for us. We have but to fly directly into that grace to experience the fullness and freedom of its abundance. We need not remain trapped behind glass, knowing of, but never experiencing, the joy of that flight. How do we fly toward the grace of God? The answer is found in Hebrews 4:16.

"Therefore let us approach the throne of grace with boldness, so that we may receive mercy and find grace to help us at the proper time" (HCSB).

We can boldly approach God and ask for His grace for every need. And as we do, His grace will fill and transform us and change us into grace-givers.

Excerpt taken from *Conversation Peace* by Mary Kassian (© 2004).

The Masterpiece of Simplicity

*To seek to lead a quiet life, to mind your own
business, and to work with your own hands, as we
commanded you. (1 Thessalonians 4:11 HCSB)*

Jesus' life was one of simplicity. Not of ease and not without complexity. But a cloth that is woven of many hundreds of knots all working together to create a pattern of simple beauty, clear and perfect. It was His willingness to die to His own will and live the will of His Father that created this masterpiece of a life.

Too often my life looks more like a jumble of threads, mismatched, hastily tied, and poorly executed. Pulling colors from here and there, I obscure the Creator's intent. I go running after my own will rather than keeping my eyes on the race that has been set before me. If I will only slow down and refer to the pattern, everything will turn out beautifully.

I have learned to ask myself a few questions before making a commitment. Maybe these questions will help you as you strive for simplicity in your own life:

1. Do I actually want to do this activity? This doesn't mean that you only have to do those things you enjoy. I don't enjoy paying our mortgage, but I am fairly certain that is not a legitimate excuse not to do so. But there are plenty of times I have agreed to completely optional activities for me or the kids only to realize we don't like doing the activity. Think about what you like to do and don't talk yourself into something for fear of being left out.

2. How will my making this commitment impact my most important responsibilities? The choices you make affect other people. It's unavoidable. I have sometimes chosen time together over strict bedtimes and sanity over well-balanced meals. But there are other times when I did something because I was afraid of being looked down on or in order to receive great recognition by those on the outside, all the while neglecting my responsibilities at home and being unkind to my family to boot. We only have so much time and energy to give, and our primary responsibilities should get first dibs.

3. What would those who know me best tell me to do? Everything I have learned about the art of discerning priorities and maintaining simplicity in my life, I learned from my husband. I hate it because I love to say yes to things, but he has been right too many times to be ignored. Now, before I sign on the dotted line, I either consult him or do my best to anticipate his response.

When in doubt, I try to go back to the example of Christ. He, just like us, had a finite amount of time on earth in which to accomplish a great deal. His work is the basis for our own and was complete and perfect while ours is not, but the purpose behind His work and ours is the same. *To establish the kingdom of God.*

Excerpt taken from *Letting Go of Perfect* by Amy Spiegel (© 2012).

The Affirmation Crusade

Therefore encourage one another and build each other up
as you are already doing. (1 Thessalonians 5:11 HCSB)

My husband is fascinated, intrigued, and still somewhat bemused by the fairer sex. He's discovered a plethora of feminine dynamics in the years we've been married that he admits he'll never fully understand. Like, for instance, why a weekend trip requires more than one pair of shoes. Or why the mere act of talking could ever be such an enjoyable hobby. He's asked me lots of questions over our years together, hoping to figure out some of these things. And yet even after my fine attempts at explanation, he tends to just smile, pat me lovingly on the cheek, and then walk out the door shaking his head in disbelief.

I guess a man will just never understand some things that are crystal clear to women.

Perhaps none more than this: the compliments one woman is allowed to give another.

He heard me telling a girlfriend not long ago that the skirt she was wearing really accentuated her pretty legs. He heard me tell another that her hair was "just lovely" in that color and style. He's seen other women come up to me expressing gratitude for a particular personality trait or just to tell me that the blouse I was wearing was really cute.

And for the life of him, he doesn't know how this works. Men just don't do this, he tells me. Never, for example, will I ever catch him praising another guy's hair, or telling a friend how that button up really brings out the broadness in his shoulders. In fact, he's made clear to me that if I ever overhear another guy complementing him on some of the things women get away with, I need to make sure that guy isn't around too much.

"That's just not something we do," he says.

But it is something *we* do, my sister friend. Something we ought to do a lot more often.

We are relational in a way most men are not. We thrive on our friendships with women and appreciate the commendation we receive from them. There's something about another woman's admiration that we can accept more fully because, for the most part, we're certain no strings are attached. No ulterior motives are underneath it. Just an honest, encouraging assertion expressed by another.

And while our self-worth should never depend on others' compliments or approval, we experience a certain depth of blessing when we are affirmed by other women. While appreciation from men is flattering, a sister's compliment carries a purity, simplicity, and gentle strength that refreshes us. It helps us feel reassured, supported, and warmly comfortable. Plus it does something else, something powerful; it diffuses any need for competition.

This should be our mandate, our campaign. A movement of women linked by our resolution and devoted to seeing it manifested in the lives of the women around us.

It can be our crusade.

Our *affirmation* crusade.

Our gift, one sister to another.

Excerpt taken from *The Resolution for Woman* by Priscilla Shirer (© 2011).

Unnecessary Risk

*"God has not given us a spirit of fear, but of power and
of love and of a sound mind." (2 Timothy 1:7 NKJV)*

The enemy wants to magnify our fears, making them appear insurmountable. He means to intimidate us with worries until avoiding them becomes our driving motivation. He wants to cripple us with anxiety, paralyze us with indecision, and leave us clinging to safety. He wants us defensive and defenseless.

The fact is this: fear is one of Satan's primary schemes for crippling God's people. I'm not talking about legitimate concern. I'm not talking about the protective warnings of wisdom and godly counsel. I'm talking about *fear.* Incessant worry. Up-all-night anxiety. Worst-case scenarios becoming the only probabilities you can think about. Fears like these, instead of simply raising our blood pressure, ought to set off some fire alarms. *Why am I feeling so paralyzed by this?*

God did not create us to be fearful people (2 Tim. 1:7). So whenever you sense a "spirit of fear" invading any particular area of your life, you can know by process of elimination that it's not coming from God . . . which only leaves one other spiritual place it could be originating from . . . which ought to make you wonder why it's there. Aren't you at least a little bit curious about what Satan's trying to keep you from experiencing?

I'm pretty sure you're familiar with the story of Moses and the children of Israel, pinned up against the waters of the Red Sea while the Egyptian pharaoh and his armies were bearing down hard from behind. Israel was fast in the process of being surrounded by people whose nation had brutalized them and their ancestors for four long, horrendous centuries. No escape. And the only direction that wasn't swarming with enemy hordes, the one path God was directing His people to go, laid straight ahead through the sea.

So these two million Hebrews had every reason to be terrified. Mortified really. There was no swimming out of this one.

And yet, in the face of such impossible circumstances, with the odds so heavily stacked against them, and with no indicator of the miracle that God had planned, Moses said to the people, "Do not fear!" (Exod. 14:13 NASB). His very first instruction to them was to *not be afraid*.

Notice that Moses wasn't telling them not to *feel* fear. The prospect of looming death will just kind of do that on its own. Fear is a natural human response to a lot of things, a Red Sea moment being one of them. So he knew they would *feel* fear, but he was telling them not to *wallow* in it. Not to choose it. Not make friends with it. Not entertain it, engage it. Because if they did, they risked not sticking around long enough to experience the stunning miracle their God was about to perform. And even more, they risked not getting to the other side. To the Promised Land. To the milk and to the honey. To destiny.

Excerpt taken from *Fervent* by Priscilla Shirer (© 2015).

Costly Love

*I know the One I have believed in and am persuaded
that He is able to guard what has been entrusted
to me until that day. (2 Timothy 1:12 HCSB)*

Many of our perils are deeply personal and out of public sight. We've each faced situations and circumstances we were not sure we could emotionally survive. We've been treated treacherously and carelessly. Or we've simply been ignored. We've ached and pined over the brevity of life and creaked and groaned when it felt unbearably long. We've hung in there when we wanted to quit. We've stayed where we wanted to leave. These things were costly.

Expensive.

You need to know that in this very season, on this very day, in this very moment Jesus counts the cost. He knows the personal price you're paying. He esteems with especially high regard when your faithfulness to Him is expensive and when you endure or do the right thing solely because you love Him. Read these next words carefully: *He also knows when our unfaithfulness and our fleeing from Him are the very things that cost us dearly.* But something miraculous and gorgeous can happen in the secret spaces of our greatest expenses. We can engage with Jesus there. We can talk to Him like people who know He really is there. Tell Him what is really going on in our minds. We can cry out or moan or just sit in tired silence and think four coherent words: *Jesus, I need You.*

You have Me. Tell Me what you need. Tell Me what you want. Tell Me how you feel. Tell Me how you don't.

We can become alert to His presence, awake and aware of our communion with Him. And we can draw from Him. We can draw bona fide strength from Him, achieving-power, sudden clarity and insight, palpable consolation and comfort. Rest for our weary souls. We can draw faith for a future that breaks the mirror of our past. We can draw the unction and the wherewithal to resist the temptation to throw something away that we know deep in our hearts we really want to keep.

And that's not all. We can draw joy from Him. Relief. Laughter. We can gulp down hope when a moment is hard to swallow. We can draw buckets from the bottomless well of His love so we have something to give the people in our lives who drain us dry. We can also draw something for ourselves when we've ground our own encouragers to dust.

Jesus is our affluence in affliction. When life gets expensive, take Him up on it. We're living like paupers in a bank vault. The resources are right there because He is right there. And He's listening. Talk to Him. This isn't your imaginary friend who gives you imaginary company and imaginary power. Christ's works have lasting effects and real life applications. No imaginary friend could have done for me what Jesus has managed to do.

We can know hope because we know Him well.

Excerpt taken from *Audacious* by Beth Moore (© 2015).

Ever Faithful

*If we are faithless, He remains faithful, for He
cannot deny Himself. (2 Timothy 2:13 HCSB)*

One day at the playground, my husband Brent and I were standing beneath the slide chatting while our son, Clark, then a preschooler, was clambering up.

"Catch me, Daddy!" Clark shouted, as he jumped from the full height down toward Brent. Brent turned to see Clark already sailing through the air and just managed to do a football-type lunge to catch him. Clark didn't wait to ask Brent to catch him. He just assumed that he would. "Daddy always catches me!"

Clark trusted his dad to catch him because his dad had always caught him in the past. His experiences had taught him that his dad was faithful and could be counted on.

To be *faithful* means:

- Unswerving in devotion
- Loyal to one's promises
- Trustworthy
- Sure
- Firm
- Certain

Faithfulness means predictability in a good, wholesome, positive sense. Those who are trustworthy are consistent in character with regard to their loyalty toward you. They are also true to what they say they will do. They will not disappoint you or let you down. You can totally trust and depend on them.

We all long to have someone in our lives whom we can count on. If a significant figure in your life has been unfaithful to you, you may struggle with fear of rejection, hurt, humiliation, anxiety, and/or feelings of inferiority. Faithlessness breeds emotional insecurities in one's life. Faithfulness, on the other hand, fosters security, confidence, permission to fail, and the ability to be vulnerable to others.

Faithfulness is one of the Father's prime characteristics. He revealed Himself to Moses as "the faithful God" who keeps His promise of love (Deut. 7:9). Paul often reminded the early believers of this trait, stating boldly, "God is faithful; you were called by Him into fellowship with His Son, Jesus Christ our Lord" (1 Cor. 1:9 HCSB).

God remains totally consistent in character (Ps. 102:25–27). He is not one way today and a different way tomorrow. His faithfulness is not affected by mood swings or circumstances. He operates with "perfect faithfulness" (Isa. 25:1). The Father is faithful without flaw. And He remains faithful forever (Ps. 146:6 HCSB).

God will never let you down. It would go against His nature. In fact, according to Paul, it is impossible for the Father to let you down. To Him, not being faithful is as remote a possibility as not loving or not being God. The Father is faithful. He is faithful because He is God. According to 2 Timothy 2:13, it is possible for humans to be undependable, inconsistent, and untrustworthy but it is impossible for the Father to be any of those things.

Second Corinthians 1:20 says, "For every one of God's promises is 'Yes' in Him. Therefore, the 'Amen' is also spoken through Him by us for God's glory" (HCSB).

Amen means "certainly, always, truly, for sure"! We can be sure, without a doubt that the Father will do what he says. Amen!

Excerpt taken from *In My Father's House* by Mary Kassian (© 2005).

God's Best

Flee from youthful passions, and pursue righteousness,
faith, love, and peace, along with those who call on the
Lord from a pure heart. (2 Timothy 2:22 HCSB)

The majority of statistics show that brain development does not stop until the mid-twenties, although drugs and alcohol can end that growth prematurely. What does this mean for your son or daughter? It means he is impulsive. It means she is insecure. It means his emotions are all over the place. It means she has a limited, sometimes very limited, awareness of long-term consequences. It means he grossly overestimates his power and grossly underestimates your wisdom.

One of the main regions of the brain that is not fully developed in teens is called the frontal cortex. The cortex is made of lobes that grow from the back to the front so the frontal lobe is last to develop. The frontal lobe is responsible for reasoning, planning, and judgment. According to an article in *Harvard Magazine*, this region is not fully developed until somewhere between twenty-five and thirty.[1]

Without the reasonable, logical portions of thinking fully developed, teens are often overcome by their emotions and impulses. These emotions and impulses only add fuel to the hormonal fire that is constantly stirring in your teen. And that's only what's happening on the inside. On the outside they've got the voices of their peers, media that glamorizes drug use, and that age-old need to live life on the edge.

Obviously peer pressure plays a major role in many teens' decisions to have sex. For many of them, it's the norm. Subsequently guys and girls feel "stupid" if they're the only one in their group of friends who hasn't. In addition, their hormones are pushing them toward sexual experiences. As they move into older adolescence, they also develop a hunger for deeper connection. Girls talk frequently about wanting to "belong" to someone. Guys enjoy being able to talk to girls and have close relationships without the ribbing that boys often do with each other when any vulnerability is displayed. As a result, everything physically, emotionally, and socially is pointing toward a longing for intimacy for many teenagers.

What in the world can you do?

One of the things you *can* do is talk to your child about expectations. They need to hear from you—not just what you expect but what you value, as well. They need to hear what you believe God has designed male-female relationships and sexual intimacy to be. They also need to know the why's behind that design. Many kids know they're not supposed to have sex, but they have no idea that God has made sex to exist in marriage for our protection. He's not just trying to protect us from physical harm like disease, but also the emotional devastation that occurs after the relationship ends.

God the Father and our Creator does have a plan for marriage. Reassure them that it is the best way, and it is for their good.

Excerpt taken from *Modern Parents, Vintage Values* by Melissa Trevathan and Missy Goff (© 2010).

---

1. Debra Bradley Ruder, "The Teen Brain," *Harvard Magazine* (September–October 2008), http://harvardmagazine.com/2008/09/the-teen-brain.html.

One Author

All Scripture is inspired by God and is profitable for teaching, for rebuking, for correcting, for training in righteousness, so that the man of God may be complete, equipped for every good work. (2 Timothy 3:16–17 HCSB)

Though the Bible has approximately forty different authors, runs the gamut of history to law, prophecy to poetry, and includes sixty-six books written over the span of sixteen hundred years, it has one Author who made every word sure and every truth proclaimed.

This is the truth Paul was reminding his young protégé of in 2 Timothy 3:16–17. It is the same truth we need reminded of as we seek to know and understand the Word of God.

This short passage packs a big punch by revealing to us a few things about itself and every other verse in the Bible. It tells us that every word of Scripture comes from God Himself, that they are "inspired" by the Holy Spirit. That looks pretty in cross stitch, but it's worth pausing for a moment to ask, "What does this sort of inspiration mean?"

When we say God inspired men to write the Bible, we don't mean it in the same way that a man may write a poem because he was inspired by a beautiful woman or a waterfall. The inspiration that the Holy Spirit provided in revealing the Word of God was direct, not indirect.

On the other hand, the inspiration that the Spirit provided in the revelation of the Word of God did not turn the human authors into automatic dictation machines. They weren't possessed—at least not in the sense of losing control over their own faculties. God used men to write the Bible, but He did so without overriding their personalities. We still see Moses' personality in the background of the Pentateuch, the preferences of each individual writer in the four books of the Gospels, and Paul's to-the-point communication style here in his words to Timothy.

When Paul taught that his biblical words were inspired by God, he meant that God took whatever care determined necessary to make sure that what Paul and all the other biblical writers said was what God wanted said.

This verse also tells us that because all Scripture is authored by God, all Scripture has authority. Through the Bible the sovereign God of the universe is declaring and commanding. But it is explicitly evident in the way Paul tells Timothy that the Word of God contains all that we need to be "complete" and "equipped for every good work." And since the Bible's help for us in these areas is comprehensive and exclusive, it is therefore authoritative.

We don't need to look outside of the Bible to find out what God deems as "need to know" knowledge. It's all available to us, smushed between the covers of God's Word. And while He may have used men like Paul, to pen the actual words, God is the author of every pen stroke of truth.

Drawing Us to Himself

*The Lord will rescue me from every evil work and will
bring me safely into His heavenly kingdom. To Him be
the glory forever and ever! (2 Timothy 4:18 HCSB)*

Paul knew without a doubt he was soon to die. Yet he was no masochist. He wasn't begging for the guillotine. He simply looked at life through the window of these words: "For to me, to live is Christ and to die is gain" (Phil. 1:21 NIV). It's a sincere statement from a changed heart. Christ had profoundly transformed Paul's attitude toward life and death.

1. Paul saw death as a departure. He did not say, "The time for my death is close." He said, "The time for my departure is close" (2 Tim. 4:6 HCSB). His entire life was a series of departures. He followed the leading of the Spirit through Judea, Syria, Cilicia, Galatia, Pamphylia, Asia, Macedonia, Achaia, and Italy. He never knew what awaited him as he entered a city, but one result was inevitable—as surely as he arrived, he would depart. God never let him hang his hat for long. "Our citizenship is in heaven," he had said (Phil. 3:20 HCSB). To him, settling in would be pointless until then. Paul had faithfully done his time in Rome and, predictably, another departure awaited him. This time, he was going home.

2. Paul saw death as a rescue. Paul didn't see death as a defeat. He did not believe the enemy finally had his way. He saw death as a rescue! We tend to define the word *rescue* an entirely different way. God certainly rescued Paul many times on this earth, just as He has rescued us, yet Paul knew the greatest rescue of all awaited him. Death was not God's refusal to act; death was God's ultimate rescue.

Oh, if we could only understand this difficult truth, how different our perspectives would be. Paul not only saw death as the ultimate rescue from evil; he saw death as a rescue from frail, limited bodies.

3. *Paul saw death as a safe passage.* Remember the words of 2 Timothy 4:18. God will not only rescue us, but He will bring us safely to His heavenly kingdom. The original Greek meaning for the word *rescue* is rhuomai, which means "to draw or snatch from danger, rescue, deliver. This is more with the meaning of drawing to oneself than merely rescuing for someone or something." God is not simply trying to snatch us from danger. He desires to draw us to Himself spiritually, then one day physically. When our ultimate rescue comes, God's purpose is to deliver us to Himself—safely.

On that day, may we echo Paul's words, confident in our Rescuer: "I have fought the good fight, I have finished the race, I have kept the faith" (2 Tim. 4:7 NIV).

Excerpt taken from *Portraits of Devotion* by Beth Moore (© 2014).

Collecting

For I have great joy and encouragement from your love,
because the hearts of the saints have been refreshed
through you, brother. (Philemon 7 HCSB)

When you collect the moments that matter, it means the moments have passed. And that's sometimes hard for me. I see the value in them, clearly, and the importance of remembering what it feels like to slide my feet in that sand and listen to my friends talk about theology and tacos and Texas; and recalling that memory, even today, strengthens me.

Why do I still feel sad today, at home in Nashville, and yet smile when I think of nights on the beach with friends? How can that be? How can sadness and joy coexist? How can a memory that makes me so happy also be a memory that brings sadness?

Paul was so faithful in his letters from prison to remind the churches, always in the first few sentences, of how he was thanking God for them and their partnership in spreading the gospel. Paul was pulling strength from these memories of friends and stories he continued to hear, even though he wasn't with them, even while imprisoned.

As you know, I'm a pain avoider, and yet I have a bad habit of tossing out the memories I need because they also hurt. But I've realized there is something beautiful, and something that opens your heart in new and deeper ways, when you open yourself up to experience pain as well as joy. I think that has to be part of all of this. Maybe that's what it means to rejoice in our sufferings as Paul says in Romans 5. Maybe when we make our hearts available to the hard moments and allow ourselves to experience God's love in new ways, we are also increasing our capacity to love others.

I was scared that collecting these moments would feel like trying to hold onto bubbles or wind or ice cream. I was scared the tighter I tried to grip the more I'd panic, and these moments would slip through my fingers; and while I'm freaking out about losing them, they would be gone. He asks me to trust Him. To let Him hold the things my hands cannot grasp. While I collect moments, He will collect friendships and make them last.

I think that may be the trick to this whole looking for lovely business. I think confessing to God when it seems hard or scary or painful, confessing what you want to do but what feels too challenging—it's what helps you finish. It's what helps you see Him in the people you meet and in the moments when you have to let them leave. So I decided to believe God, that He is who holds all things together, including my friendships, those memories, and my heart.

Excerpt taken from *Looking for Lovely* by Annie F. Downs (© 2016).

Man, Oh Manna

But solid food is for the mature—for those whose
senses have been trained to distinguish between
good and evil. (Hebrews 5:14 HCSB)

Paula Deen. Maybe you've seen her on the Food Network. That southern accent and down-home charm are as delectable as the food she serves up. But I wonder what Mrs. Deen would do if she had nothing to work with but manna? Could she make it into something special without having butter, shortening, and bacon drippings on hand? It's doubtful.

So what do we make of this manna that was supposed to keep them satisfied for forty years in the wilderness? Were they just supposed to doctor it up and somehow imagine they were eating what they really wanted? Was their only hope to engage in some sort of mind game, tricking themselves into believing that this inferior and incessant ingredient was (repeat after me) "the best stuff on earth"?

This may not be the answer you're wanting, but it was Israel's reality, and it's ours too. In fact, it's the gospel truth: God's manna does take some getting used to. It's an acquired taste. It is solid food "for the mature, who because of practice have their senses trained to discern good and evil" (Heb. 5:14 HCSB).

I'm not saying for one second that God's supply can't hold a candle to Satan's tantalizing feast. Satan is *forced* to rely on that wildly spinning mix of options. He needs all of those whipped-up concoctions to keep his plan on track, to keep us enticed and addicted to his wide menu of offerings. Only God can be so assured of the superiority of His provisions that He can present it to us in its simplest, purest form and blow us away with the difference that one tiny taste of His presence can make.

Listen, the simplicity and singleness that was characterized by God's daily manna was a symbol of Jesus Christ who was to come—the beautiful one-way plan for extending *to* us and establishing *for* us true abundance of life. The question is not whether a good God could possibly be so restrictive as to confine our path of redemption to one available option. The better question, after all that we've done to resist and reject Him, is why He chose to open the one path He did.

He is our "bread of life" (John 6:48). He is heaven's ultimate manna. And while the manna of the wilderness could not provide eternal life, the living "bread" (v. 50) did and will to anyone who will receive it. He is God's miraculous portion given not to bore us but to show us a little more of Himself every day. He does not become dull and tasteless by being our "narrow way." Rather, He becomes a daily expression of the unfathomable love of God, served fresh with the morning dew, the way only a caring, compassionate Father would do it.

Excerpt taken from *One in a Million* by Priscilla Shirer (© 2010).

Ineffective Anchors

We have this hope as an anchor for our lives,
safe and secure. It enters the inner sanctuary
behind the curtain. (Hebrews 6:19 HCSB)

As sure as God has a plan for us, the enemy has his own. He does everything he can to convince us God's steadfast love is weak and deficient. He calls into question the integrity of the anchor of our souls.

Can it really hold?

Are you sure this is the right anchor for this vessel?

If the enemy can get us to forsake the true anchor for a substitute, he has us right where he wants us: ineffective and defeated, adrift on a tumultuous sea, thrown by every wave, aimless and in danger of breaking into pieces on the rocky shore. Why is it important to him for us to be ineffective?

If you'll remember in the account with Eve, the serpent suggested God was afraid that she and Adam would become like Him. But that was God's plan all along. He made them both in His image. To bear His attributes on earth. To be His representatives in the world.

The enemy hates God and since he knows he has no power over Him, he believes the next best move is to mar God's image in His image bearers. He decides to make ineffective imagers by baiting them with ineffective anchors.

You see, he wanted to test our faithfulness. Would we be content being like God or would we want to *be* God? His gamble paid off. Adam and Eve took the bait. So have we.

We are meant to show His attributes in how we are fruitful and multiply and how we fill and subdue the earth. He gave us the ability to reflect His creativity by the miracle of human conception and birth and by creating pieces of art or building something with our hands or constructing ideas that improve our life and others' lives.

More often than not, though, fear wins. I tend toward defeat and self-pity more than accomplishment and self-praise. It's weak pride, really. I buy into the lie that I should be more than what I am. I am convinced that the giftedness given to me by God isn't enough; it should look like hers, or his.

I anchor my soul to what I am and what I can do and am paralyzed, rendered impotent. Ineffective anchor. Image marred.

When the Spirit eventually confronts me with my pride, He gives me the chance to do it differently. I get the opportunity to confess my unbelief, to say that I questioned God's good purpose in how He made me. I admit to Him that I want to *be* Him more than I want to be *like* Him. I also get the pleasure of thanking Him for how He has made me, how He delights in my using the gifts He's given me to make much of Him. The true anchor is restored and I am freed to be like Him.

Excerpt taken from *Steadfast Love* by Lauren Chandler (© 2016).

An Inconvenient Truth

Endure suffering as discipline: God is dealing with
you as sons. For what son is there that a father
does not discipline? (Hebrews 12:7 HCSB)

Upon entry to the Kiddie Casino (i.e., Chuck E. Cheese), I am immediately deemed the "Best Mom in the Whole World." I am showered with thank-yous, hugs, and kisses. Today is officially declared the "Best day ever!" However, as the moment of our departure nears, I brace myself for battle. For as soon as I say it's time to go (and mean it), I am immediately dethroned as Queen Mommy. Gone are the hugs and kisses of gratitude. They are supplanted by pouting lips, crossed arms, and other forms of sulky defiance. Gone are the shouts of joy and pleasure. Now there are only cries of lament and accusatory whining.

As much as I am annoyed by this behavior, aren't I often guilty of the same attitudes and assumptions, only perhaps more cleverly disguised? When God tells me it is time to leave the green pastures and head for the Valley of the Shadow of Death, don't I, too, stomp my foot and mutter under my breath? In part, I assume that if God loves me, He will give me what I want. Not what He knows I need, or what is best for me, but what I desire. And if He withholds those things from me, it must mean that He doesn't care, or that I have done something to displease Him and therefore I am being punished. I may not affirm these things with my lips but in the secret places of my heart, I am on the floor, kicking and screaming, desperate to get my own way.

When suffering of both the inconvenient and downright serious variety comes into our lives, our hearts cry out that we must be unloved and forgotten. Our minds give birth to thoughts of bitterness and envy. Who does God think He is, bringing us to our knees with cellulite or unemployment or loneliness or disease?

Well, He thinks He's God. He thinks He is the Creator of all that we see and so much more. The question isn't who does He think He is but who do we think *we* are? We call ourselves His children yet when He treats us like His own, we cry foul.

We simply need to look at Jesus, the Son of God, in order to see what we can expect as part of God's family. No bed of roses for the Messiah but rather a cradle of dirty straw. No crown of gold for the King of the Jews but rather a crown of thorns. So why on earth would we expect to be treated any differently? The suffering in our lives is not a sign of neglect or displeasure but a confirmation that we are His own.

God's Word acknowledges that suffering is painful by definition, but is the seed not the fruit. Sticking it out yields a bumper crop of peace and righteousness (Heb. 12:11). Endure!

Excerpt taken from *Letting Go of Perfect* by Amy Spiegel (© 2012).

Purpose in Pain

No discipline seems enjoyable at the time, but painful. Later on, however, it yields the fruit of peace and righteousness to those who have been trained by it. (Hebrews 12:11 HCSB)

A friend of mine once said, "I do not welcome pain, but I do not fear it. Pain is an excellent teacher." Another friend told me that the most godly people she knows are people who have walked through the deepest valleys. The people familiar with pain.

Pain was not a part of life in the garden of Eden. Pain became a reality upon the entrance of sin into the world. Ultimately, the Father will do away with pain. At the end of time, when the dwelling of the Father is with His children, "He will wipe away every tear from their eyes. Death will no longer exist; grief, crying, and pain will exist no longer, because the previous things have passed away" (Rev. 21:4 HCSB).

Tears will dry.

Death will die.

Grief, crying, and pain will pass away.

Until such time, pain is a reality with which we all must wrestle. Because pain is an ever-present reality, the Father allows and uses it in the lives of His children for His own redemptive purposes. The following list represents some of the ways God uses pain in our lives:

- To bring correction to our behavior (Ps. 119:67).
- To teach us something about His character (Job 42:3–5).
- For testing and purification (Ps. 66:10).
- To bring us closer to His heart (Rom. 8:35–39).
- To increase our dependency upon Him (2 Cor. 12:9).

- To increase our maturity and wisdom (James 1:2–5).
- To strengthen us (1 Pet. 5:10).
- To reveal His power and glory (John 9:1–3).

God desires to use your pain to fulfill His purpose for you. That is one of the ways He protects you. He may not always protect you from pain, but He will protect you by redeeming the pain and changing it into something of eternal value. He uses what Satan meant for evil to build goodness in your life.

The choice to let the Father work in this way is yours. Contrast two passages of Scripture. Of those "who love God" and who "are the called according to His purpose," Romans 8:28 says, "all things work together for the good" (HCSB). On the other hand, in the parable of the soils Jesus told of one who received the seed that fell on rocky ground (Matt. 13:20). That person received the word with joy, but when persecution came, Jesus said, "Yet he has no root in himself, but is short-lived. When pressure or persecution comes because of the word, immediately he stumbles" (v. 21 HCSB).

In the one case, the person who loves God allows the Father to use pain and suffering for good purposes. In the other, the persecution serves only to destroy the person's faith. In either case we see that the Father uses affliction. The question becomes, will affliction make your faith strong or simply point out where you're weak?

Excerpt taken from *In My Father's House* by Mary Kassian (© 2005).

Make Straight Paths

Therefore strengthen your tired hands and weakened knees, and make straight paths for your feet, so that what is lame may not be dislocated, but healed instead. (Hebrews 12:12–13 HCSB)

The way back to God is often described as being "straight." When the Israelites wandered in the desert after their escape from Egypt, their winding way was a result of God's dealing with the idols still left in their hearts and their refusal to trust Him for the Promised Land. He was squeezing what was left of Egypt out of them. For forty years they wandered in the wilderness until Moses died and God appointed Joshua to "arise, go over this Jordan, you and all this people, into the land that I am giving them, to the people of Israel" (Josh. 1:2 ESV).

It was that simple. Arise and go because I, the Lord, am going with you. And they did. And it wasn't easy. Straight doesn't mean easy, but we can definitely make it more challenging.

A friend of mine and I love to run together at night after we put our kids to bed. The problem with running at night is that not all paths are well lit.

On one run, we were chatting away when suddenly my friend was no longer in sight. I looked to the space beside me where she had been seconds before and she was gone! I stopped in my tracks and turned around. She was laid out in the grass giggling uncontrollably, her palms raw and knee bleeding.

"What happened?!?"

"I tripped over something and couldn't keep myself from falling!"

She and I inspected the sidewalk behind us. On the side where she had been running was a narrow manhole that protruded several inches above the concrete.

From then on, we tried to make straight paths for our feet. We adjusted our routes and times and did what we could to avoid dimly lit sidewalks, protruding manholes, and narrow shoulders.

Scripture implores us to do what we can to make straight paths for our feet. There are some things that aren't sinful in and of themselves but serve as distractions. We can be distracted from God's leading and thus miss His best. Too much television and time on social media keeps me focused on the temporary instead of digging deep into His Word. I can find myself honing in on what to remodel in my house, what kind of boots to wear now, where someone has been invited to go (and, humph, I haven't!), what such-and-such has to say about this Scripture, what's the latest cause to undertake, and on and on it goes. They are potholes that slow my walk with Christ. When I'm willing to resist the temptation to "just check quickly" what's going on in the digital world, I find my heart is more at peace and primed to meet with the Lord and be led by His Word.

Excerpt taken from *Steadfast Love* by Lauren Chandler (© 2016).

A True Miracle

*Make sure that no one falls short of the grace of God
and that no root of bitterness springs up, causing trouble
and by it, defiling many. (Hebrews 12:15 HCSB)*

Forgiveness is a miracle. It really is. It's a supernatural outworking of God's Spirit through you, enabling you to extend something you could never do apart from His indwelling activity. He alone can compel a grieving mother to forgive her child's killer, or a betrayed friend to forgive an act of emotional disregard and cruelty, or a deceived wife to welcome back the one with whom she exchanged those first vows.

Only one power, one invisible force, one miracle can clear away the eroding illness that robs you of peace and love and the enjoyment of life. Only one substance is heavy and blanketing enough to douse the raging fire of resentment that burns away your joy, the flames that have left behind nothing but scraps and soot and the ashy remnants of what your life could have been.

Only God can alter your pattern, quicken your step, expand your reach . . . and get you out of those circles.

By no means am I suggesting that these steps are simple or easy to do. I'm only proposing, by the authority of God's Word, that it is worth it. Being a woman resolved to forgive can save your marriage, restore your relationship, rebuild your life, refurbish your business, reestablish your work, and help you regain your very self, allowing you to live freely. Lovingly. With joy.

Forgiveness is designed to rescue *you,* while bringing with it the added by-product of extending the impact of your grace toward those you love.

"Just as the Lord has forgiven you, so you must also forgive" (Col. 3:13 HCSB).

We extend forgiveness just as He has so wonderfully, abundantly, and outlandishly poured it out on us.

Now I'm certain this is not the first thing you've ever read or the first message you've ever heard on the topic of forgiveness. I'm fully aware that this theme and need are as ancient as the Bible itself. There's nothing innovative or particularly brilliant about what I've shared—no formerly unknown secret, no 1-2-3 formula for unlocking yourself from a prison of bitterness.

You've known all this. But what have *you* done with it?

Have *you* resolved to be forgiven, as well as to forgive? Taking the steps to do it makes all the difference.

Therein lies the secret you've possibly been waiting to discover—the promised opportunity to change the geometry of your life from endless circles into the best shape your heart has ever been.

- Prayerfully consider: Who, if anyone, are the people you harbor unforgiveness toward? How have you seen this affect your life?
- Grab your Bible and choose one passage to read and study on forgiveness.
  - Mark 11:25–26—making reconciled relationships a regular part of our praying.
  - Matthew 6:14–15—how our forgiveness of others relates to God's forgiveness of us.
  - Hebrews 12:14—the blessing that flows from pursuing peace with everyone.

Excerpt taken from *The Resolution for Women* by Priscilla Shirer (© 2011).

The Scarlet Cord

May the God of peace, who through the blood of the eternal covenant brought back from the dead our Lord Jesus, that great Shepherd of the sheep, equip you with everything good for doing his will, and may he work in us what is pleasing to him, through Jesus Christ, to whom be glory for ever and ever. Amen. (Hebrews 13:20–21 NIV)

Her name was Rahab, and I must say, she's one of my favorite heroines in Scripture. Leading up to her story, remember Moses had died without ever entering the Promised Land. His successor, the mighty warrior Joshua, was planning to invade Canaan. Before doing so, he sent two spies to focus on Jericho, to scope out the land.

While they were there, the spies stayed at the home of a prostitute named Rahab. It's been speculated that they chose to stay there as they were unlikely to be discovered in a brothel. Regardless, by the end of their time there, they'd changed the course of Rahab's life, and in a sense, all our lives.

When the king of Jericho learned of two spies in the land, he sent representative to Rahab's house. But instead of turning them in, she lied to the king's men, telling them the spies had been there, but were now on their way out of the city. While the guards rushed after them, Rahab crawled up to her roof where she'd hidden the men under stalks of flax. She told them she knew what the Lord had done for them, parting the sea, and she believed He was on their side—that theirs is "God in the heavens above and on the earth beneath" (Josh. 2:11 ESV). Essentially, she believed in God more than she feared for herself. So she lied to protect these strangers because she wanted to be on the right side of their God.

She promised to keep them safe as long as they promised not to harm her family when they stormed the city. They agreed. She let down a cord from her window and helped them escape out of the city. They explained that they'd be back to battle shortly, and in order to save her family, she must do one thing: gather them into her home and then drop a scarlet cord from her window—signifying that their house was to be spared in the fighting.

It wasn't the first time the Lord used a symbol like this, foreshadowing the blood shed by Christ. Remember Passover in Exodus 11? The blood of a lamb . . . the scarlet cord . . . the cross at Calvary . . .

This is what I love most about my Jesus. He's the God of redemption: He loves to take the underdog and show them they're not who they thought they were. He took a woman living a sinful life and blessed her because she believed in Him with holy, reverent fear. God didn't just "let" her into the story. He *chose* her for the story.

He chose you, too.

Excerpt taken from *Mended* by Angie Smith (© 2012).

Joyfully Ever After

Count it all joy, my brothers, when you meet trials of
various kinds, for you know that the testing of your
faith produces steadfastness. (James 1:2–3 ESV)

Contentment is a character trait, and character traits are developed over the years by practice. When circumstances don't play out like we had hoped, we can choose to be content in the midst of our circumstances. Whether in good times or seemingly bad, James 1:2–3 reminds us to consider it all joy. The Greek word for "joy" is *chara* (khar-ah´), which means "cheerfulness" or "calm delight." The Greek word for "steadfastness" is *hupŏmŏnē* (hoop-om-on-ay´), which means "cheerful (or hopeful) endurance," "constancy." Calm delight. Constancy. Where do I sign up? Joy, chara, is still around when the happy dance ends.

The pursuit of happiness is based on external circumstances. Joy and contentment come from an internal, settled peace that resides deep within our souls. That peace comes from looking to Jesus, the founder and perfecter of our faith, who for the joy (*chara*) that was set before Him endured the cross (Heb. 12:2). It puts things into perspective when we think of Jesus demonstrating a "calm delight" in going to the cross to pay for sins He didn't commit. He was able to see past the moment of the cross and set His eyes on the long-term reward—being seated at the right hand of God. But let's not forget that He was human just like us. In the garden just prior to His crucifixion, He prayed, "My Father, if it be possible, let this cup pass from me" (Matt. 26:39 ESV). Ultimately, He forfeited happiness in the moment for the joy set before Him and endured the cross.

"Nevertheless, not as I will, but as you will" (Matt. 26:39 ESV). We can put away our "if only" lists because, praise be to God, Jesus put away His.

Hans Christian Anderson once wrote, "Every man's life is a fairy tale written by God's fingers." God holds the pen, but we determine the mood and tone of each chapter. It's time to let go of the fairy-tale expectations we once imagined for our lives. Happily-ever-after is a choice, not a prize offered to a chosen few who find the fairy tale. Let's quit chasing a temporary brand of happiness when joy can be ours today. True joy can only be found in Jesus Christ. Those who make Him their pursuit will experience the greatest riches this earthly life has to offer.

Why settle for a fairy-tale pipe dream when God has written us into the greatest story ever told—*His* story? Let us reflect daily on the beautiful love story of redemption. No fairy tale can match the rescue mission that took place in God's story. "But God shows his love for us in that while we were still sinners, Christ died for us" (Rom. 5:8 ESV). Our Prince awaits. Ever after . . . begins today.

Excerpt taken from *Everyafter* by Vicki Courtney (© 2016).

Trials and Joy Are in Cahoots

Consider it a great joy, my brothers, whenever you experience various trials, knowing that the testing of your faith produces endurance. But endurance must do its complete work, so that you may be mature and complete, lacking nothing. (James 1:2–4 HCSB)

In a jail cell she awaits her trial. She was arrested for keeping ten children's Bibles at her nursery school. Steadfast in her faith, she ponders her prison term with one guarantee—God is present with her and will give her the strength to endure. This trial has forged her faith like steel in a refiners fire. She wouldn't make a different choice, even if she could.

A man heads home in his car with his personal effects in a box in the back seat. He refused to do something he thought was unethical, so his boss fired him. He thinks about his wife and three kids at home, and he wonders how he will support them now, but he is amazed by the peace that seems to be coursing through him. God has provided for his family before. He will continue to do so. The man is not afraid. He's actually even a little bit excited to see what God will do next. He knows from God's long track record of faithfulness, that He never asks His people to jump without being their parachute.

A mom is in the thick of the little years. Day after day looks like an endless list of tasks that are never full done: laundry, dishes, nose to wipe, mouths to feed, and feed, and feed . . . These are not easy years, but they are fruitful years. She trusts that each day she is making deposits in the savings accounts of her children's hearts, and of her own, as she trusts God to bless the monotony of it all. Some day, she is confident, God will give a return on her investment with interest. She's seen Him do it time and time again.

A woman lies in a hospital bed receiving chemotherapy. She hopes the medicine works and the cancer cells are sent running into remission. But her hope is not in whatever is dripping into her body through the IV. Her hope is in Jesus.

James addresses his letter to the Jewish Christians who live outside of Palestine, scattered abroad. James exhorts these believers to view each trial with joy versus dismay. Trials serve as an opportunity to grow and mature as a believer's faith is tested by everyday human events, even persecution.

Is it possible that joy and trials can coexist?

Instead of being enemies, could they be in cahoots for our good?

James tells us that as we press through times of trial, we emerge with stronger faith and character. Though we are tempted to rail against trials, question God, and worry ourselves sick, we can choose instead to grow in patience and endurance. Jesus exemplifies perseverance under trial, thus we look to Him for strength and joy in our times of stress.

Excerpt taken from *100 Days in the New Testament* (© 2016).

Faith vs. Faithfulness

For you know that the testing of your faith
produces steadfastness. (James 1:3 ESV)

A mother eagle is fiercely intent on guarding her eaglets. She builds her nest high above the ground, safe and protected from intruders, then lines it with a layer of soft, comforting materials. Makes a nice, cozy resting place for her young.

But an eagle's nest contains more than meets the eye. Underneath this coating of soothing comfort, she has constructed the base of her nest with rocks, sticks, and other sharp objects—a rather ironic fact that her growing brood will soon come to discover. For when she deems the time appropriate, the mother eagle will shake up the nest, turning it almost inside out, exposing the bristly underside to their soft, young backsides. No longer is it a place of comfort for her babies; it is now extremely *uncomfortable,* a place they'd like to get away from.

For yes, a mother eagle is fiercely intent on guarding her eaglets. But she is equally determined to see them reach their full potential. So her job is not complete until she's caused them enough discomfort to make them ready to experience the reality of what God created them to do.

To stand to their feet.

To spread their wings.

And fly.

The concept of faithfulness, much like an eagle's nest, also entails more than meets the eye. It isn't merely the comfortable, untested summary of someone's beliefs—her faith—but rather a physical outworking of her actions. It's more than just having a firm persuasion; it's moving that firm persuasion into forward motion. Having a strong set of beliefs is one thing. But standing tall on them, making decisions according to them, and adjusting your life to line up with them—that's quite another.

That's faithfulness.

Faithfulness is born when the outward expressions of your beliefs are lived out over time. Often through difficulty. For difficulty is where faithfulness is honed and brought to life. You'd never classify someone as being faithful unless you'd seen her stand firm during a season when it would have been much simpler to throw in the towel.

Hopefully you're a person of faith. But heaven is calling you to be a person of *faithfulness* as well. When you're at your job. When you're struggling financially. When you're faced with a tough decision. When you're doing your daily life and wish you were doing somebody else's. By resolving to be *faithfully* His, you are deciding to allow everything you believe about God and His Word to consistently guide your feet, your hands, your mind, your heart— despite anything and everything that may point to the contrary.

In a world marked by constant change and incredulous options, a woman who is resolved to live faithfully is an irony. A mystery. But being different is worth the cost of being diligent and strong. Being uncharacteristic is worth the cost of feeling complete and lacking nothing, prepared by God for the great work He has for you.

Excerpt taken from *The Resolution for Women* by Priscilla Shirer (© 2011).

The Path of Sin

But each person is tempted when he is lured and enticed by his own desire. Then desire when it has conceived gives birth to sin, and sin when it is fully grown brings forth death. (James 1:14–15 ESV)

This is not a happy birth story. Sin is conceived in our bellies as a result of an unholy desire. When that desire is fully developed, it is born as sin. And that sin always grows up to be a rebellious teenager that will be our undoing.

Sin starts when we are lured and enticed toward it. Satan has a history of doing the luring and enticing in moments when we are alone or feel separated from the people God has put in our lives as a safety net. But the temptation itself is not a sin. Eve could have had that conversation with the serpent with a very different outcome. The ticket to being lured and not devoured is to tell God and to tell others.

James goes on to give Christians these instructions: "Therefore, confess your sins to one another and pray for one another, that you may be healed. The prayer of a righteous person has great power as it is working" (5:16 ESV).

There's healing when we tell. There's power when we tell. There's pain and isolation when we stay silent. But as individuals we refuse to get real about our sin. We want to keep up appearances at church. We'd like people to think we're really good people and that church is just a country club where we wear our best clothes, including a pretty mask, instead of a hospital where we can get bound up and healed through the loving care of others.

And so we surround ourselves with people who all want the same thing. The mood is light, but they're not really connected. At the end of the day, the sermon, the service, the game, they will go back home to their lonely lives with the same sense that they could never tell what's really going on.

That kind of thinking will get us isolated from the herd every time, like antelopes. Sure, antelopes are pretty. People like to look at them, but they are easy targets because they are quickly separated from their community. Refusing to tell your sin to others will keep you an antelope forever.

Are you lonely? If so, is it possible sin is the root cause? Can you look back and see that Satan waited for moments when you were outside your community? He attacked and then he lied to you, telling you your shame should banish you to the bushes, making you feel even more alone.

It's time to fall into the safety net of your community. Seek God and ask Him to reveal the sin in your life. Confess it to Him right then and there. Don't hide yourself or your junk. Tell someone. Keep telling until you see the lion pride slink away and set their sights on a different antelope.

Excerpt taken from *Connected* by Erin Davis (© 2016).

Grace Alone

*For just as the body without the spirit is dead, so also
faith without works is dead. (James 2:26 HCSB)*

Faith is a gift. Not a gift we give ourselves or a reward we somehow earn, but an actual grace—by definition, undeserved. We know this because Scripture tells us so.

Perhaps the most familiar evidence of this is a passage from the book of Ephesians:

> *But God,* who is rich in mercy, because of His great love that He had for us, *made us alive* with the Messiah *even though we were dead* in trespasses. You are saved by grace! . . . For you are saved by grace through faith, and *this is not from yourselves; it is God's gift*—not from works, so that no one can boast. (Eph. 2:4–5, 8–9 HCSB, author emphasis)

We were dead. God made us alive. This salvation "by grace through faith" is His gift to us. Seems clear enough, huh?

This passage in Paul's letter to the Philippians is another:

> Just one thing: Live your life in a manner worthy of the gospel of Christ. Then, whether I come and see you or am absent, I will hear about you that you are standing firm in one spirit, with one mind, *working side by side for the faith that comes from the gospel,* not being frightened in any way by your opponents. This is a sign of destruction for them, but of your deliverance—and this is from God. *For it has been given to you on Christ's behalf not*

only to believe in Him, but also to suffer for Him, having the same struggle that you saw I had and now hear that I have. (Phil. 1:27–30 HCSB, author emphasis)

Here, Paul instructed the people of the church at Philippi to work together "for the faith" (Phil. 1:27 HCSB), while at the same time contending that faith is a gift from Christ (v. 29). These are not mutually exclusive assertions; faith is a gift, and we are to work for it, or on its behalf. But nowhere does God's Word tell us that faith is a result of the working. Instead, Ephesians 2:9 states the opposite: ". . . not from works, so that no one can boast" (HCSB) (along with Rom. 11:6; Gal. 2:16; and Titus 3:5).

As for me, there must be some glitch hardwired into my brain. Even amid all the evidence to the contrary, I am still quick to see the connection between works and faith as causative (works acting as the cause or producer of faith) rather than symptomatic (works acting as a sign of faith).

The Bible is not teaching that works give life to faith, but the other way around. A faith that is living will produce works just as a body that is living will produce breath. If a body is not breathing, it is not alive. If a faith is not working, it isn't alive either.

Excerpt taken from *She Reads Truth* by Raechel Myers and Amanda Bible Williams (© 2016).

Steering in the Right Direction

Now when we put bits into the mouths of horses to
make them obey us, we also guide the whole animal.
So too, though the tongue is a small part of the body,
it boasts great things." (James 3:3, 5 HCSB)

Words are powerful.

Patrick Henry's historic words, "Give me liberty or give me death!" inspired a nation to fight furiously for freedom. Mother Teresa's challenge, "Let's do something beautiful for God," stirred many to contribute to the needs of the poor in Calcutta. Successful advertisers know that words influence the purchase decisions we make. Words *are* powerful. Cold words freeze people, and hot words scorch them. Words can heal, soothing with balm, or cripple, drawing blood like a dagger. They make or break relationships—build up or tear down, bring peace or conflict, determine the destiny of individuals, families, and nations. That two-ounce muscle between your teeth is more powerful than any other muscle in your body! That's why it's so important to control it.

James maintains that a controlled tongue is like a well-trained horse. When we put bits into the mouths of horses and train them to obey us, we are able to turn the direction of the whole animal. A trained animal can pull a plow or a wagon, or carry a rider to his destination. The energy of an untrained horse can't be harnessed for productive work. Loosed, it would run through the street wildly, causing damage and chaos. And it would probably injure itself.

It's the same way with our tongues. Free and untamed, our words can cause lots of damage. According to James, godliness involves bridling the free, uninhibited nature of the tongue and actively controlling the direction of our speech so that it becomes productive instead of destructive. To harness the power of navigation, we need to put our hand to the reins, take control of our words, and steer them in a positive direction.

How we choose to use our tongues—for good or for evil—affects our whole lives. It affects the type of person we become and the type of experiences we will have. In Proverbs 12, Solomon compares and contrasts the characteristics and life experiences of those who use their tongues for evil with those who use their tongues for good. The former are reckless with their words. Their speech pierces like a sword. They are impatient, deceitful, duplicitous, uncaring, and vindictive. Solomon says that they will be trapped by their sinful talk. Because of their words, they will be despised, overthrown, and have their fill of trouble.

Those who use their tongues for good, on the other hand, will stand firm. Their speech will be righteous, truthful, and kind. They will promote peace and healing. Because they use words wisely, they will escape trouble. Their gracious speech will result in all sorts of awesome rewards. According to Solomon, there is joy in store for all those who promote healthful conversation.

One direction leads to conflict and chaos. The other leads to peace and joy.

Excerpt taken from *Conversation Peace* by Mary Kassian (© 2004).

He Won't Let Go

You are being protected by God's power through
faith for a salvation that is ready to be revealed
in the last time. (1 Peter 1:5 HCSB)

We were created to hold tight.

If you've spent much time around newborns, you may have noticed that when you place your finger or a toy in their palm, they will involuntarily close their fingers around it. Amazingly, this grip can be tight enough for the baby to support its full body weight—though it's probably best for you to just take my word on that.

As early as eleven weeks in utero, and until they're about six months old, babies demonstrate a critical developmental reflex known as the Palmar Grasp.

Holding is as natural as breathing.

Even before we took our first breath, our fists have been naturally exercising the motion of grasping and holding. Well into adulthood we continue to employ that instinctual motion, and without it, our function would be deeply limited. The truth is, real-world holding tight is often associated with anxiety or fear—we're trying to prevent something bad from happening.

We hold our people tight—holding hands as we cross the street, and supporting our grandparents as they proceed cautiously down a set of stairs. Even when we hold tight out of affection, there's always still an element of fear—of not wanting to lose something.

Parent-child relationships can be beautiful examples of how we relate with God. But when it comes to the realities of permanent and passing away, even the most enduring love of a parent cannot hold up. It's not that way with God.

Because everything in this world is fragile, there is no real-life metaphor for holding tight to something that is actually secure. We hold out of fear, we grip out of anxiety or prevention, and we eventually lose our grip every time. But because the gospel of Jesus Christ is permanent, it is not subject to the same shortcomings of anything that is passing away.

Hear that. The gospel is not passing away.

God does not let go.

The very nature of the gospel is different than anything else around us. Scripture calls our gospel inheritance "a living hope." Not a dying hope. The apostle Peter describes it as, "imperishable, undefiled, and unfading, kept in heaven for you." And the hope of the not-passing-away gospel is literally being "guarded" by God Himself (1 Pet. 1:3–5 ESV).

Our eternal hope is guarded in heaven by God's own power. No wonder He tells us not to fear. No wonder He promises we can stake our lives on His Truth.

The gospel is good news. It is not scary news.

The gospel calls us to hold tight, yet reminds us we're already being held.

By holding tight to the Permanent Thing you're trusting Him to hold on to all of the rest—with your very life, and all of the blessings and burdens that come with it. You aren't holding them together— you are holding tight to Him alone, asking Him to carry the rest.

Excerpt taken from *She Reads Truth* by Raechel Myers and Amanda Bible Williams (© 2016).

Inward Beauty

Your beauty should not come from outward adornment,
such as elaborate hairstyles and the wearing of gold jewelry
or fine clothes. Rather, it should be that of your inner self,
the unfading beauty of a gentle and quiet spirit, which
is of great worth in God's sight. (1 Peter 3:3–4 NIV)

My hands don't look like kid hands anymore. They don't look bad or weird or ugly; they just don't look young anymore. Getting older is a weird thing. In a Western culture that teaches that beauty is found in youth, the process of slowly seeing that fade away is interesting and different from what I would have predicted.

I've been a nail-biter most of my life. As an elementary-age student, I bit and picked at my nails until they bled. I bit my nails when I was nervous, bored, sad, lonely, busy, scared—it really didn't matter. I bit them down until you could see the tips peeled to deeper levels and the nail bed would be revealed on each finger. It was ugly. So now I paint my nails. Depending on my mood, the weather, the season, or the event.

First Peter 3:3–4 speaks of not focusing too much on your outward appearance. It was a warning, at the time, to the women of Israel to not become like the Egyptian women and spend hours focused on outer beauty. Instead, Peter says, spend time on who you are on the inside.

I used to not like these verses. (Am I allowed to say that?) They didn't resonate with me because I thought about all the time I spent in church and all the time I spent trying to be the "right person," but I never felt like I had a gentle spirit, and I continued to hate my body. But what I have learned of late is that when I focused on the inside, the outside changed, too. The focus isn't on clocking time with God just for the sake of checking off your daily responsibilities. *"Did I pray today? Did I read my Bible? Did I journal? Okay, then I'm good!"*

I tried that for a long time. I thought that was building my strength. But it wasn't. When I'm doing the hard work of healing, letting God dig down into the hurt places, my body responds with health as well. But when my inside is neglected and hurting, it shows in my hands and in my eyes. Not in the crow's-feet, but in the sadness that can't be denied when someone looks right at me.

I love how Scripture shows us what true beauty is—the kind that lasts forever. It doesn't mean I'm going to stop painting my nails or working out or brushing my hair. It just means I see those things for what they are, and put them in their appropriate place, behind the focus of a healthy body, soul, and spirit.

Excerpt taken from *Looking for Lovely* by Annie F. Downs (© 2016).

How to Be Hospitable

Above all, maintain an intense love for each other, since love covers a multitude of sins. Be hospitable to one another without complaining. Based on the gift each one has received, use it to serve others, as good managers of the varied grace of God. (1 Peter 4:8–10 HCSB)

The essence of hospitality is a "heart open to God," and it begins at home. The Scriptures speak clearly about the methods of the hostess.

She is to serve with love (Gal. 5:13).

She is to maintain calmness and self-control (Luke 10:41–42).

She is to work energetically and heartily (Col. 3:23).

She is to present her gift of hospitality "as something done for the Lord" (Col. 3:23).

And as 1 Peter 4:9 reminds us, she is to offer her hospitality without grumbling.

To invite someone into your home offers an opportunity to take the challenge of lifting that person's happiness quotient for as long as he or she is your guest.

The hostess becomes a steward of the resources of her home (1 Cor. 4:2). The major benefit of her wise stewardship and willing service is the delight of serving. Time is the first resource, and it is given equally to all to appropriate as God directs. The psalmist calls on us to "give them [your] food at the right time" (Ps. 104:27 HCSB). You may be tempted to take for granted the simple task of providing balanced, nutritious meals for your family and guests. When I am preparing a festive meal for family or friends, I try to set aside a block of time just to set my tables, prepare place cards and favors, arrange china and flatware, fold napkins, and coordinate the entire culinary journey. On a really special occasion I may give as much time to these finer touches as to cooking the food.

Money is another resource (Acts 2:45) often required for hospitality. We work within our respective budgets to use our resources to bless others.

Energy must also be appropriated in any sincere efforts at hospitality (Titus 2:4). Whether preparing food, decorating tables, or planning activities, there is a price to be paid beyond dollars and cents. Using our limited energy to serve others is a sacrifice necessary to demonstrate true hospitality.

Underlying the investment of time, money, and energy is the attitude of love. This love is action with feeling and feeling with action. No hostess will be ultimately effective unless she loves her guests.

Jesus is the very best example of hospitality. He frequently fed people, but even more important was His determination to go beyond the physical needs of His guests for food to offer answers to deeper needs of the heart and spirit in the midst of His genuine and complete hospitality.

"'I am the bread of life,' Jesus told them. 'No one who comes to Me will ever be hungry, and no one who believes in Me will ever be thirsty again'" (John 6:35 HCSB).

Excerpt taken from *A Woman Seeking God* by Dorothy Patterson (© 2013).

The Rock That Will Stand

"But the Day of the Lord will come like a thief; on that day the heavens will pass away with a loud noise, the elements will burn and be dissolved, and the earth and the works on it will be disclosed." (2 Peter 3:10 HCSB)

This world is ever-changing. It's passing away. We calculate our risks and evaluate our next steps, trying to hold on to the reins. But in the calculating and the evaluating and the holding tight we can let go of the reason it all matters to begin with. We focus on facts, forgetting the truest Truth.

When consumed with fear, I can't see the faithfulness of God and His covenant.

When I'm determined to figure out my piece of the puzzle, I fail to see how the picture has been steadily coming together since the beginning of time.

When I grip too tightly the things I think I control, I lose touch of the eternal Truth—it's God who holds all things together.

But when I zoom out to see the fullness of God's promises—to remember His covenant that He has upheld for generation after generation—the Truth comes into view. Only then do I see that those blurry parts of the picture do not change the glory of the whole. The uncertain places I so desperately want to bring into focus do not change what's true.

Our circumstances are also real. The anxiety you experience, the pain your body feels from illness, the tragedy your family has endured, or the financial hole you're digging out of—those are real too. The facts in our lives that we try to keep orderly and under control, that we use to measure our days, do not disappear or change just because we will them to.

Trusting in God's Truth does not mean ignoring everything else. We don't have to explain our fears away in order to earnestly believe God's promises to us. It's not an either/or situation. It's both/and.

We're afraid, AND God is trustworthy.

Awful things happen, AND God is wholly good.

We're sick, AND Jesus is the Great Physician.

The world is passing away, AND God's Kingdom will stand.

Truth is not diminished when we stand it next to our doubts, questions, and fears.

Like the rock that withstands the raging fire, the Truth will remain. Everything around it will perish, but the Truth—and the One who gives it—will remain.

The prophet Isaiah stated it plain as day: "The grass withers, the flowers fade, but the word of our God remains forever" (Isa. 40:8 HCSB). Jesus said the same to His disciples: "Heaven and earth will pass away, but My words will never pass away" (Matt. 24:35 HCSB).

The stuff of our temporary lives will melt away with the heat, and then what will be revealed? Is my life hidden in the immovable, imperishable rock of God and His Word, or am I climbing hills made of lesser things, hoping for the best?

Jesus alone is our hope for an eternal tomorrow.

Excerpt taken from *She Reads Truth* by Raechel Myers and Amanda Bible Williams (© 2016).

Out of Darkness

*But if we walk in the light as He Himself is in the light,
we have fellowship with one another, and the blood of Jesus
His Son cleanses us from all sin. (1 John 1:7 HCSB)*

The dark can hide all kinds of ugly. The light fixture in our master bathroom did a good job of lighting the room but left much to be desired aesthetically. No fear, online shopping is near! I clicked on a lovely substitute, dropped it in the digital basket, and checked out. My purchase would arrive only a few days later.

The box was a bit smaller than what I expected, but I gave a shrug and bounced to the bathroom. I set it aside until our friend Ron could install it. He arrived with tools in hand. I didn't want to be in his way so I busied myself in the kitchen. Once the installation was complete, Ron called to me. I couldn't wait to see the beauty hanging above our mirror.

My wide-eyed smile folded into a furrowed brow.

The light fixture might as well have been a night-light. I could barely see a thing!

I didn't have the heart to inform Ron that his work was in vain. So any time I really want to see to put my makeup on, I go to my daughters' bathroom. They have a large window and bright lights that show me everything my mirror doesn't. I'll be honest, at times I'm afraid to go in their bathroom. I fear what I may find on my face that has been obvious to everyone else: a weird hair or blemish or something worse.

To be brought into the light can be frightening. It means we will have to face what we haven't had the courage to acknowledge. We will see the ugly with our own eyes. We will see our rebellion. We will see every jagged edge of that hurt, every hideous consequence of our obsession, and every grotesque inadequacy.

Yet, God is illuminating light. If He is light, then we know light is good. What does it mean to walk in the light? It means we stand in front of the well-lit bathroom and look. We invite others to look with us. We tell the hurt. We expose what's hooked us. We confess all the ways we can't get it right.

I recall a moment when I was afraid to give voice to a deep, dark secret. I feared the atmosphere wouldn't be able to handle it and would rip in two. To my surprise, the air held together when I brought the secret to light. Even more astonishing, the women with whom I shared didn't look at me like I had grown an extra head. They nodded compassionately and we went on to the next person.

I was shocked and simultaneously relieved. My ugly was out in the open and no one recoiled. They knew they had their own ugly, and they knew Christ's blood is enough to cover us both.

Together, we walked in the light where God already is.

Excerpt taken from *Steadfast Love* by Lauren Chandler (© 2016).

Called and Loved

*We have come to know and to believe the love that God has
for us. God is love, and the one who remains in love remains
in God, and God remains in him. (1 John 4:16 HCSB)*

Do you find it at all peculiar that John alone called himself "the
one Jesus loved"? (John 13:23 HCSB). If we believe the Gospel
of John was inspired, however, then we must accept that the detail
of John's self-identity was also inspired. Not because Jesus' love for
John exceeded the others but because God purposed the reader to
know how John saw himself. At first glance we might be tempted to
think John a bit arrogant for terming himself such, but God would
never allow a man who received such revelation to get away with
that kind of self-promotion.

I'd like to suggest that John's evolving identity over the course of
those decades came out of the opposite kind of heart. God is far too
faithful not to have greatly humbled John before giving him such
surpassing revelation. Paul describes a similar humbling in
2 Corinthians 12:

> Therefore I will boast all the more gladly about my
> weaknesses, so that Christ's power may rest on me. That
> is why, for Christ's sake, I delight in weaknesses, in
> insults, in hardships, in persecutions, in difficulties. For
> when I am weak, then I am strong. (vv. 9–10 NIV)

I believe quite possibly the heightened positions of Peter and
Paul in the era of the early church coupled with the impending
martyrdom of each apostle fed abasement in John rather than

exaltation. Surely he struggled with terribly perplexing feelings of fear that he, too, was doomed to martyrdom—and yet fear that he wasn't. Does that make sense?

But as the years went by and the virile, youthful fisherman grew old and gray, I am convinced that John's weakening legs were steadied and strengthened on the path by the constant reassurance, *"Jesus, You chose me. You keep me. And above all else, You love me. You love me! No matter what happens or doesn't, Jesus, I am Your beloved."*

If any of us had been John during the years conspicuously silent in Scripture, we might have given up. Or at least dropped into a lower gear. Not John. He knew two things, and I believe he grabbed on to them for dear life. He knew he was called to be a disciple. And he knew he was loved. Over the course of time, those two things emerged into one ultimate identity. "I, John, the seed of Zebedee, the son of Salome, the brother of James, the last surviving apostle am he: the one Jesus loves." Beloved disciple. Somewhere along the way, John, that Son of Thunder, forsook ambition for affection. And that, my friend, is why he was sitting pretty when some of the most profound words ever to fall from heaven to earth fell first like liquid grace into his quill.

Excerpt taken from *Portraits of Devotion* by Beth Moore (© 2014).

Do You Love Me?

We love because He first loved us. (1 John 4:19 HCSB)

Throw back the calendar several thousand years and shift the scene from a restaurant to a shore in Galilee. Look for smoke coming from a charcoal fire and the bones of grilled fish picked white and clean. Find Jesus in the scene first. He's both host and cook. Then study the other men until you find the one whose hair is damp. That will be the guy who threw on his robe, dove from the boat, and swam like a madman in the nippy waters of early spring.

At some point in the scene, one of the fishermen on board, the ablest to see the shore with the youngest set of eyes, says to the one named Simon Peter, "It is the Lord!"

And Simon Peter? He up and jumps overboard. I love how Scripture words it. He *plunged into the sea.* Hence, the wet head.

The rest of the guys get *out on land,* we're told, and Jesus invites them over to the charcoal fire where He's grilling fish and baking bread. This is the precise place our opening scenario originates. Read it for yourself in John 21:15–17 (HCSB):

> When they had eaten breakfast, Jesus asked Simon Peter, "Simon, son of John, do you love Me more than these?"
>
> "Yes, Lord," he said to Him, "You know that I love You."
>
> "Feed My lambs," He told him.
>
> A second time He asked him, "Simon, son of John, do you love Me?"

"Yes, Lord," he said to Him, "You know that I love You."

"Shepherd My sheep," He told him.

He asked him the third time, "Simon, son of John, do you love Me?"

Peter was grieved that He asked him the third time, "Do you love Me?" He said, "Lord, You know everything! You know that I love You."

"Feed My sheep," Jesus said.

Not *Do you believe Me?* Not *Do you worship Me?* Not *Do you respect Me?* All those questions have profound placement in the life of faith but they are not synonymous with the one Jesus deliberately, repeatedly asked Peter. The question was, *Do you love Me?*

With every ounce of conviction in my soul, I believe Jesus brought you and me to each side of these pages to ask us the exact same question.

Here's the beauty of it: not one word of the divine inquisition is for sake of judgment or condemnation. Not one iota for the purpose of provoking guilt. Not one whit to expose failure or weakness. Jesus ties up the three-question divine inquiry with two words to Simon Peter: *"Follow Me!"* (John 21:19 HCSB). Following Jesus is meant to be driven and drawn by love. Audacious love. We get to love Him because He loved us first. And now we get to walk with Him, to follow Him.

Excerpt taken from *Audacious* by Beth Moore (© 2015).